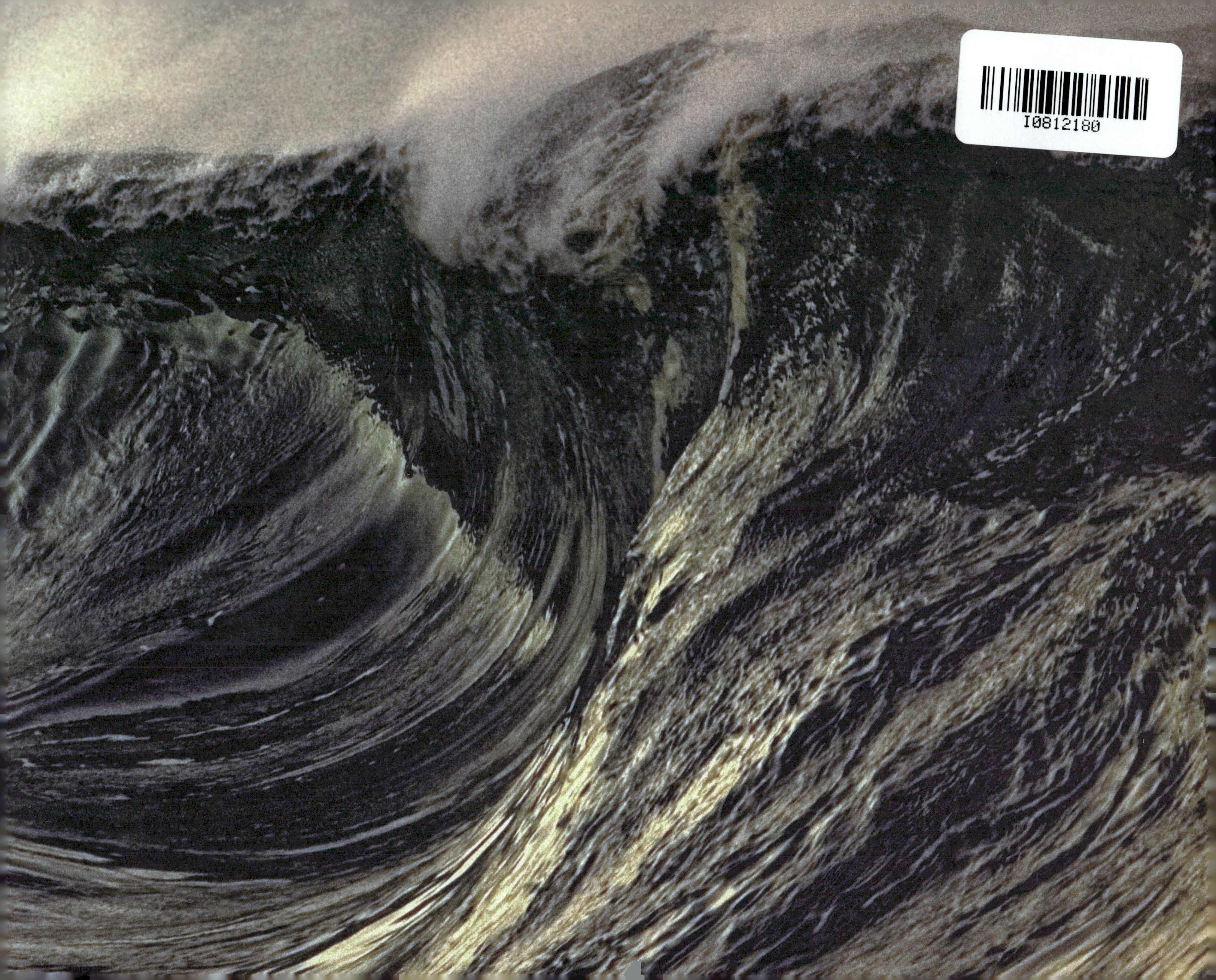

Flying Through the Clouds

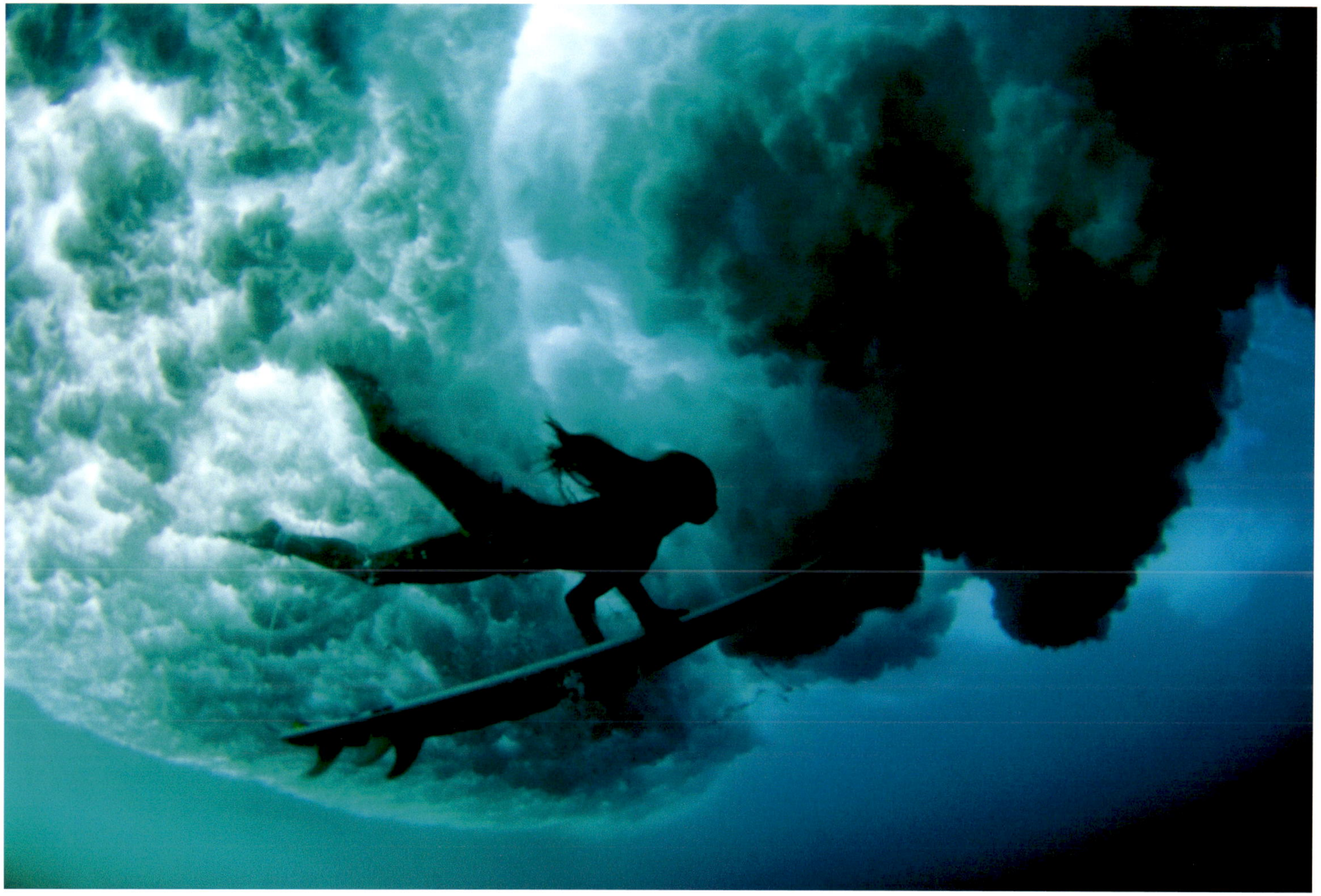

Surf Photography of Jim Russi

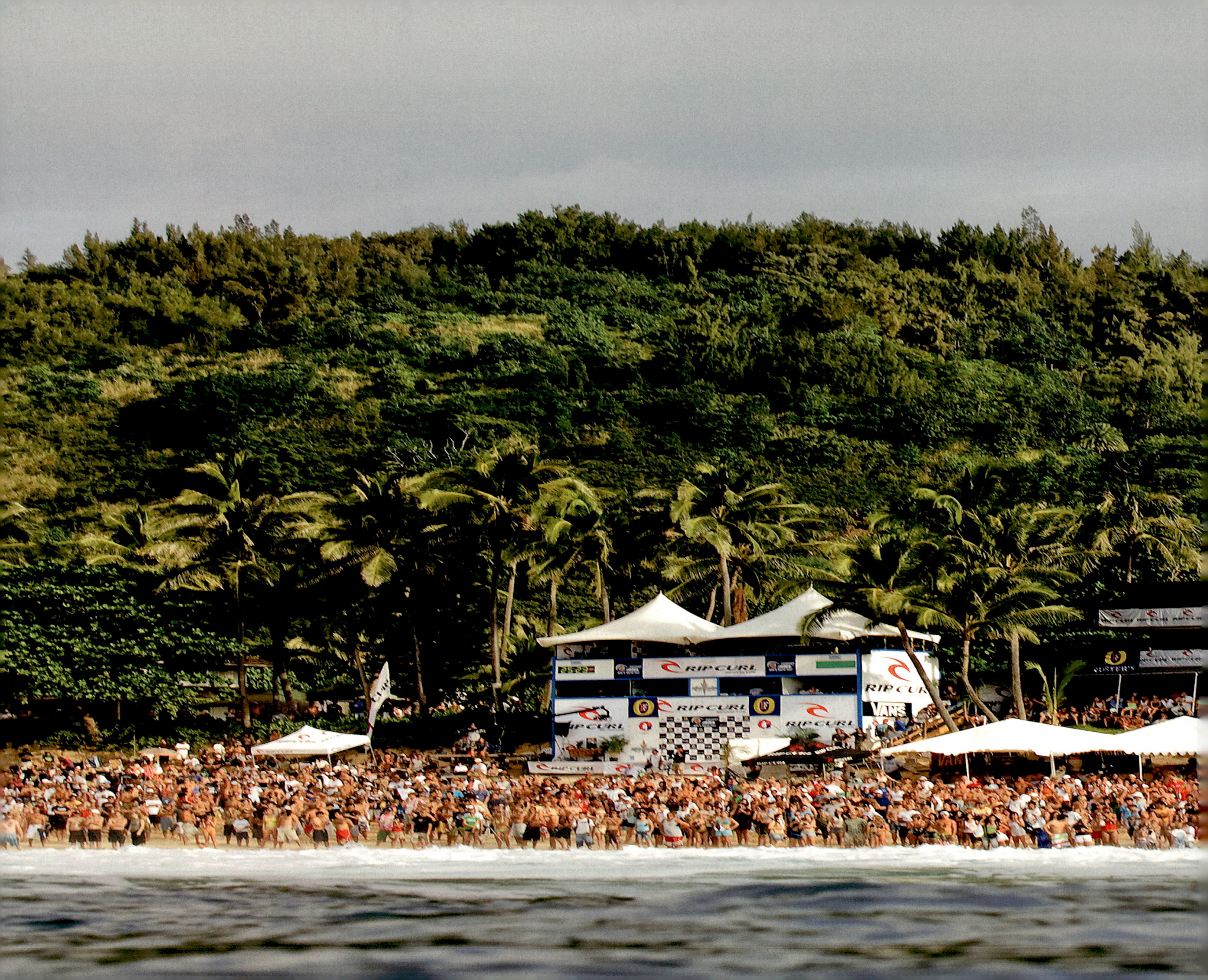
RIP CURL
VANS

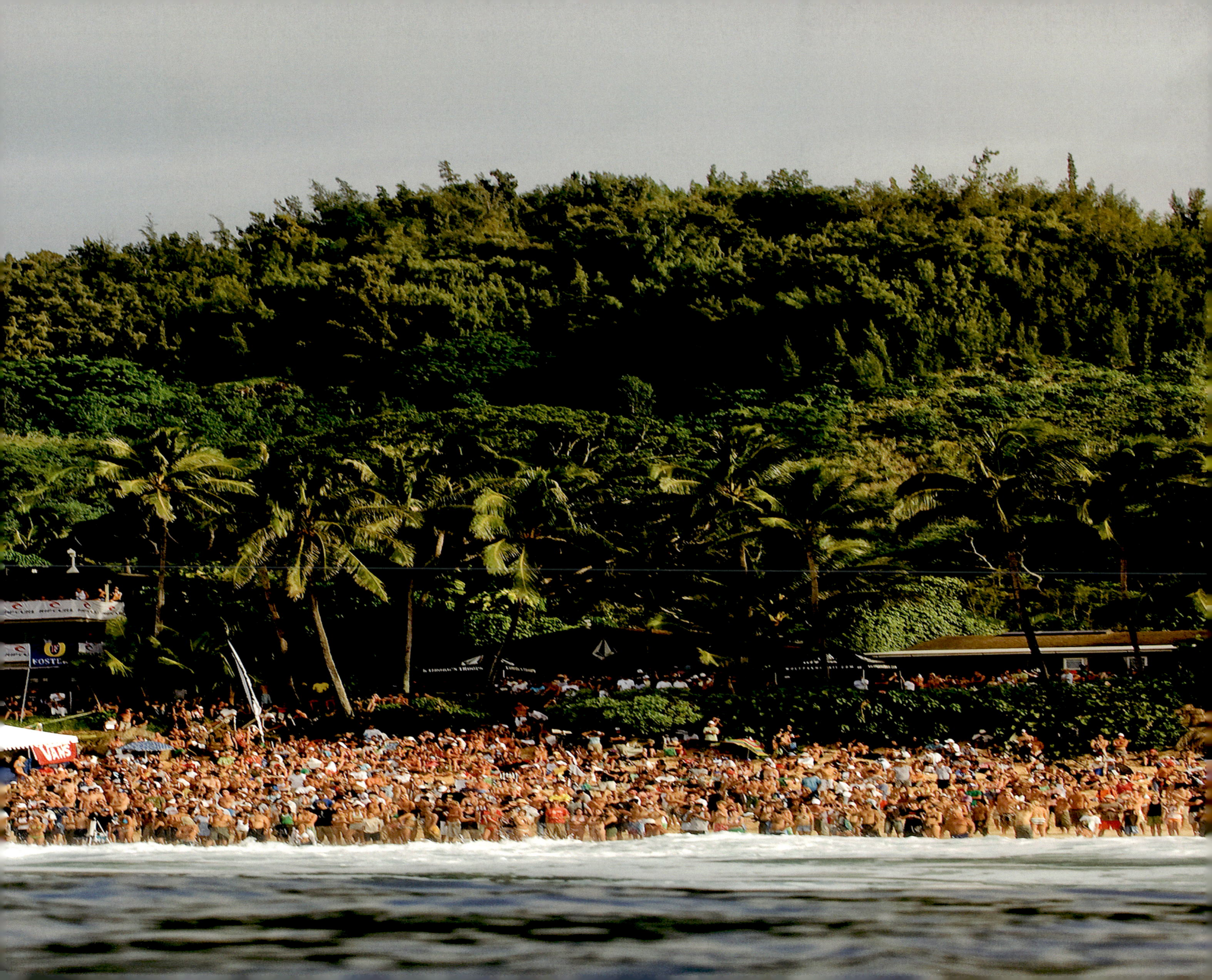
VANS

FLYING THROUGH THE CLOUDS

PHOTOGRAPHY BY JIM RUSSI

INTRODUCTION BY SCOTT HULET, EDITOR THE SURFERS JOURNAL

ART DIRECTION BY TOM ADLER

PROJECT COORDINATION BY KATE RUGGIERO

Schiffer Publishing Ltd®

4880 Lower Valley Road Atglen, Pennsylvania 19310

Library of Congress Control Number: 2011928837

Type set in Humanist 521 BT

ISBN: 978-0-7643-3861-8
Printed in China

Schiffer Books are available at special discounts for bulk purchases for sales promotions or premiums. Special editions, including personalized covers, corporate imprints, and excerpts can be created in large quantities for special needs. For more information contact the publisher:

Published by Schiffer Publishing Ltd.
4880 Lower Valley Road
Atglen, PA 19310
Phone: (610) 593-1777; Fax: (610) 593-2002
E-mail: Info@schifferbooks.com

For the largest selection of fine reference books on this and related subjects, please visit our website at **www.schifferbooks.com**
We are always looking for people to write books on new and related subjects. If you have an idea for a book please contact us at the above address.

This book may be purchased from the publisher.
Include $5.00 for shipping.
Please try your bookstore first.
You may write for a free catalog.

In Europe, Schiffer books are distributed by
Bushwood Books
6 Marksbury Ave.
Kew Gardens
Surrey TW9 4JF England
Phone: 44 (0) 20 8392 8585; Fax: 44 (0) 20 8392 9876
E-mail: info@bushwoodbooks.co.uk
Website: www.bushwoodbooks.co.uk

Cover photo: Kelia "Sister" Moniz, Flying Through the Clouds. North Shore, Oahu.2009. Inside front cover: Pipeline Masters, Surfer's Perspective. 2007. Inside back cover: For all my boys, you know who you are. Mahalos. Back cover photo: Rosy Hodge, Pulling In. Backdoor, HI.2008.

Dedication

For my wife, Mia, who stands behind me strong and loves me completely. Your love and laughter are my backbone.

For my mother and father who have always believed in and supported all of my endeavors.

For my sons, Kaden Ku'oko'a and Kona James, and my daughter Brooke, who keep me laughing and make me rich.

For my Lord Savior Jesus Christ, without whom I would be forever lost.

I am ever grateful. I have been blessed with unconditional support and love from each of you.

This book is for all of you. Thank you.

Introduction

Scott Hulet
Editor, *The Surfers Journal*

If you've spent any time at all in the surf publishing game, you learn that there's a bird in the forest so rare that it doesn't even have a name. I'm talking about the photographer with both artistic merit and business acumen—a contributor you can count on when you need museum-grade results quickly, efficiently, and with a minimum of drama. The book you're currently holding assembles the work of just such a fellow.

Growing up in the oceanfront enclave of Palos Verdes, young Jim Russi honed his surfing on the grunting right point waves at Lunada Bay. Yes, he was a local there, a place known for an intolerance for outsiders bordering on the pathological. Times changed and so did Jim. At a spot infamous for anti-media hysteria, Jim picked up a camera. He also felt a special relationship with nearby Paddleboard Cove, home of the legendary Palos Verdes Surf Club in the 1930s. This is where original surf photographer Doc Ball stuck his tripod legs in the sand. Russi is honored to be a part of that lineage, and has a keen understanding of surf image history. Formal training at the estimable Brooks Institute gave his nascent talent teeth. His analytical nature assured him of a rapid growth curve. After all, he was born to a rocket scientist father and a mathematician mother.

Soon enough, he was one of less than a dozen photographers working the North Shore of Oahu. It was the early-1980s, and he was living on a shoestring. This was a time when the North Shore was still a wild and lawless place. Surfing companies did not yet control the oceanfront houses between Log Cabins and Ehukai. Individual surfers making it their crusade to ride as many waves as possible at Banzai Reef rented the houses at Pipeline. Jim became a sort of staff photographer for this Pipeline Underground, shooting the likes of Brian Bulkley, Adam 12, and Doug "Roach" Brown. He lived with them, partied with them, and surfed with them when the light wasn't up to his standards for shooting.

It was a good life, rich with experience but marred by some bad choices. What can you say? Russi decided to clean up his act, becoming a youth pastor at his local church. But the call of photography was strong. In 1991, the first longboard magazines were forming in California. Jim became a contributor to both of them, eventually aligning with *Longboard* as a senior staff photographer. His work grew by leaps and bounds, and he quickly became longboard surfing's most prolific documentarian. Whether it was Joel Tudor at Windansea, Herbie Fletcher at Reunion Island, or Josh Baxter at Makaha, Jim nailed down the most vibrant moves in the most lavish color.

His work was marked with an exacting technical proficiency. His use of the beautifully grained Fuji Velvia film wasn't itself unique. What gave Jim a real signature was that the highly saturated look yielded matched both his aesthetic and his subject matter hand-in-glove. As a result, Jim became the visual master of the longboard renaissance. Almost all of that era's peak moments were seen through his viewfinder.

Be it Grajagan and the North Shore in the '80s, international destinations in the '90s, or high end commercial work in the now, Russi's hallmark has always been a preoccupation with perspective. Many surf photographers do just fine with a couple of angles: from the beach with long glass, or into the tube with a water housing. Not Jim. He constantly entertained "what-ifs." "What would surfing look like from below, as the sea turtles see us?" "What would this moment look like from far away, as if seen by a voyeur?" "What does a seagull think of a ridden wave, viewed from above?" No sooner would he ask these questions than he'd set to work chasing those self-same POVs. It was never indulgent or contrived, and his technical skills led to a rather amazing success rate.

Jim has a tremendous work ethic. When on assignment, he's up hours before dawn checking batteries, loading water housings, cleaning lenses, and packing backups for his backups. By the time golden light hits, he's been ready for half an hour. By noon he's ready for a break. By early afternoon, he's going through the preparation ritual once again, getting ready for evening light. At night, the flash unit comes out for portraits and lifestyle. He's usually asleep by ten.

A committed Christian, Jim finds no need for weed or alcohol, but is fond of huge, stinking Cuban cigars from Bolivar or Romeo y Julieta. He never curses, instead employing defaults like "Gosh darn it" issued through clenched teeth. He is a careful dresser, always put together neatly. He has a horrible temper, but tries to keep it in check. Sometimes he snaps, which can be a thing to witness. That said, he is a loyal and fair fellow, willing to take a flyer on projects that seem chancy and with little hope for fiscal return. To that end, he's often seen shooting groms and girls.

Today he lives on the beach between Rocky Point and Pipeline with his wife and their two children. Such a family has always been his dream, and he seems happier now than ever before. As a result of his broad portfolio and professional ethic, he has been working with Quiksilver's female surf brand Roxy for over a decade, responsible for shepherding their models and surfers on assignments and catalog shoots at beautiful places around the globe. He takes this work as seriously as ever.

Placed in the context of today's top surfing lensmen, Jim is in the top ranks. He brings the quest for ice-pick sharpness exemplified by Bob Barbour, the range of Aaron Chang, the creative open-mindedness of Jeff Hornbaker, and the longevity of Art Brewer. That he's popularly viewed as a specialist irks Russi. A pass through his files—and indeed, this book—spotlights one of the most well rounded portfolios in "surfdom." In the way that Ron Stoner made the 1960s longboard scene his own, Jim did with the 1990s. Odds are strong that he'll put a similar stamp on an epoch not yet known by us.

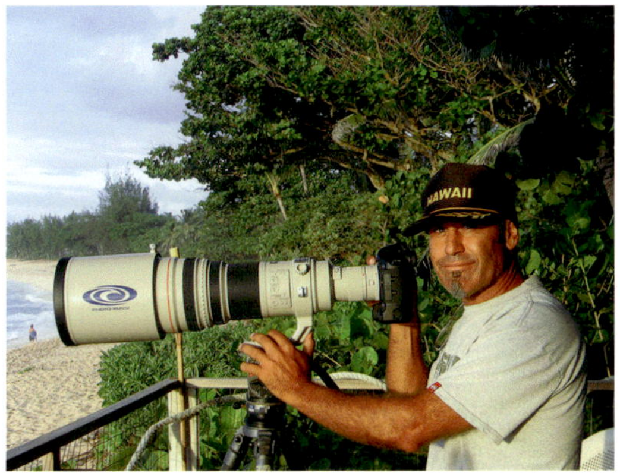

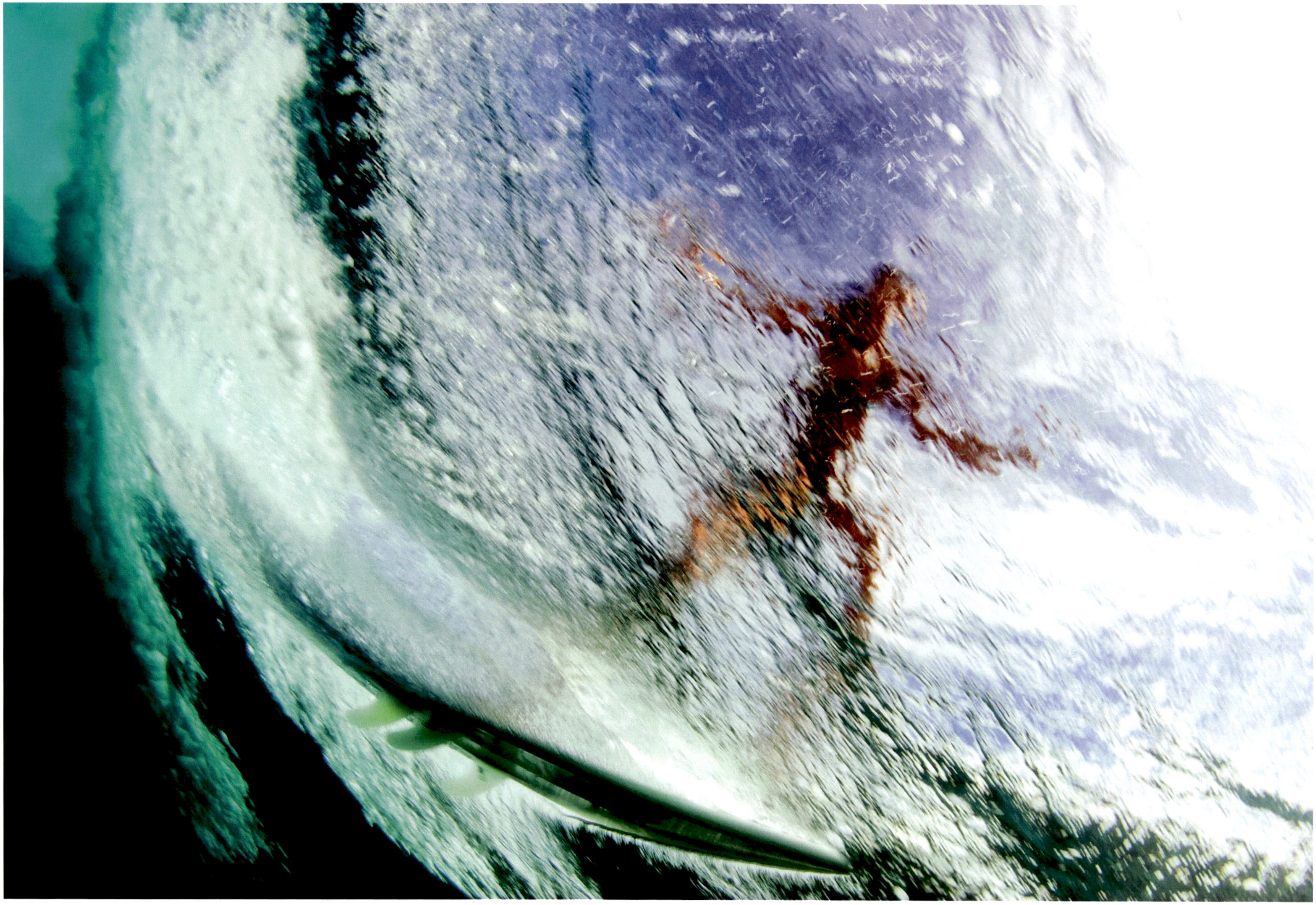

Crystal Dzigas, Crystal Clear. Hawaii. 2005.

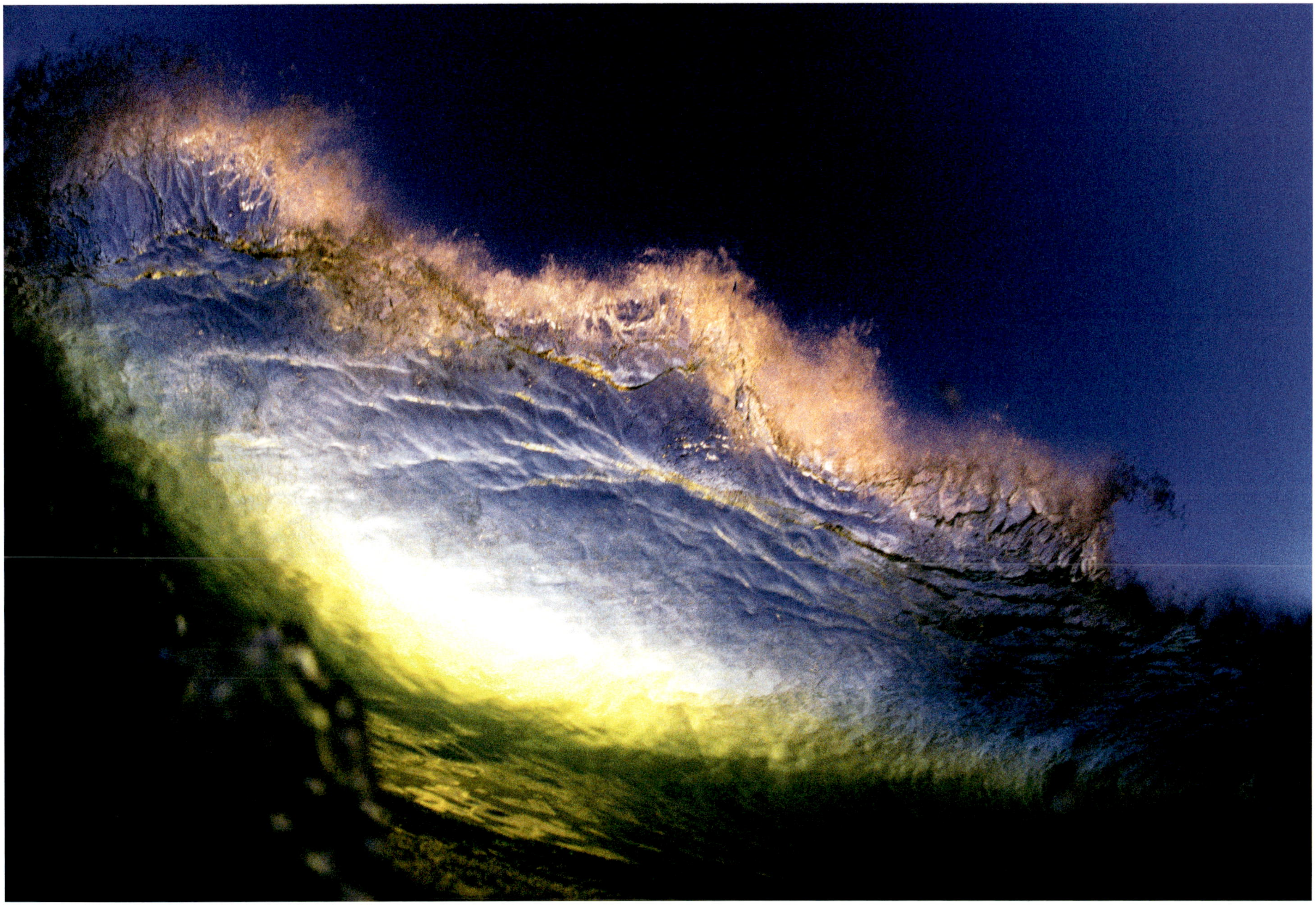

Liquid Sunshine. Gas Chambers, Puerto Rico. 1999.

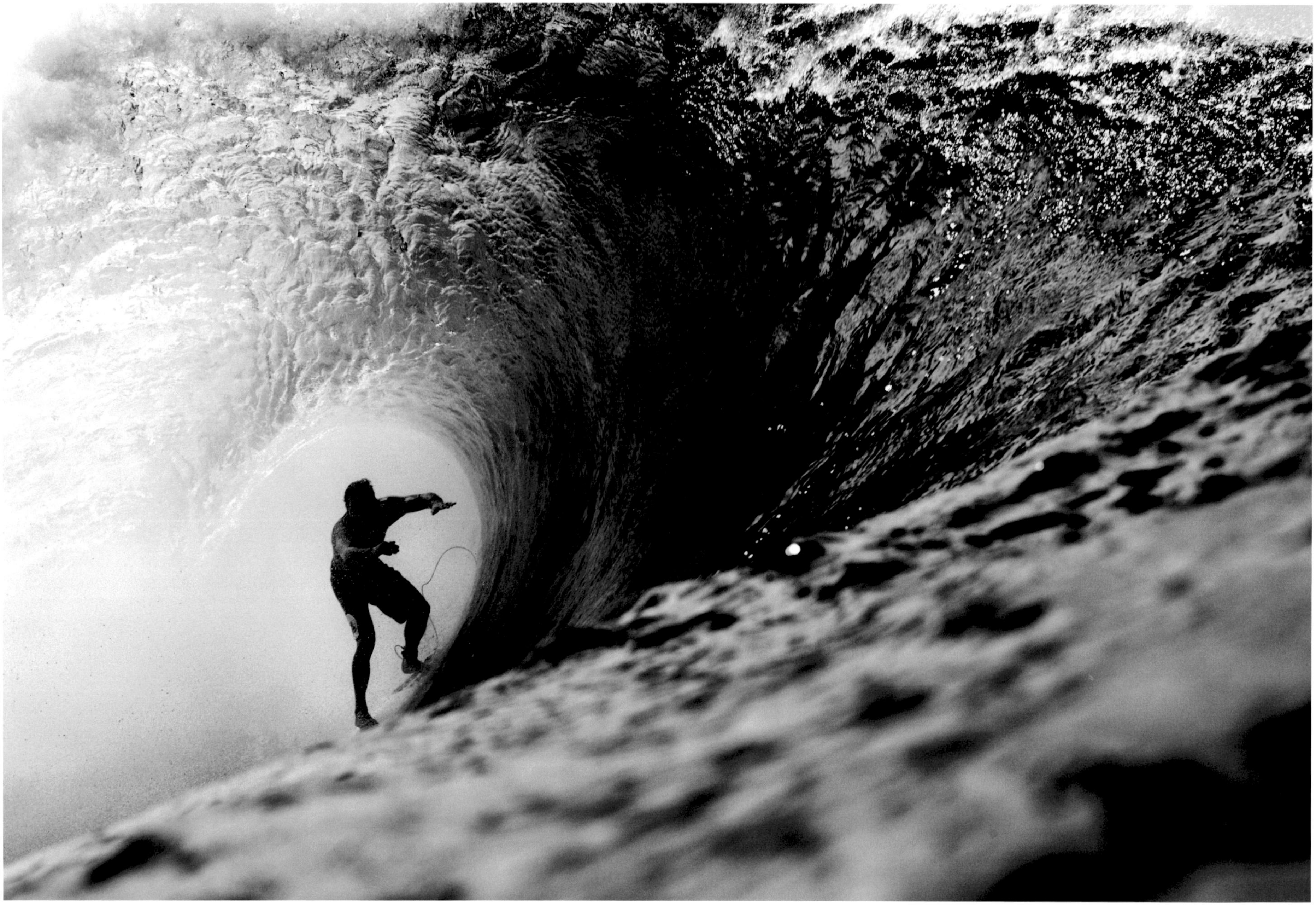

Nathan Fletcher taking a deep breath. Pipeline, HI. 2005.

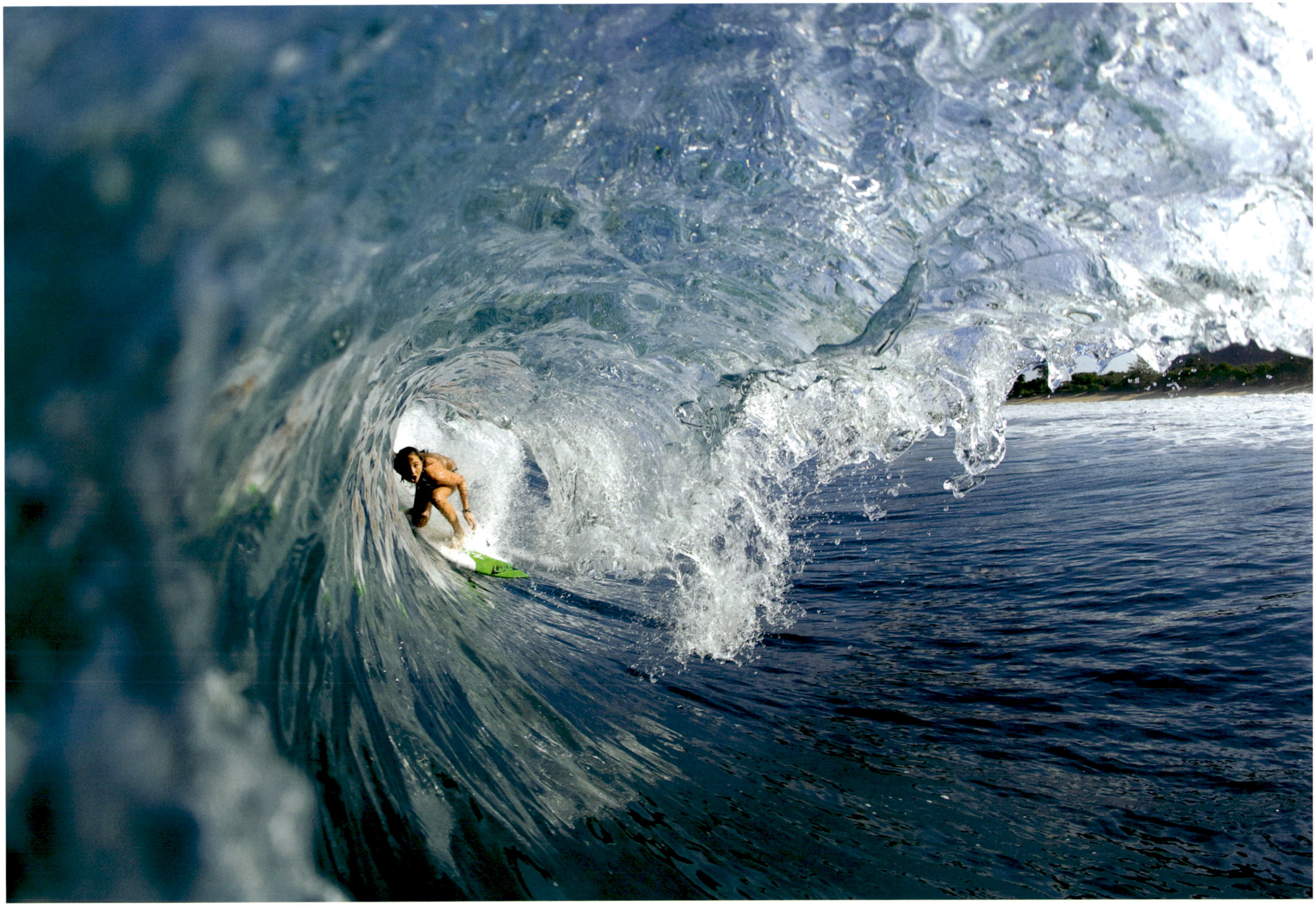

Carissa Moore age 14. Deep Thinker. Velzyland, HI. 2006.

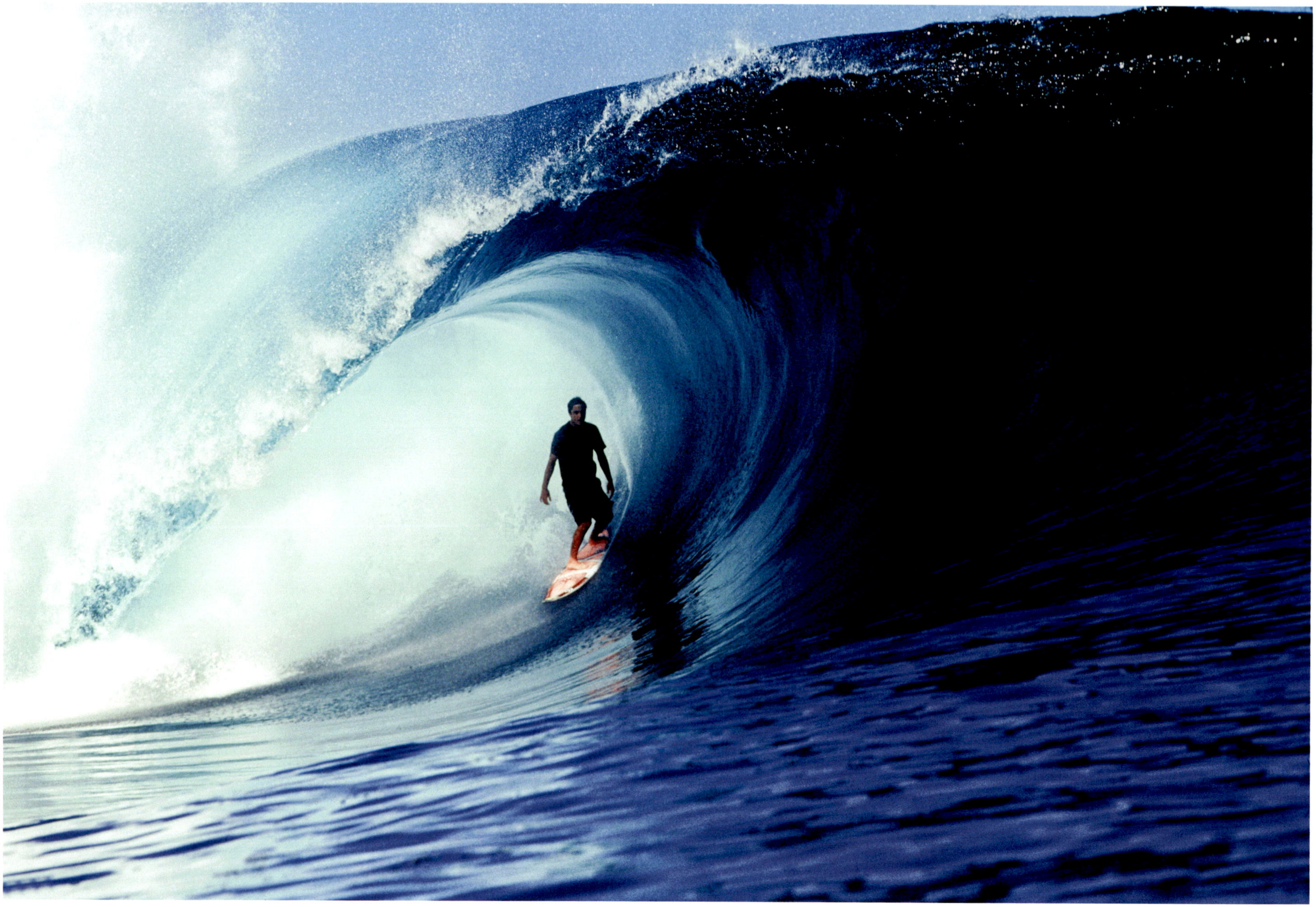

Mikey Todd, standing tall. Teahupoo, Tahiti. 2001.

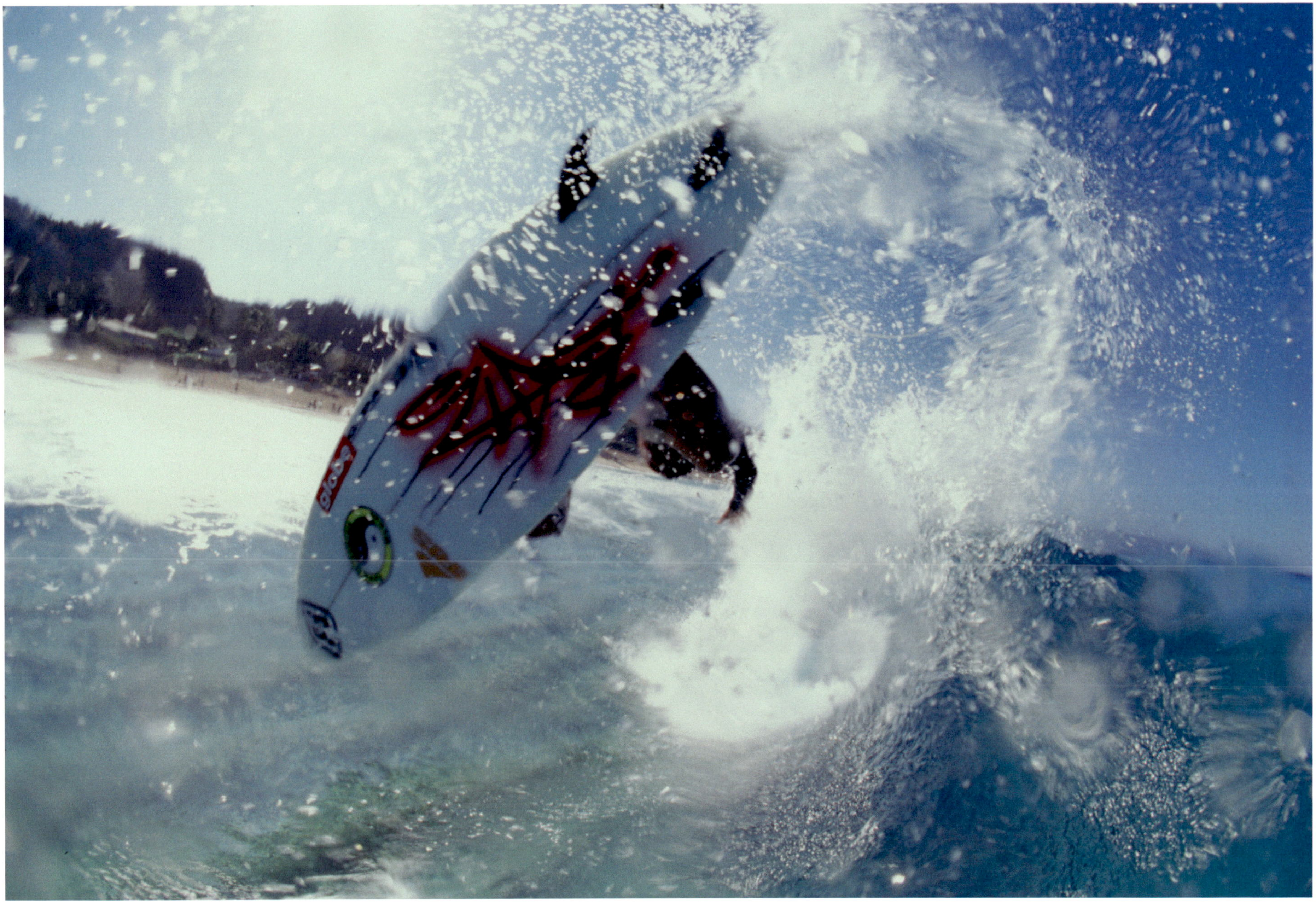

Jason Shibata, in your face. Rocky Point, HI. 2006.

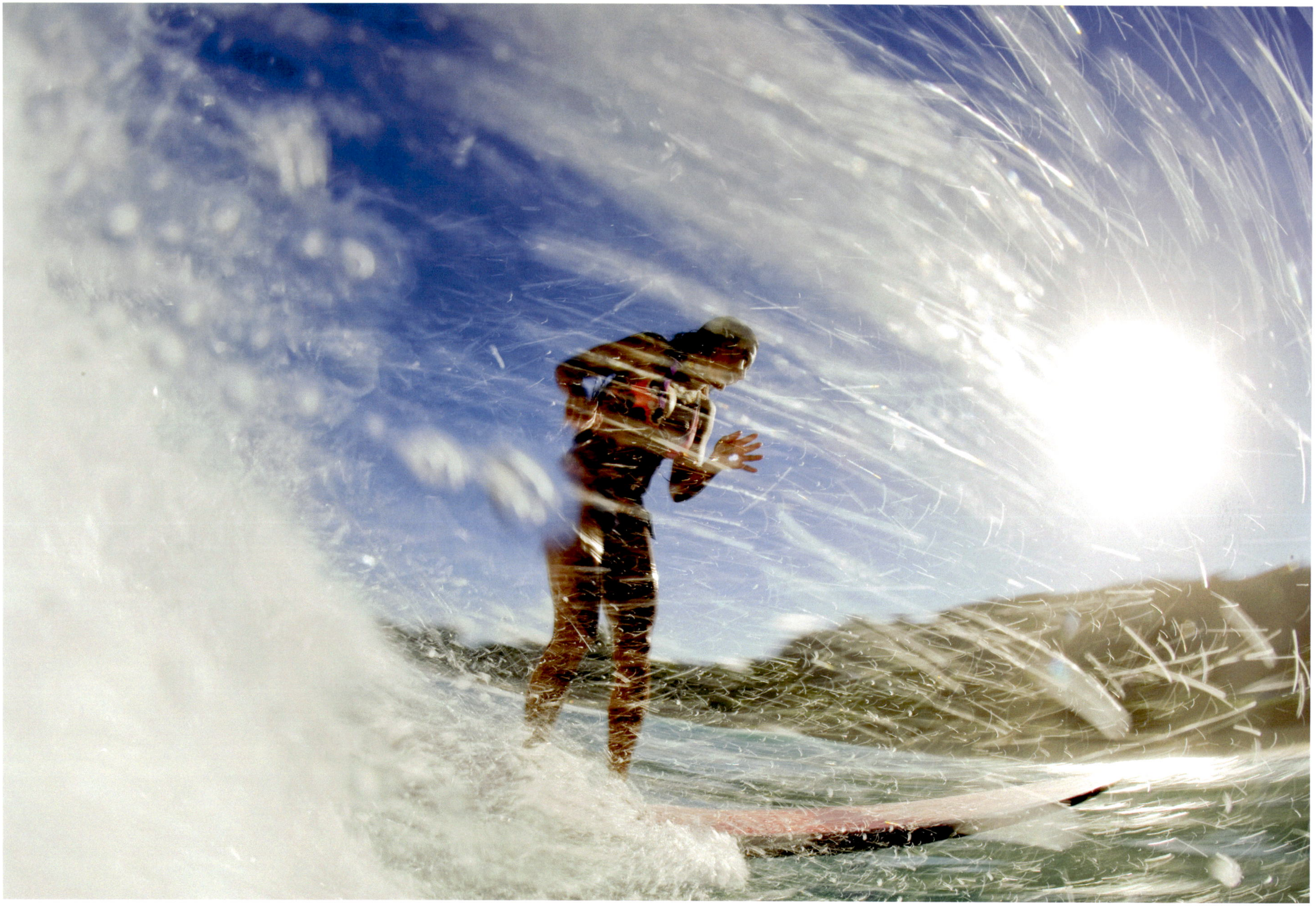

Crystal Dzigas, Racing The Sun. Ehukai, HI. 2005.

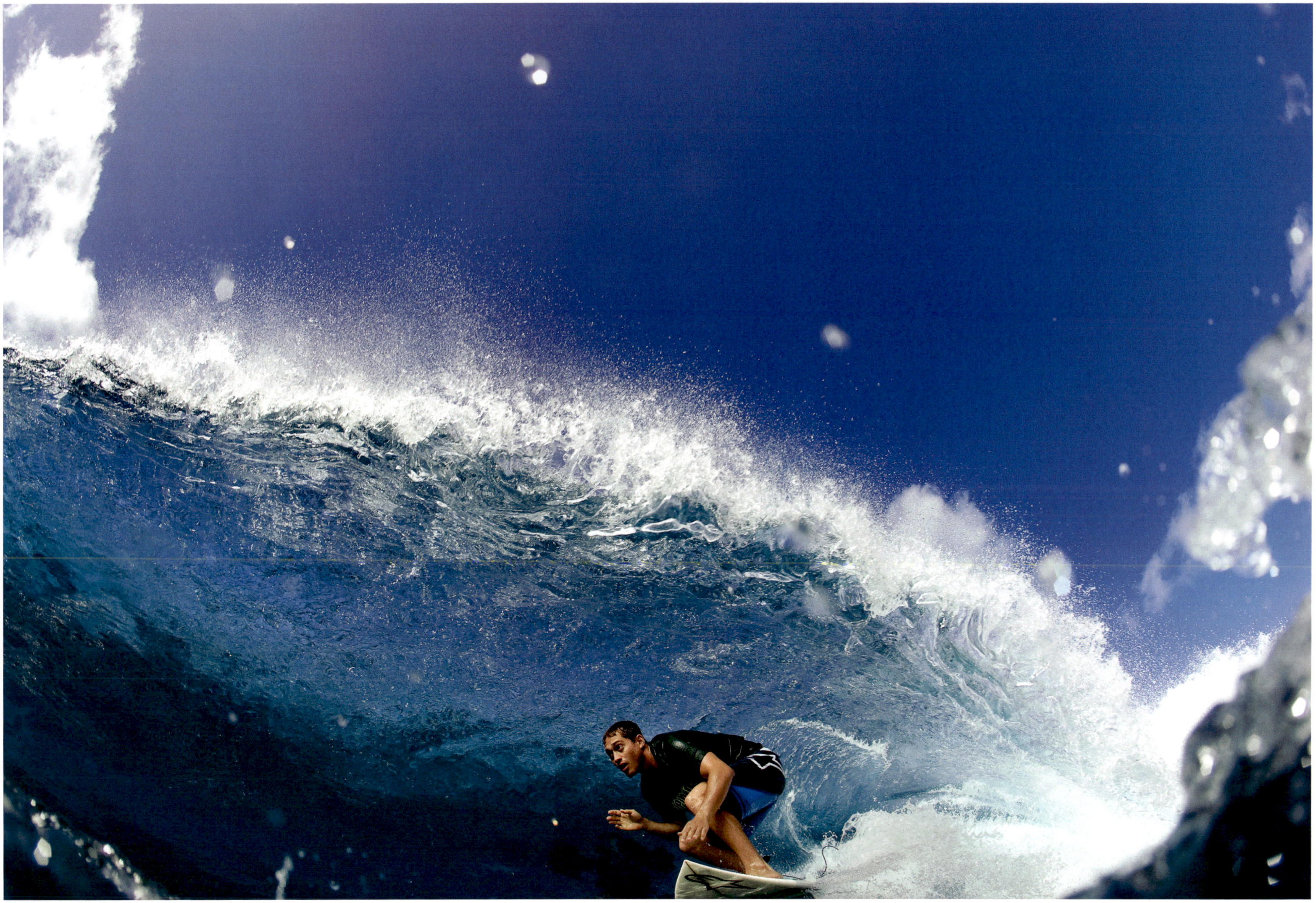

Makua Rothman, taking cover. Backdoor Pipeline, HI. 2007.

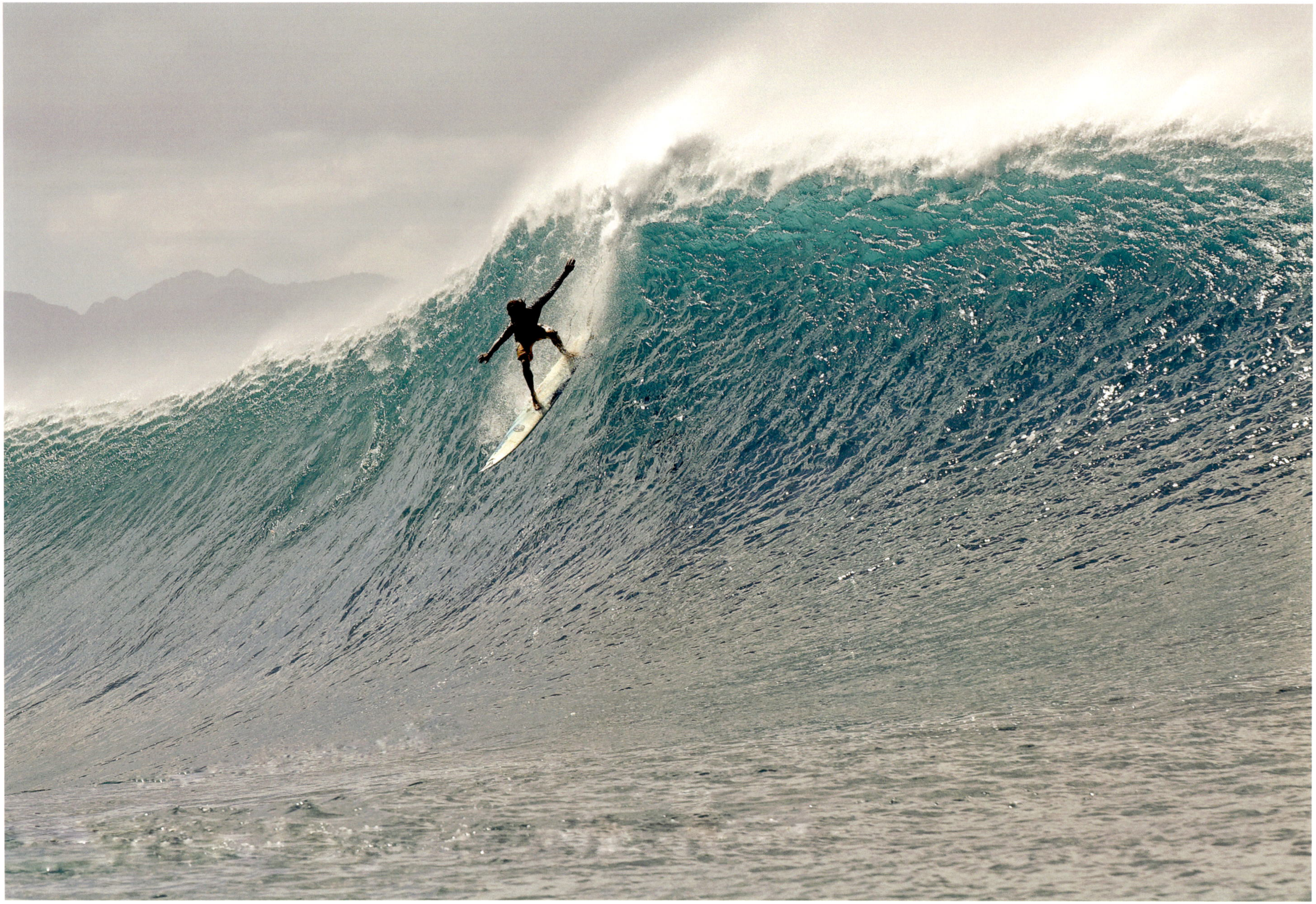

Jake Kirschenbaum, airdrop. Pipeline, HI. 2007.

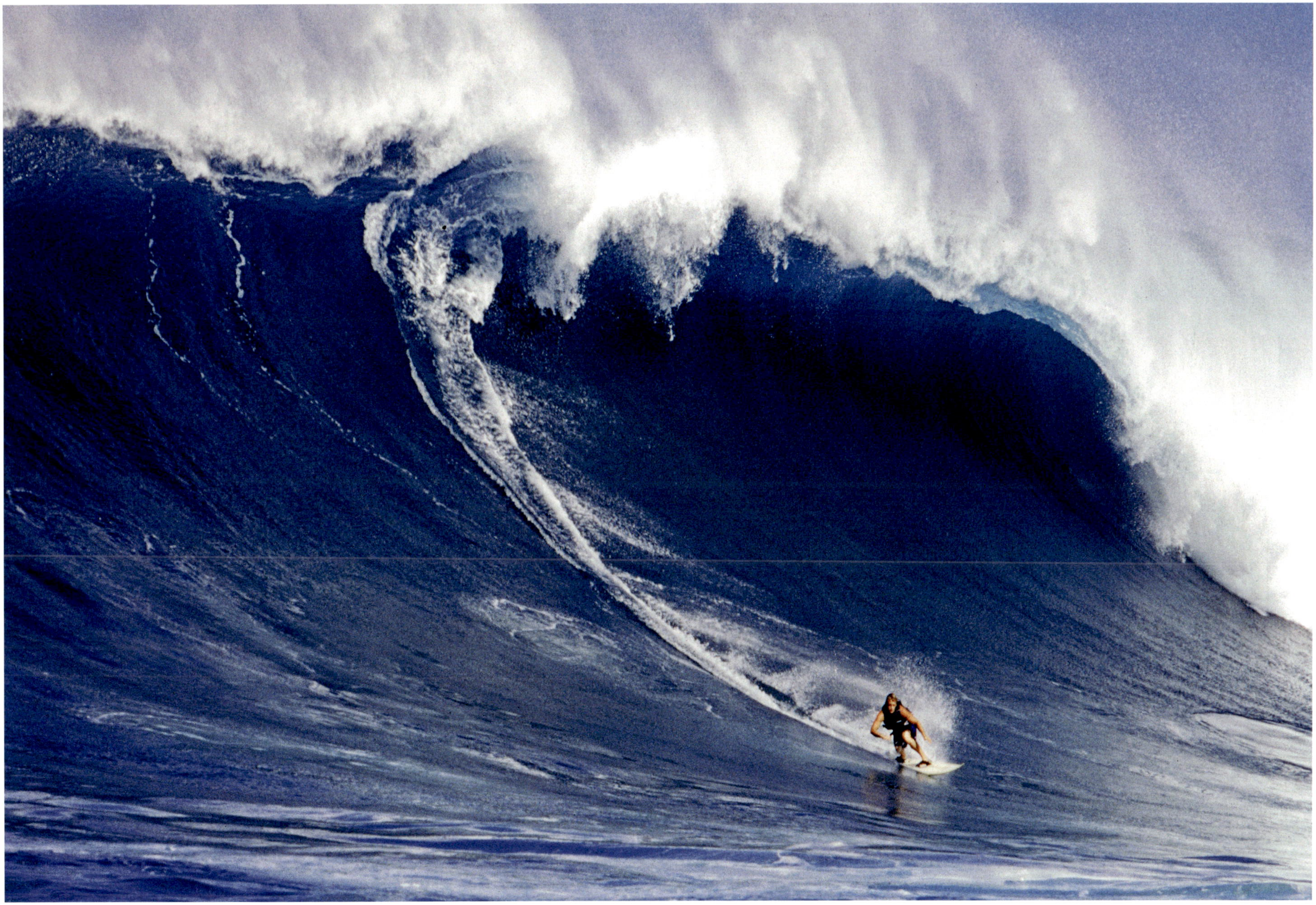

Todd Morcom. Outer Reef, North Shore, HI. 2002.

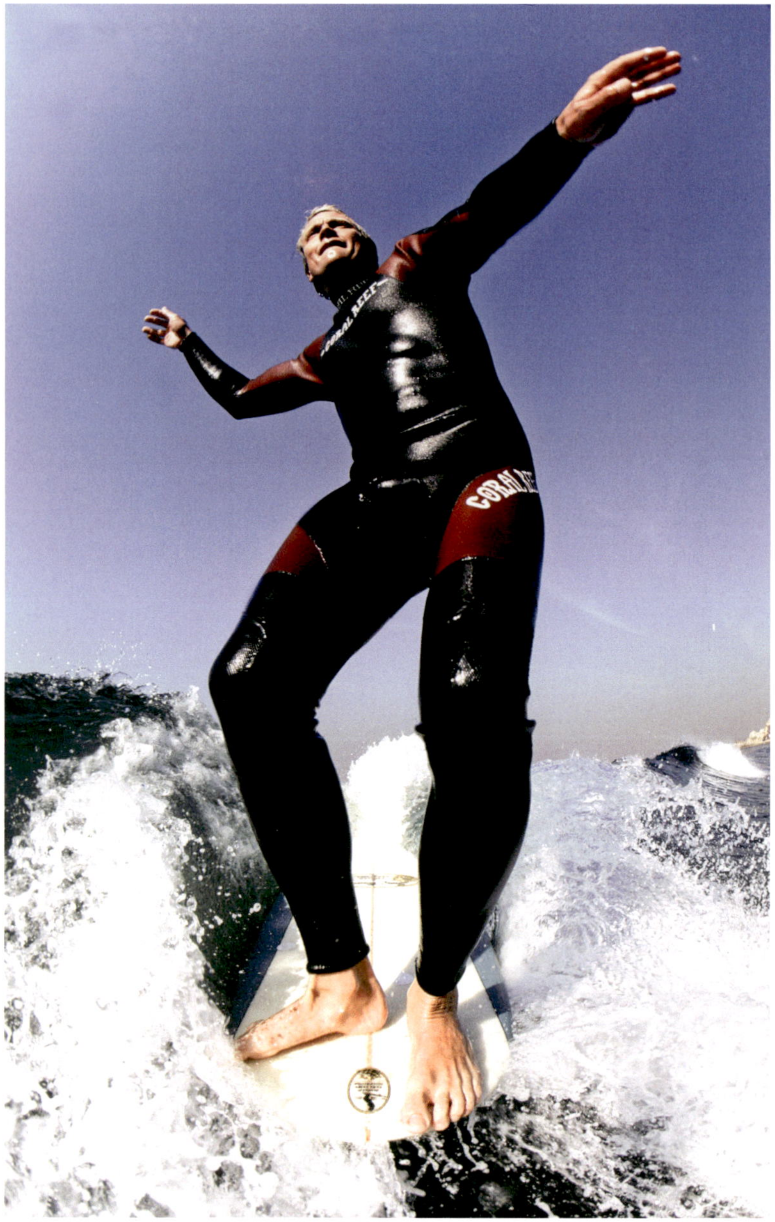

Tom Wegener. Remote camera board. Palos Verdes Cove, CA. 1996.

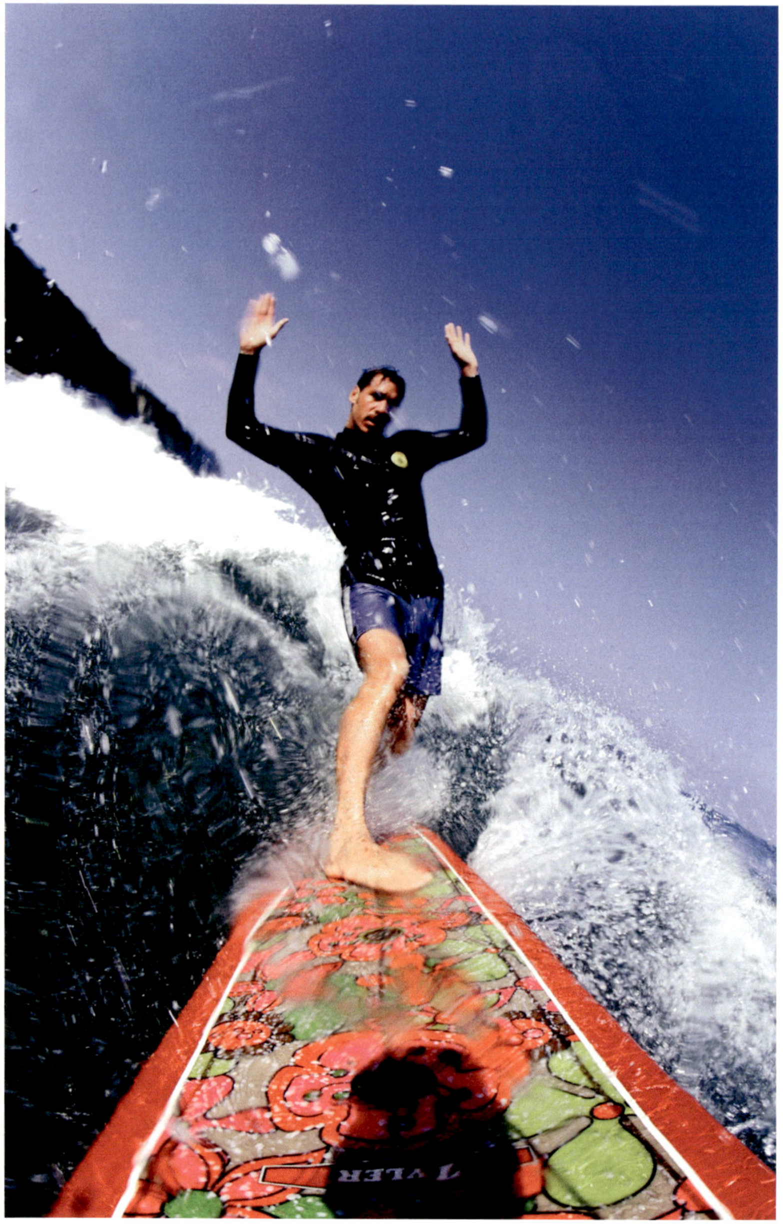

Tyler Hatzikian. Master of Style. 1998.

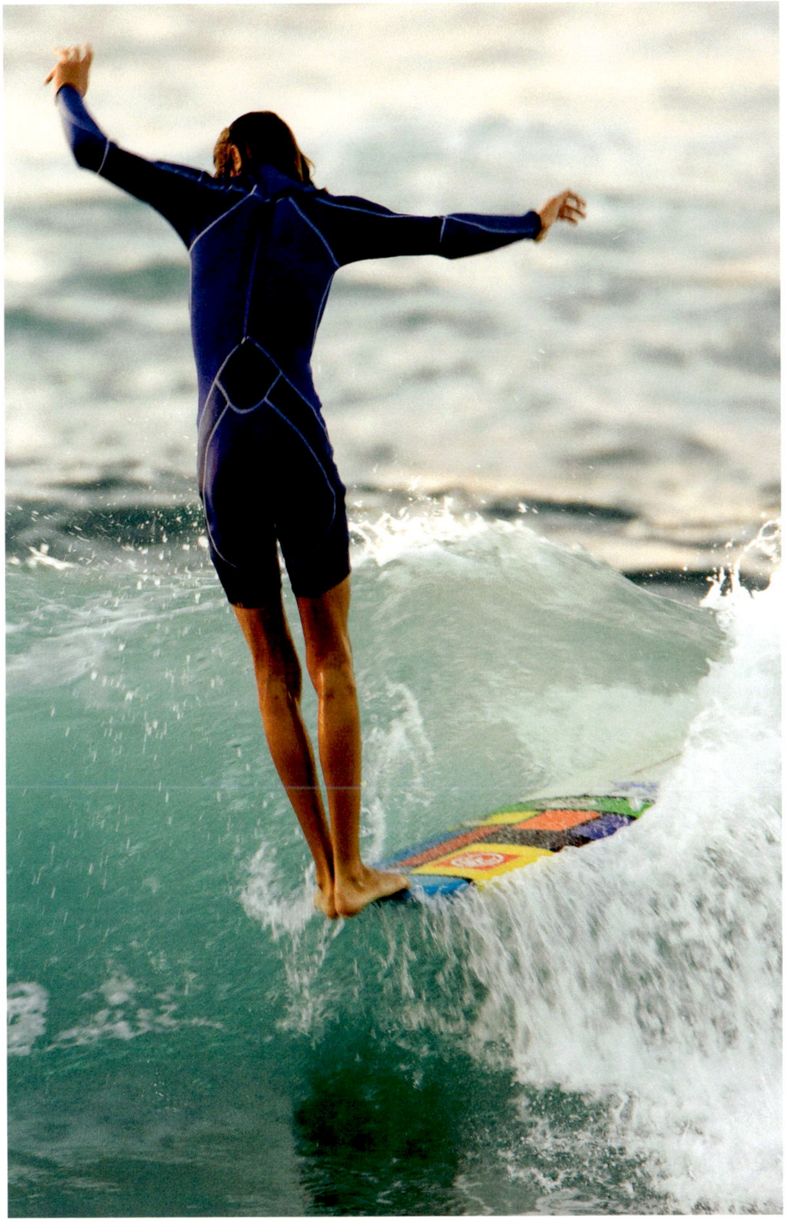

Joe Aaron. Hanging Heels. Chuns Reef, HI. 2006.

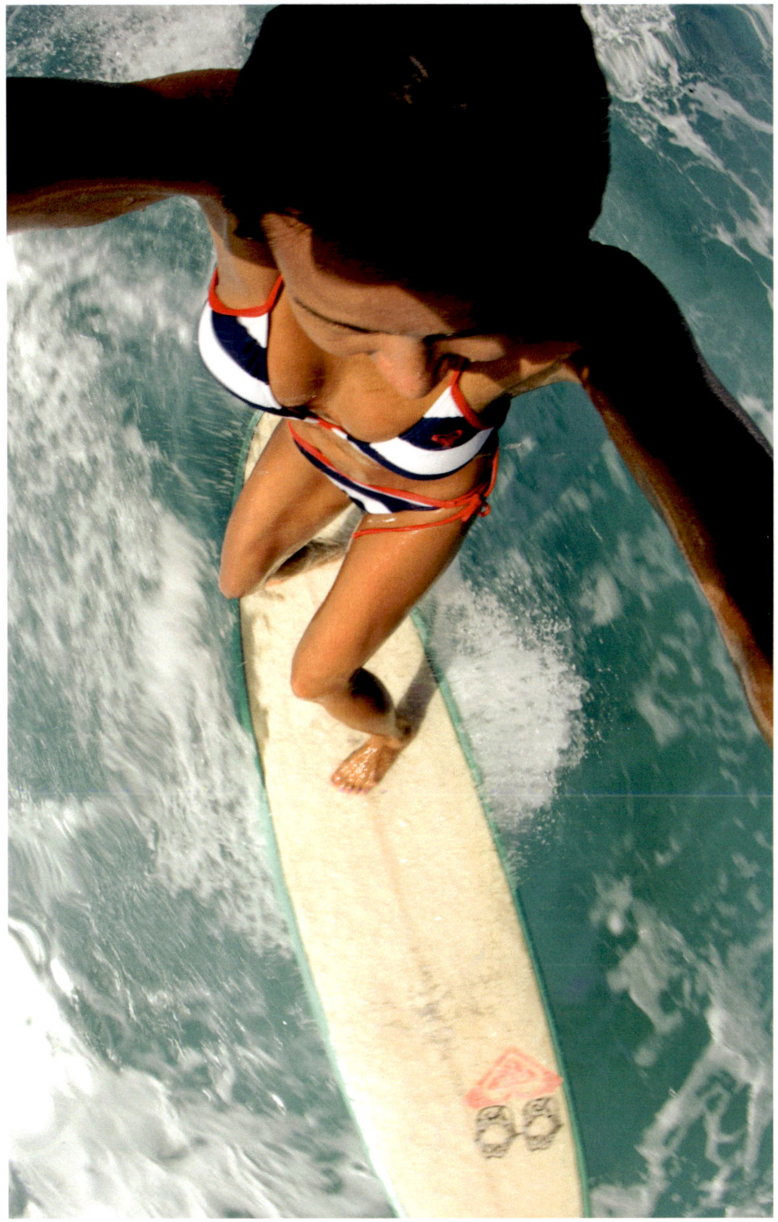

Crystal Dzigas self portrait. Waikiki, HI. 2007.

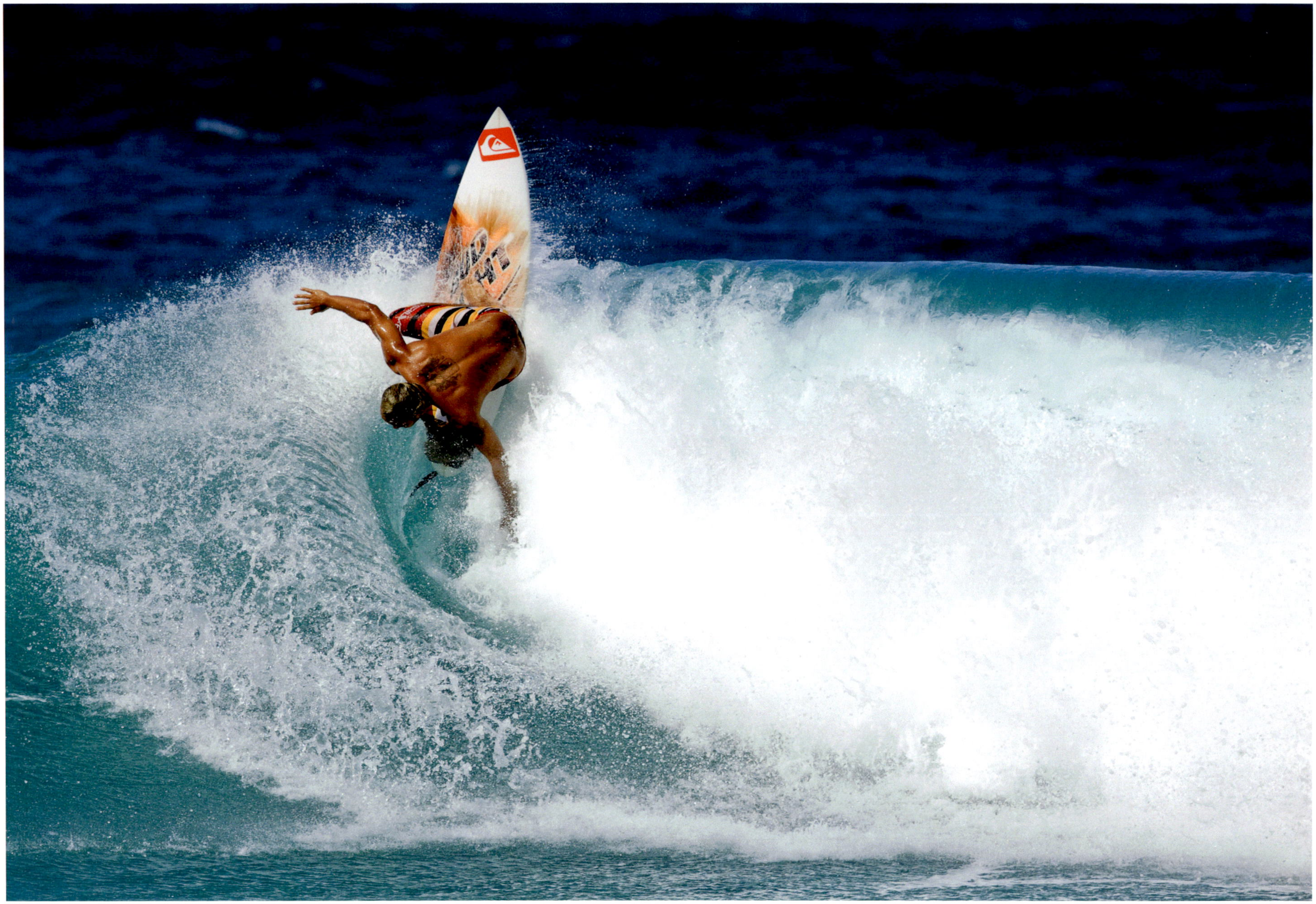

Freddy Patacchia striking high noon. Rocky Rights, HI. 2008.

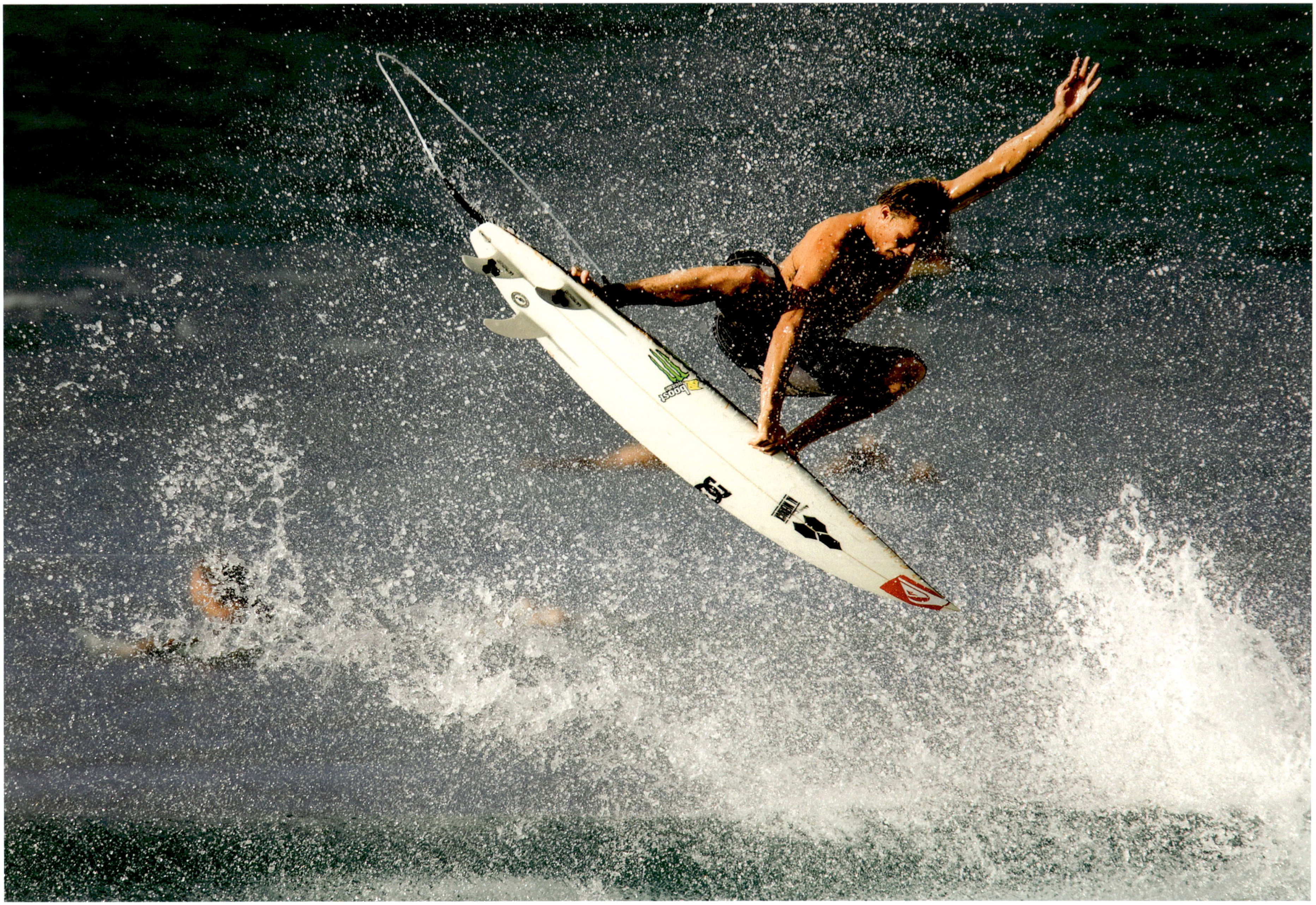

Dane Reynolds. Big hand on the twelve, Little hand on the five. Pupukea, HI. 2006.

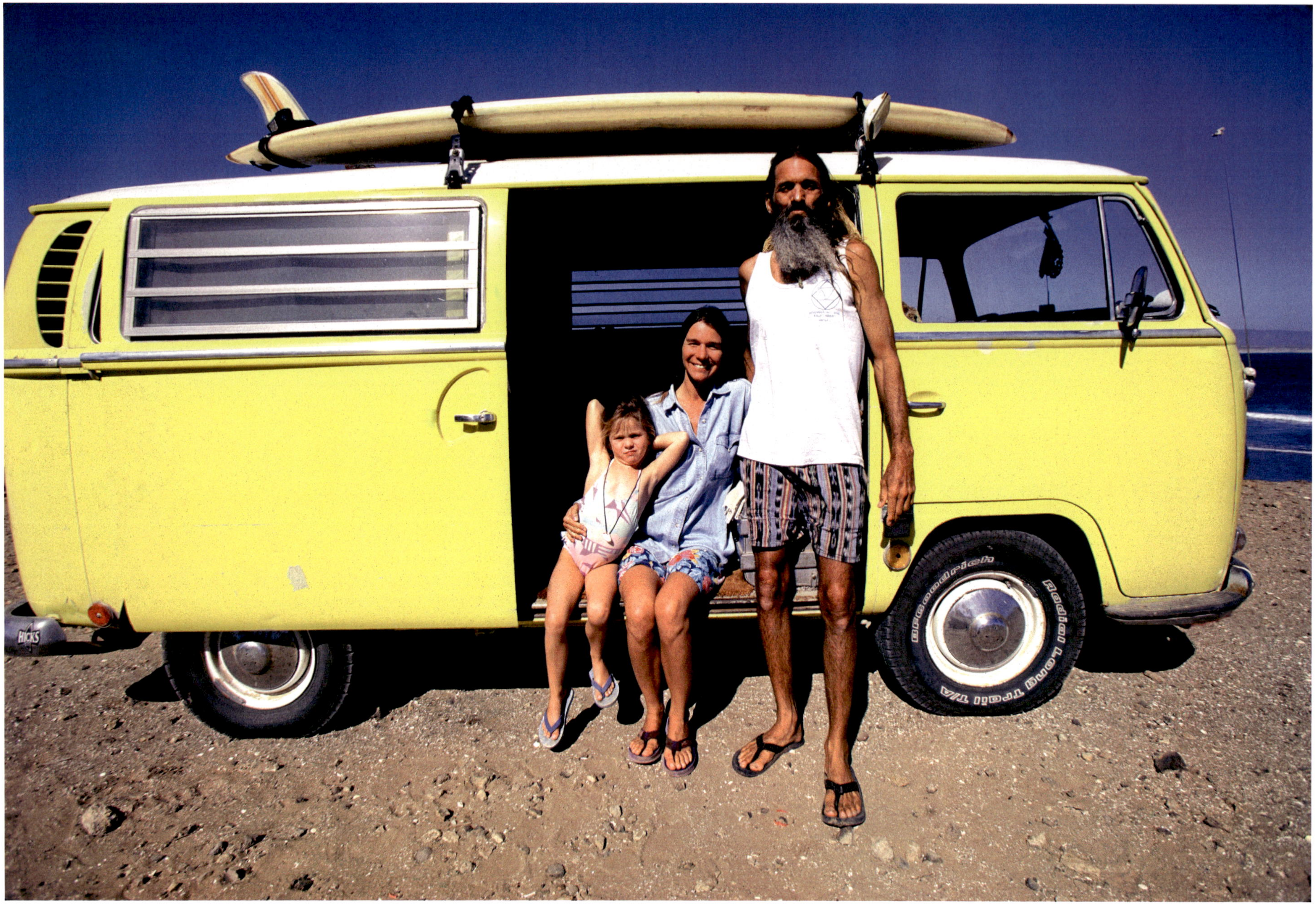

John Peck & friends. 1968 VW Bus. Deep Baja expedition. 1998.

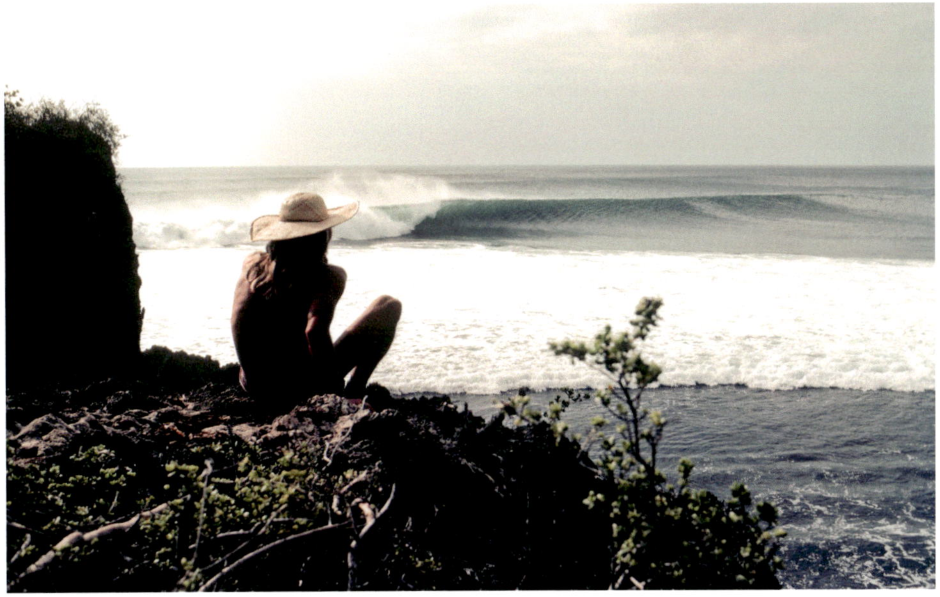

Outside the Bubble

When I was six years old, I got my first board and started surfing. Like so many other California kids, that marked the beginning of a lifelong adventure. Equally important was an early exposure to travel. For me, this started with long, cross-country road trips, seeing the world from the back of my parents' station wagon. They loved traveling and camping. Often times, we'd pack up on the weekends and go to Mexico. With my brother and I, and our surf boards in the back, we caravanned through the Baja landscape. I remember my mom and dad asking me to bring along some of my clothes and toys. We would stop along the way and give them to kids there who were less fortunate. Sometimes I passed on some of my favorite things. My parents taught me to share and made it clear that no one was better than anyone else, and that we needed to have compassion for others. Looking back as an adult, I see that these trips were about so much more than getting good surf. They were a chance to see, to learn, and to experience. There was always a sense of adventure and the unknown. The colors, scenes, and people I saw from the backseat of that car had me wanting more. Surfing turned out to be a great way for me to do just that.

While Mexico is where my traveling started, it was just the beginning—what a perfect introduction. That country is full of amazing surf and gracious people, and I still find myself returning there again and again, particularly the area in and around Puerto Escondido. Later in life, I fell deeply for Indonesia, traveling through Bali, Java, and the remote islands of the Mentawais. I've also been fortunate enough to have spent time in Tahiti and Fiji, particularly the island of Tavarua, one of my favorite spots in the world. My surf and photography circuit also included Australia, the islands off of South Africa, Madeira, La Reunion, and much of Europe. But there is no place I love more than Hawaii. Indeed, there's no place like home.

I am so grateful that I have been able to travel the world and shoot photos and meet people from every imaginable walk of life and geographical area. The following is a glimpse of where I've been over my decades of traveling for the surfing magazines. I hope they bring you joy.

David Kelly and no one out. Padang Padang, Bali. 1980.

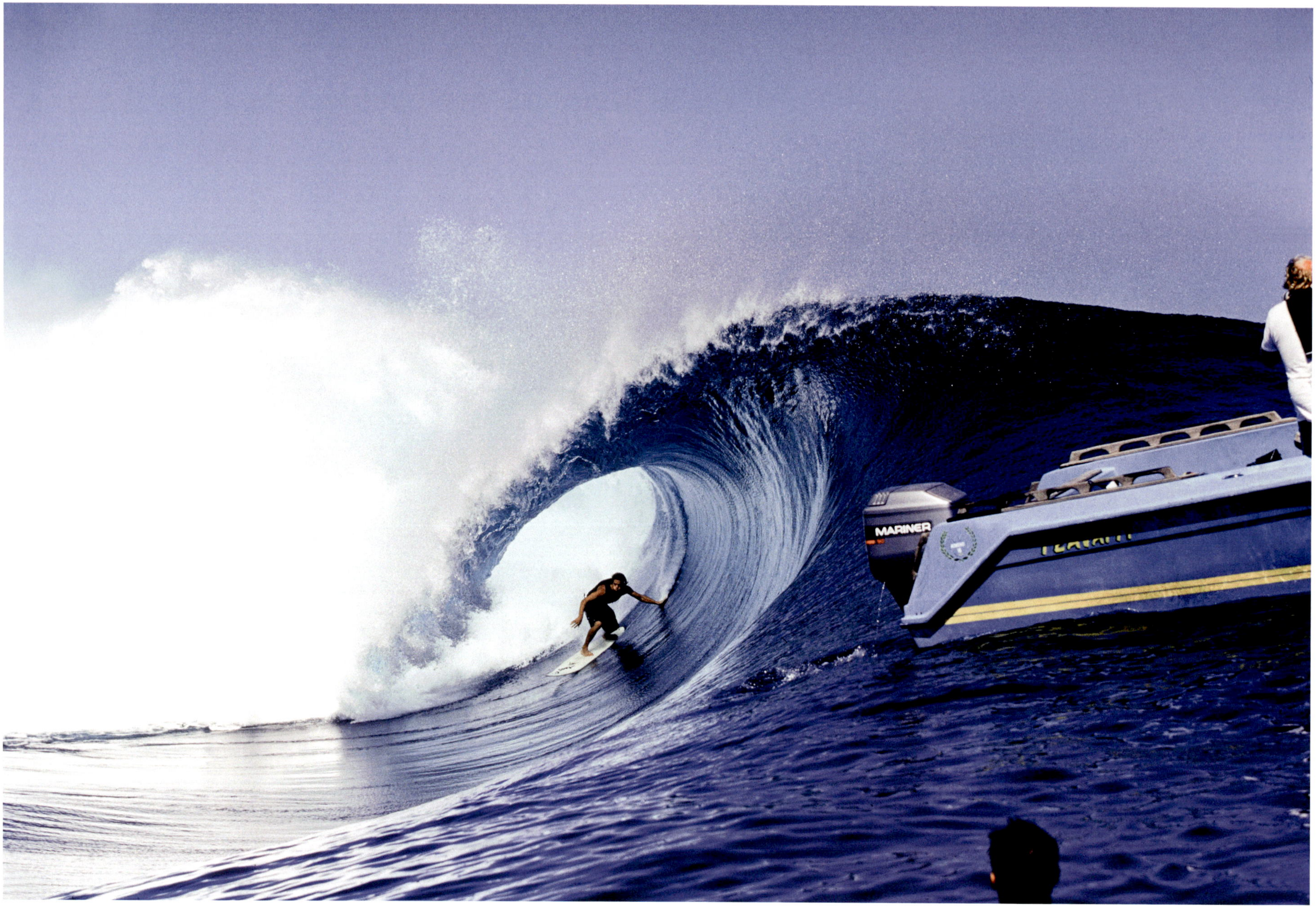

Malik Joyeux surfing on earth. Teahupoo, Tahiti. 2001.

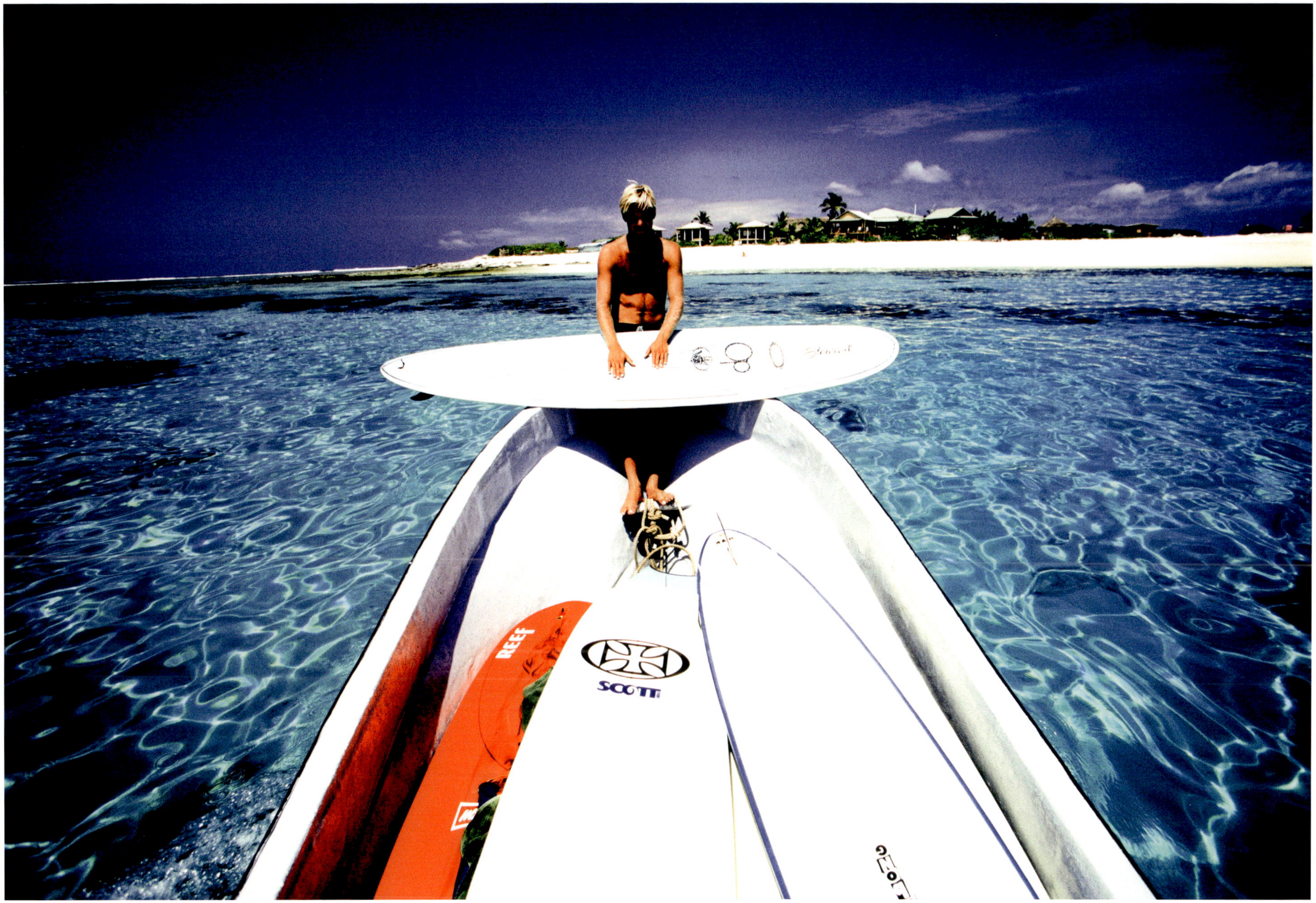

Colin McPhillips. Swimming pools, Namotu Island, Fiji. 1996.

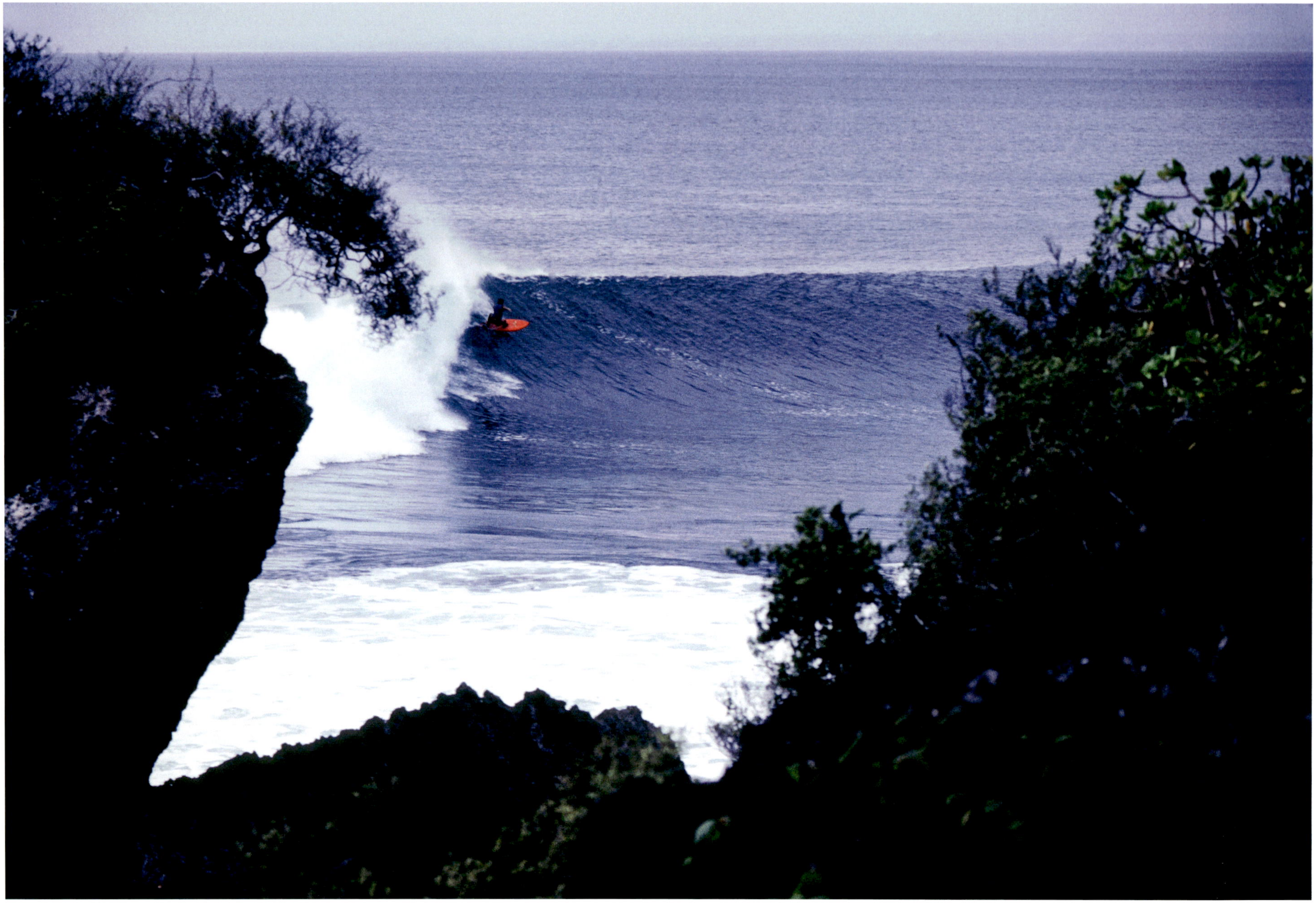

Rick Rasmuson, last session. Padang Padang, Bali. 1980.

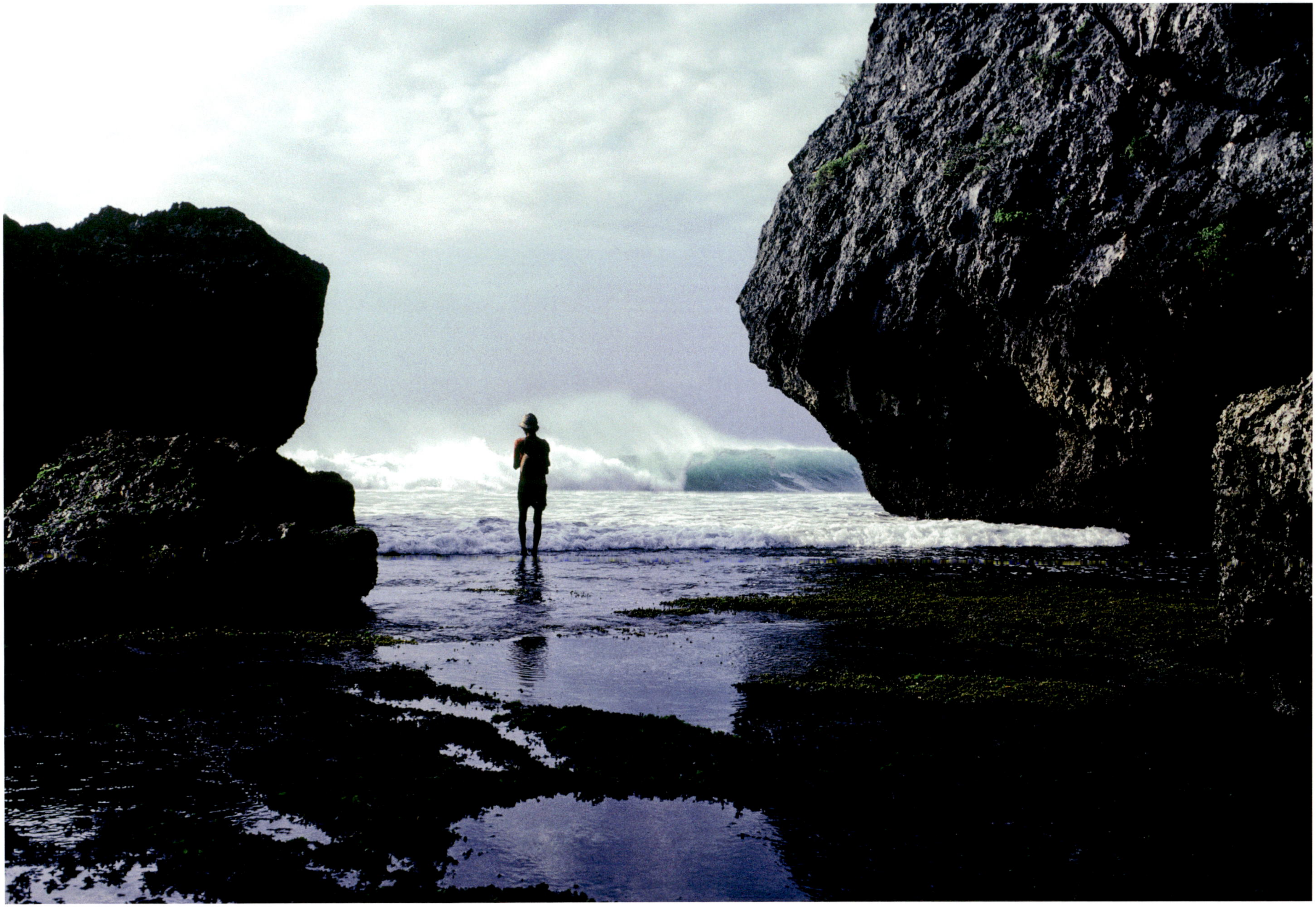

Balinese Fisherman. Uluwatu. 1980.

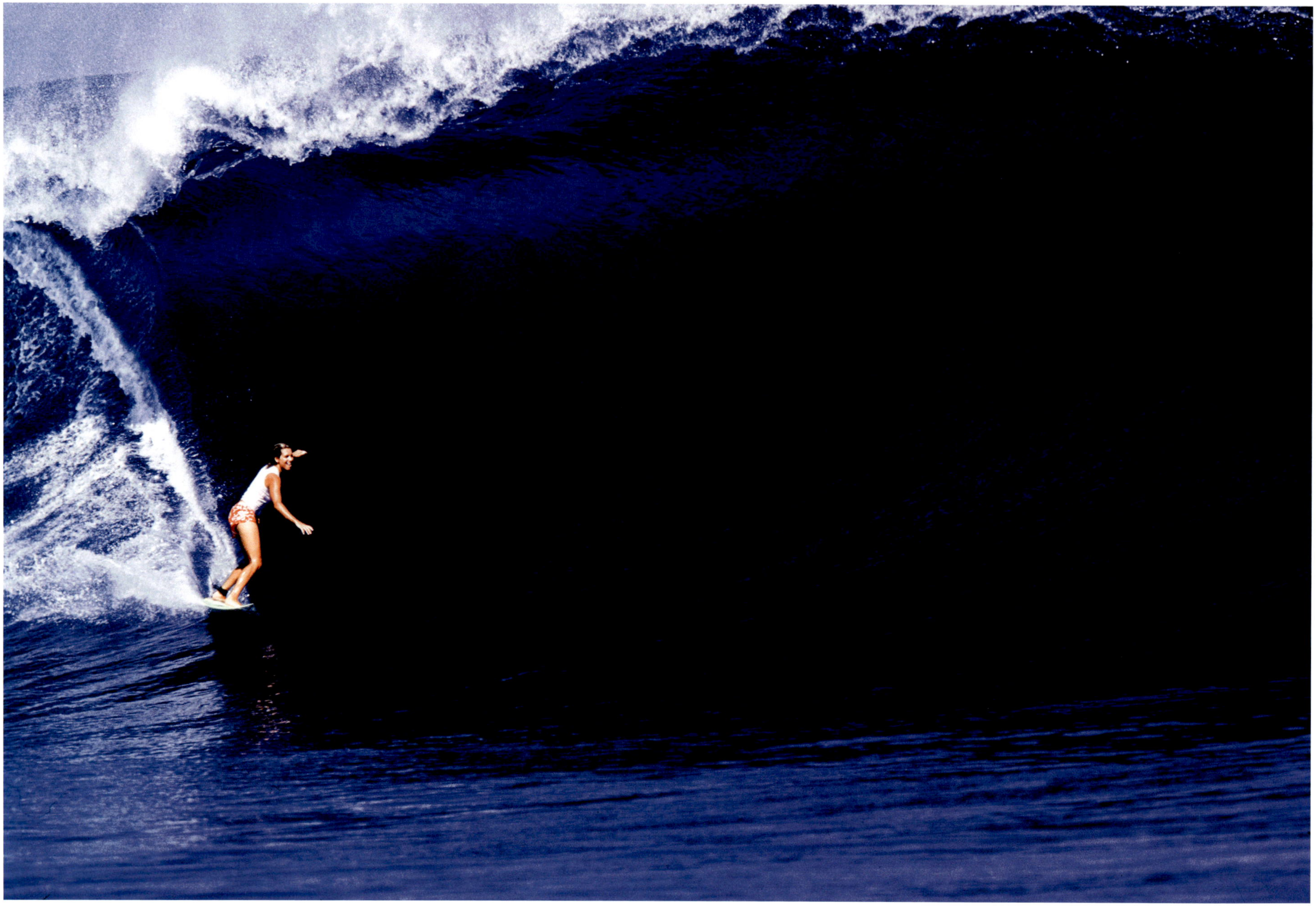

Jodie Nelson, first female tow-in session. Outer Reef, Tahiti. 2001.

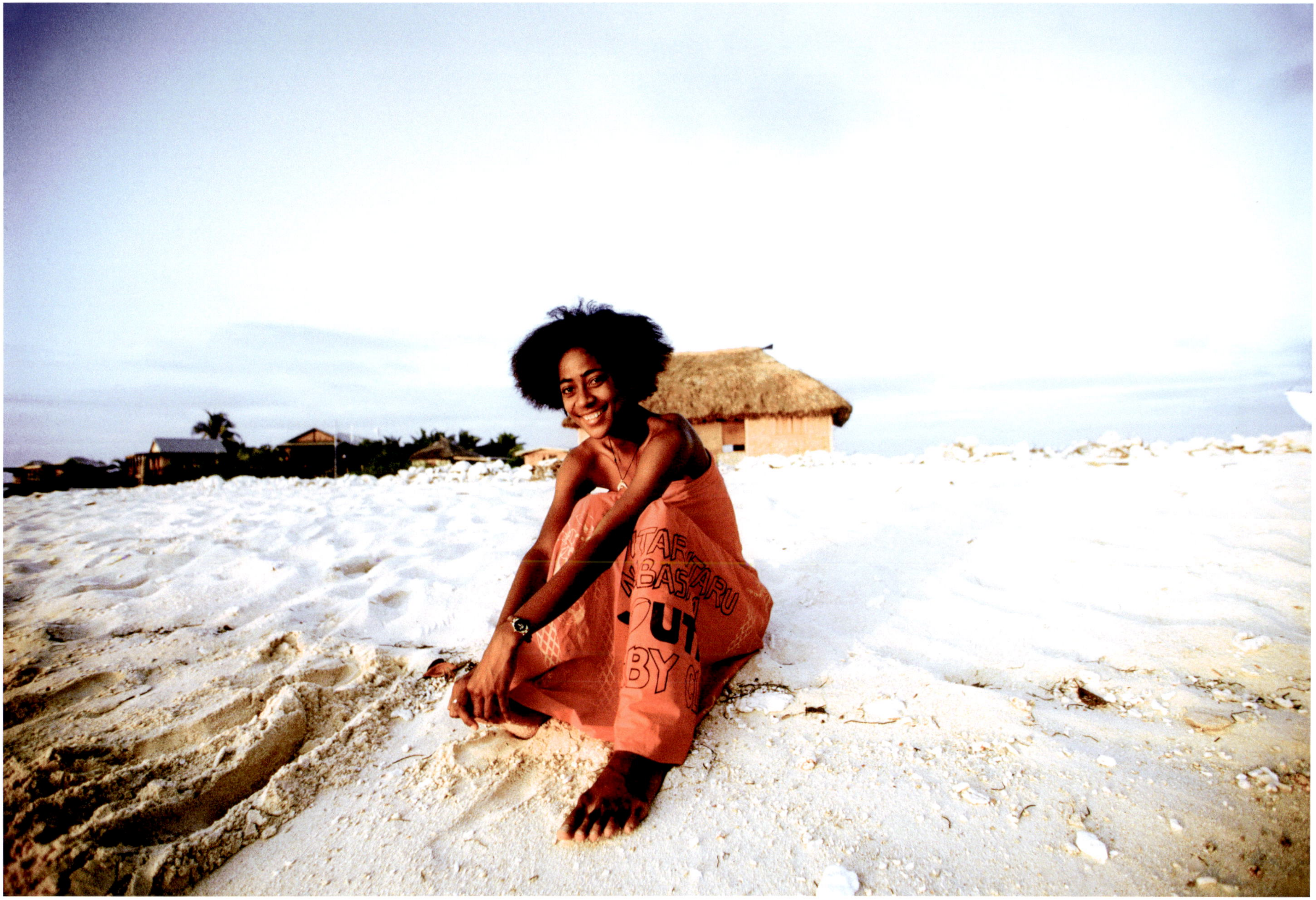

Welcome to Fiji. Namotu Island. 1996.

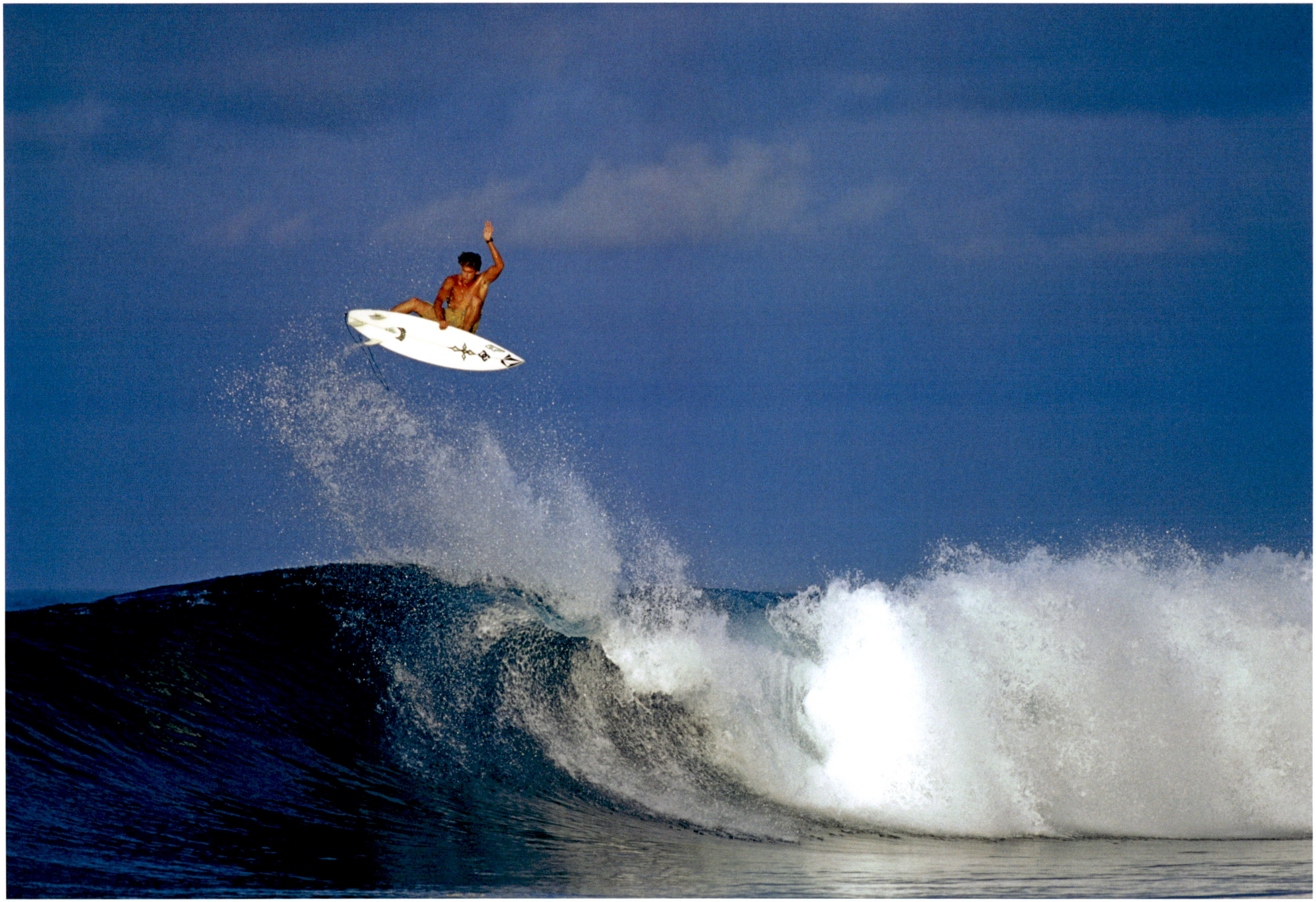

Bruce Irons, hangin' at Hollow Trees. Indonesia. 2000.

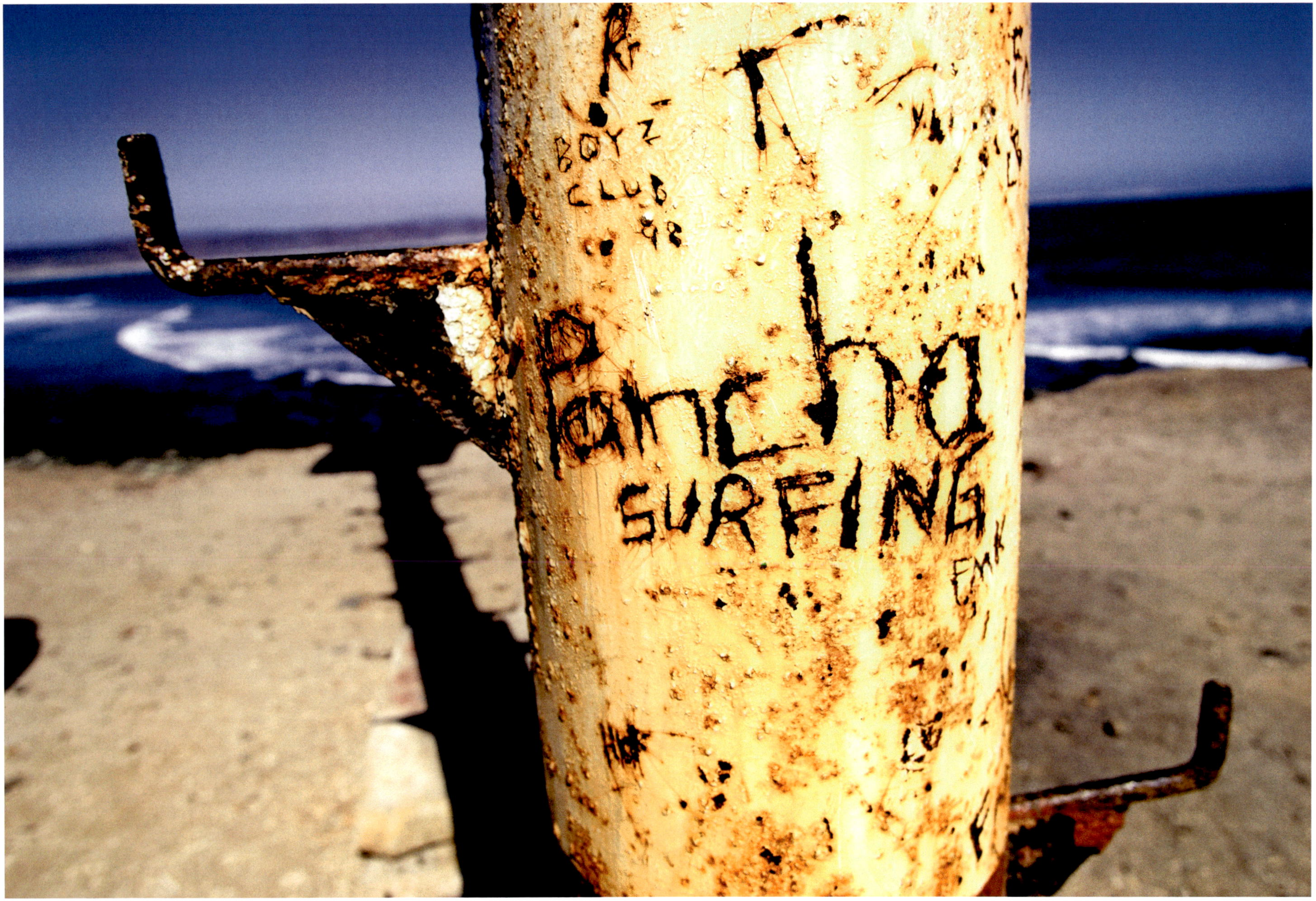

Mexico, 1998.

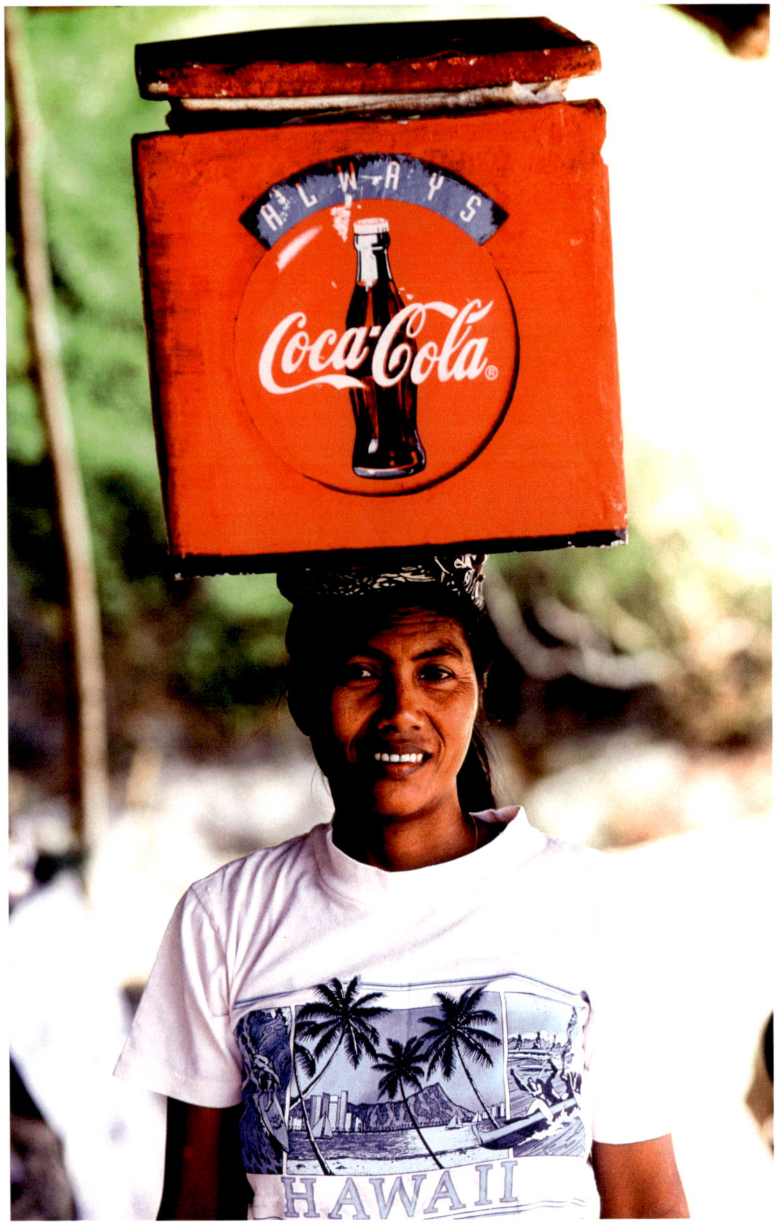

A Coke and a Smile. Bali. 1994.

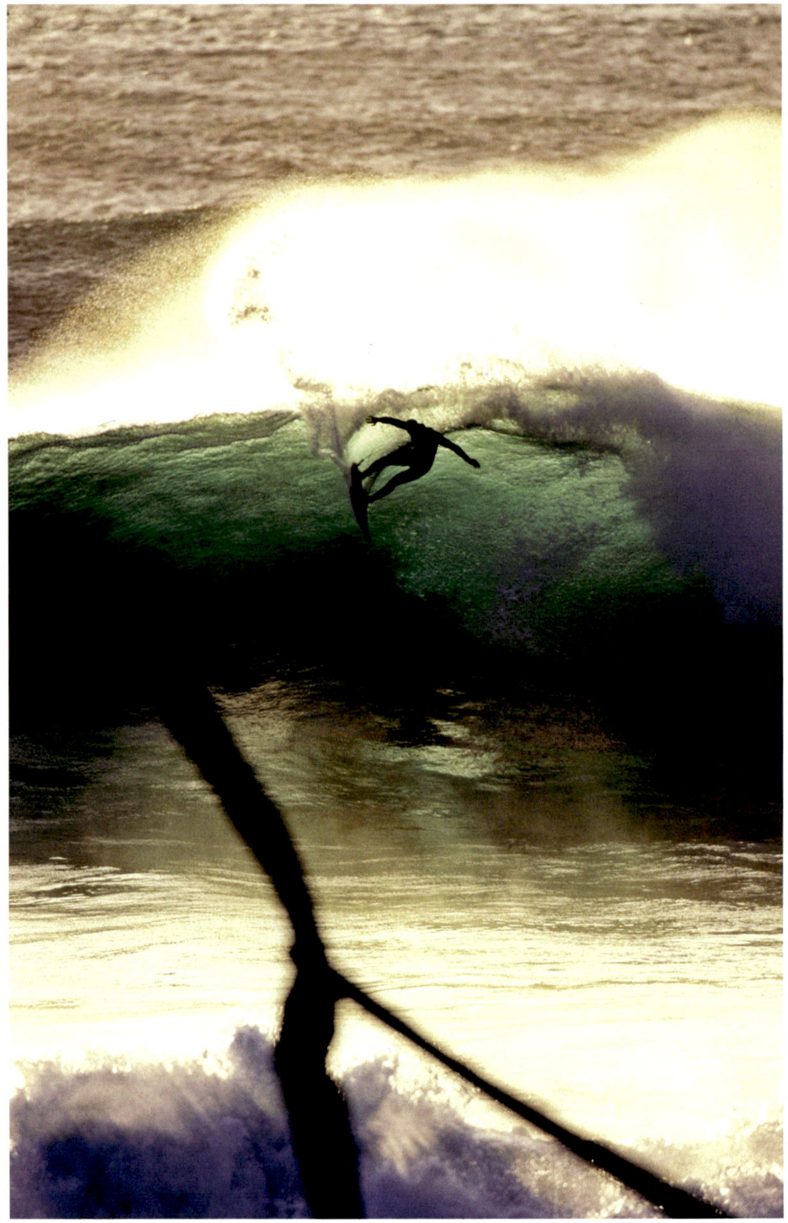

Todd Chesser, surf in peace. Madeira Island. 1996.

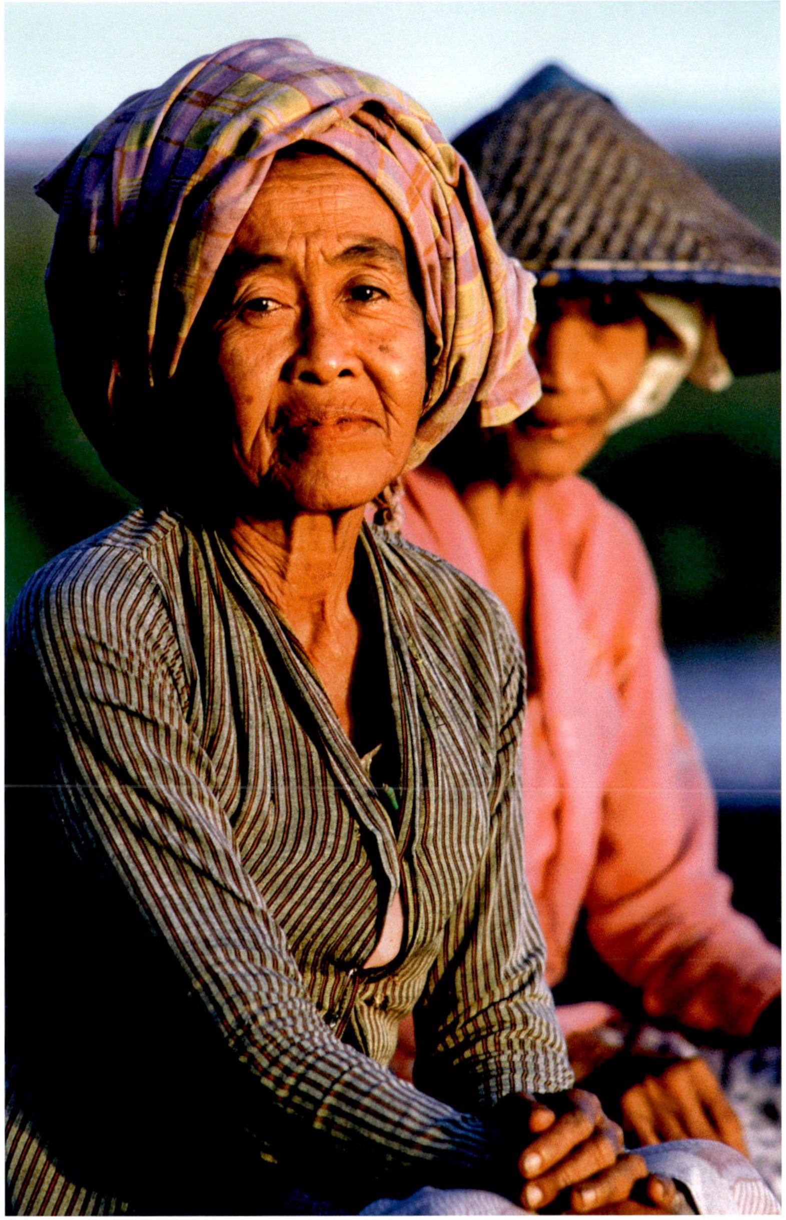

Java Locals. Grajagan Bay, Indonesia. 1980.

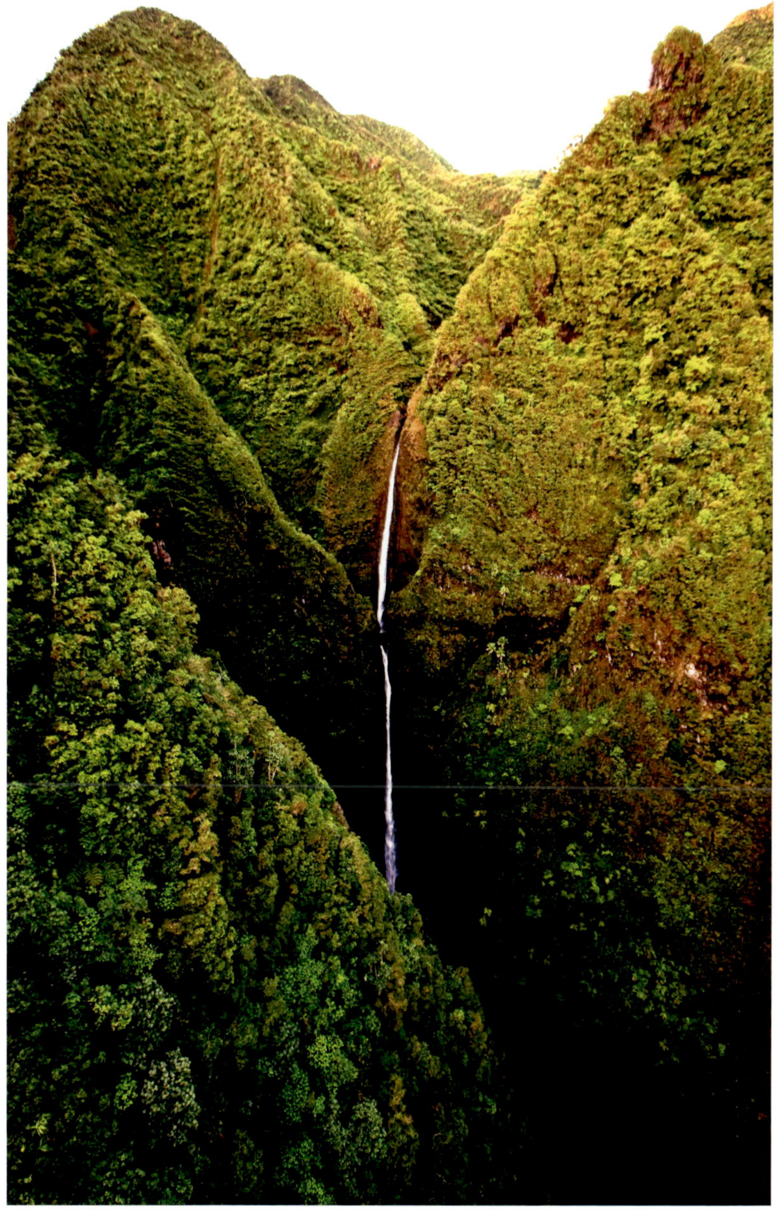

Jimi Hendrix may have been singing about this one. Eastside Oahu, HI. 2007.

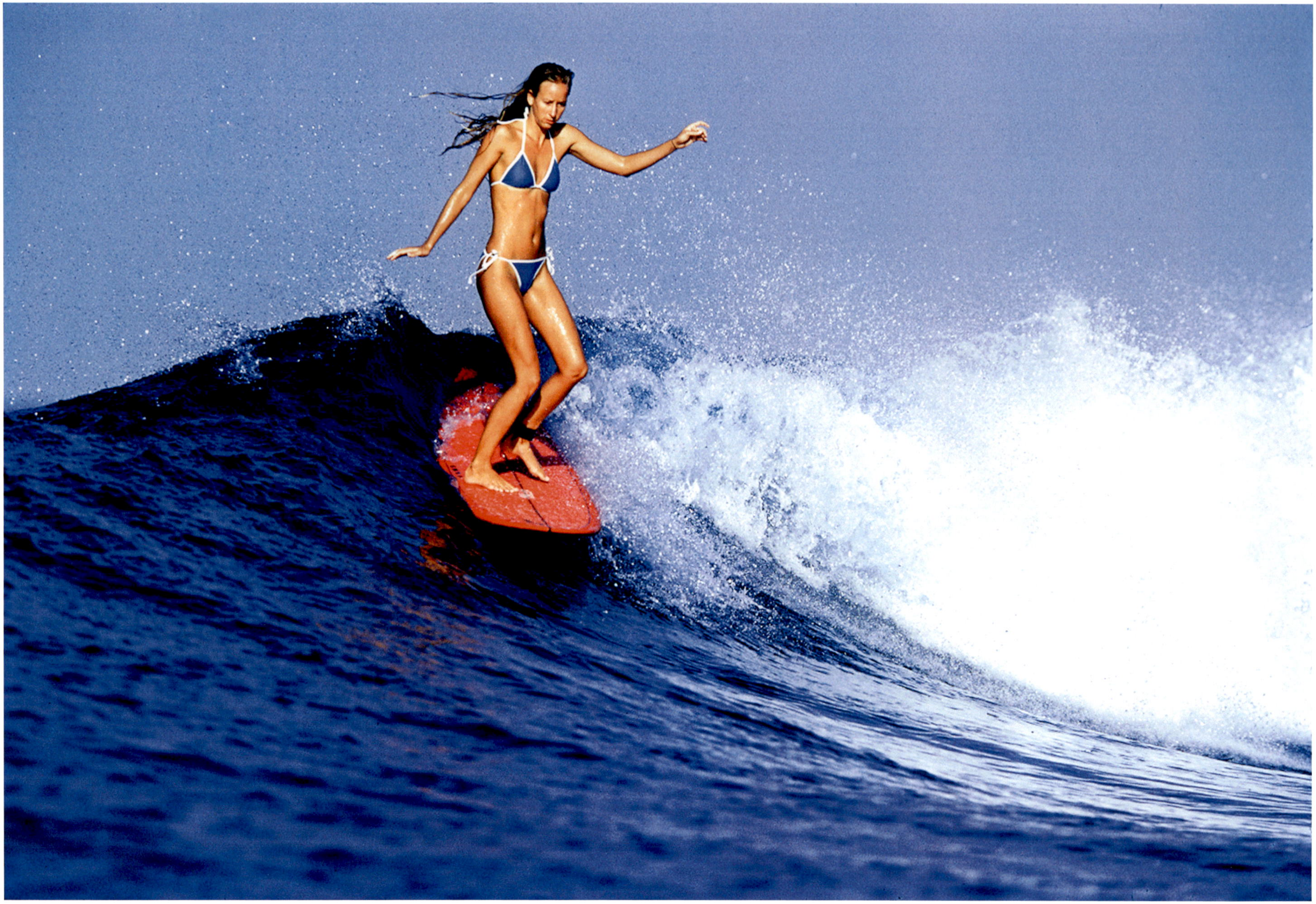

Daize Shayne Goodwin. Last day of world innocence. Namotu, Fiji. Sept. 10, 2001.

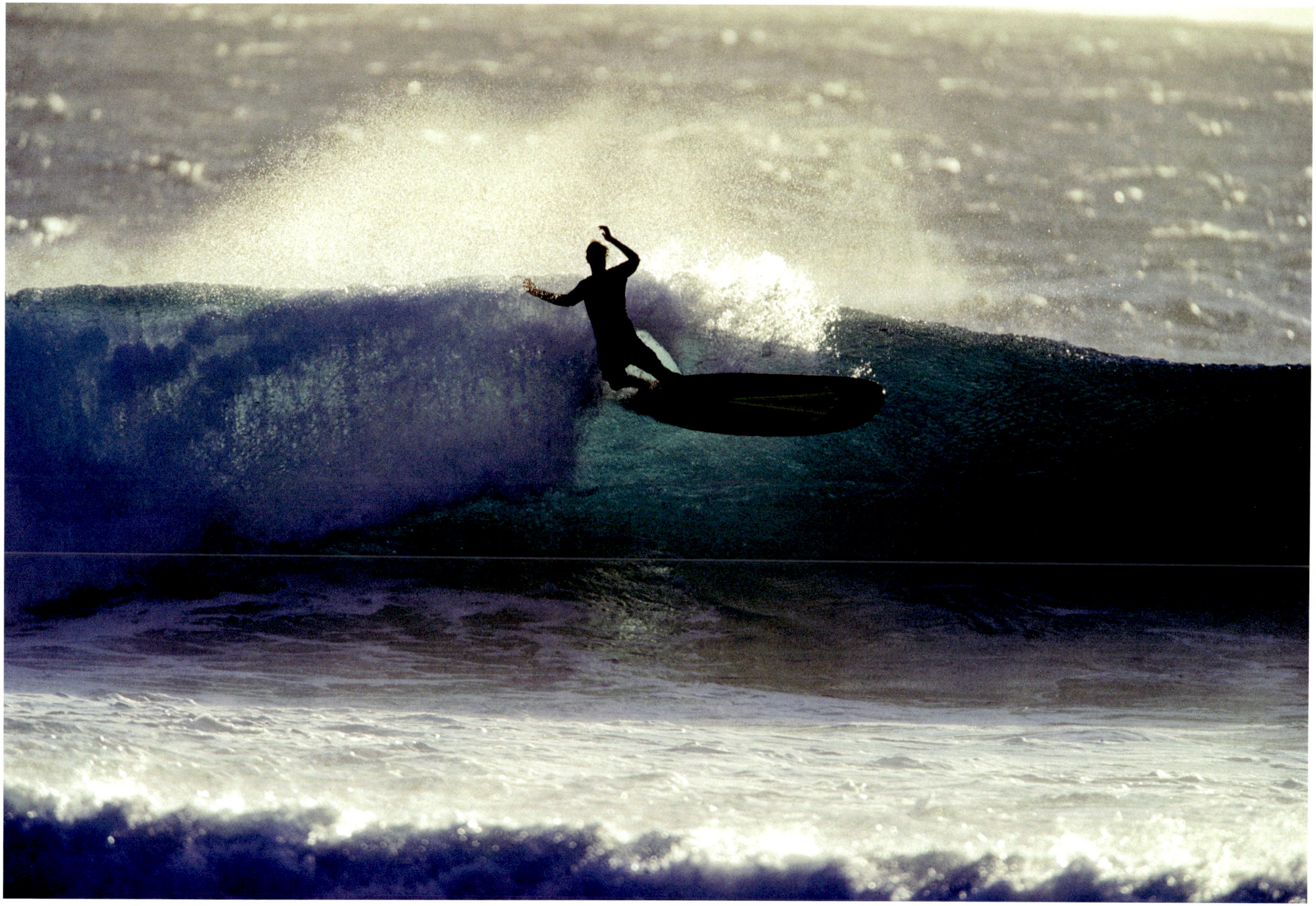

Herbie Fletcher. The Thrill is Back. St. Leu, La Reunion Island. 1995.

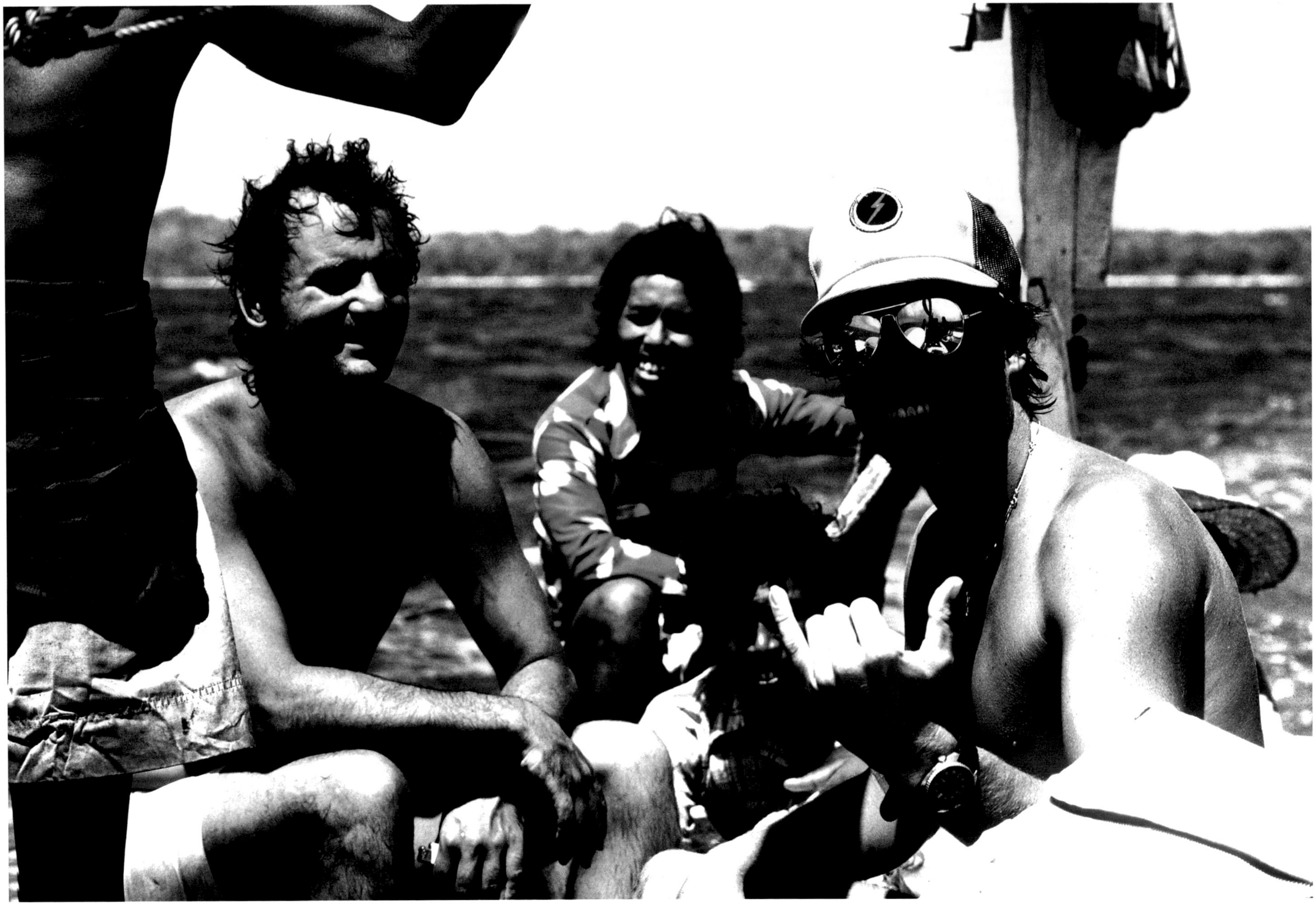

Bill Murray and Rory Russell. Boat ride to G-Land. Grajagan Bay, Indonesia. 1980.

Strange Days

Among the many travels I was blessed to experience, some journeys stand out more than others. One, in particular, is impossible to forget. The first time I went to Bali was in 1980; it was an overwhelming, amazing experience. I was fascinated with the culture and decided to stay for several months. During this extended visit, I ended up spending time with Rory Russell, a classic Pipeline surfer and Gerry Lopez's right hand man on the original lightning bolt surf team. One night Rory and I were out at a restaurant in Kuta Beach called Poppies, at that time the only game in town. Many of the waiters were lifeguards we knew from the beach, so we were in familiar company. While we were sitting at the bar, one of the waiters ran by and was raging about how he was going to have to beat someone up. We heard lots of noise and commotion from the dining room and got up to find a white man standing on his chair in the middle of the restaurant, howling some crazy old song at the top of his lungs. He had a wad of rupiah bills and was peeling them off and throwing them in the air. He was surrounded by a band of rough-looking Balinese guys, all clearly insulted and angry. Americans were rare in these parts, and we wondered what this guy was up to. The Balinese were offended and on the verge of teaching him a lesson. Rory looked over at me in confusion and said, "Dude, that's Bill Murray!" As soon as he said that, it registered. But this wasn't Live From New York, it was Live From Downtown Kuta Beach, and the locals were seething.

Rory and I quickly ushered him down from the chair and pulled him into the bar. We explained that he couldn't act that way here in Bali. We asked what he was doing here. He told us he was here from New York while a big actors strike was going on at the time. He was frustrated by the strike and fed up with the city and had blindly put his finger on the other side of a globe and landed here in Bali. He was curious why we were there. Rory explained that we were heading to Java to film a surf movie and shoot photos for *Surfer* magazine at G-land, a surf camp on the edge of a jungle full of monkeys and snakes and tigers.

Directly in front of the camp is one of the best tube riding waves in the world. Murray asked if we'd mind if he came along. Rory made the arrangements, got Murray an old longboard, and we took him with us.

We traveled in vans over land and then boarded an overcrowded ferry across the channel to Banyuwangi, Java. Now, traveling across Java, whenever we stopped on the roads crowds of curious Javanese surrounded our van. In 1980, there were not many white people traveling through Java, so we were quite a novelty. Bill would jump out of the van to entertain the locals with yoyo tricks and crazy songs. We arrived in the Graiagan village to make ready for yet another open ocean crossing, this time in large dugout canoes, across Graiagan Bay to G-Land; when we arrived having survived our crossing of the bay, we landed through the surf a half mile down the beach from the surf camp. As the boat drivers and crew carried our surf boards and duffle bags up the beach to the camp, I noticed Bill Murray had three Javanese guys carrying cases of champagne and a case of Stolichnaya vodka. I knew we were in trouble. Ten days in a tree house with Bill Murray, Rory Russell, Peter McCabe, Duane Webster, and a couple other guys in close quarters was like a live version of *Caddyshack*. One night after dinner, Rory was regaling us with stories of his adventures and the wild trips he'd been on. Bill sat there looking at him skeptically and finally interrupted Rory and said, "So I guess you're like the kingpin then, right?" Murray's tone was super sarcastic. Rory, after a few too many, didn't get the sarcasm and replied, "Well yeah, I guess I am." We all lost it, breaking out in crazy laughter. The big Bintang beers were spewing out of our noses and we were all in hysterics. The whole trip was like that.

Towards the end of our stay, we decided it was time for Bill to get his surf lesson. Outside, there were some ten-to-twenty-foot bombs peeling off and pushing water over the reef into the lagoon, making a nice, mushy, reform wave. Rory paddled Bill out across the lagoon at high tide and pushed him into the very first little wave that came to them. Bill stood up, parallel stance, feet forward, raised both hands in victory signs, and rode the wave into the lagoon, in classic Murray style.

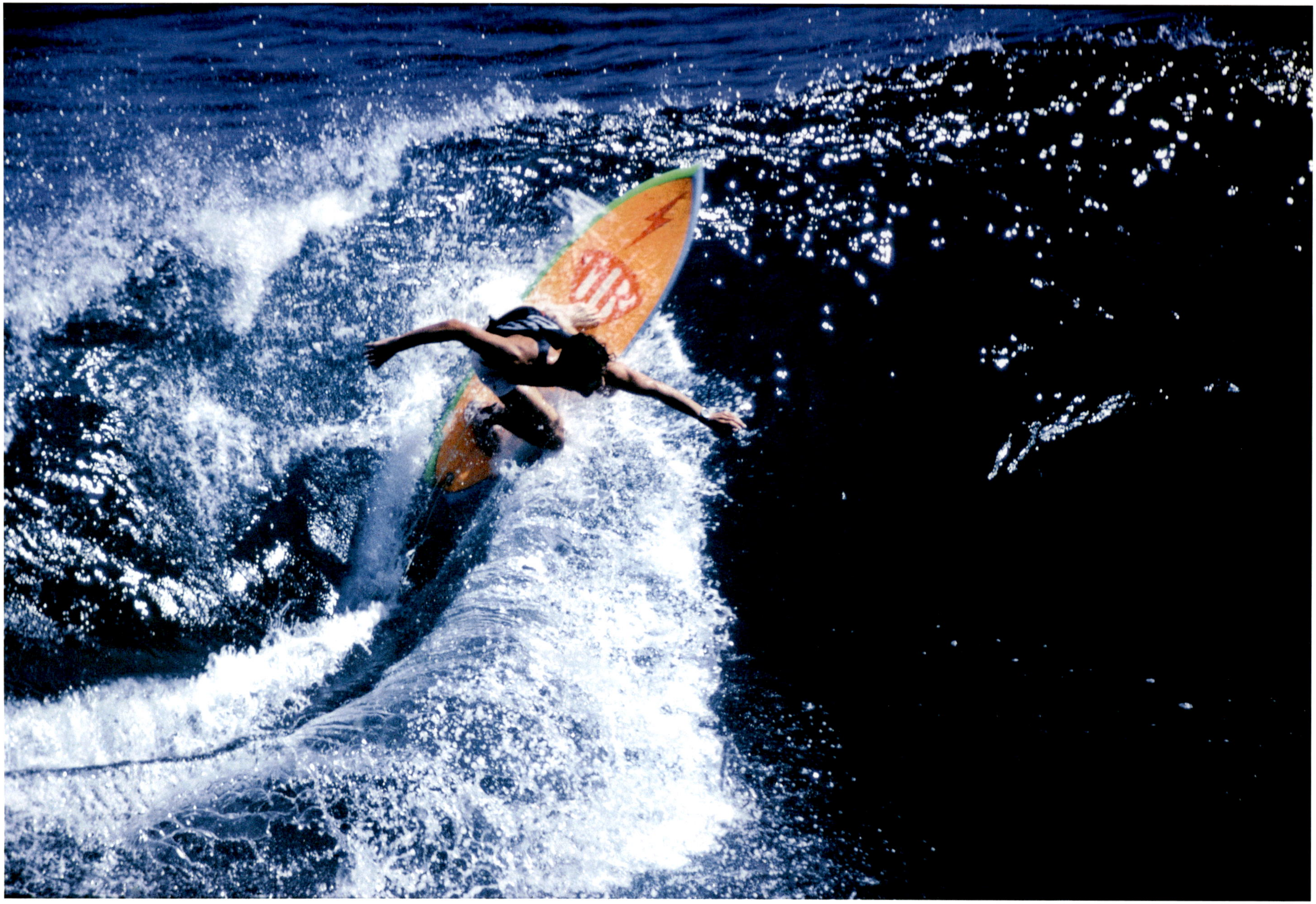

Mark Richards, my first cover shot, *Surfer Magazine*. Uluwatu, Bali. 1980.

Way Outside the Bubble

I stayed in Indo as long as I could. Finally, after three months in Bali and with $100 left in my pocket, I decided it was time to head home. It took a couple of days to get back to the States, with several layovers and a two-day stay in Singapore. I remember the captain's voice over the intercom as we were arriving in Singapore, urging everyone to ride in marked taxis and only stay at official hotels. I got into the airport and saw the long taxi-line, I was not about to turn down a ride. I was beat. A Singapore man approached and offered a cab ride without the wait. As we approached his car, I asked him why it was unmarked, and he said, "it was a private cab company." I thought it was a little strange but was exhausted and got in the cab. He stopped at a payphone and "helped" me call the "official" hotels to find out about vacancy. Strangely enough he said they were all full. He offered to take me to a place he knew had available rooms. I agreed but started to sense something wasn't right when he told me the cab fare would be $40. I had been told it was no more than $10 to any hotel in the area and only had $100 left in my pocket to get home. When we arrived at the hotel, which was an odd building that did not resemble a hotel, he dropped my bags in the lobby and the woman at the counter told me it would cost $100 for a room. I started to panic.

Then I remembered a note from an airline stewardess I had met from Holland, with a contact number in Singapore in case I was ever in trouble. Her name was Hanikah Peters and she had given me the contact information for an older couple she knew in Singapore. I called them and explained where I was and that I was a friend of Hanikah Peters. The man on the other end of the line told me to grab my bags and wait outside to meet the town car he was sending to pick me up.

After an altercation and scuffle with the cabdriver, who was trying to take off with my camera equipment, I got my bags and met the driver of the black limousine that had come to meet me. The driver got out and screamed at the woman and the cab driver as they were all screaming at me. The driver took me across town to a beautiful home where I met the man I had spoken with on the phone. I had been traveling for months through Indonesia and had lost about 25 pounds; I looked as scraggly as you might expect. But because I was a friend of Hanikah's, they took me in as their own. I thanked them profusely and we headed out to a fancy hotel, the Shangri-La for dinner. They treated me to an amazing meal, checked me into the hotel for two days, and prepaid for my stay and meals. I asked them for their address, since I wanted badly to repay them when I got back home. They said they would come by the next day for lunch and we could sort it out and I could get their address. I never saw them again. When I got back to the States, I tried desperately to get their contact information through Hanikah, but never could find a way to repay them. Maybe they were angels in disguise. I don't know what to make of it, but God was looking over me for sure, even in my stupidity.

I arrived back home in California, exhausted and underweight. My mother and girlfriend were super relieved to see me home safe after three months of adventure. I was in some crazy hippy Euro outfit speaking pidgin English with an Australian accent and a smattering of Indonesian. I had gone troppo, but now I was back in the California mainstream.

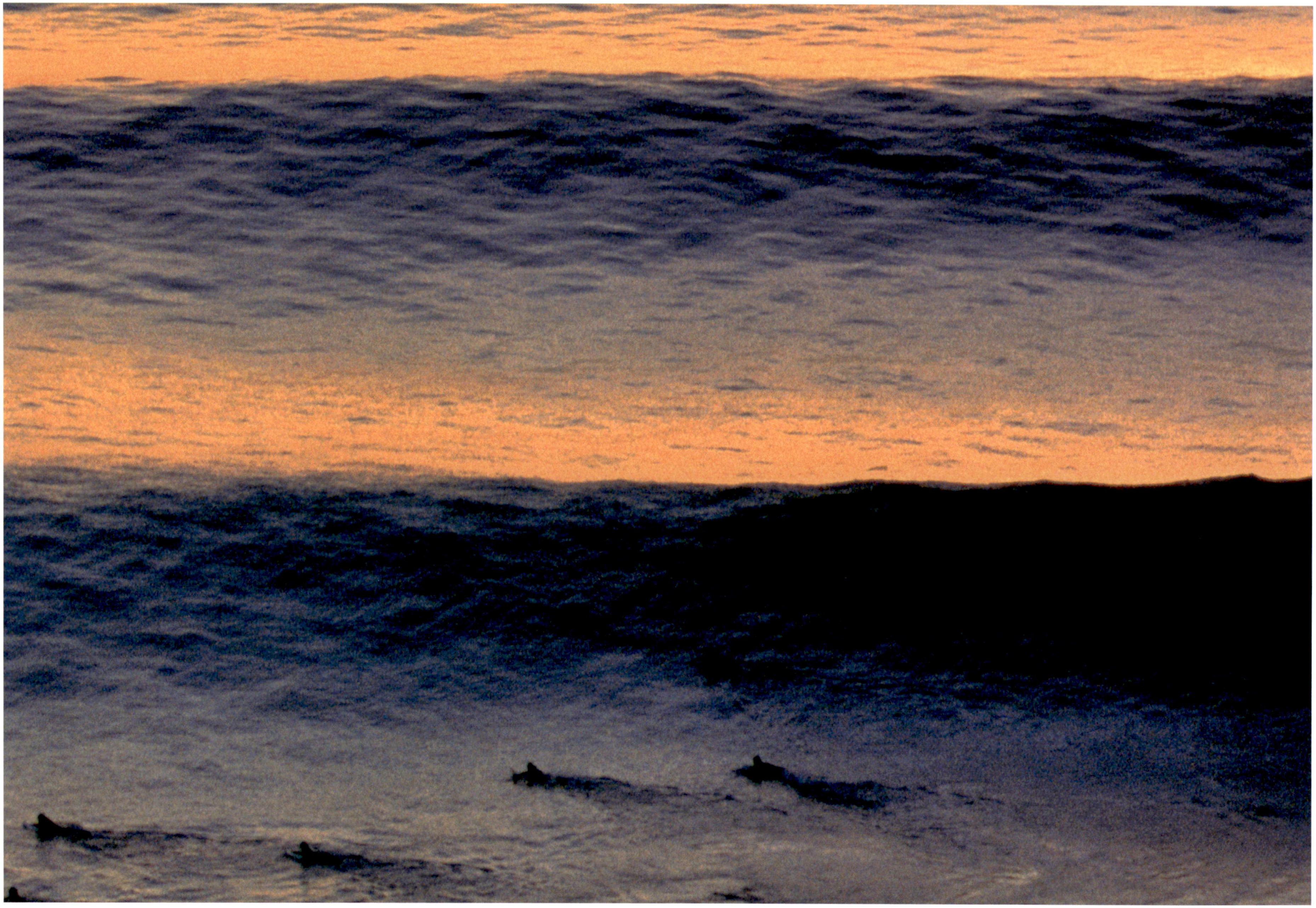

Los Angeles County, CA. California Dreaming. 1979.

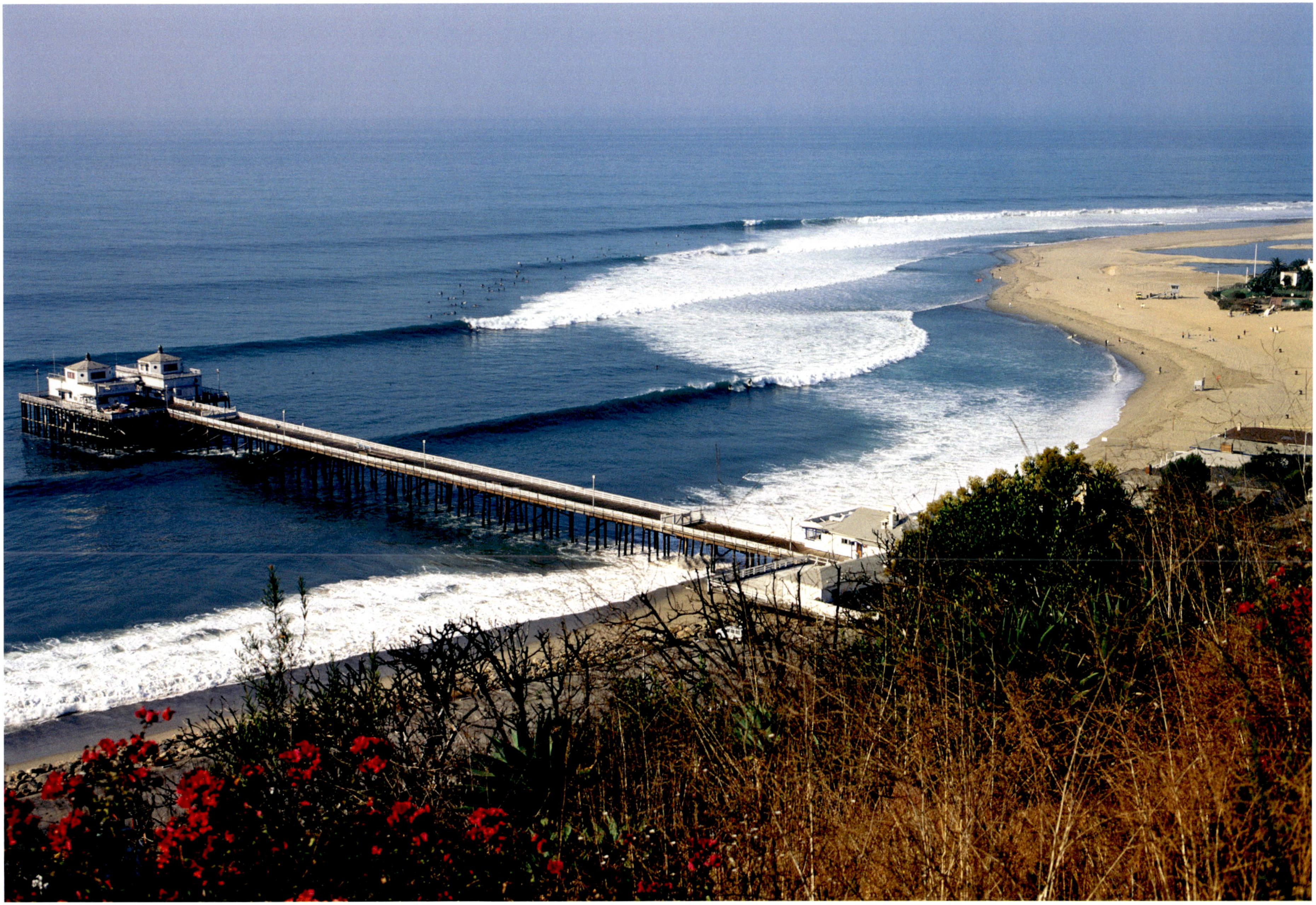

California legend. Malibu, CA. 1990s.

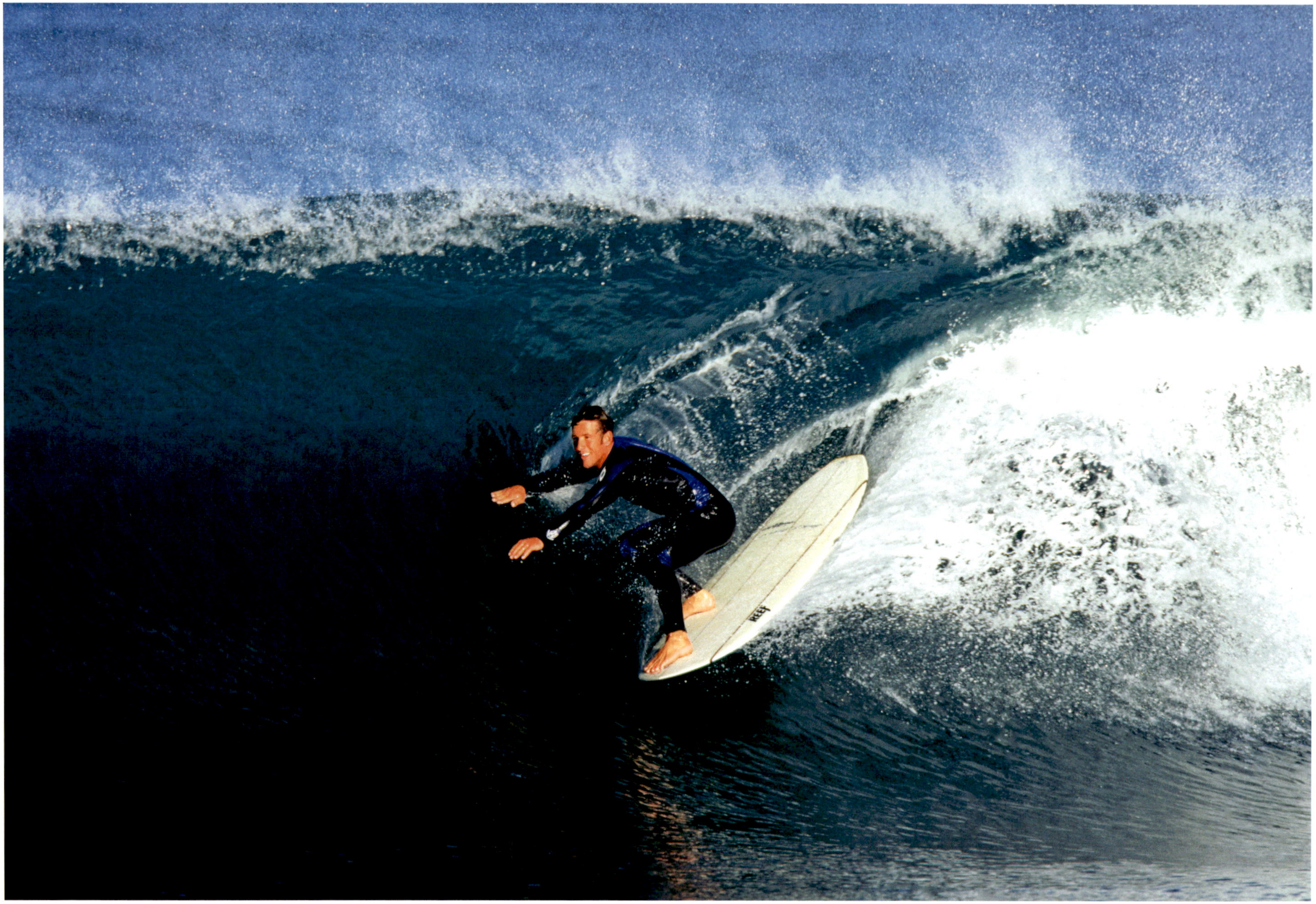

Wingnut cruising the central coast. 1999.

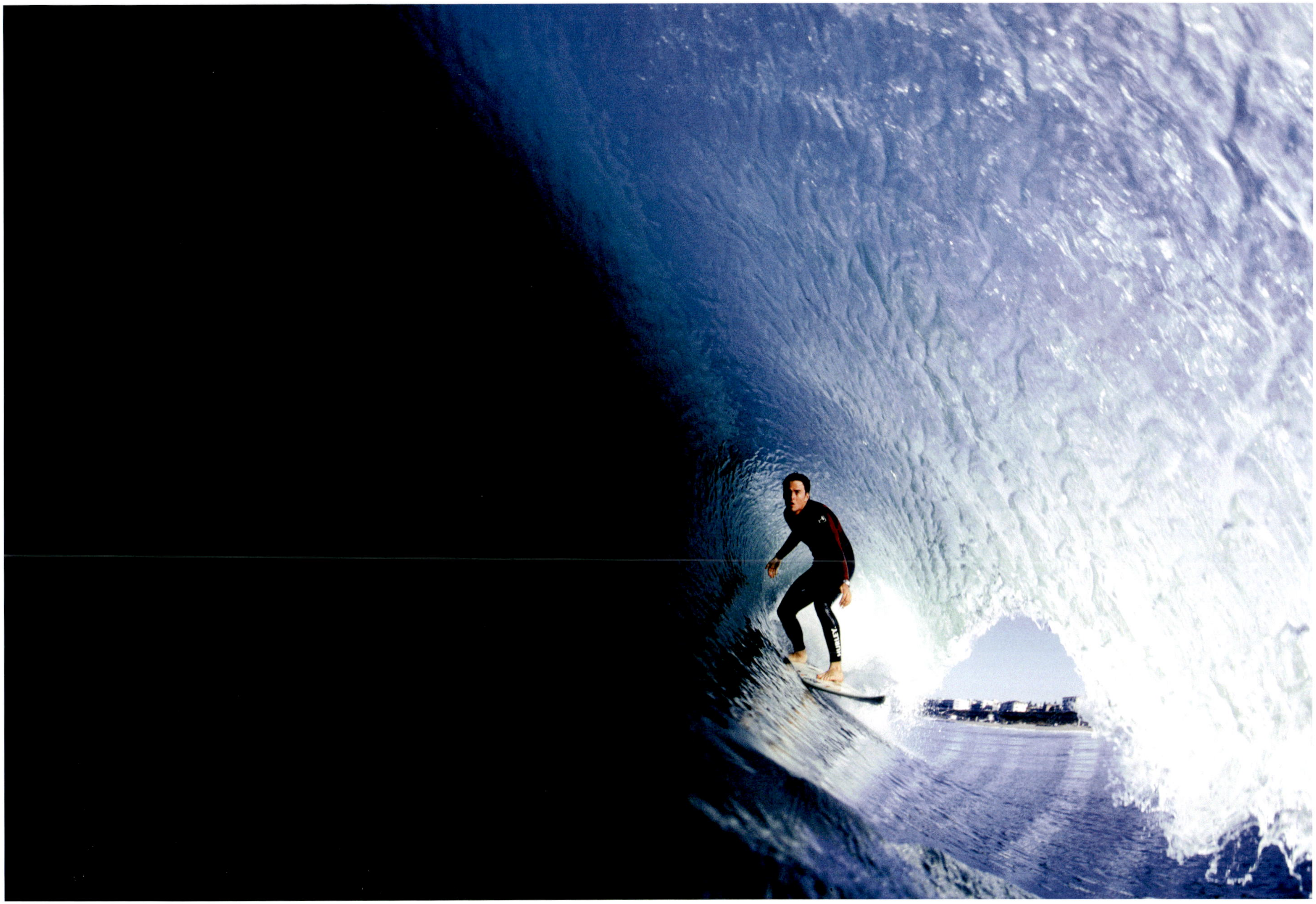

Dan Malloy visiting L.A. county. 1998.

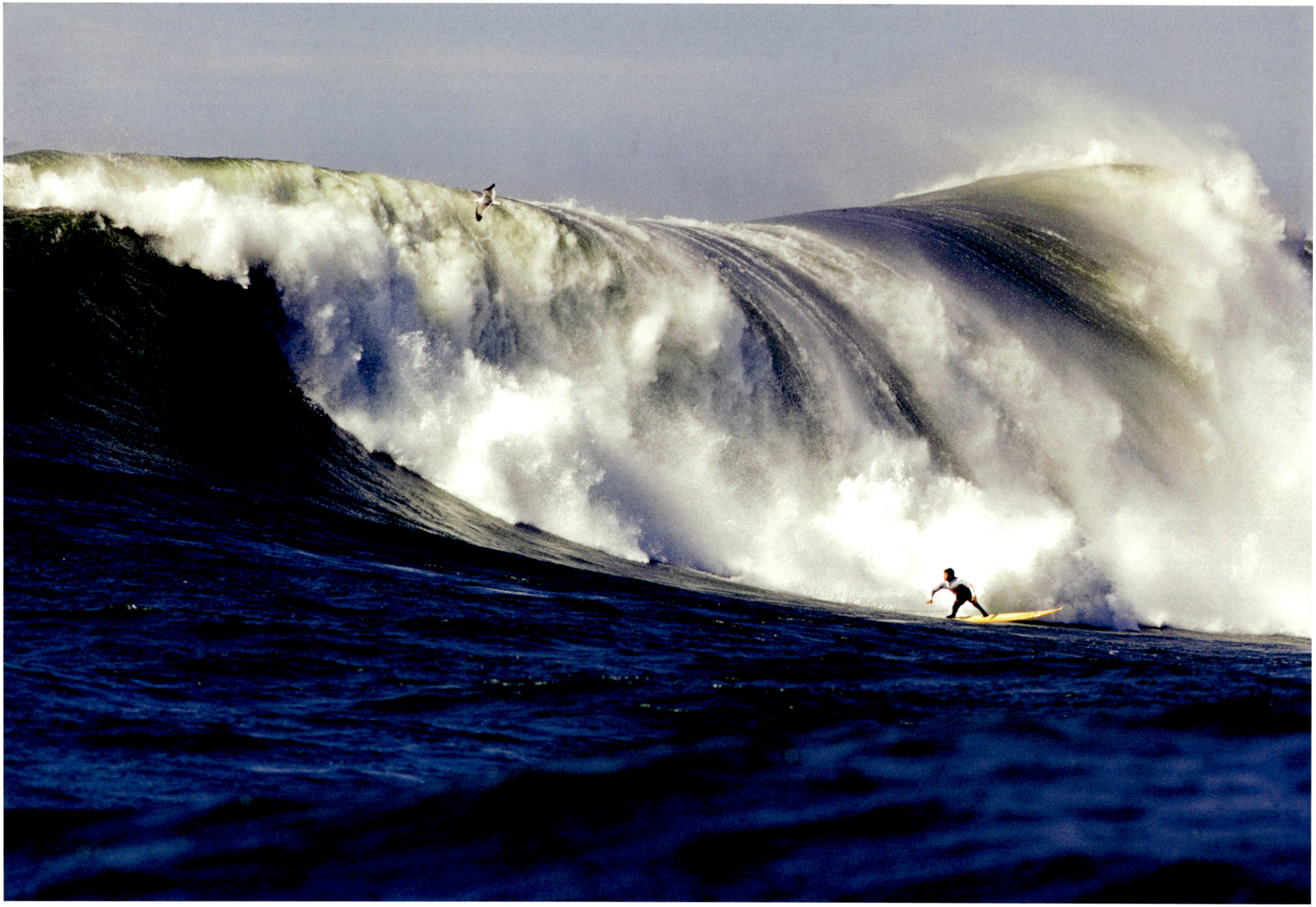

Flea Virasko sharing a wave at Mavericks. 2000.

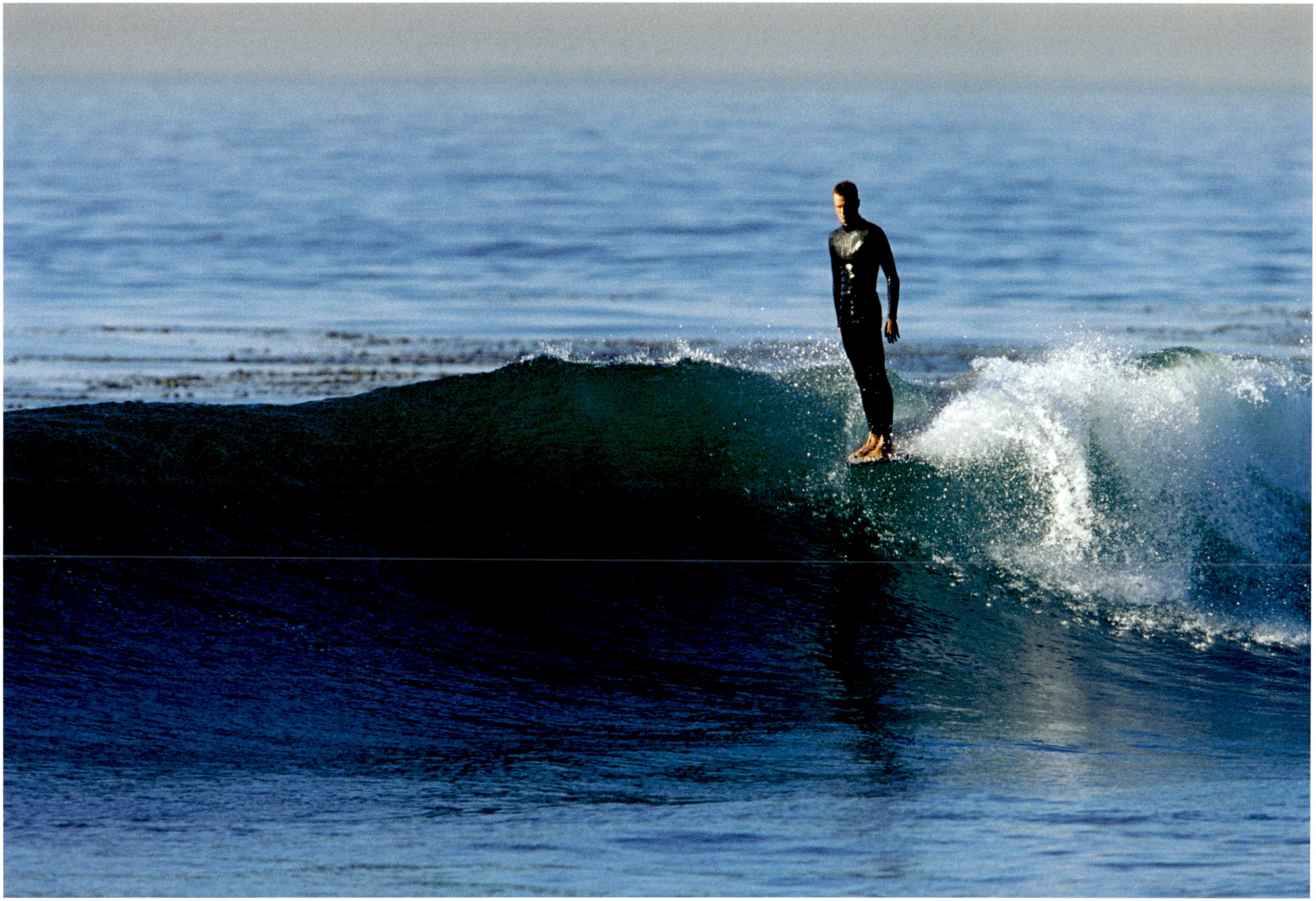

Mitch Abshire counts to ten. County Line, CA. 2005.

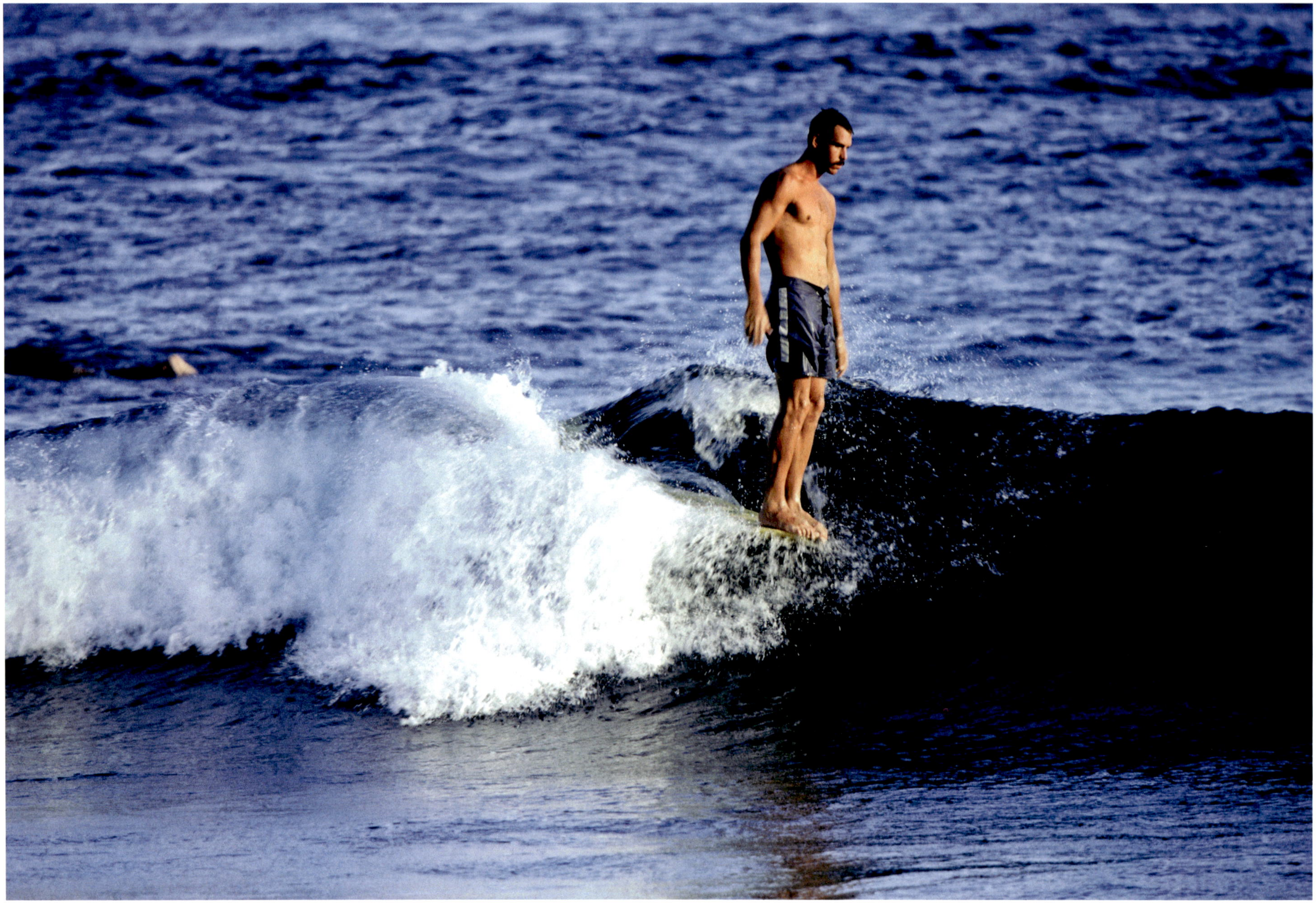

Tyler Hatzikian at home with his size 14's. El Segundo, CA. 1998.

The Golden State

California was a safe haven. I had enjoyed an unbelievable childhood, surfing the beach breaks of Manhattan every day with all my friends out. I was inspired by some great traditions there in the South Bay. In the 1960s, South Bay was truly the surfing capital of the world. All the major surf shops and board builders were down in Hermosa Beach at this time. The scene was enhanced by the presence of legends like Hap Jacobs, Greg Noll, Dewey Weber, and countless others. When I was six years old, I can remember seeing Greg Noll and Mike Stang out at Manhattan Beach Pier surfing and working as life guards.

Later on in Junior High School, I moved to Palos Verdes and remember well the hike up and down the cliffs to surf secluded glassy point breaks. Some of my fondest memories are changing into my wetsuit, down on the rocks, and surfing secret spots with just my friends out. While Hawaii has been my home since the late '70s, California will always be my roots. My closest friends from that California era, like Joe Bark, Frankie Ferrara, and Steve Fairbrother, always pushed me to ride big waves. These guys were a great influence on me. The surf mags and films showed me that there was more influence out there in a world much larger than my own. Near the end of the 1970s I decided it was time to go check it out.

Under The Influence

When I first came out to Hawaii, I found some new friends who were doing exciting things in the field of surf photography. I had just graduated from Brooks Institute with a Bachelor's degree in fashion and advertising photography. I planned to head out to Hawaii for a week to surf and then go back to LA and build a studio there to become a fashion photographer. That never happened. After a few nights of couch crashing, I was offered a room at a friend-of-a-friend's. I woke up the next morning in surf photographer Jeff Hornbaker's house and we instantly hit it off. While I was strict and regimented based on my formal photographic education, Jeff was stoked and passionate, having learned the craft on his own. He had great ideas and his enthusiasm was addictive. He was a skilled waterman, as well. Through Jeff, I met two other extremely talented photographers, Aaron Chang and Dan Merkel.

Dan was a hero to me and he took a great interest in my work. He spent time looking at my photos and offering me invaluable criticism. He also helped me break into the surfing industry by sending out letters of introduction to the surf mags. He got me in touch with Art Brewer at *Surfer Magazine* and Larry "Flame" Moore, the photo editor at *Surfing Magazine*. Later on I worked closely with Jeff Divine at both *Surfer* and *The Surfer's Journal*. These guys never quit on me and were rightfully hard on me at first. Aaron Chang has been a lifetime mentor and friend, teaching me all I know about the business. They helped me in so many ways to perfect my craft and hone my skills as a surf photographer. More recently, Scott Aichner, whom I consider to be one of the finest water photographers in the world, has immensely influenced me. He has pushed me to a new level.

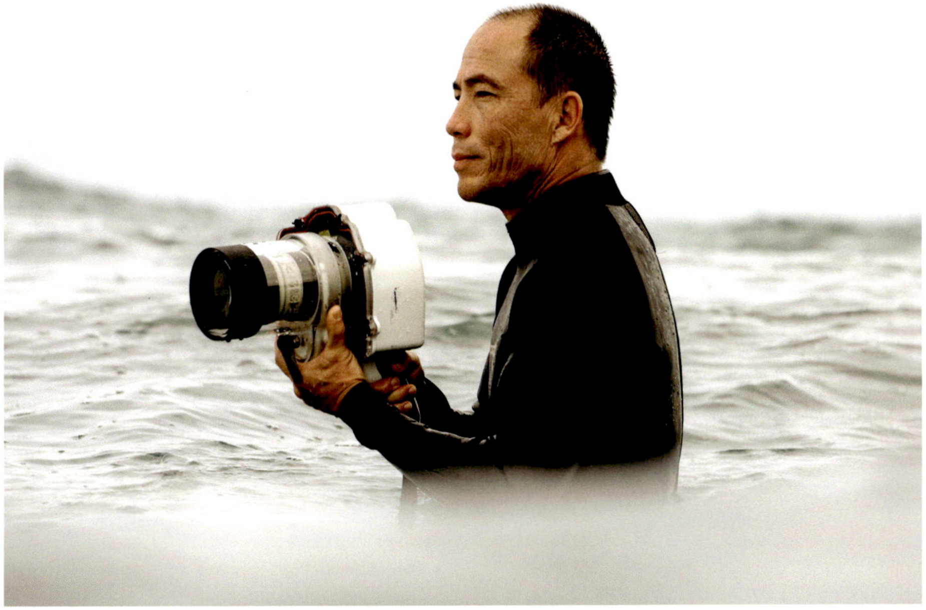

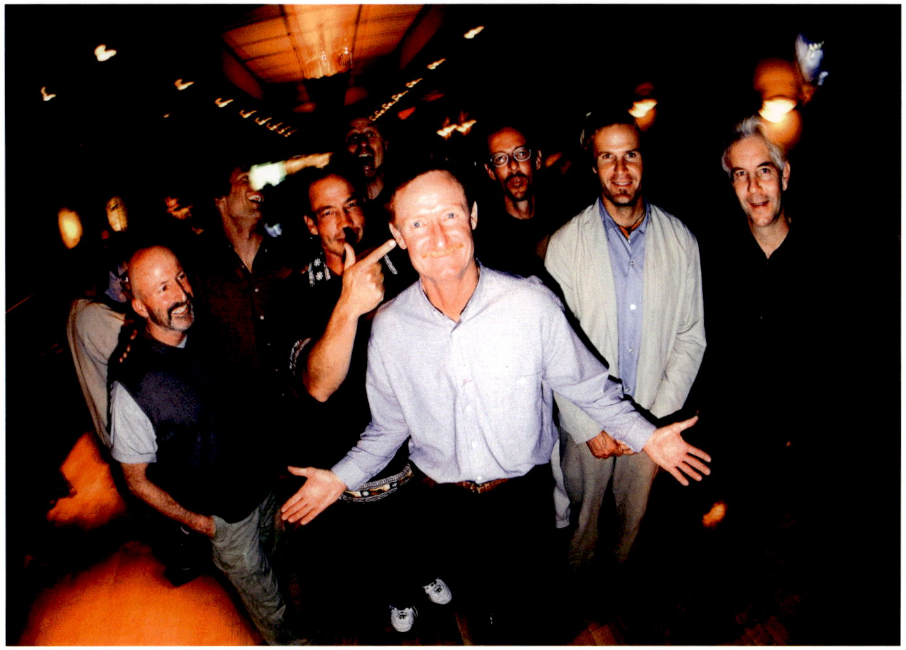

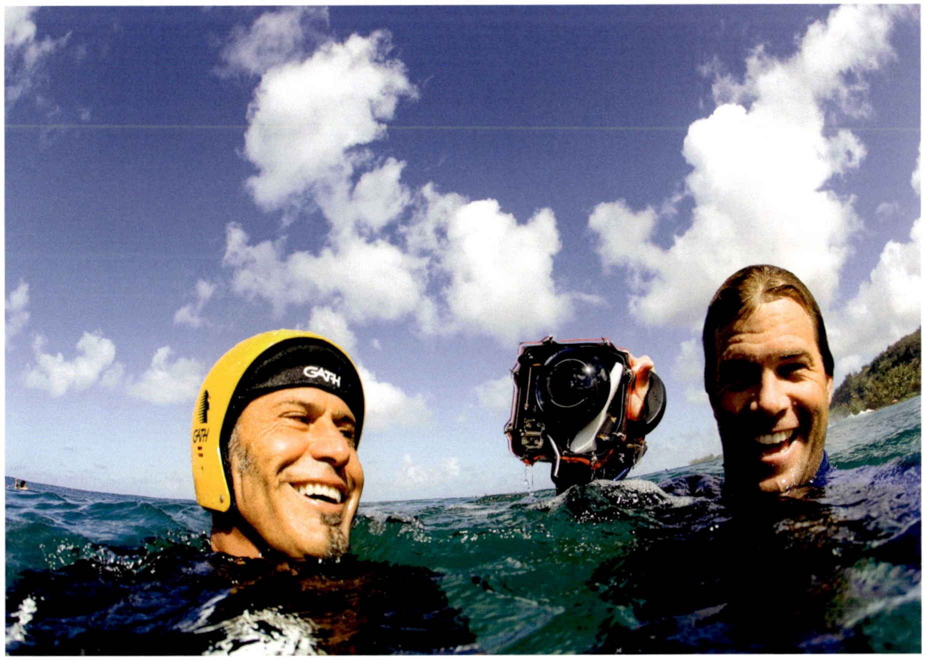

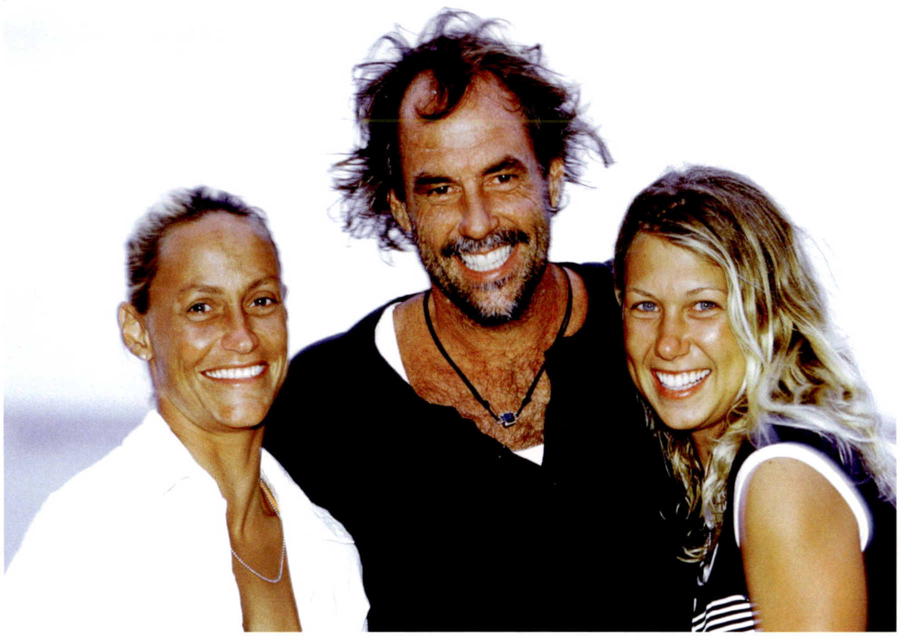

Clockwise from top left: Aaron Chang, Larry "Flame" Moore, Jeff Hornbaker with Lisa Andersen and Veronica Kay, Jim Russi and Scott Aichner.

Roxy Tribe

When I was a kid, I had no idea that I would spend the rest of my life in the water, eventually building a career out of it. The last ten years of my life have been devoted to the Quiksilver Roxy Advertising Campaign.

Working with some of the finest minds in the business, Randy Hild, Tom Adler, Danielle Beck, and Jim Poore, the Roxy team enabled me to showcase my talents in a new way. All those things I had learned and experimented with could now be put towards a campaign showing surfing and lifestyle in a way I understood. Roxy was able to put surfing in a new light by emphasizing the fun and beautiful lifestyle side of surfing. Collaborating with the team, I've created images that show the athleticism of the sport as well as the spirit and soul behind the act.

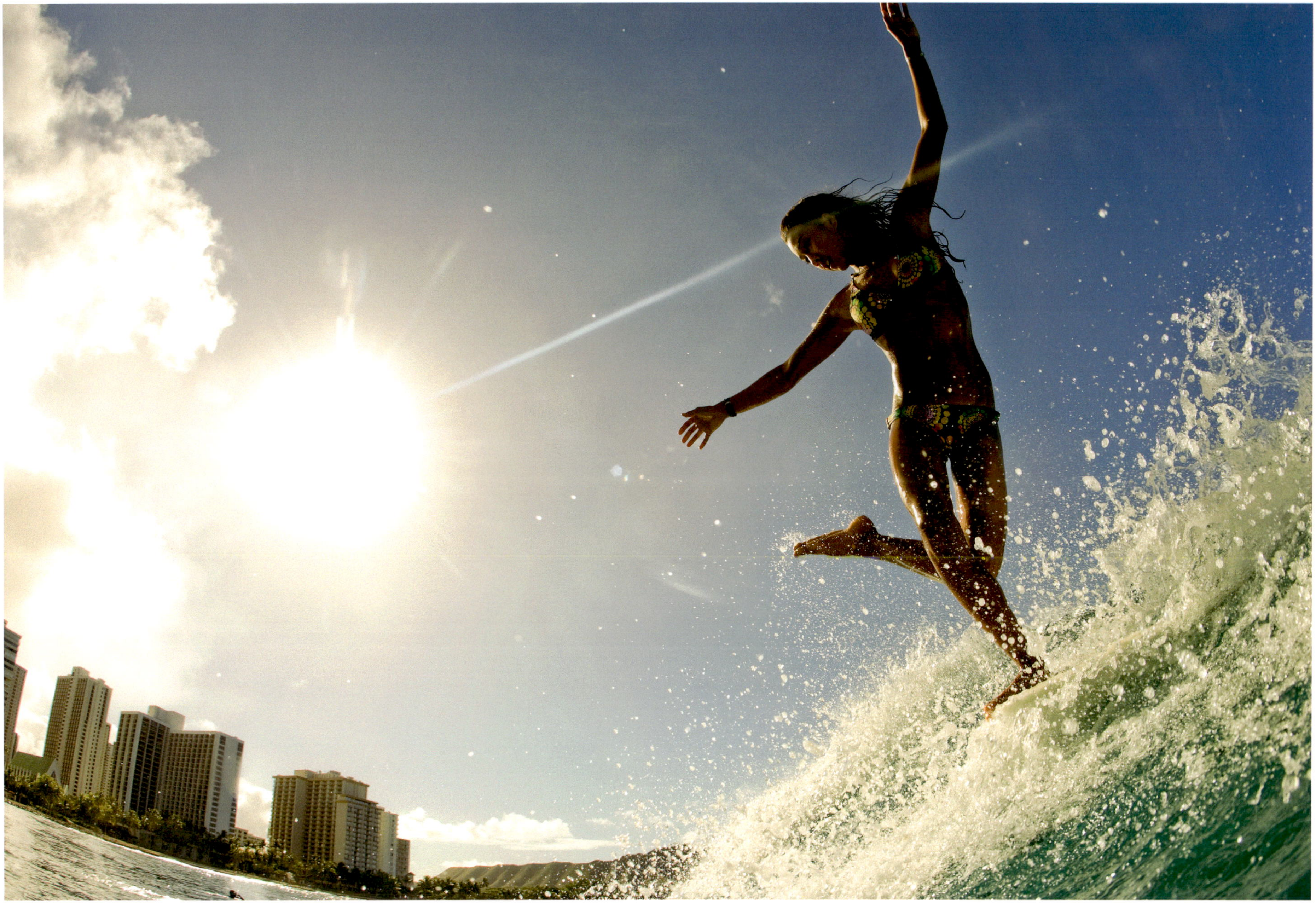

Kelia "Sister" Moniz, Water Ballet. Waikiki, HI. 2008.

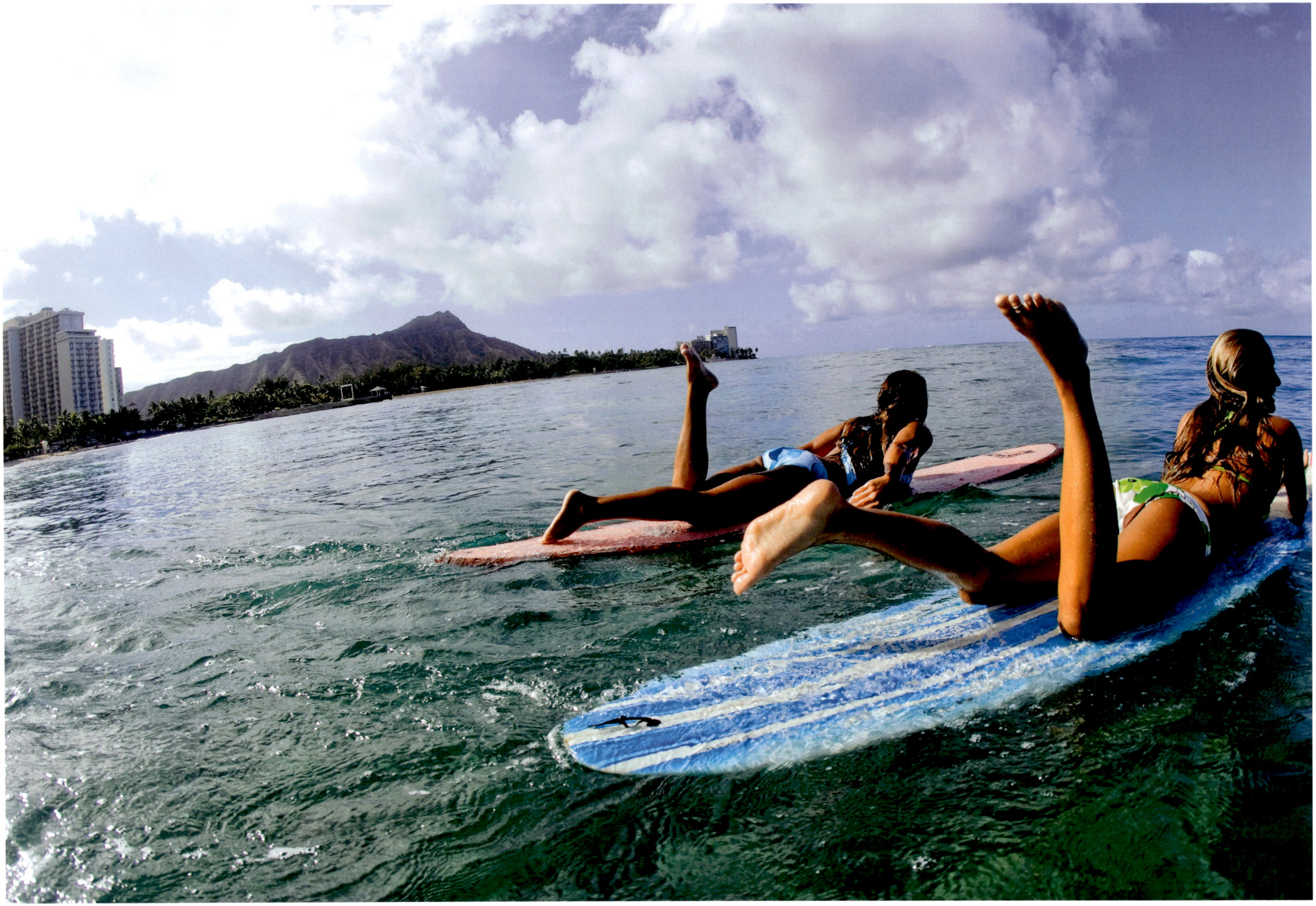

Kula Barbieto and Crystal Dzigas. Summer pastime. Waikiki, HI. 2005.

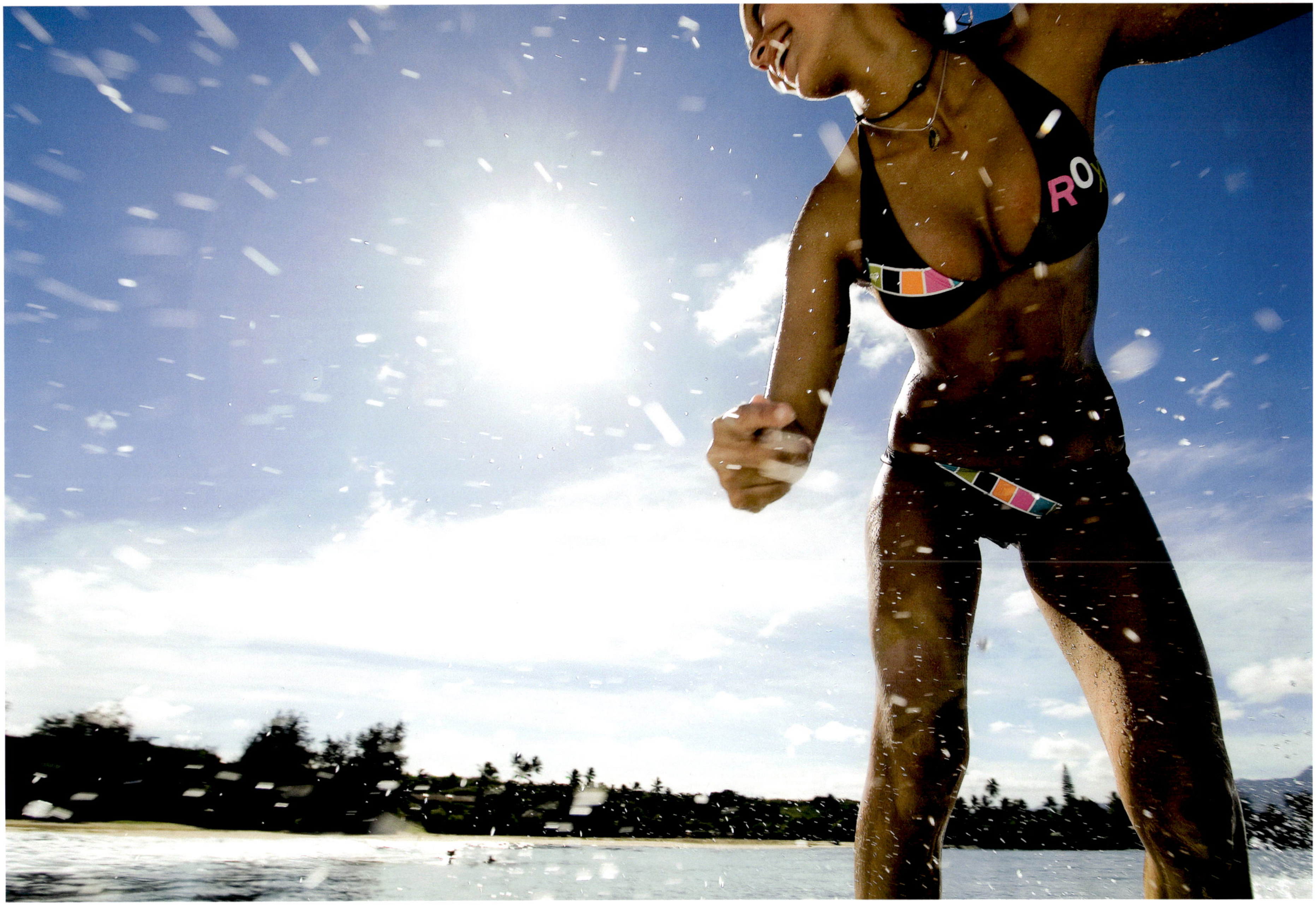

Kassia Meador, Sun Child. Chun's Reef, HI. 2005.

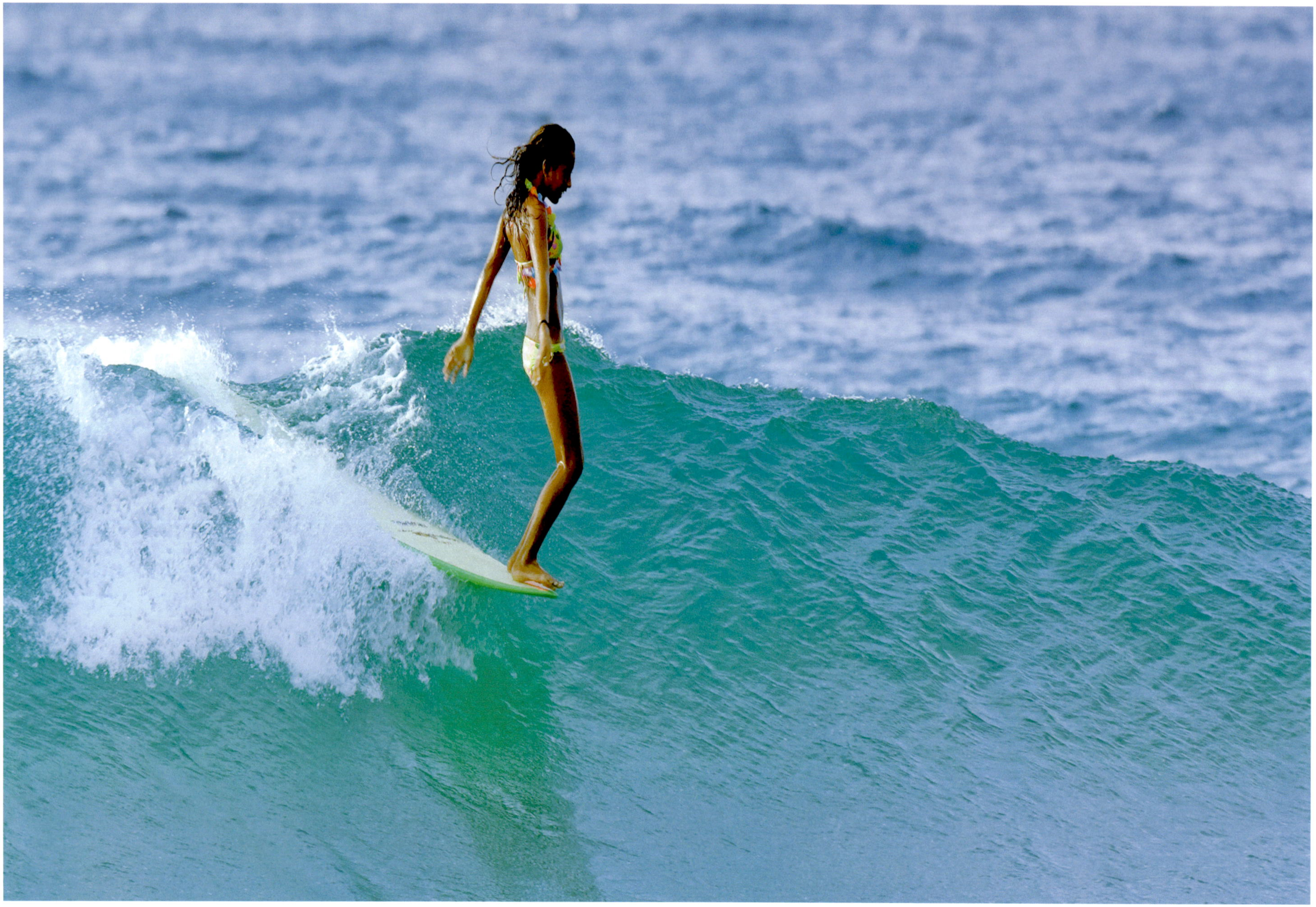

Kelia "Sister" Moniz, well balanced at age 14. Ehukai, HI. 2007.

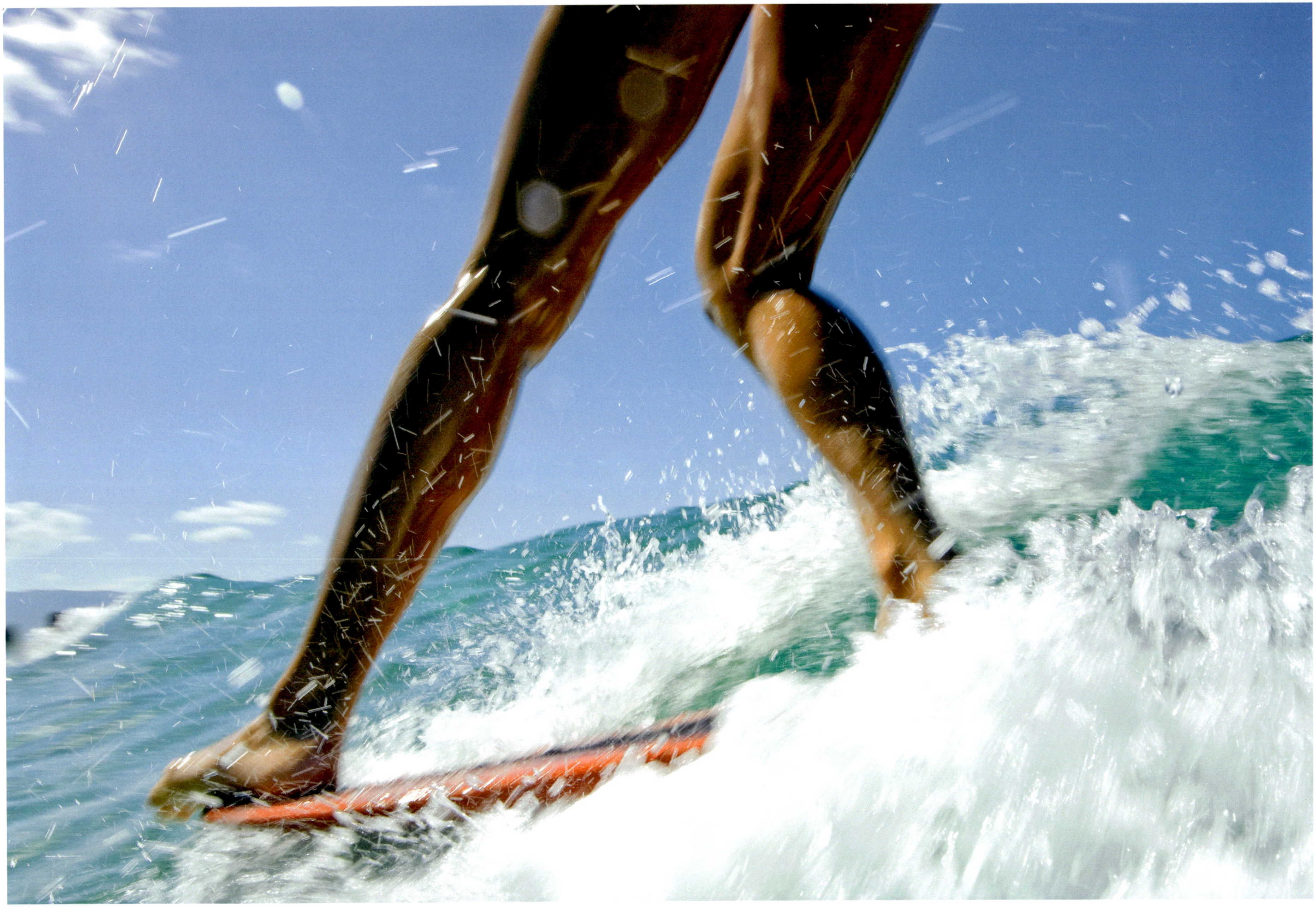

Crystal Dzigas, Roxy Legs. Pupukea, HI. 2008.

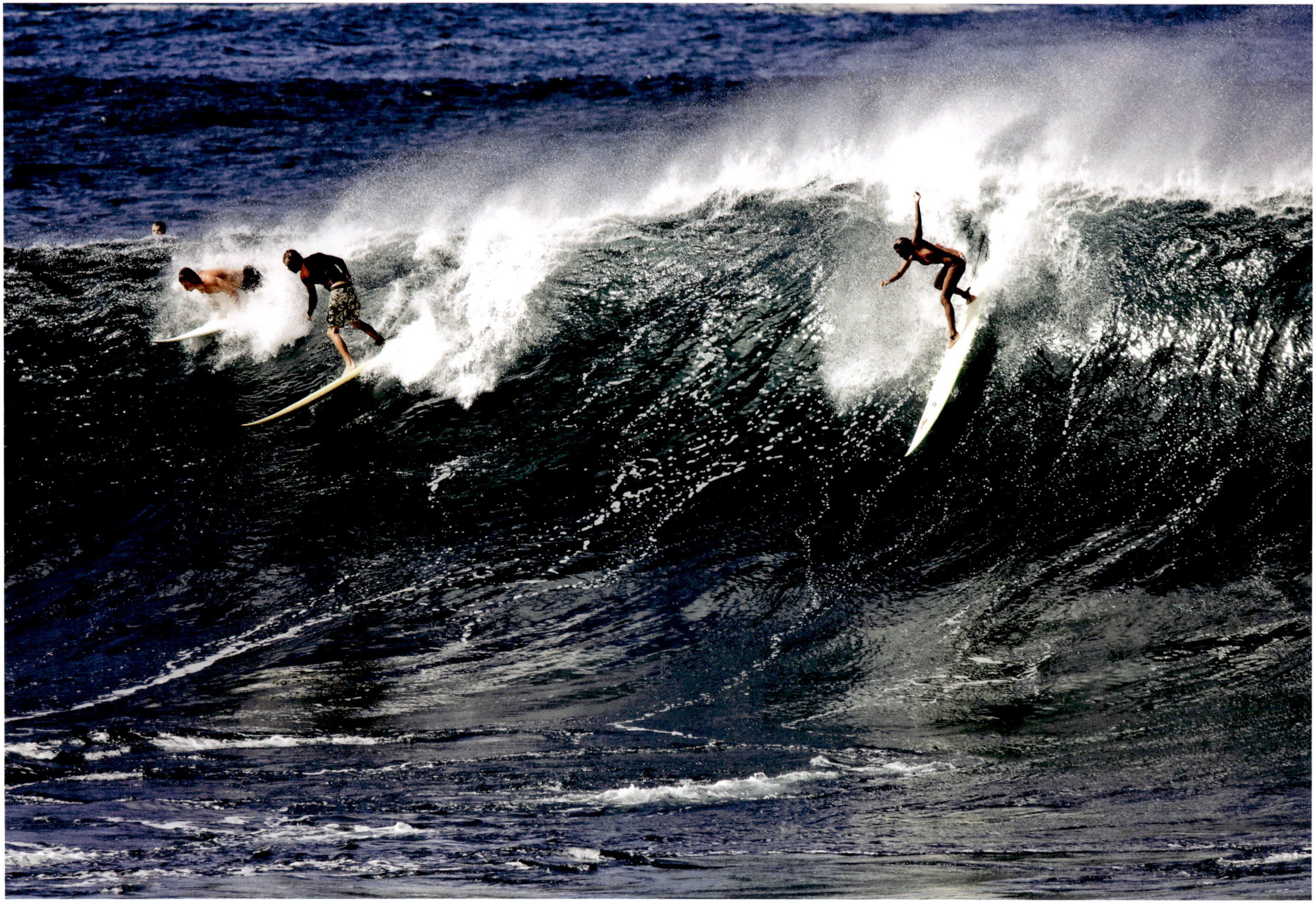

Jenny Useldinger, deeper than the boys. Waimea, HI. 2007.

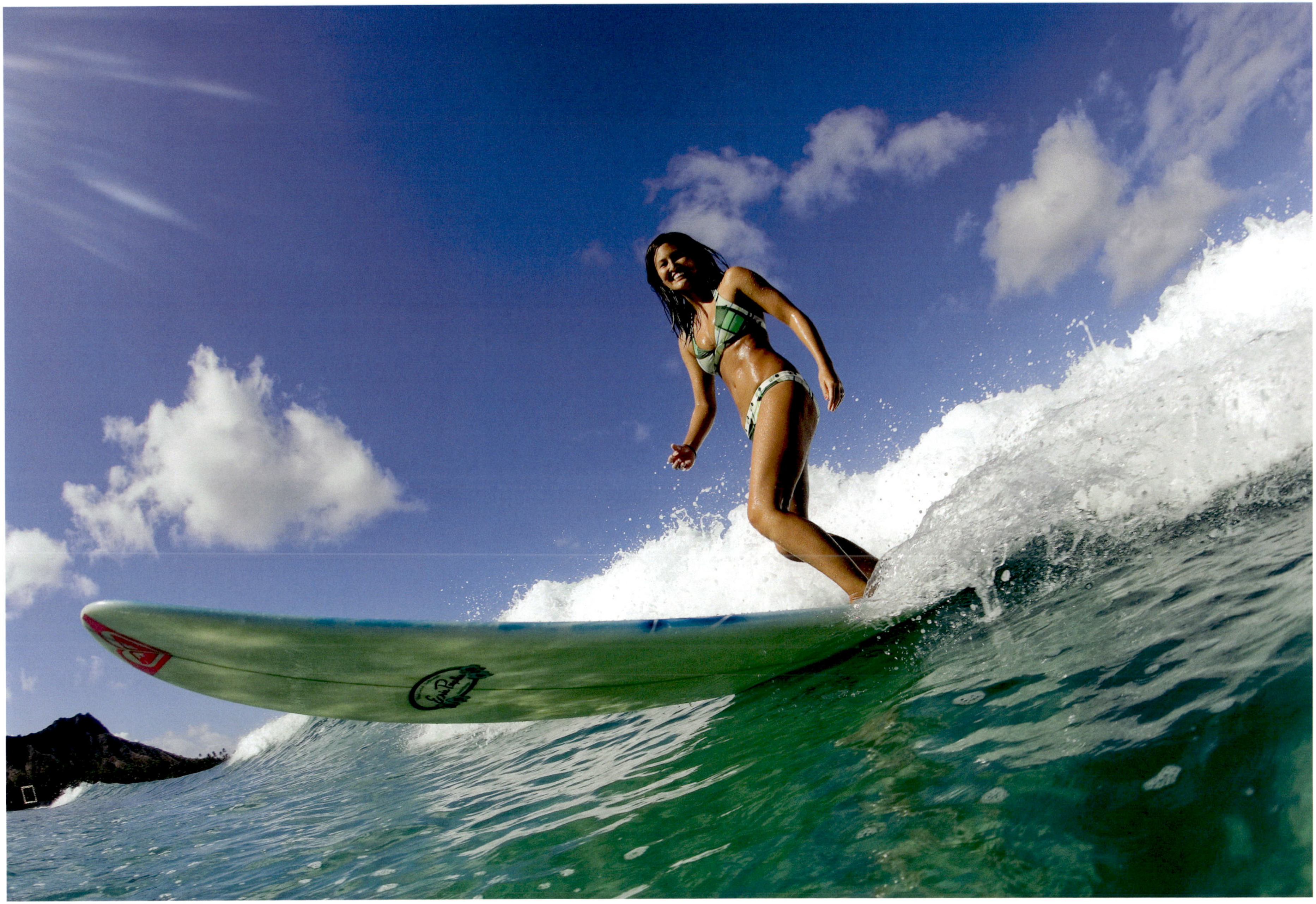

Aimee Vogelsang, Leiahi. Waikiki, HI. 2005.

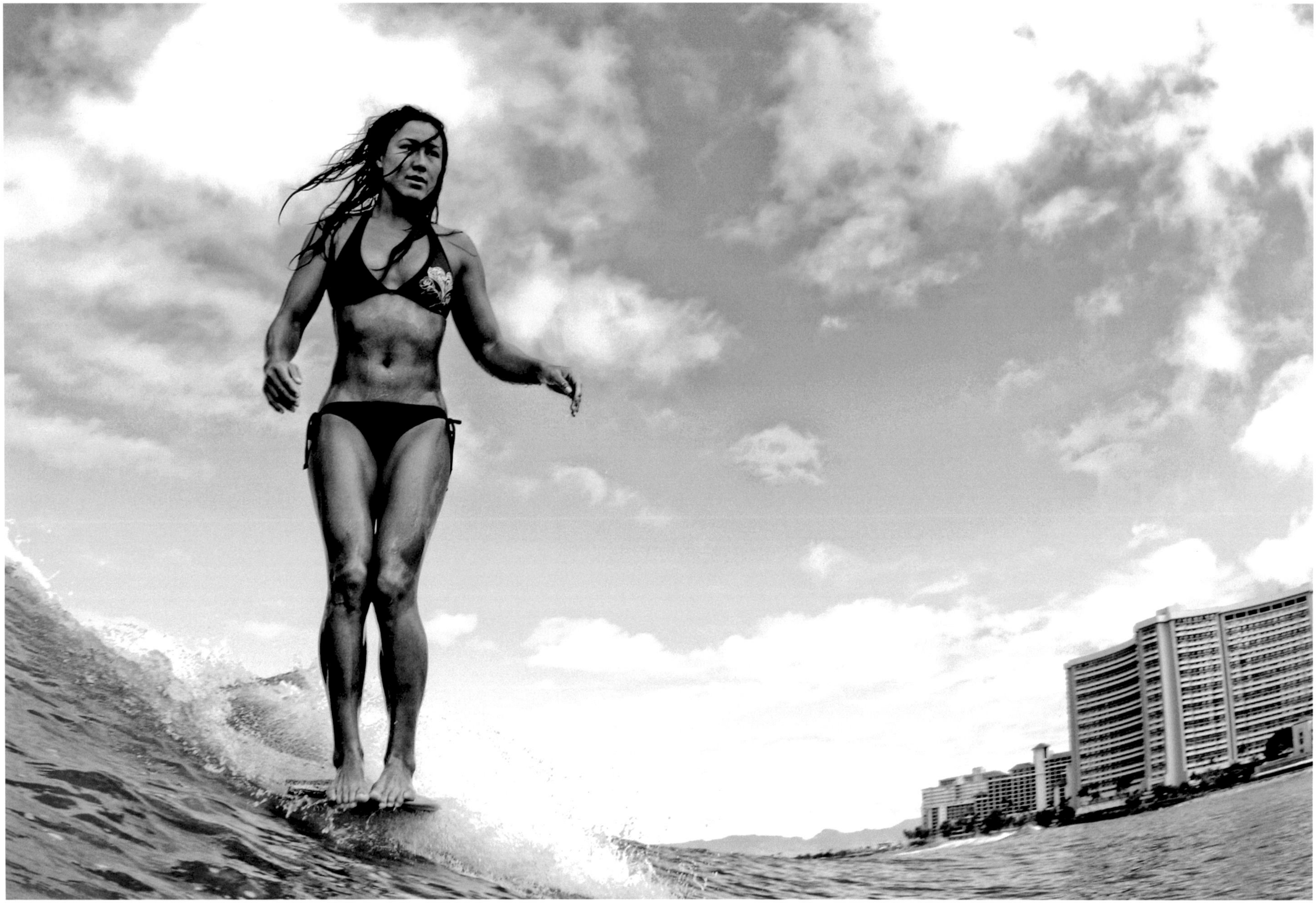

Crystal Dzigas, Hawaiian Pedicure. Waikiki, HI. 2007.

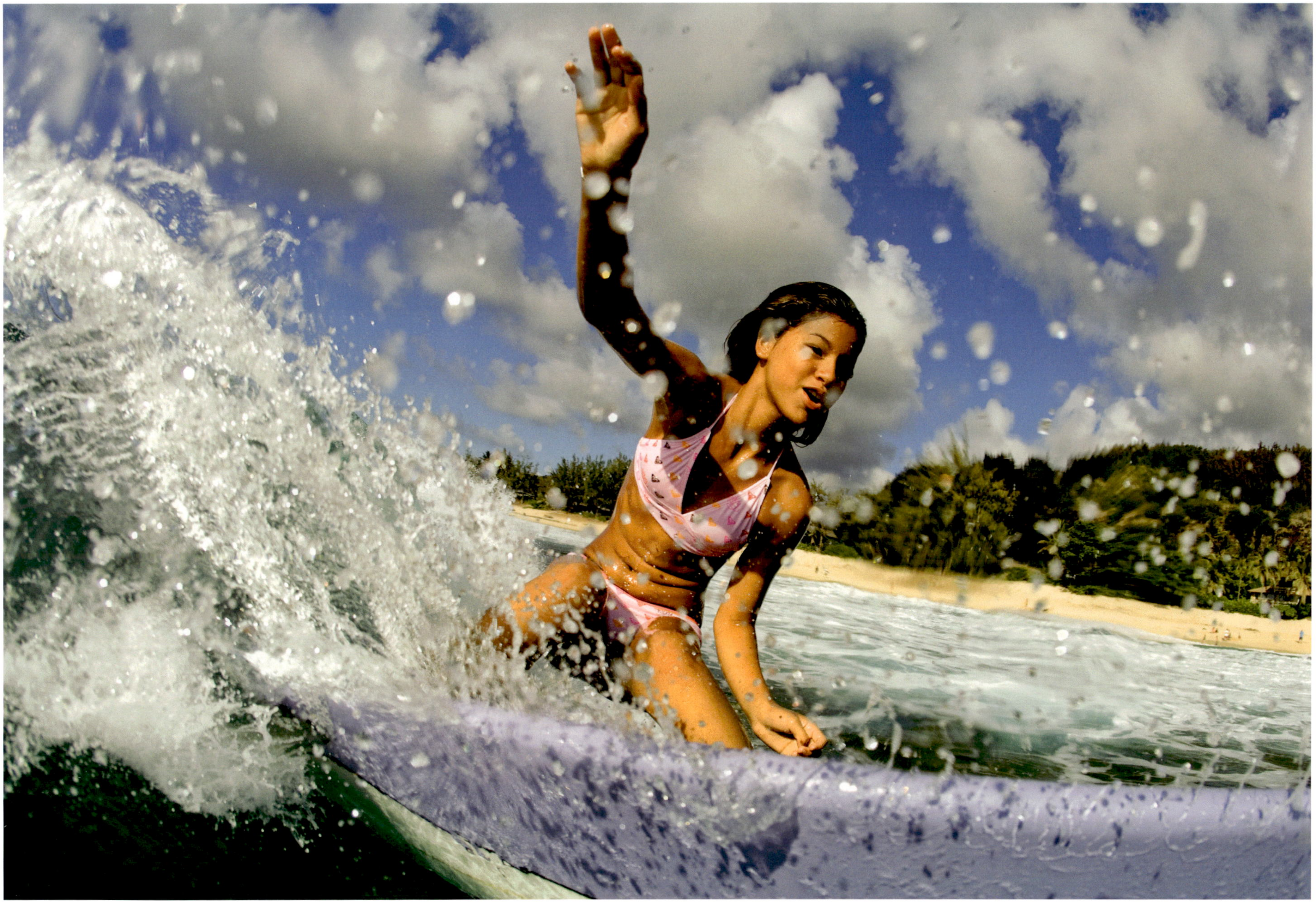

Alisha Gonsalves, rail turns at age 13. Beach Park, HI. 2006.

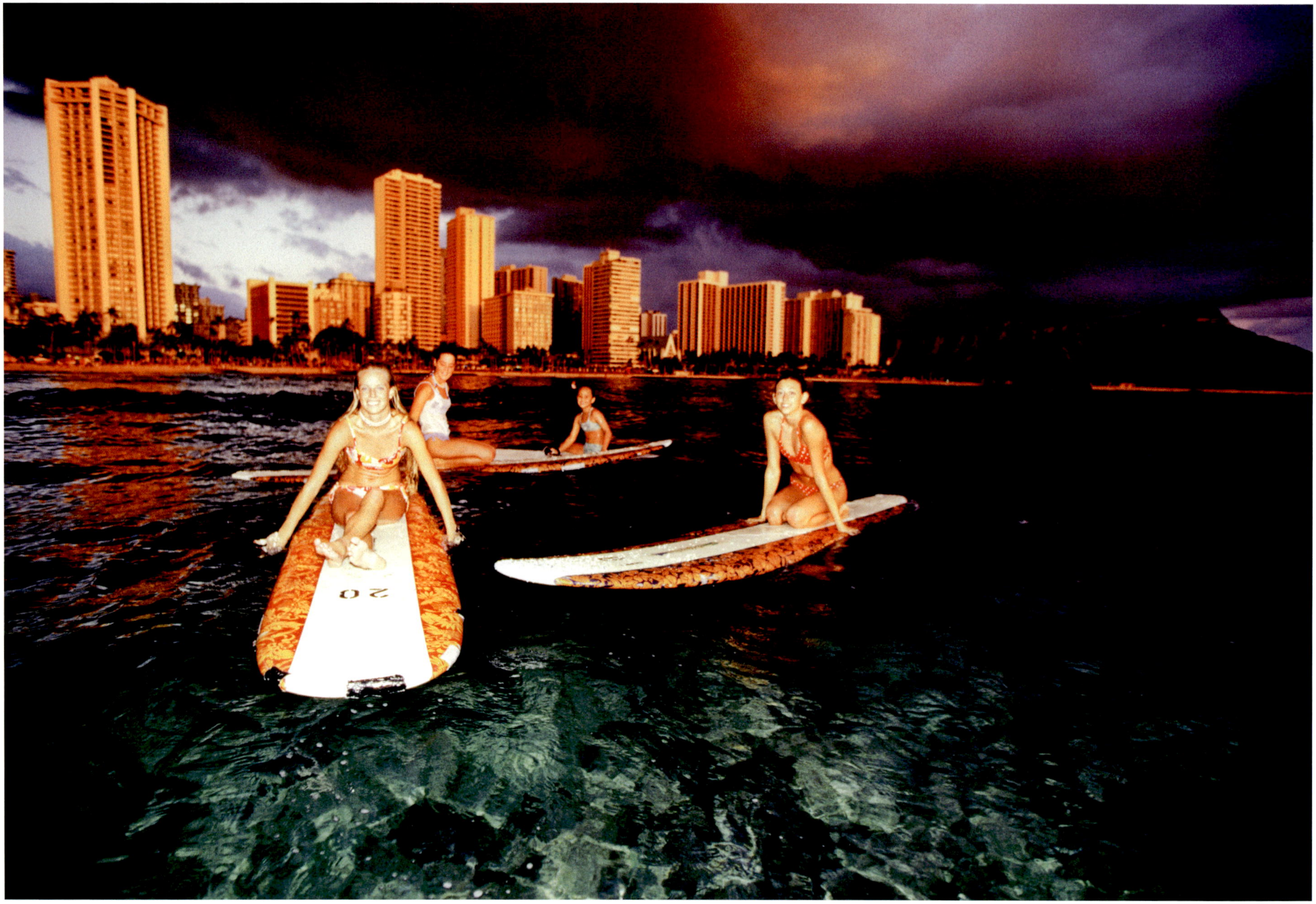

Clockwise from left: Rachel Grath, Koral McCarthy, Carissa Moore, Christiana Jansen. Waikiki, HI. 2000.

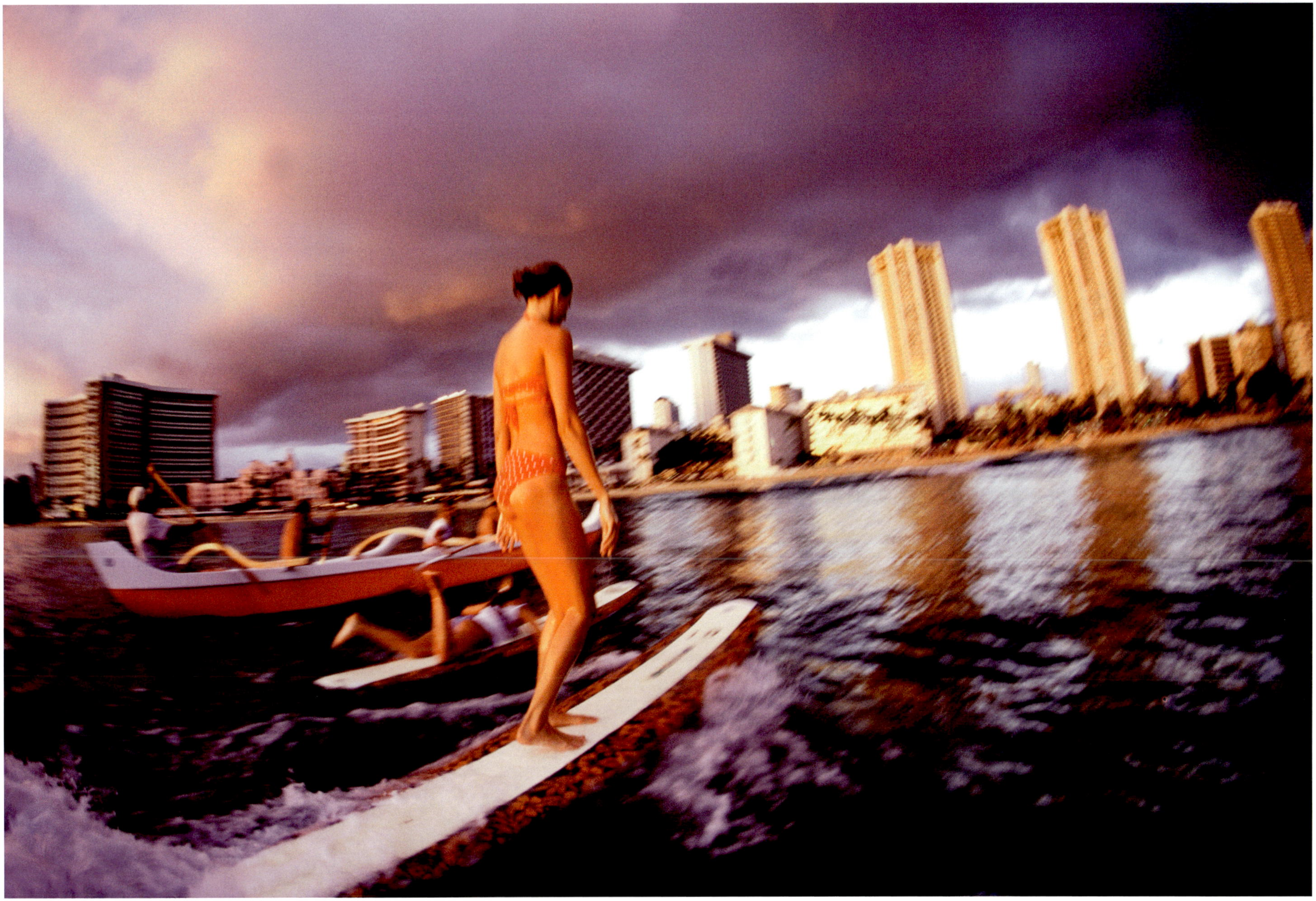

Christiana Jansen, Afterglow. Waikiki, HI. 2000.

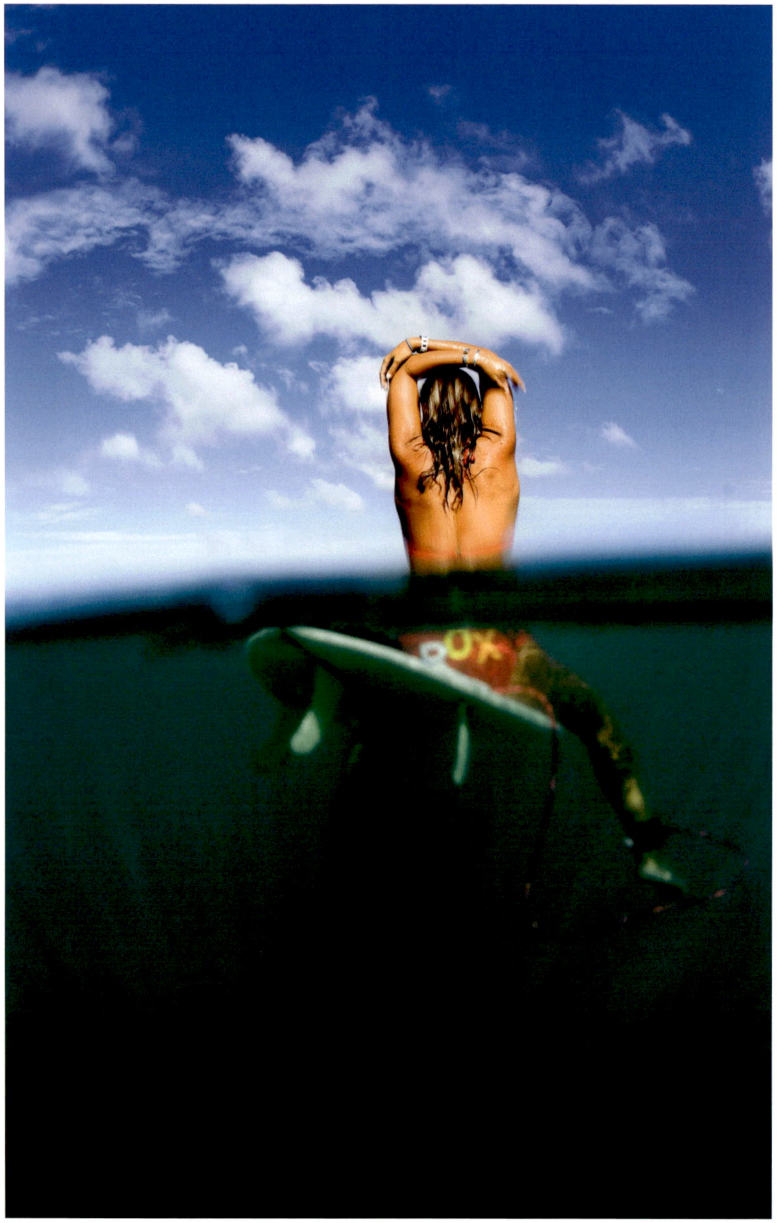

Jenny Useldinger. Hawaii. 2006.

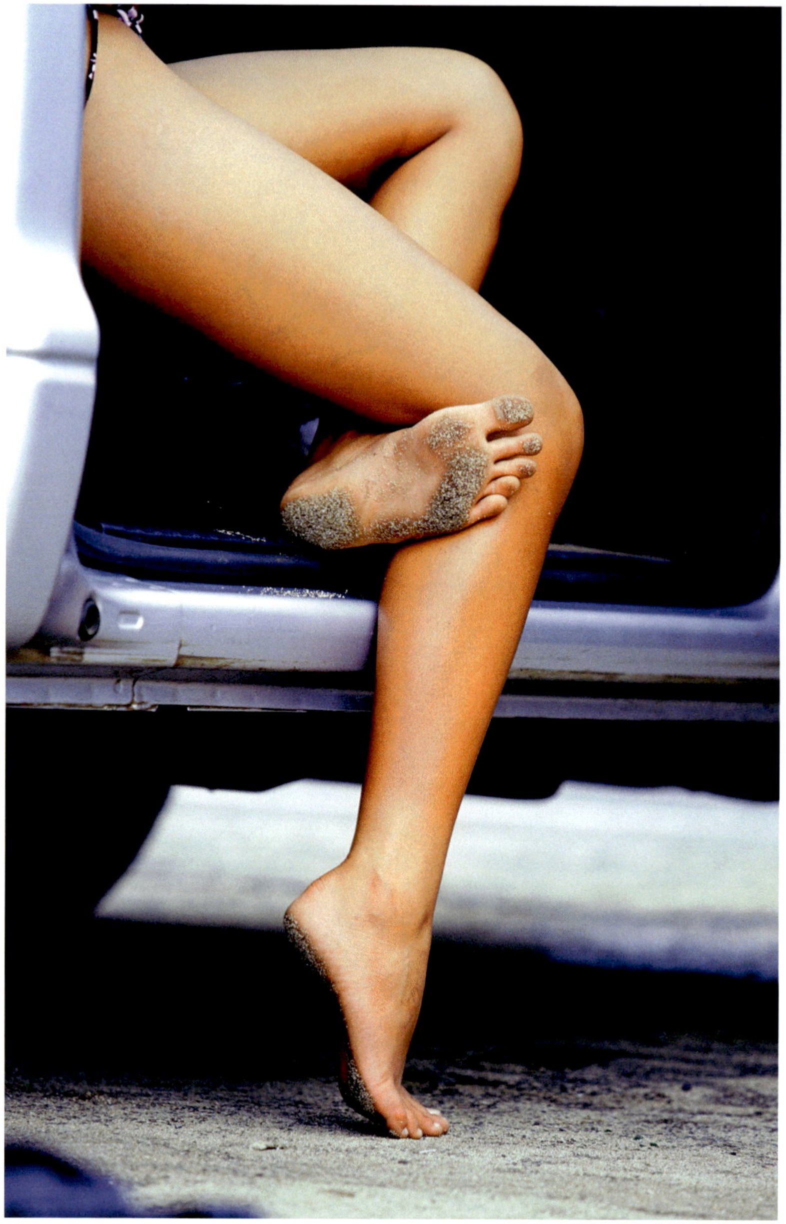

Veronica Kay. Makaha, HI. 2002.

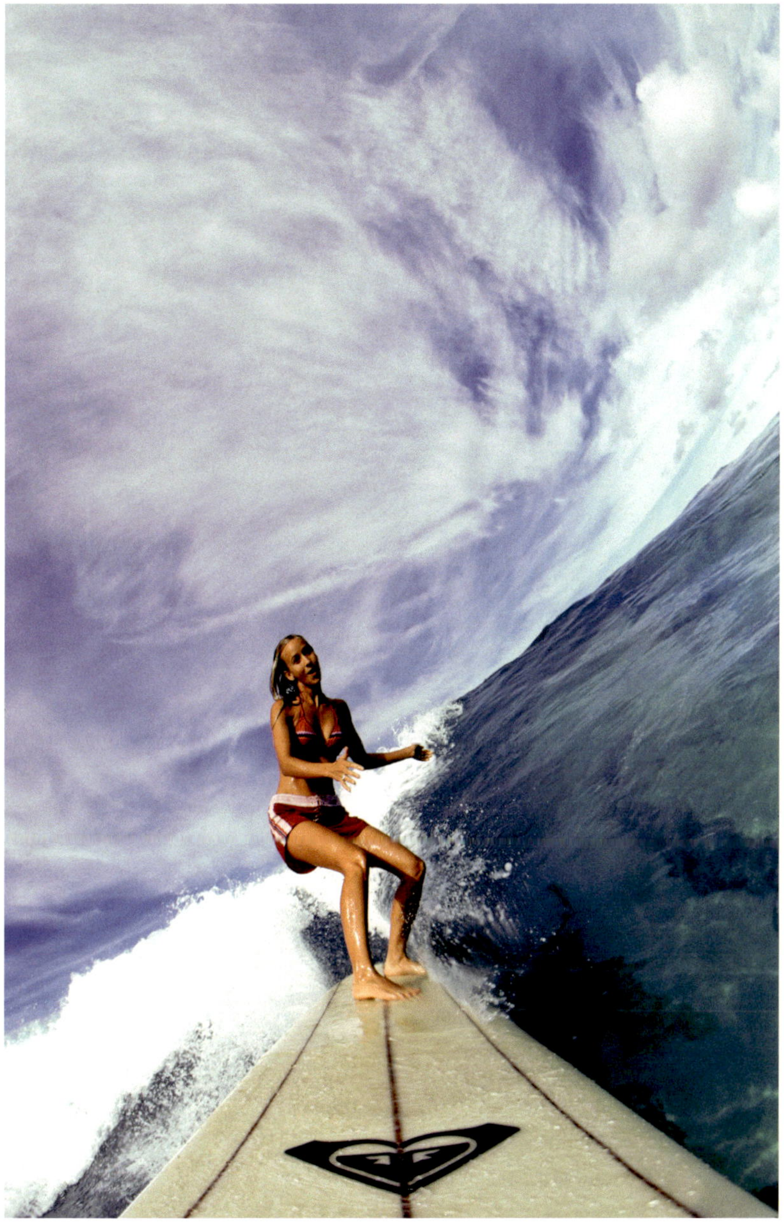

Daize Shayne Goodwin. Pupukea, HI. 1998.

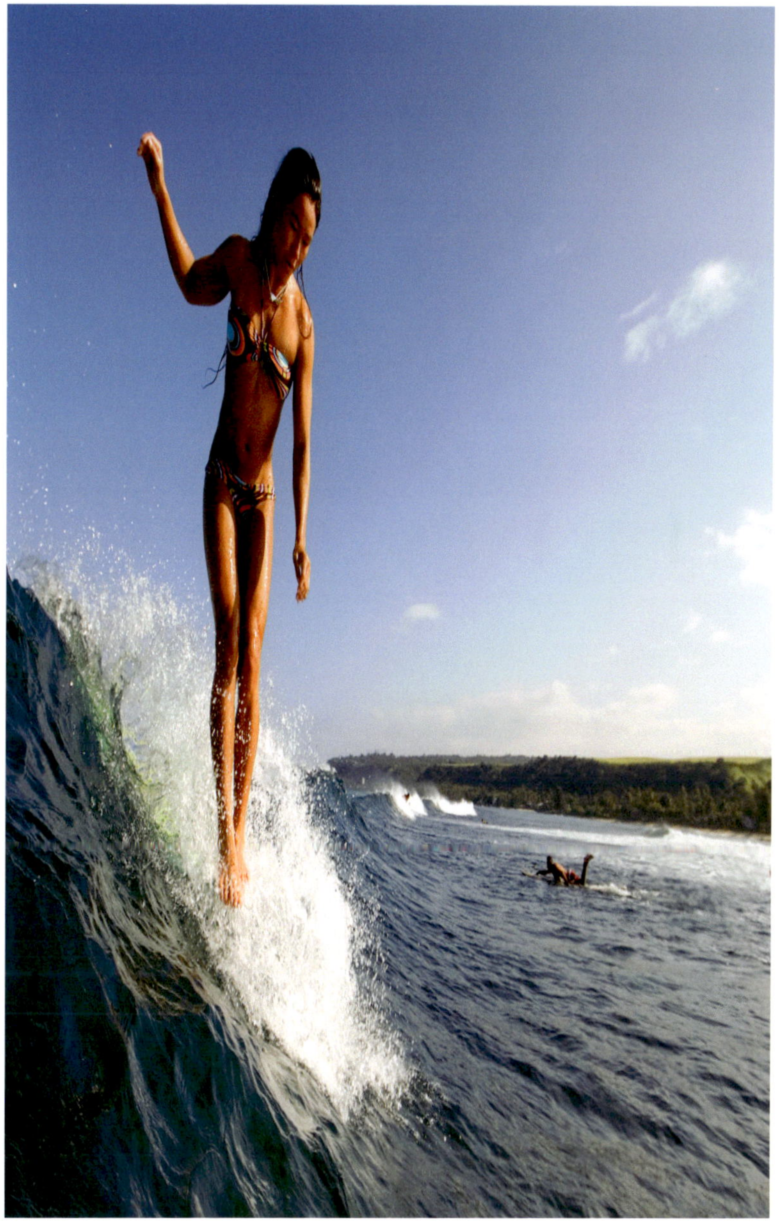

Crystal Dzigas. Chuns Reef, HI. 2005.

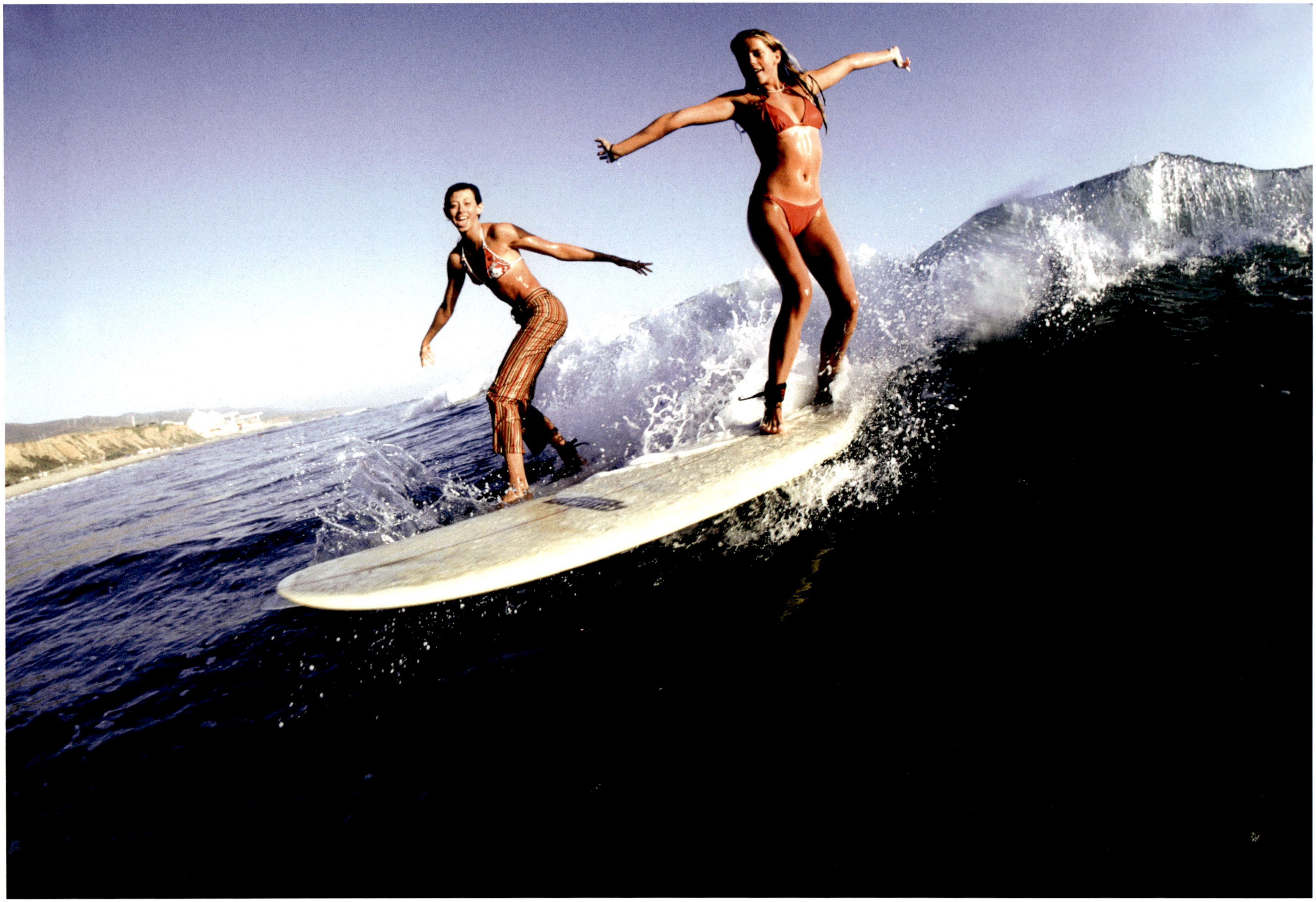

Christiana Jansen, Missy Gibson. The Birth of Fun. San Onofre, CA. 1998.

Gotta Have Fun

For 20 years prior, I had been shooting for the surf magazines and random companies within the surf industry. I never worked heavily for one ad client, developing a theme and maintaining that theme throughout an entire campaign. In 1997 I was hired on a day rate by Roxy to shoot surf action shots of the girls from the water to accompany the land fashion shoot by Dewey Nicks. Nicks, a fabulous NYC & LA fashion photographer, had developed a brilliant look for the company early on. Randy Hild invited me out to a beach house down in Newport Beach where Nicks was shooting the girls for the day. Roxy wanted to incorporate surf photos along with the fashion shots. As a core surfing brand, they didn't want their image to revolve solely around fashion; they needed the authenticity of real surfing.

Randy asked me to photograph the girls in the water out front of the beach house, near 56th street in Newport Beach. That day it was mostly pounding barrels and as I started shooting I was only able to get the girls going over the falls and getting cleaned up in the shorebreak. I could tell it wasn't working. I asked Randy to let me bring the girls down to San Onofre at the end of the day so I could capture them in good evening light and small waves. I wanted to get some longboards and show them really having fun. Unfortunately Randy told me he couldn't keep the girls past 4:00 PM on that shoot day. After I explained what I had in mind, he agreed that it was worth a try. Randy rounded up Missy Gibson, Veronica Kay, Cristiana, Daize Shayne, and a few others. That photo shoot ended up being a landmark moment, creating a distinctly Roxy look.

I had been working with a pole cam, which is basically a water housing with a wide-angle fisheye camera on a stick with a shutter release on the bottom of the pole. This allowed me to get the camera up high and over the wave. To show the line, we had the girls wear the clothes in the water. They ended up surfing in fun, crazy combinations of pants, dresses, shirts, hats, and leis. Randy wanted the girls to be involved and loose, clearly having a good time. It felt like you were really right there with them as the photos were completely full of life and in that moment.

When I brought that series of images to Roxy the following week, they immediately said it was exactly what they'd been looking for. They wanted me to create these images for them solely and have it be the unique look of the Roxy campaign. I was more than happy to join them. I had worked on and off for Quiksilver since the 1980s and loved the company and what they were doing.

That day out at San Onofre in 1997 was the beginning of a theme for me and my work: the simple fun of surfing—showing a lifestyle that anyone could relate to, appealing to hard-core surfers and to dreamers as well. Roxy's world market is 99% girls who just want to live that lifestyle and have fun (as opposed to a market of hard-core surfers who already get their clothes free because they're sponsored). That said, Roxy sponsors the top world champions, putting more money back into the sport than anyone through sponsorships and subsidizing contests. I've always admired the blend that they successfully maintain as a brand with the Roxy campaign—a combination of professional women surfing and everyday girls just surfing and playing in the water, all for the love of the sport.

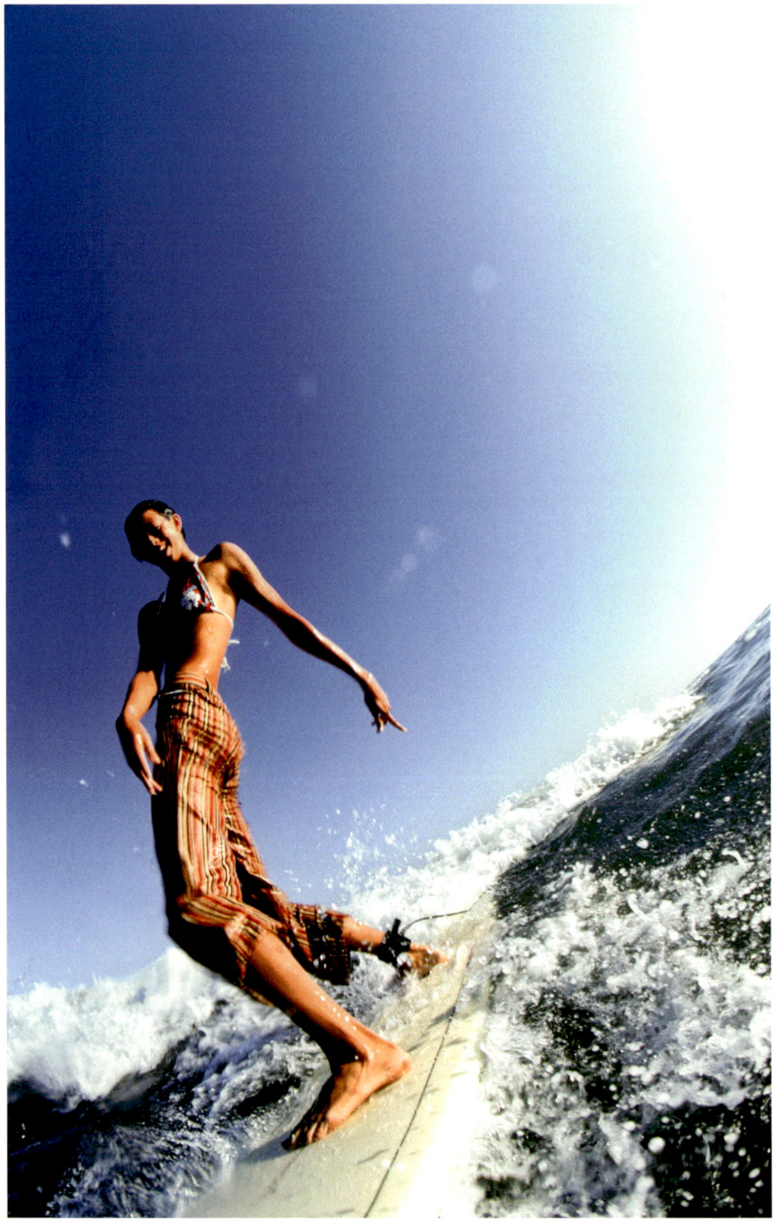

Christiana Jansen. San Onofre, CA. 1998.

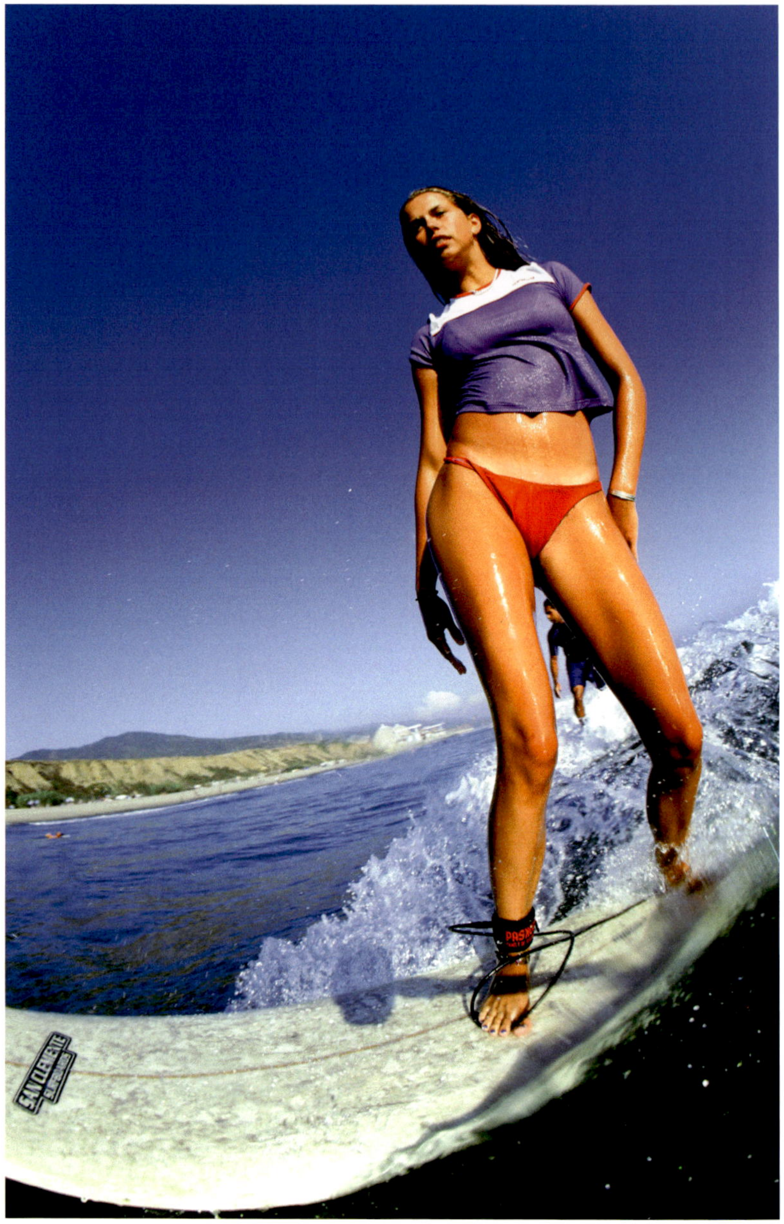

Missy Gibson. San Onofre, CA. 1998.

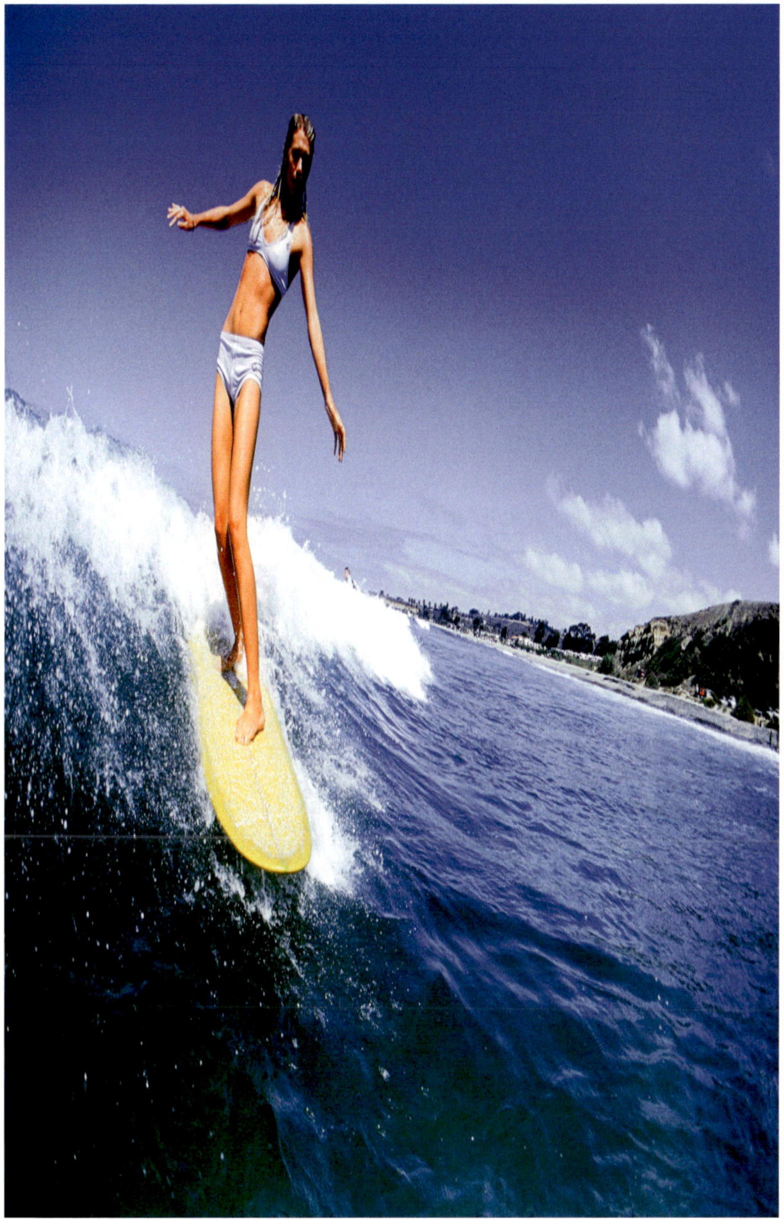

Veronica Kay. San Onofre, CA. 2001.

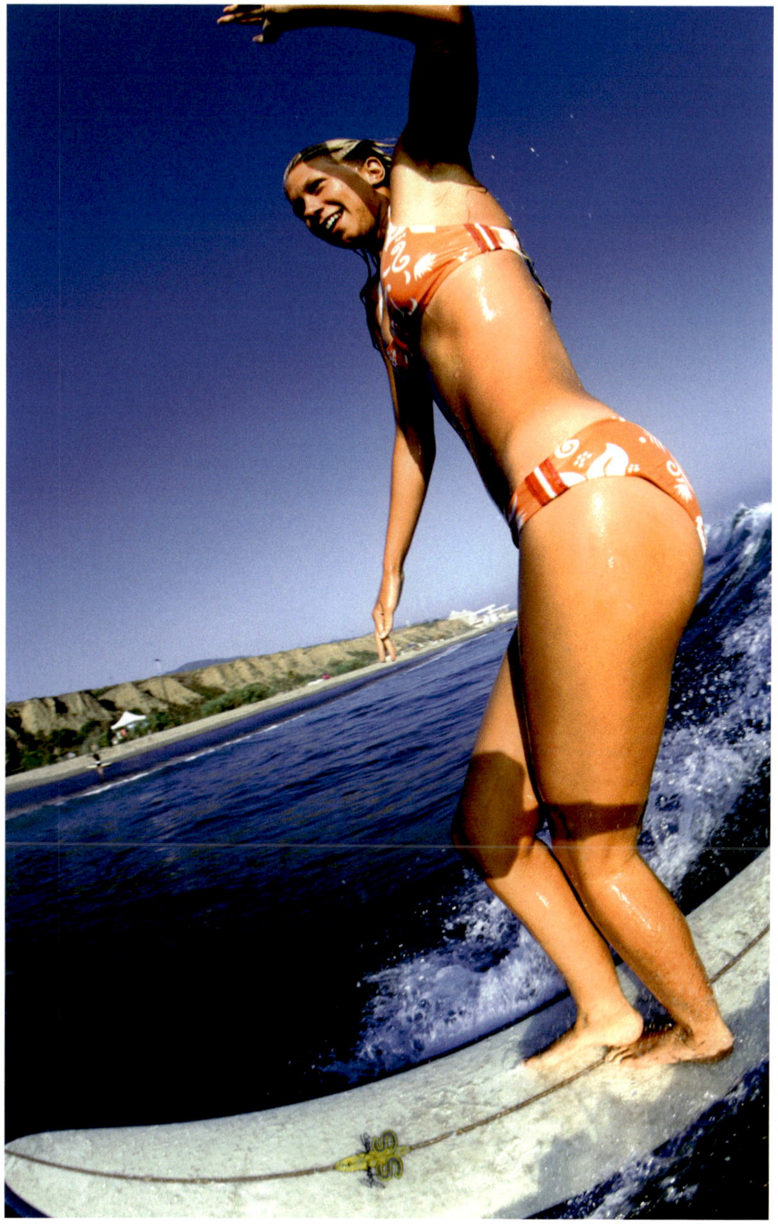

Veronica Kay. San Onofre, CA. 1998.

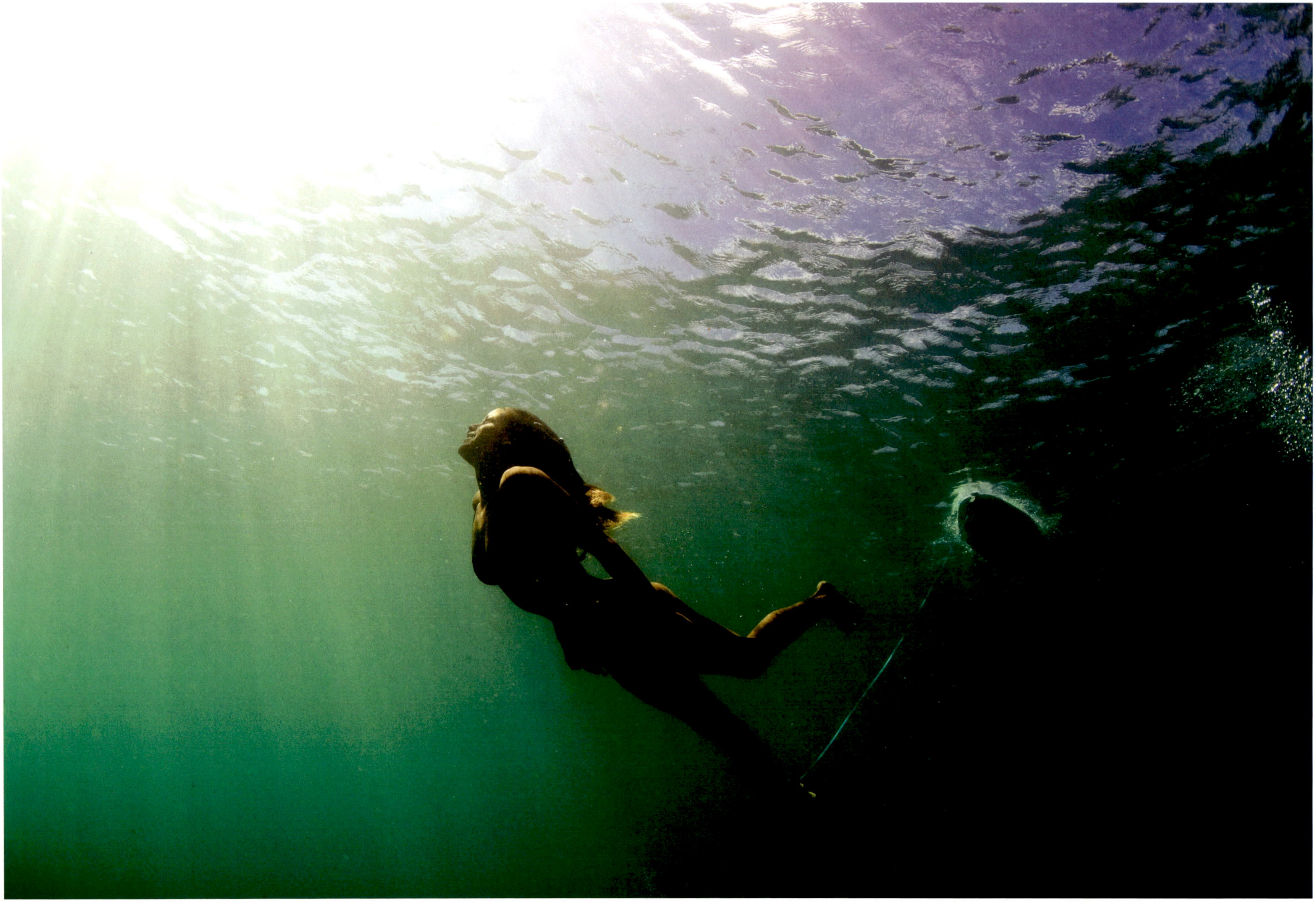

Jenny Useldinger. Into the LIght. Hawaii. 2006.

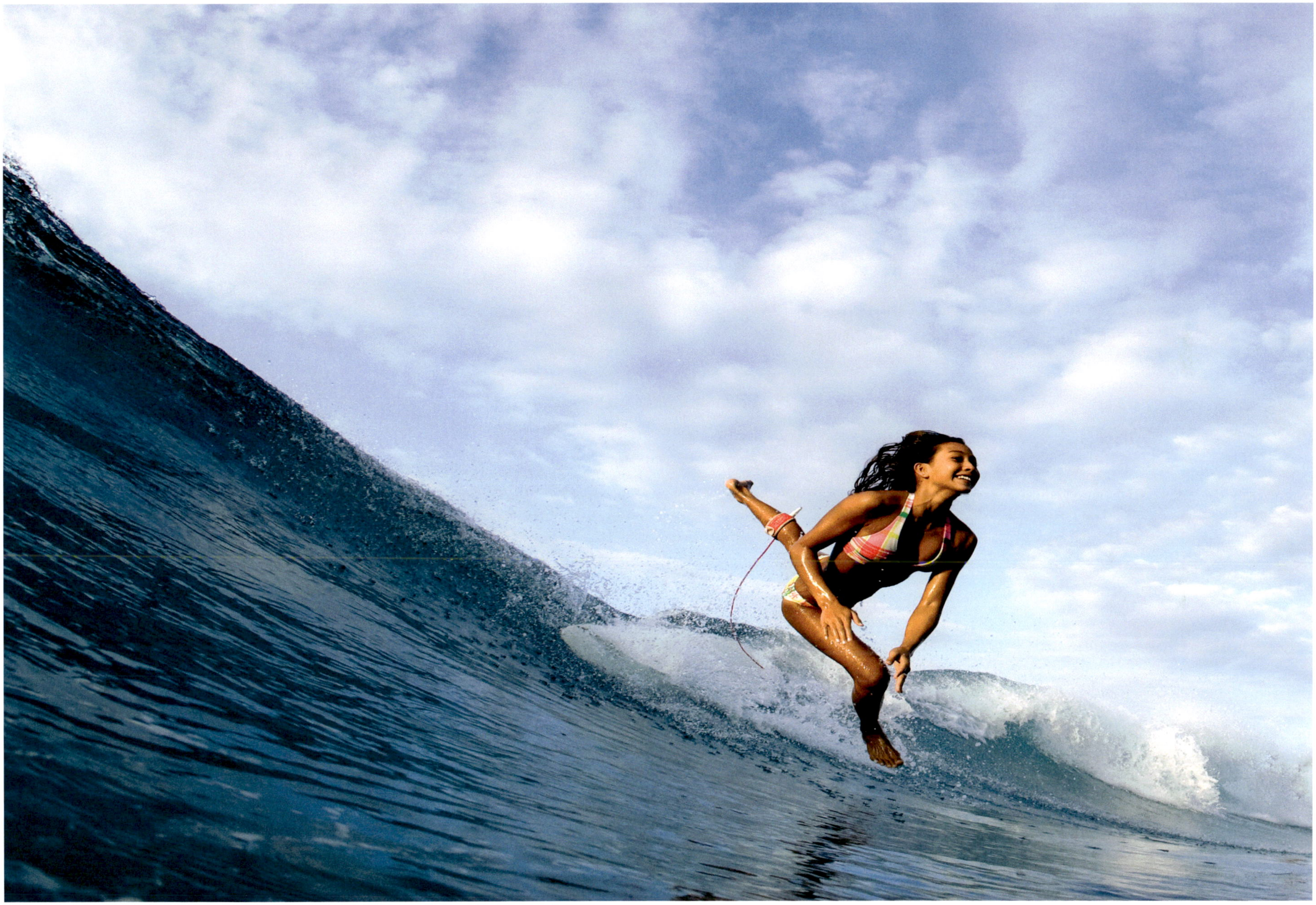

Kelia "Sister" Moniz, Walking on Water. Pupukea, HI. 2008.

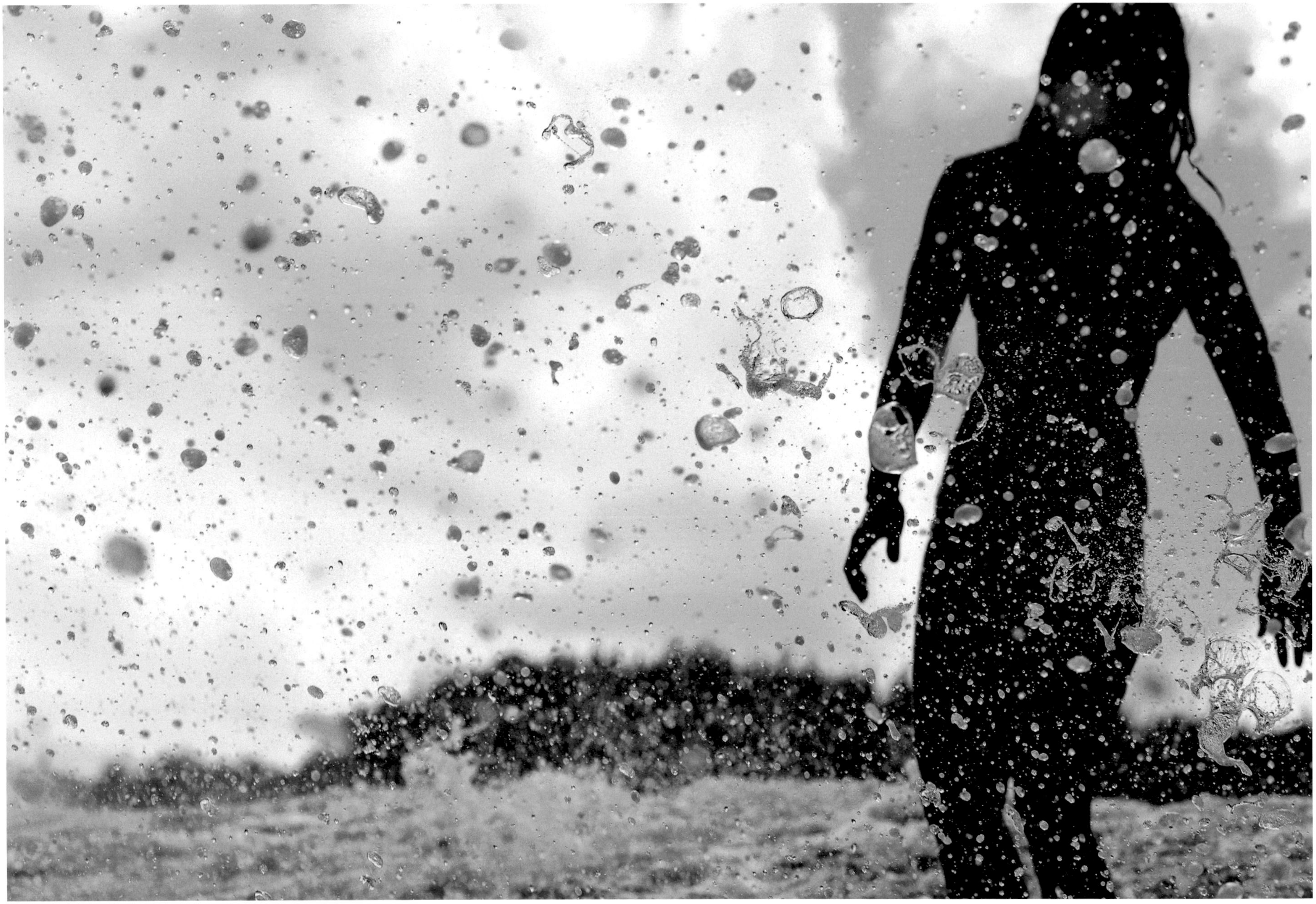

Megan Abubo. Bubble Bath. Hawaii. 2006.

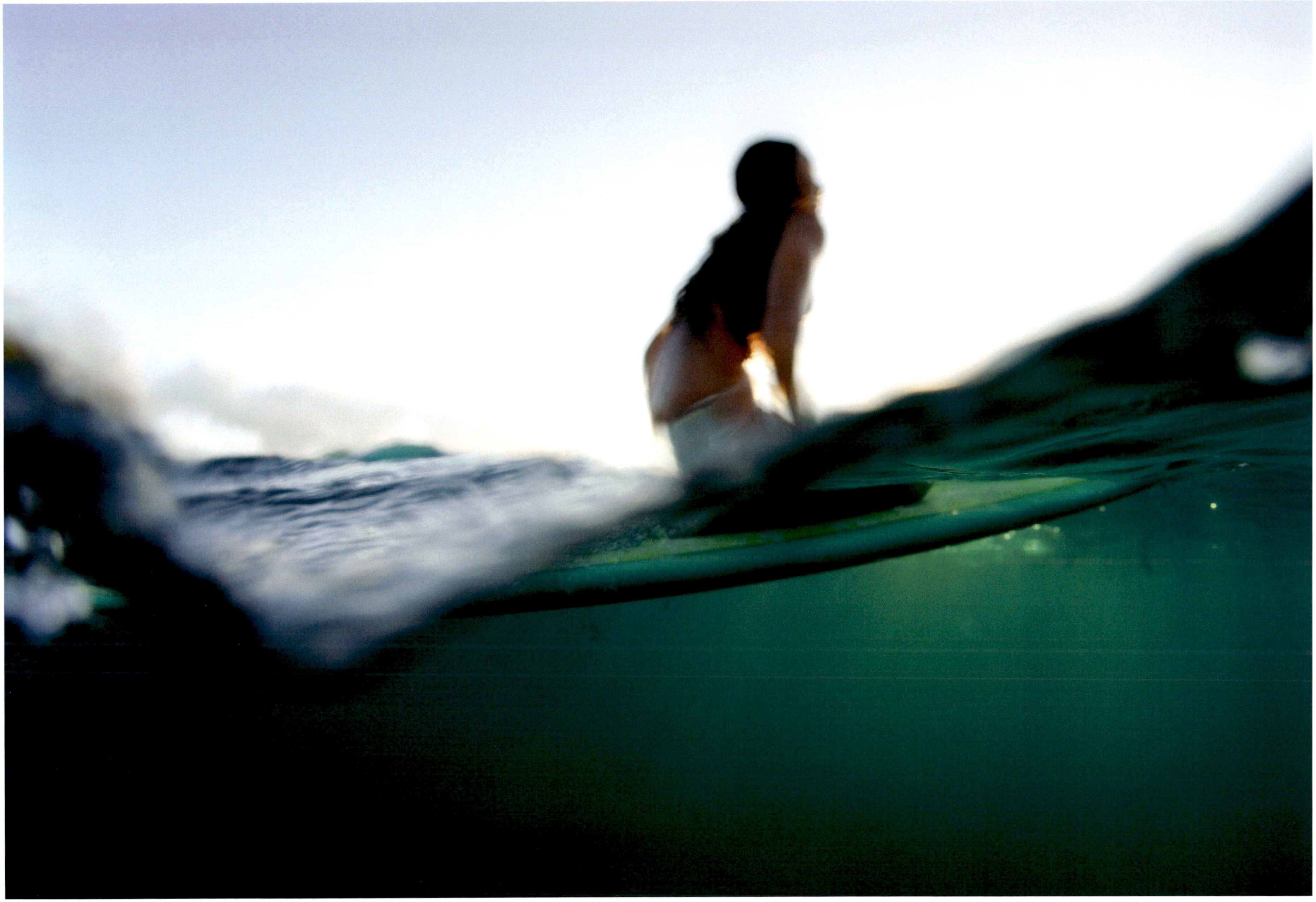

Crystal Dzigas. Warm Water. Hawaii. 2005.

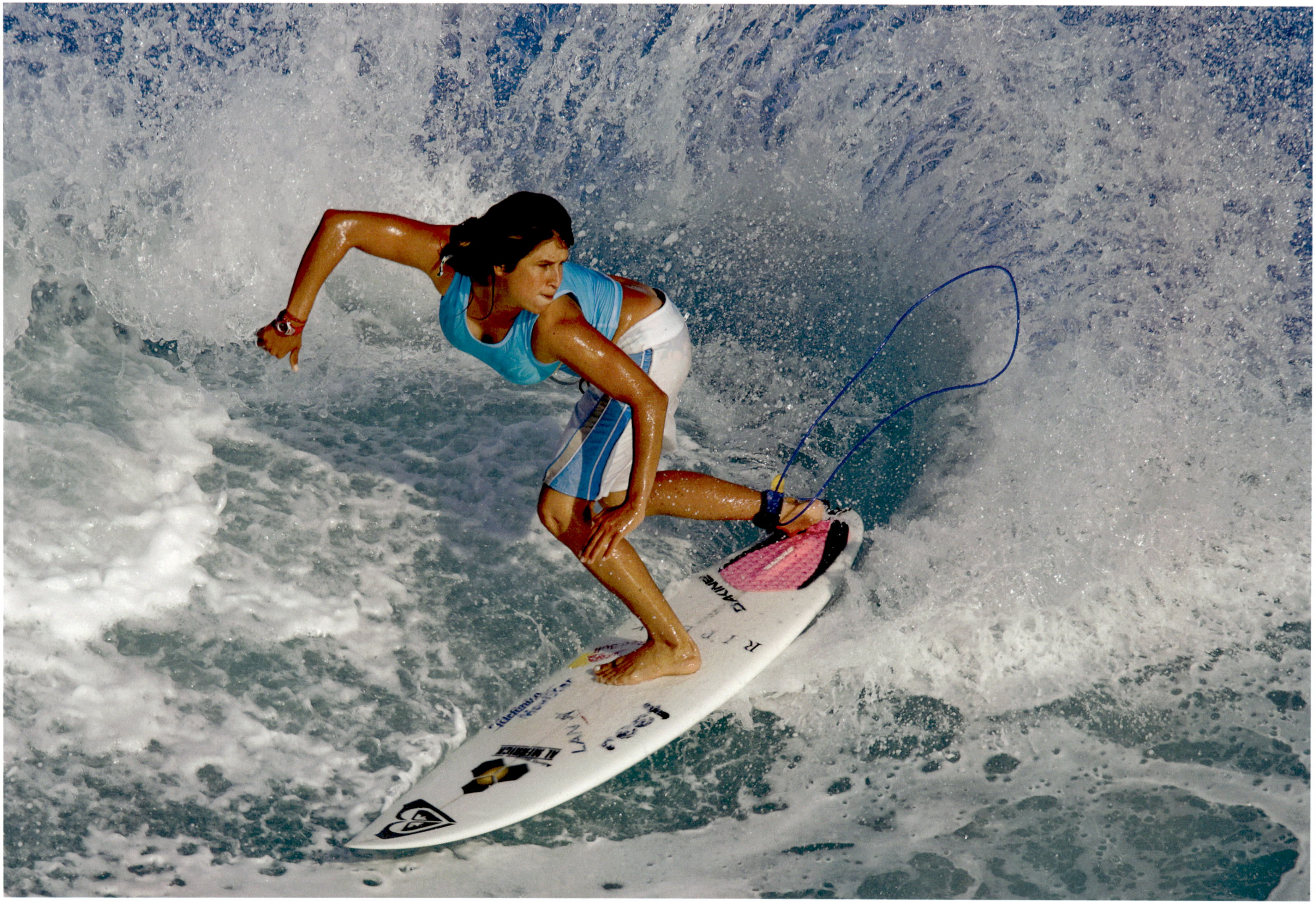

Sofia Mulanovich. Emptying the Pool. Hawaii. 2004.

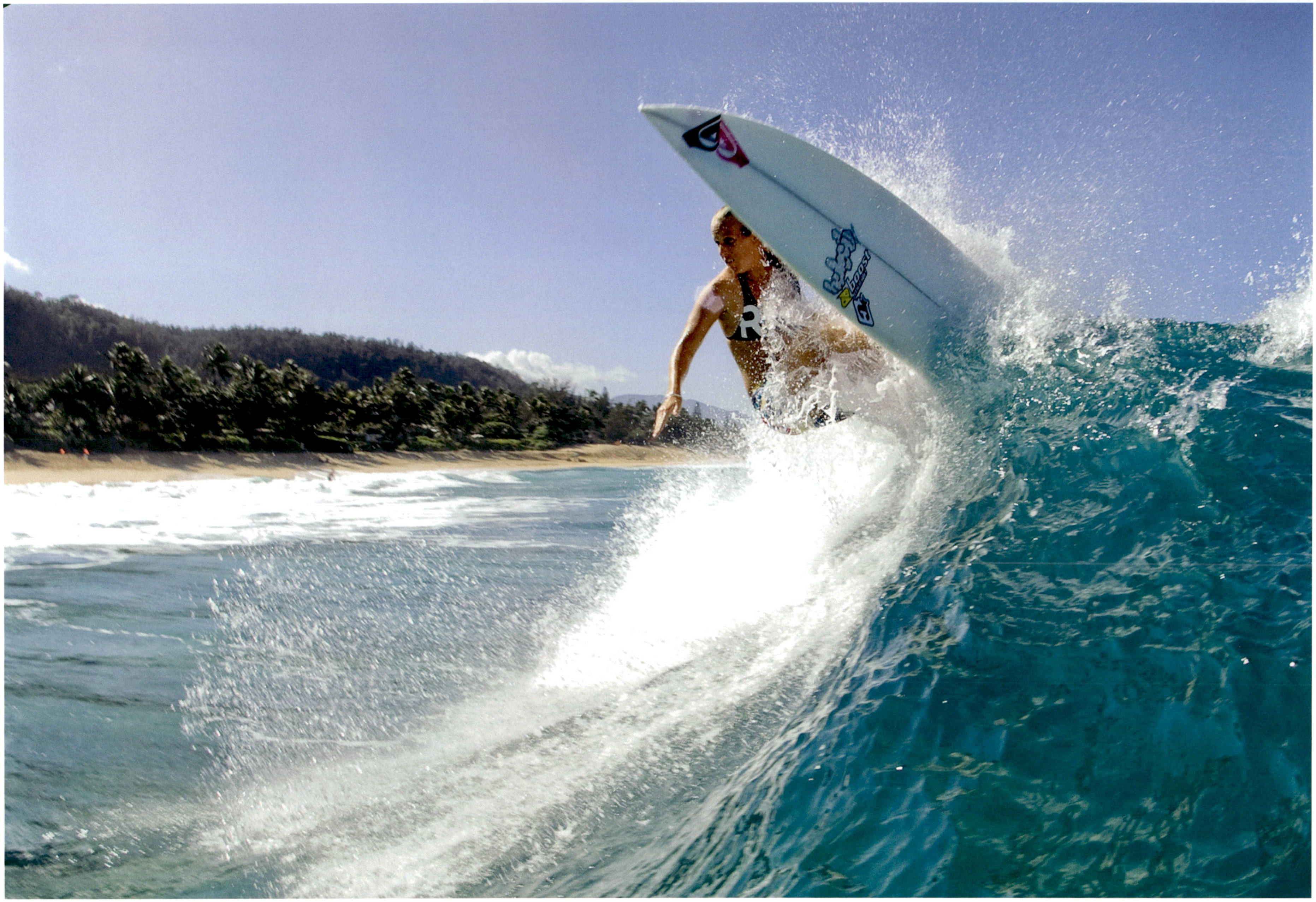

Chelsea Hedges. Snapping. Pupukea, HI. 2005.

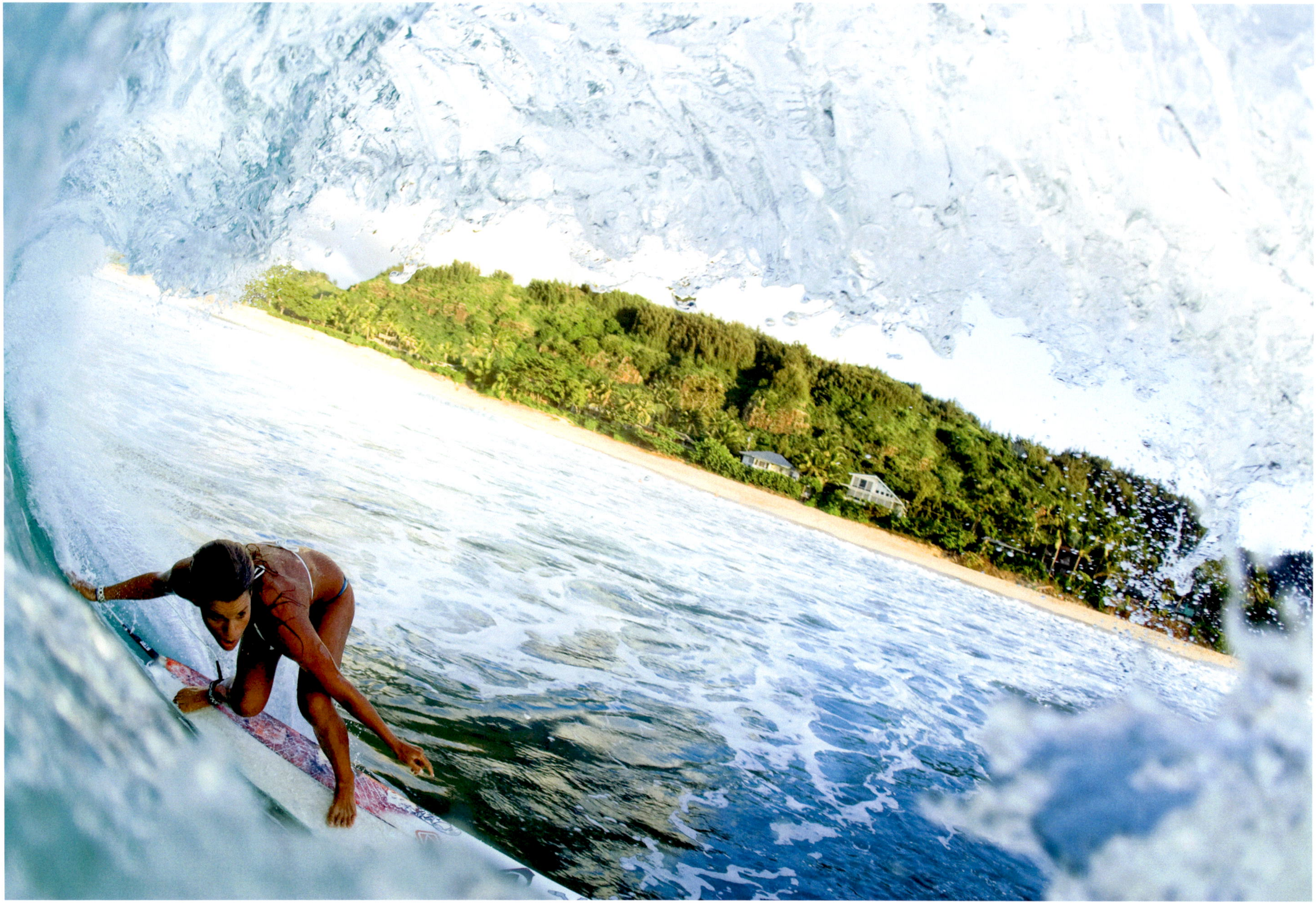

Jenny Useldinger. Duck for Cover. Off the Wall, HI. 2006.

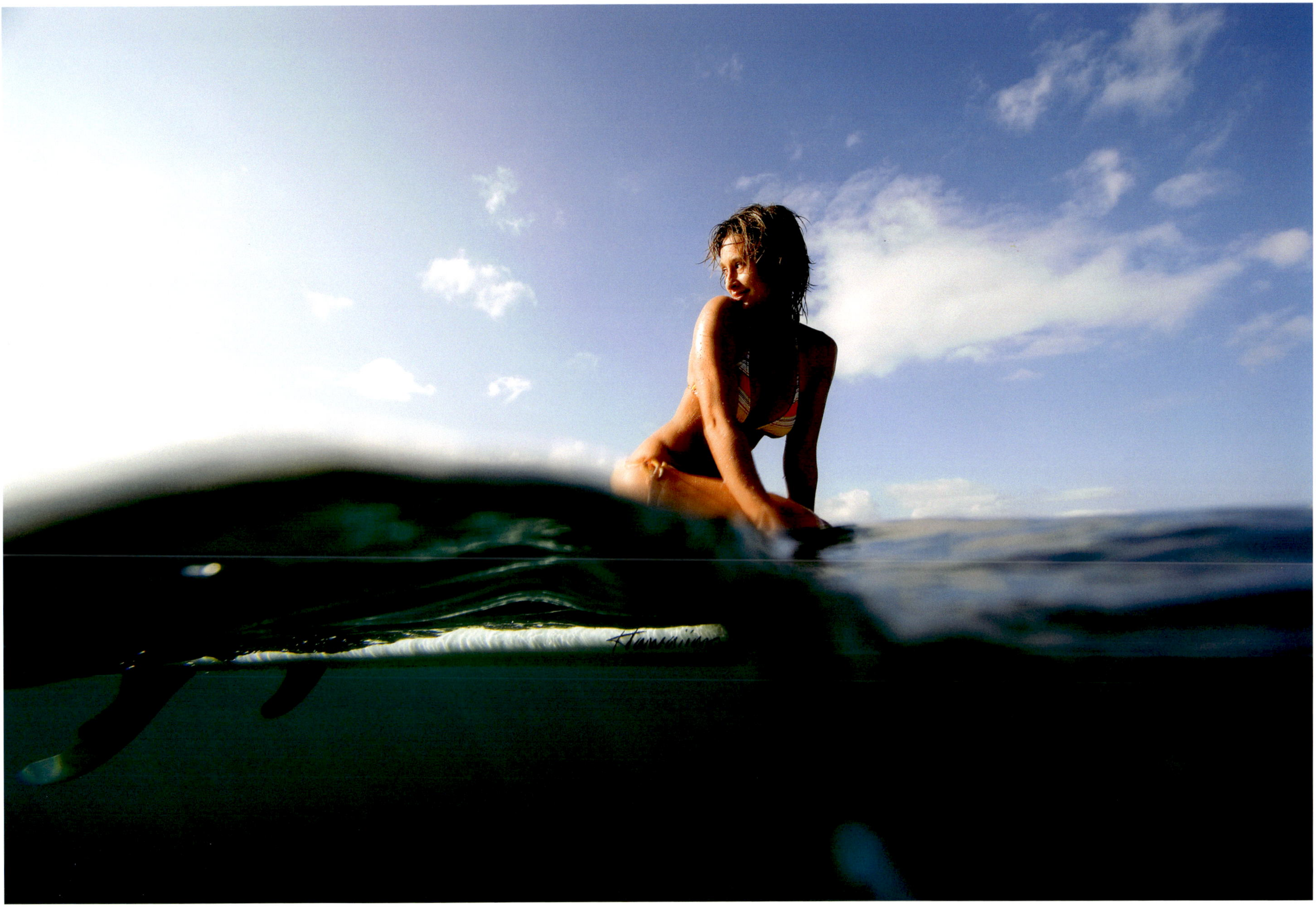

Kassia Meador. Beautiful Water, Beautiful Spirit. Hawaii. 2005.

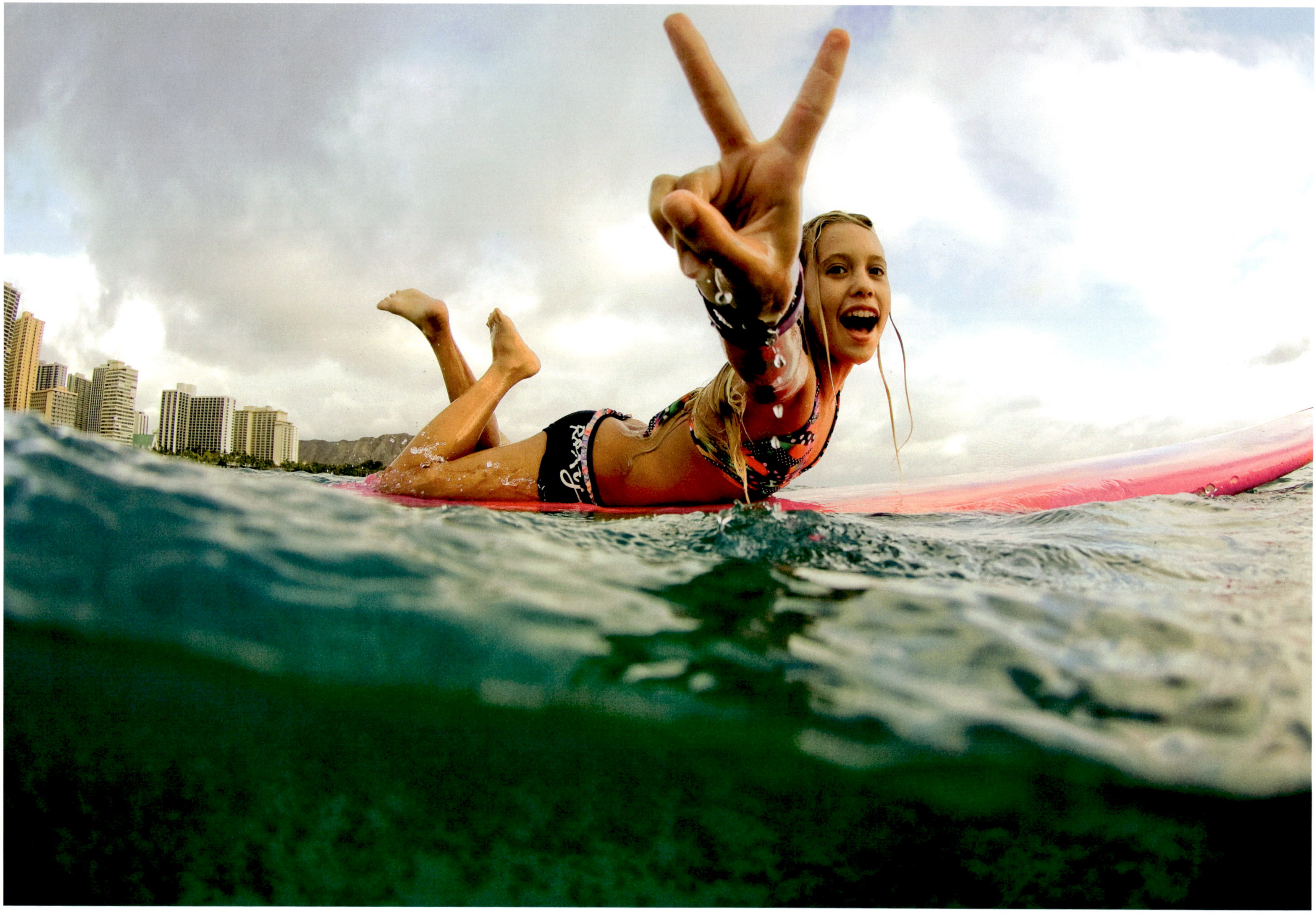

Vanina Walsh. Makes my job not a job at all. Waikiki. 2010.

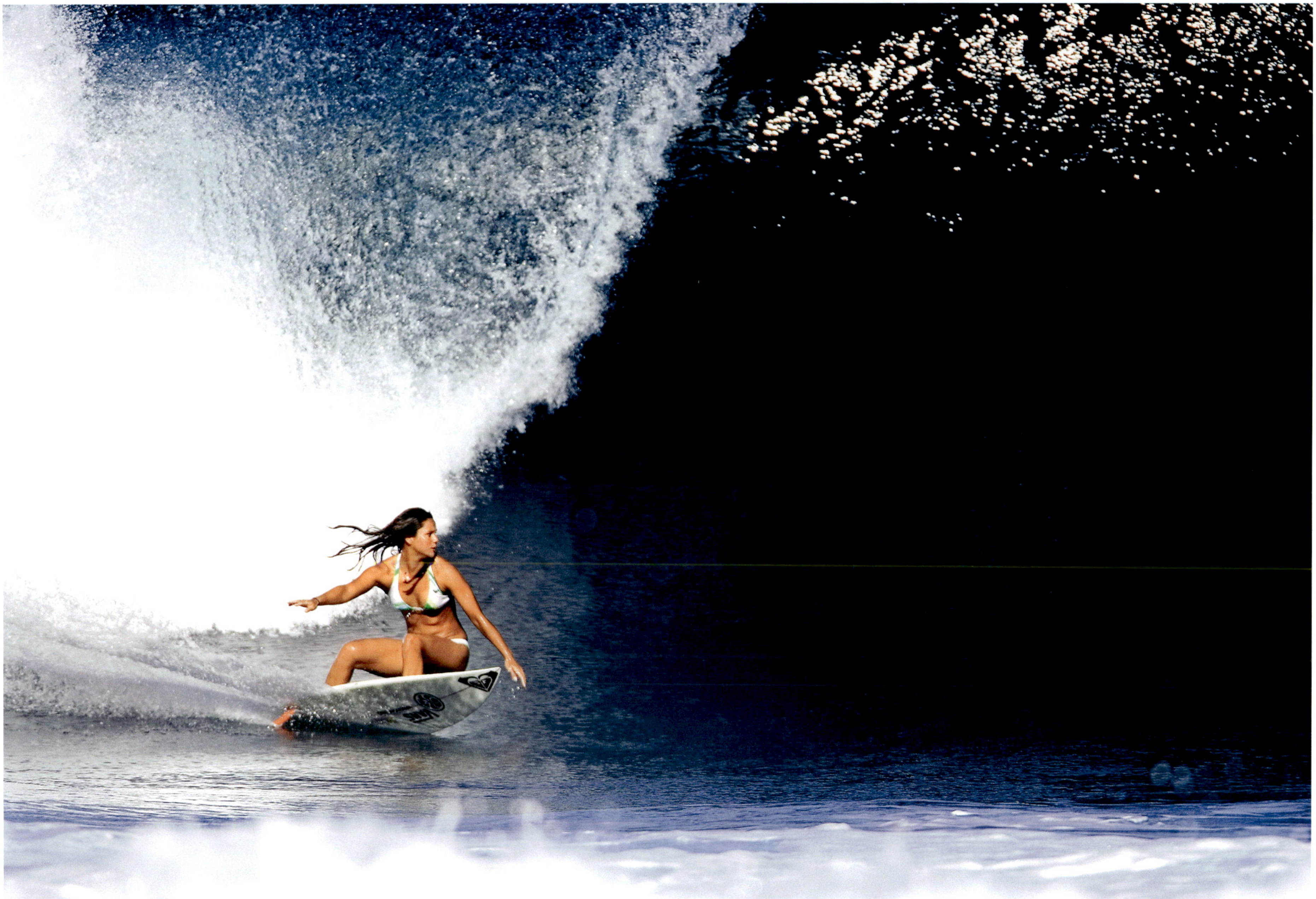

Megan Abubo. Rocky Lefts looking like "Pipe," HI. 2005.

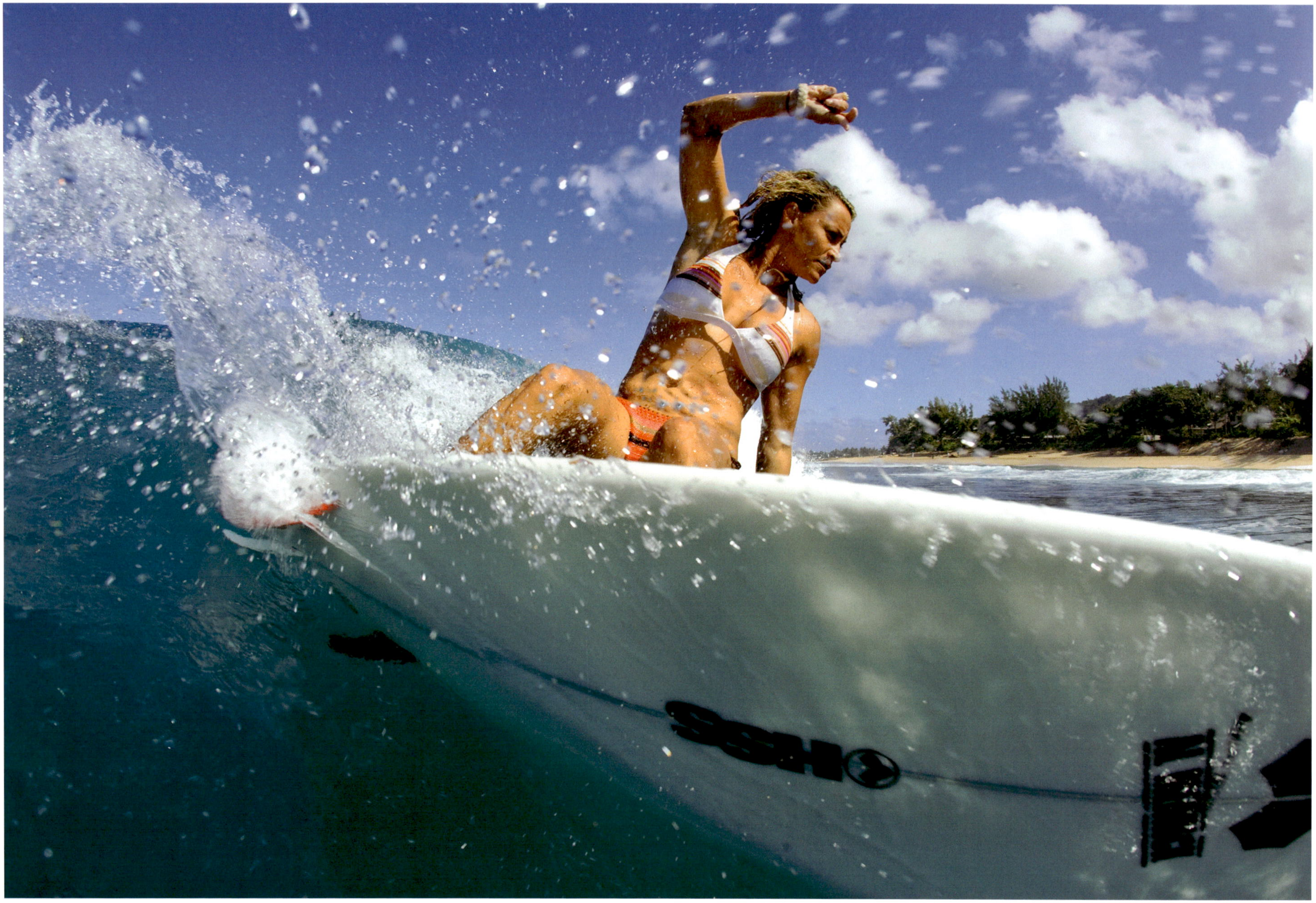

Lisa Andersen. Look what she started. Gas Chambers, HI. 2006.

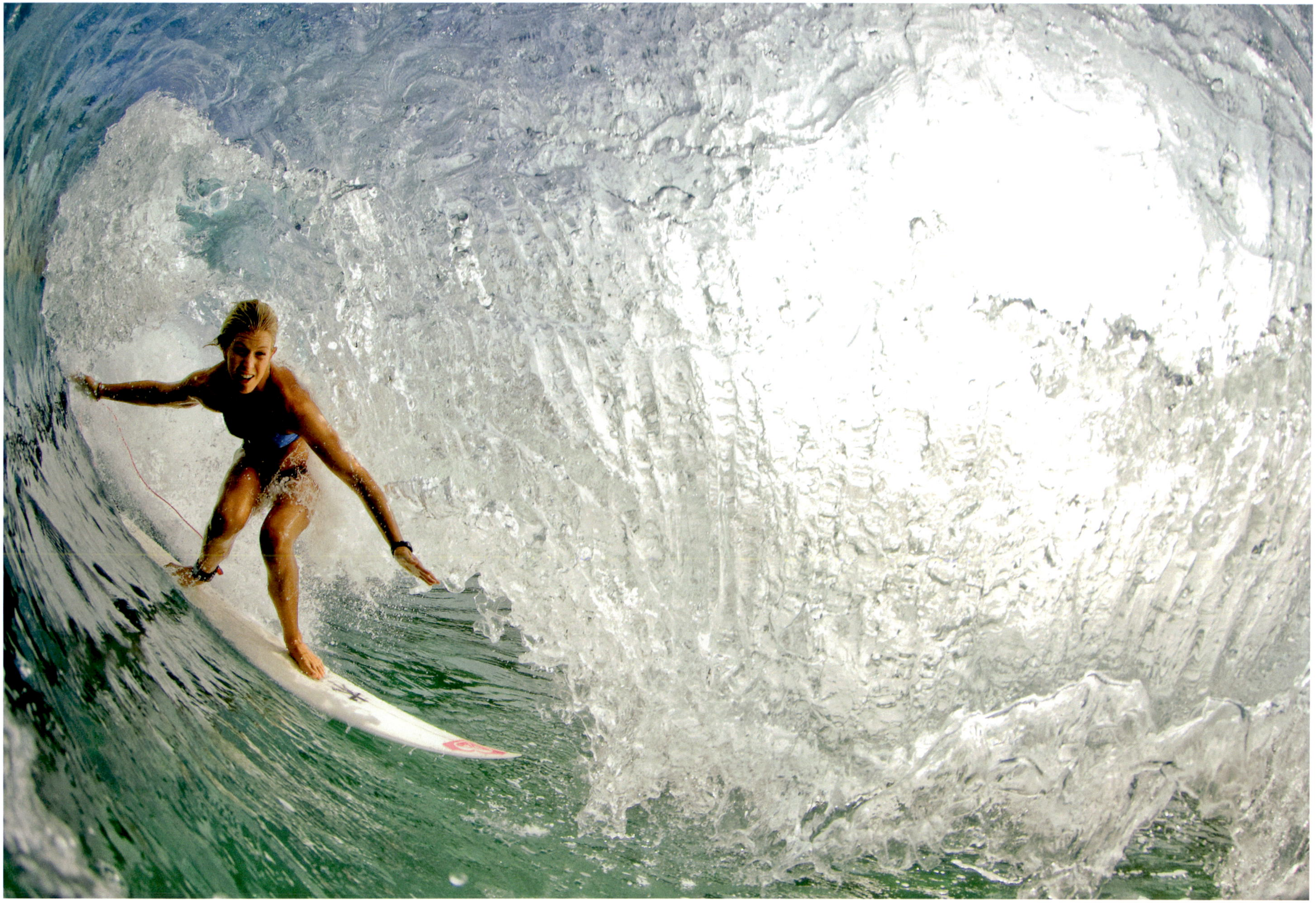

Rosy Hodge. Too legit to quit. Off the Wall, HI. 2008.

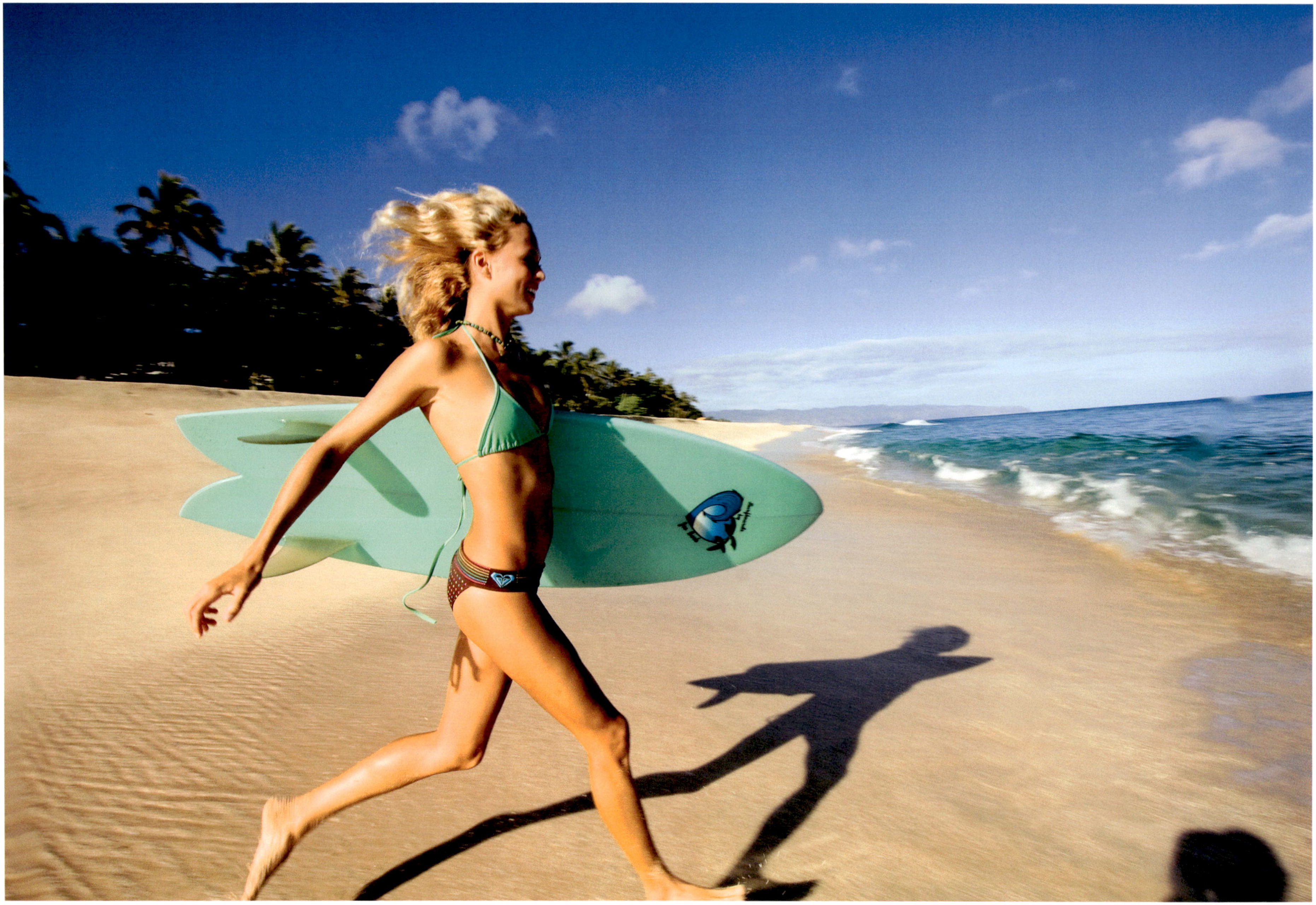

Rachel Spear. Girls just wanna have fun. Pupukea, HI. 2008.

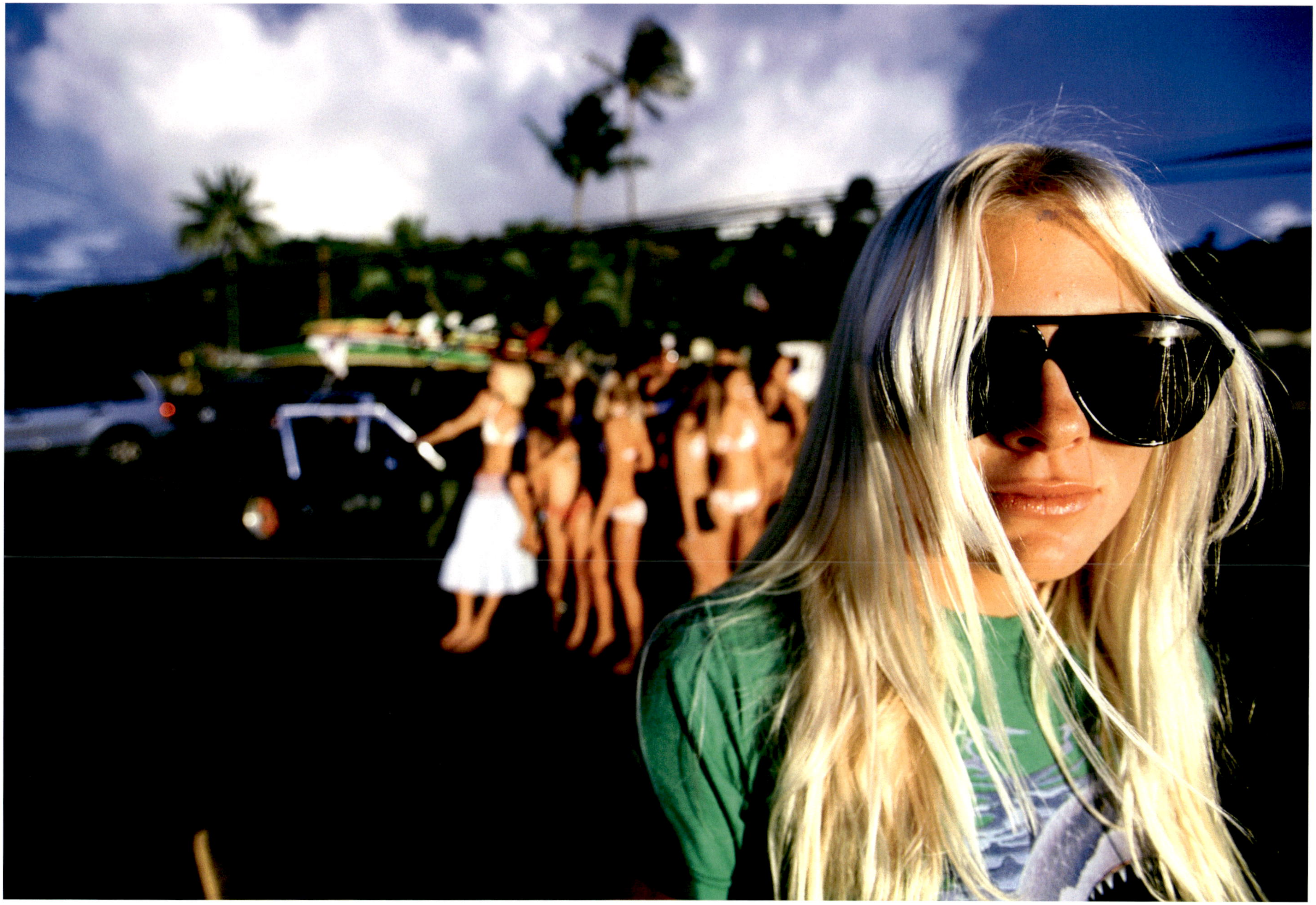

Roxy girls. Cruisin' da North Shore. Hawaii. 2002.

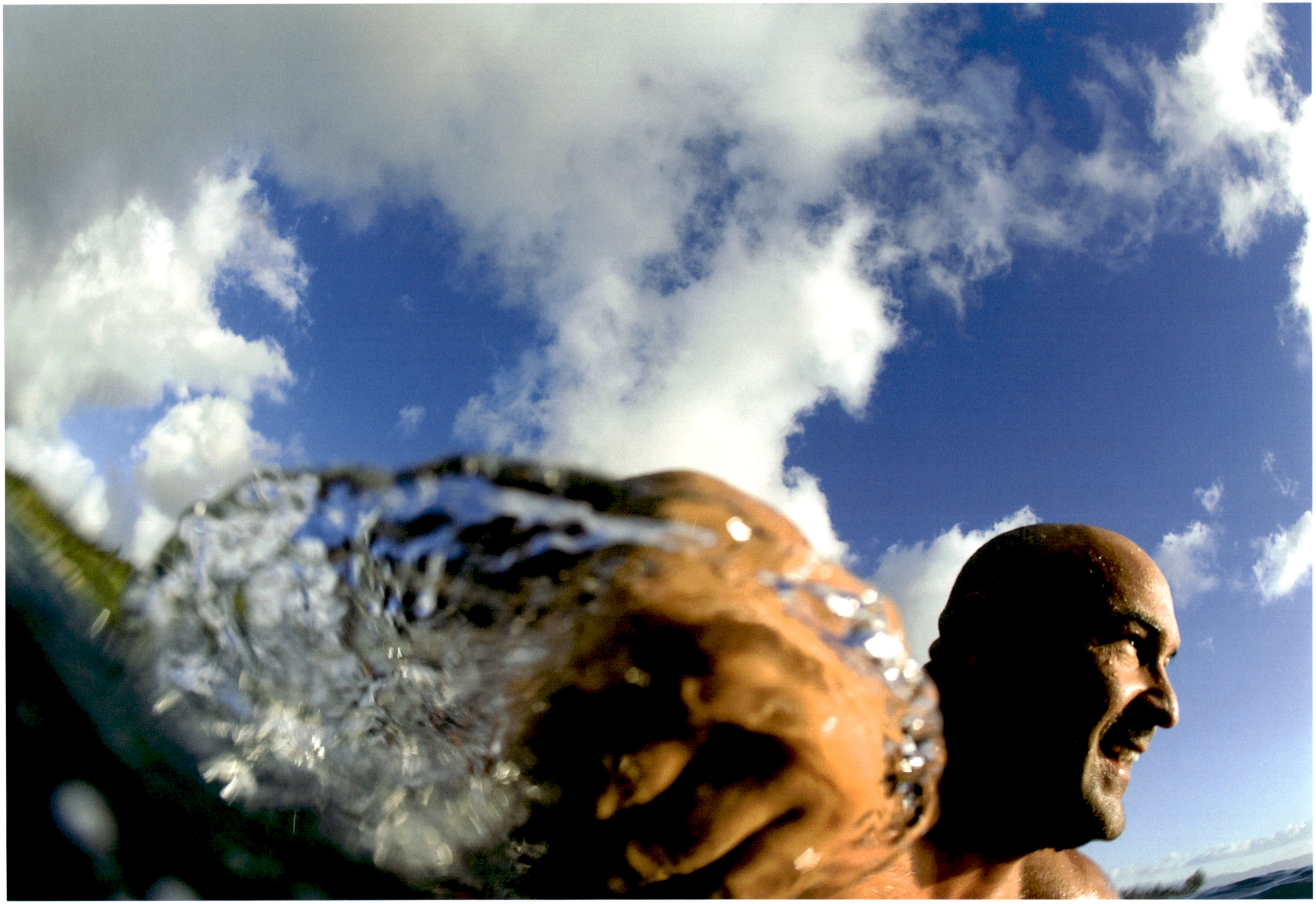

Johnny Boy Gomes. Some guys neva saw dis one comin'. V-land, HI. 2006.

Welcome to Hawaii

I first came out to the North Shore while still in high school in 1972 after seeing the movie *Five Summer Stories*. The film was full of amazing shots of the waves at Pipeline and one particular guy who later became my hero and mentor, Gerry Lopez. Being a goofy foot myself and growing up on a right hand point break, I always dreamed of surfing Pipeline frontside, Lopez style. I was determined to move to Hawaii straight out of high school, but my parents pleaded for me to stay and go to college. The day after I finished Brooks I was off to Hawaii. Being a young haole guy here in the late-'70s, the North Shore was a fairly dangerous place. Some local people who lived here did not like the influx of mainland surfers who were coming over in droves to catch their waves and so they were "regulating" it to a degree. I considered myself sort of an ambassador of understanding on how localism works.

Having grown up at a very localized spot and then traveling a lot, I believed I knew well how not to piss off the locals and how to show respect for the people who lived here. Being a photographer didn't hurt me any, as I was always able to help supply the locals with photos of themselves. However, I realized early on living in Hawaii that I was not immune.

One day, a few friends and I were searching for good surf and spent the whole day driving around the island trying to find a spot where the wind wasn't blowing onshore. Reese Patterson and David Kahanamoku were both with me and we spent hours driving until we found a spot on the west side that looked good, a perfect left hand point break at Maile Point. We were all jonesing to surf so we parked, grabbed our boards, and paddled out. Foolishly, I had my trunk full of camera equipment, but being with David, the "Duke's" grandson, I guess I assumed I had it all wired and that I was above reproach. I caught my first wave and remember looking up to see my old grey Volvo being driven out of the parking lot. I headed to the beach and met a group of young local guys standing there in the dirt parking lot laughing and pointing at me, mocking me as the dumb haole who got his car stolen. A cop car was driving by and I flagged him down and told him my car had been stolen. He replied, "Are you Russi?" He told me someone had already called it in, which was pretty unusual for the Westside.

He had an idea where the car may be. I barely squeezed in the cop car with my 6'2" board and he drove me up a side road towards a mountain full of burned out, stripped cars. I noticed the road had curbs and street lamps but no houses. I spotted my old car halfway up the road. Maybe I got lucky, I thought, since the trunk was still closed and it had only been a few minutes since the car was taken. As we got closer I saw the keys dangling from the trunk and knew everything was gone. My entire livelihood was gone—water housings, lenses, tripods, camera bodies—all of it.

Since moving to the island, I had gotten to know a few of the guys in the black shorts, Da Hui. So I drove my car back to the North Shore and went to the leader of Da Hui's house. I asked him what could be done. He turned to a young man that was sitting on the couch in his house and said, "Jim, meet Johnny Boy." He was eighteen years old from the west side, and had just gotten out of juvenile hall. The next day Johnny Boy and I drove back out to Maile Point. When we got there I saw the same group of guys hanging out there in the parking lot and they were all laughing, seeing me pull up again in that old grey Volvo. When we got close enough for them to see Johnny Boy riding shotgun, their smiles disappeared, and two of them took off running. Johnny Boy told me to cut them off, so I gunned the old Volvo and did a big brody around them. In a huge cloud of dust Johnny jumped out of the Volvo, tackled one of them, and started pounding him. He came back to the Volvo a few minutes later and told me to wait there while he went to get my camera stuff. I remember sitting in that car for nearly an hour, gripping the steering wheel, the guys in the parking lot were silently giving me stinkeye. With only one road in and one road out, I was wondering how in the world I would get out of there if things got ugly. About forty-five minutes later Johnny Boy rolled up with a car full of guys. They backed it up to my car and unloaded all of my gear into my trunk.

Back on the North Shore I thanked my friend for loaning me Johnny Boy. He said, "Ok, but here's the deal. Johnny Boy gets to live with you for the winter. He's only eighteen and just got out of juvenile hall and he's ready to start back up his surfing career so I want him to stay with you." It was an offer I couldn't refuse. That winter I fed him and photographed him, eventually shooting his first photo sequence of a "barrel roll" for *Surfer* magazine. This was a good thing, as being friends with Johnny Boy is a lot better than being enemies. Mahalos Johnny Boy. You da man!

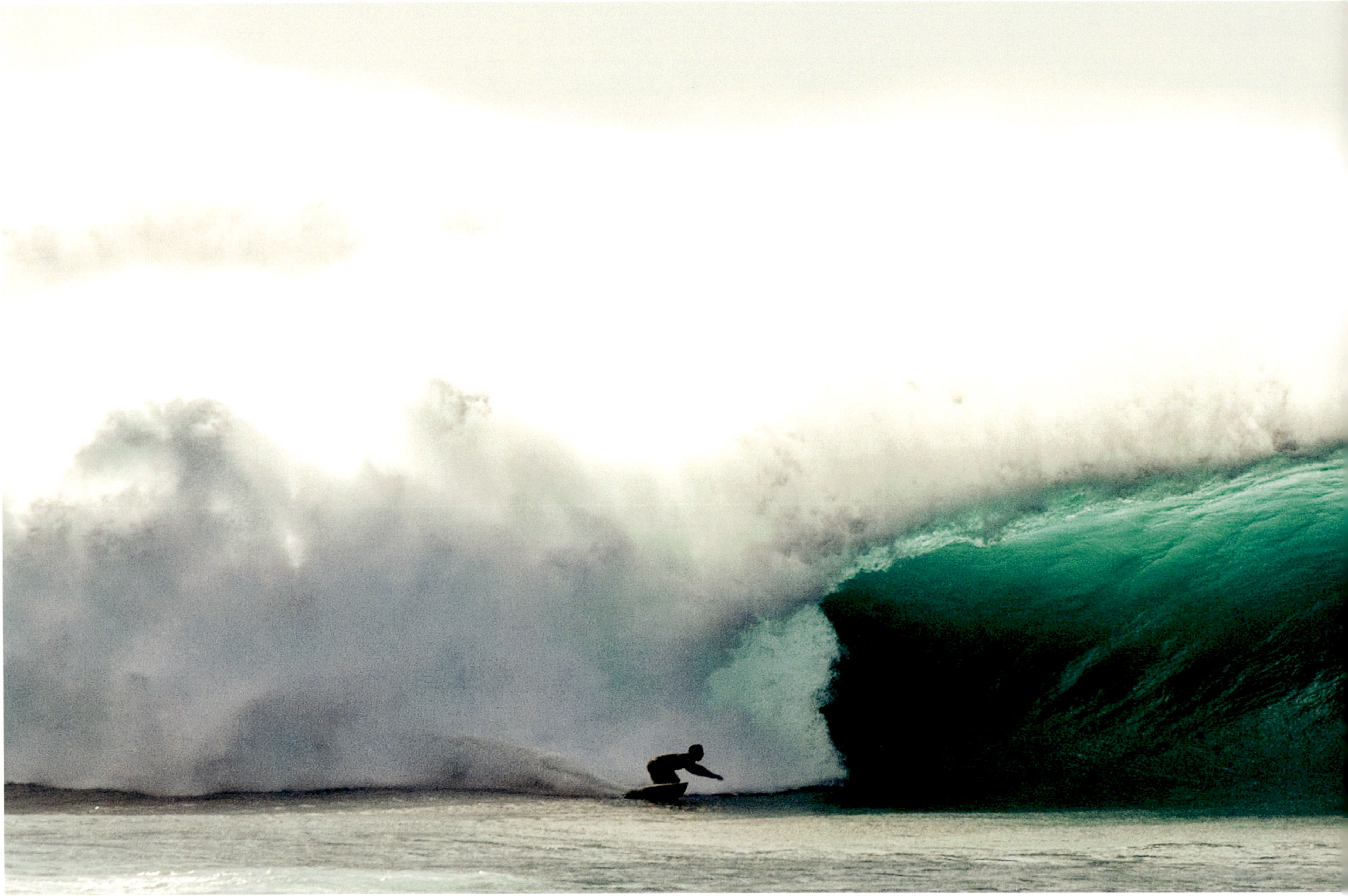

Should I stay or should I go now? Pipeline, HI. 2005.

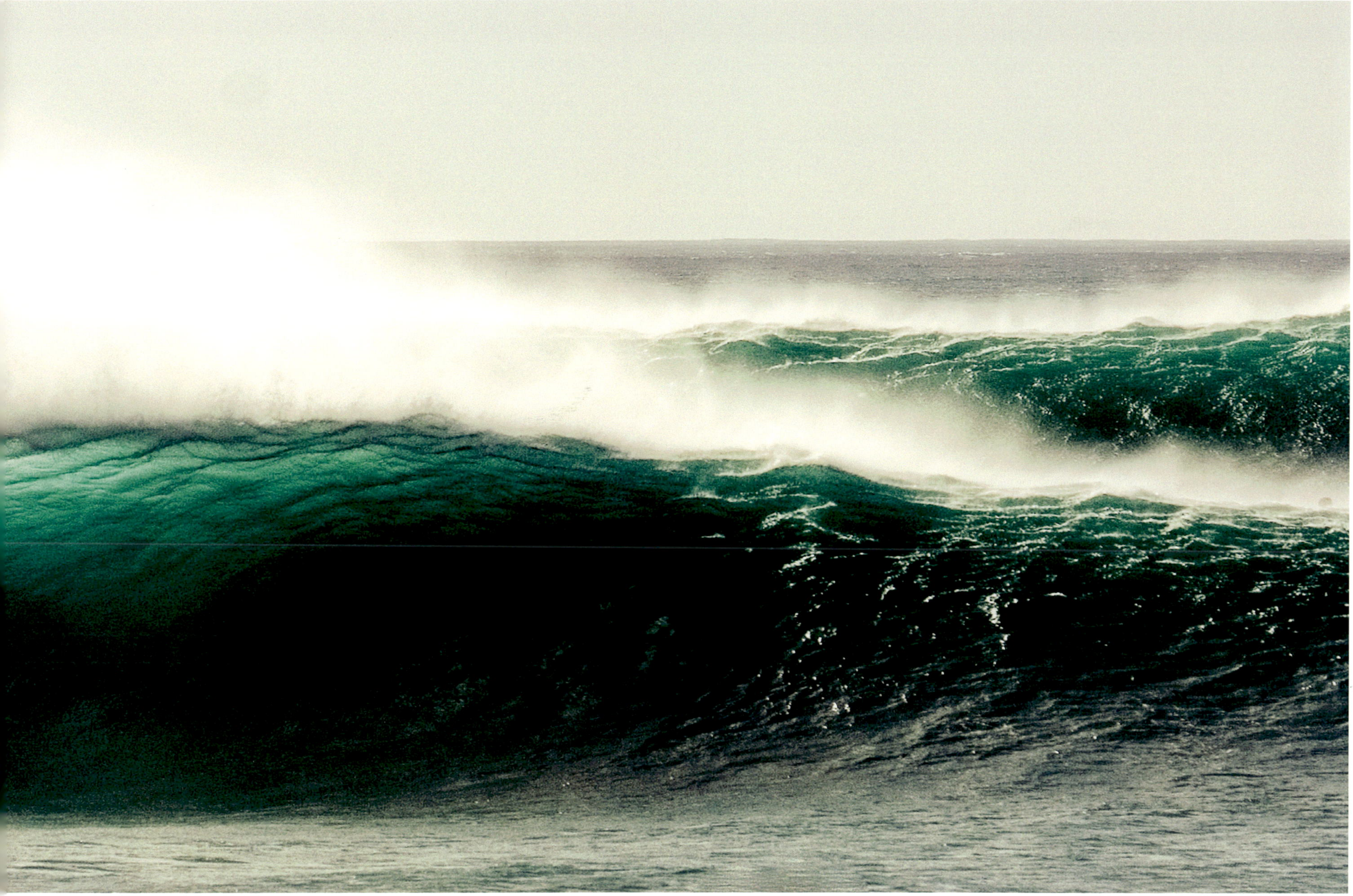

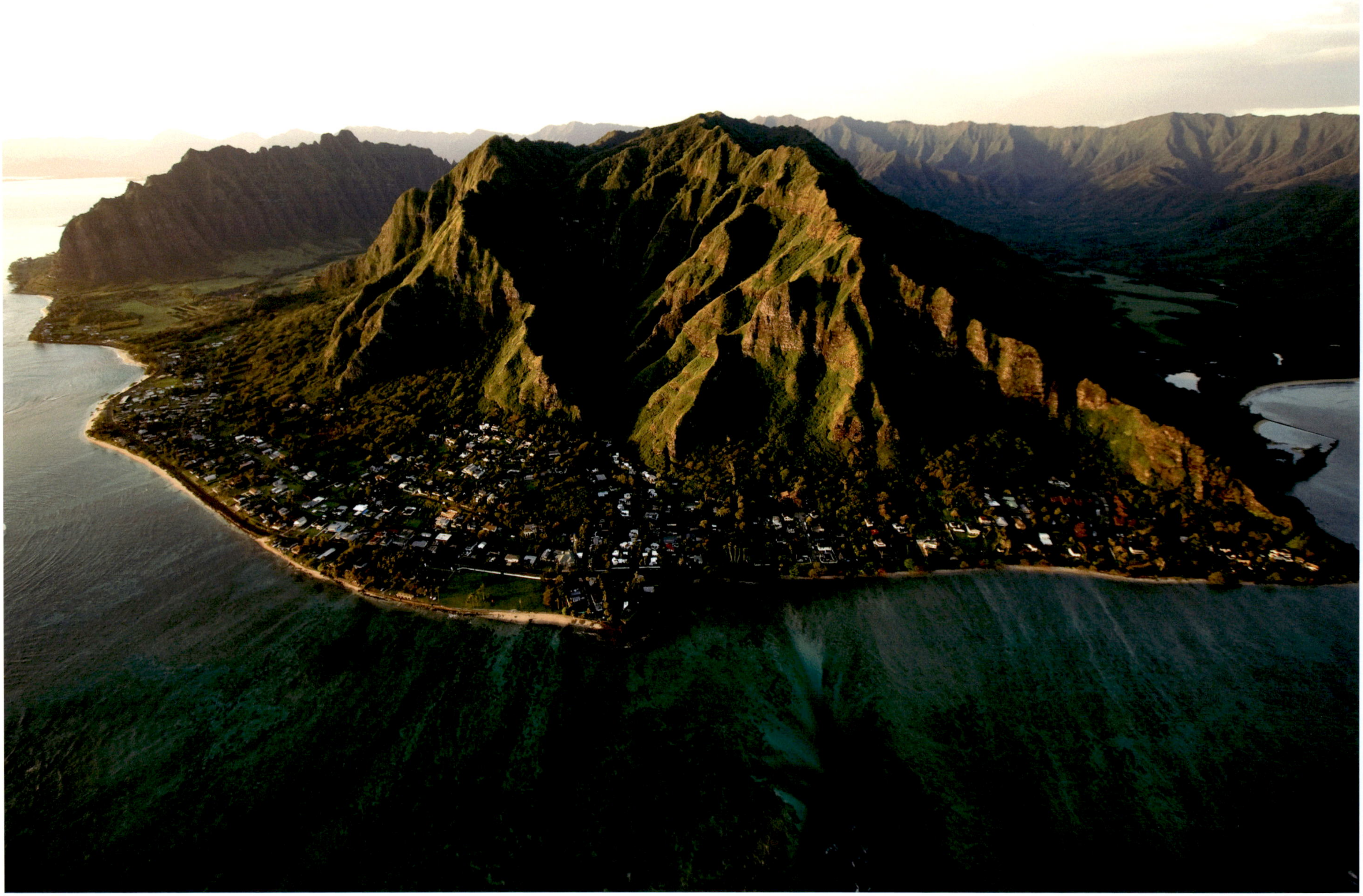

And God said, "Let the water under the sky be gathered to one place and let the dry land appear." Eastside Oahu, HI. 2007.

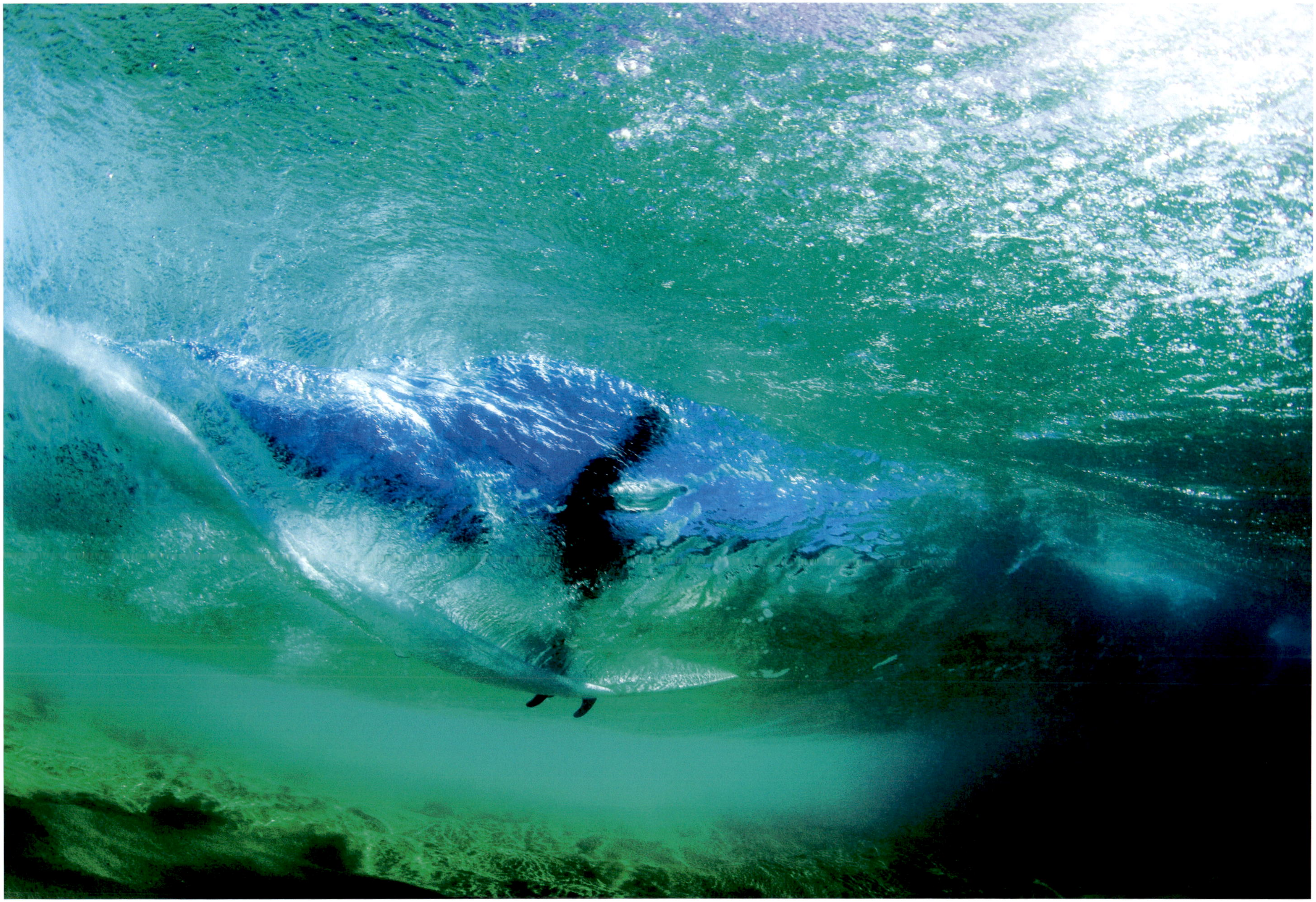

Boy in the Bubble. Hawaii. 2007.

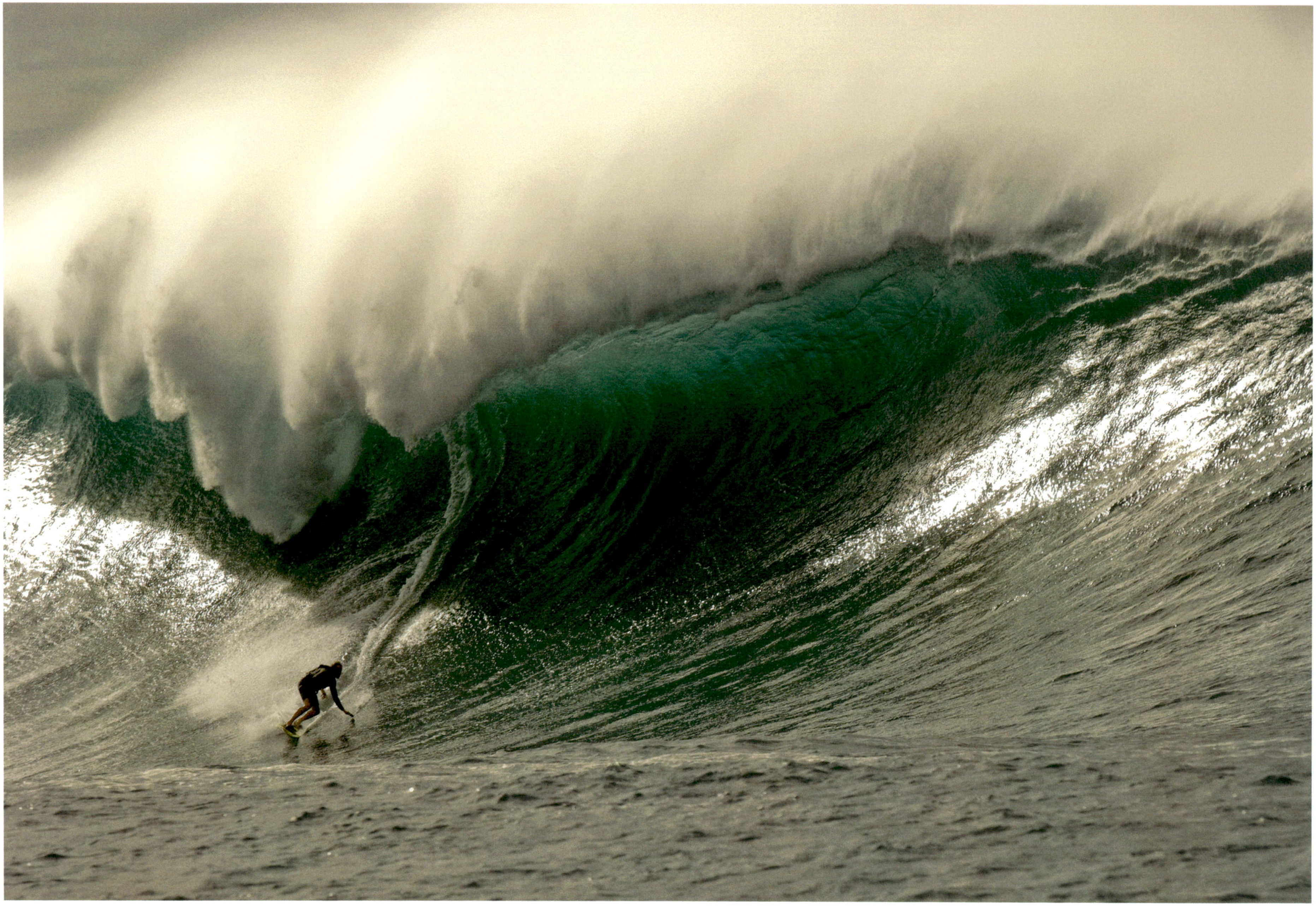

Troy Alotis. Facing the left at Phantoms, HI. 2008.

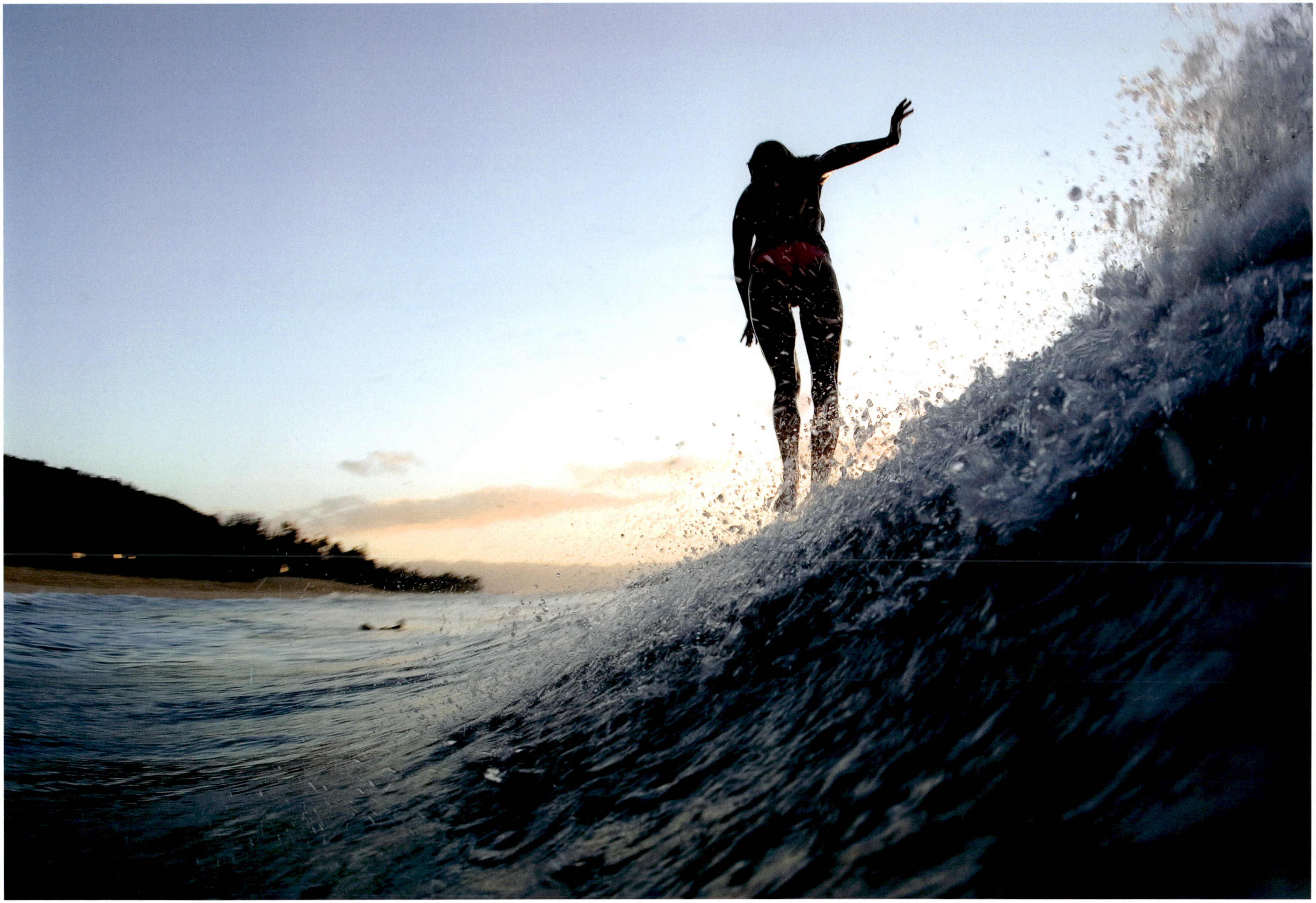

Alex "John Mom" Florence. Pupukea, HI. 2005.

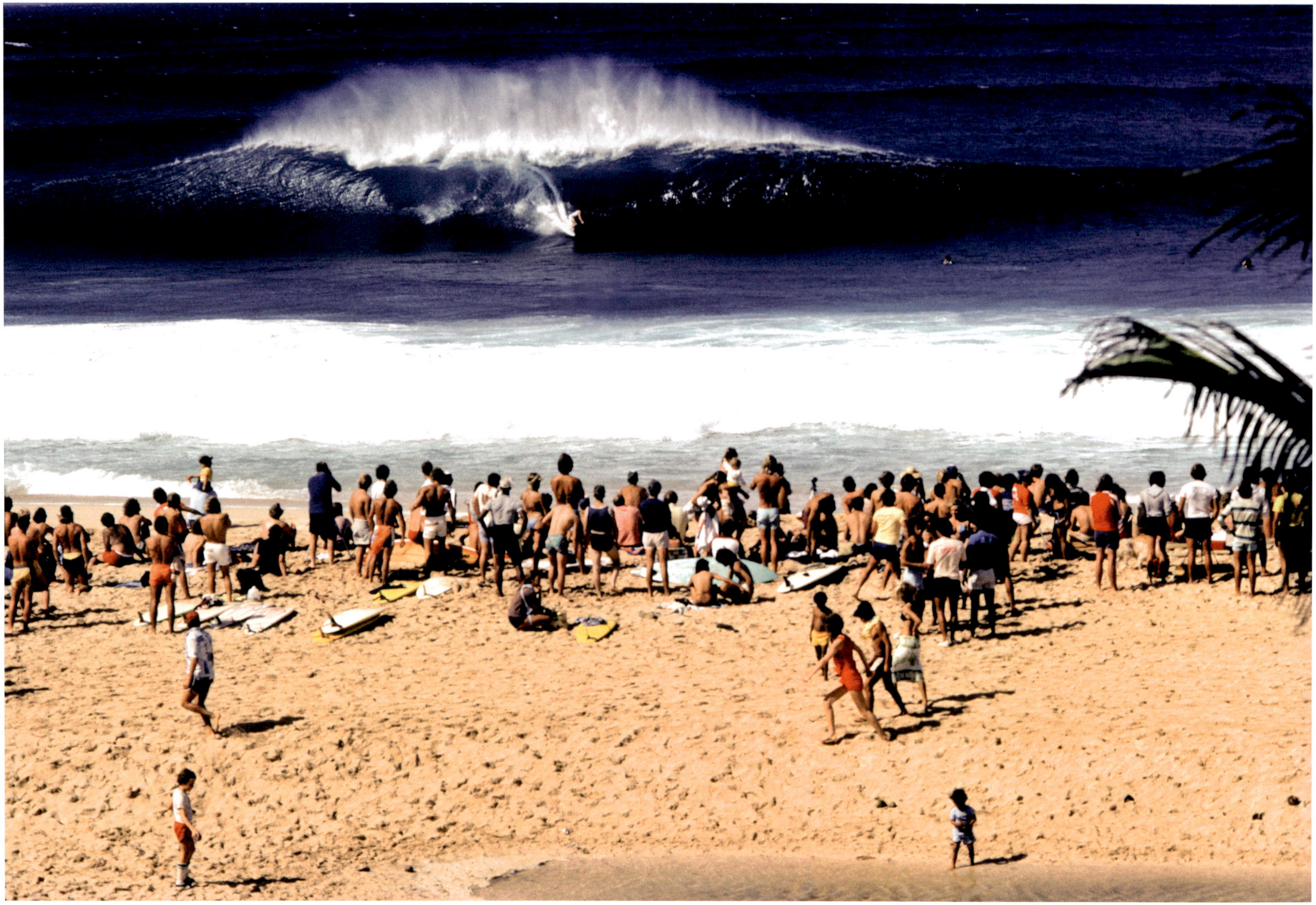

View from my bedroom window. Pipeline, HI. 1981.

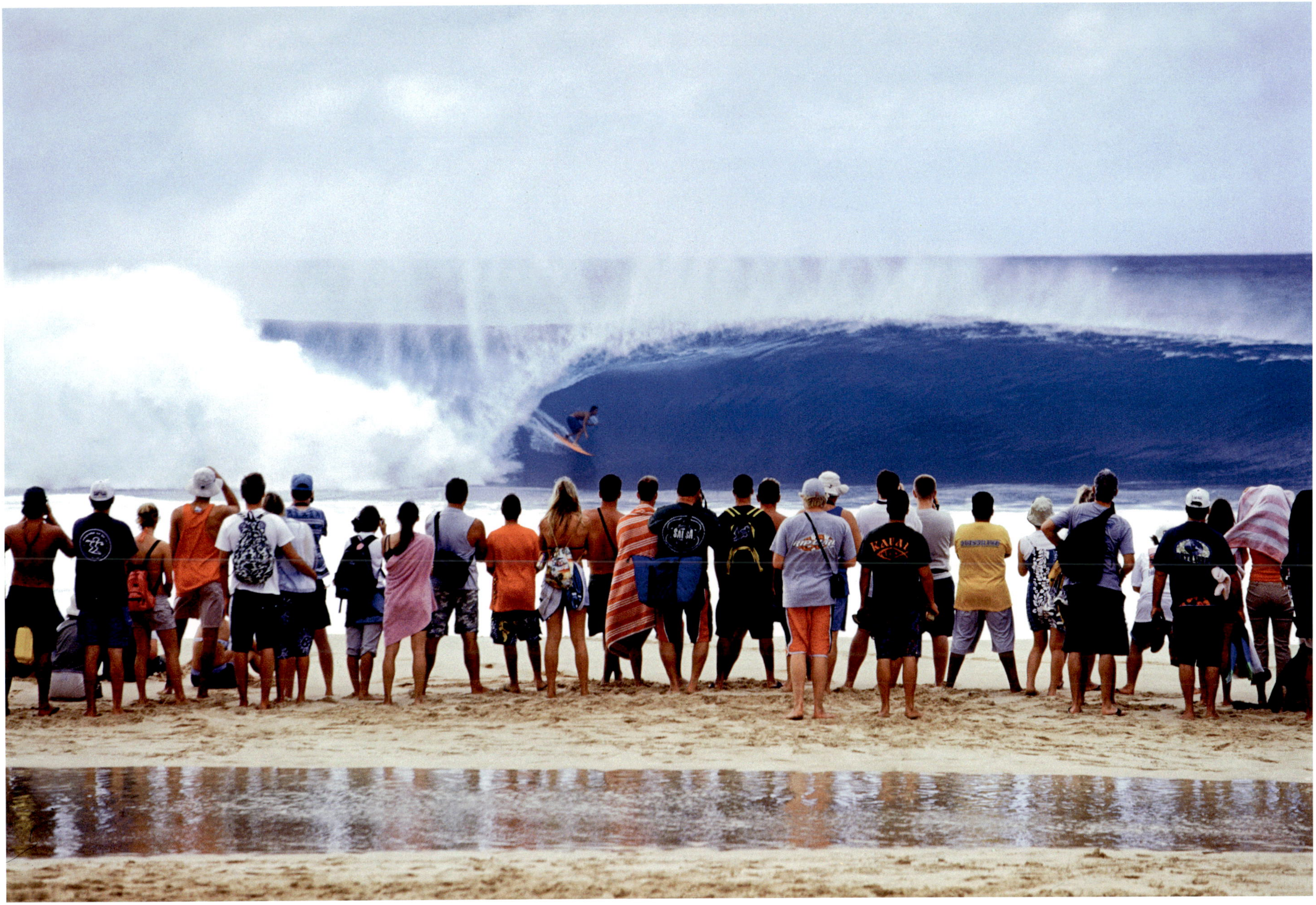

Danny Fuller. The waves remain the same, only the players have changed. Pipeline, HI. 2001.

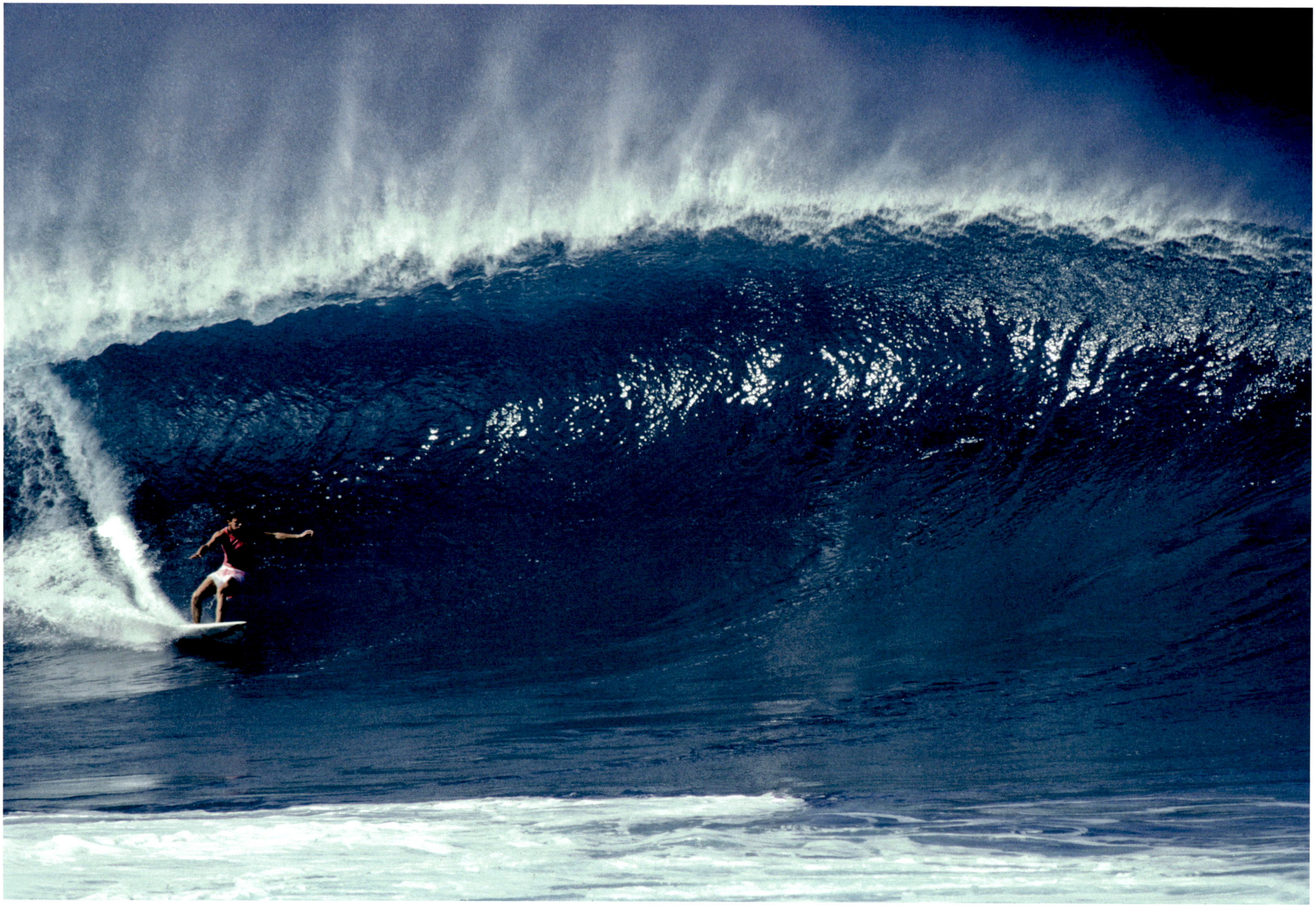

Wayne "Rabbit" Bartholomew. Pipe Masters, HI. 1984.

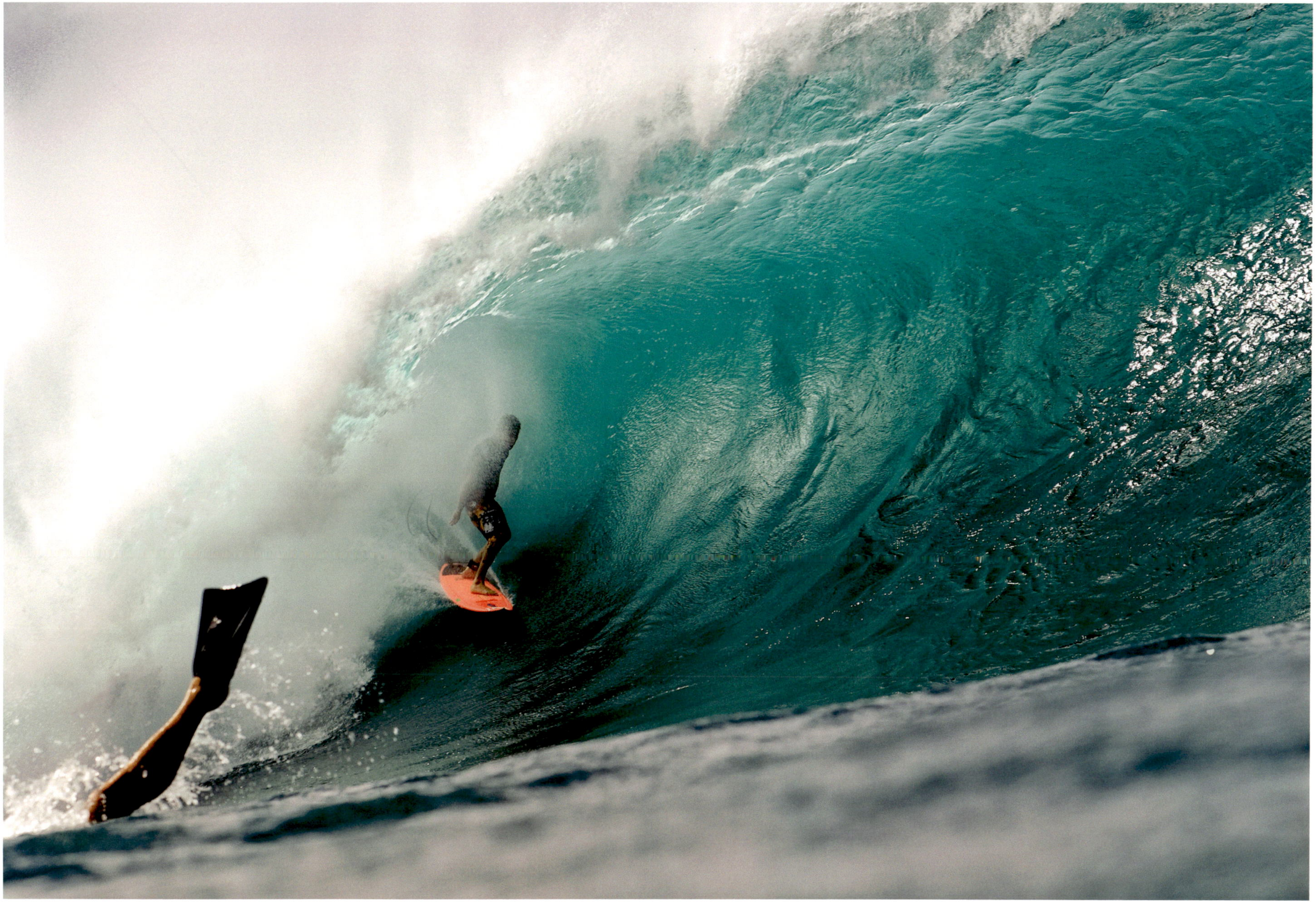

Jamie Sterling with one of his biggest fans. Pipeline, HI. 2005.

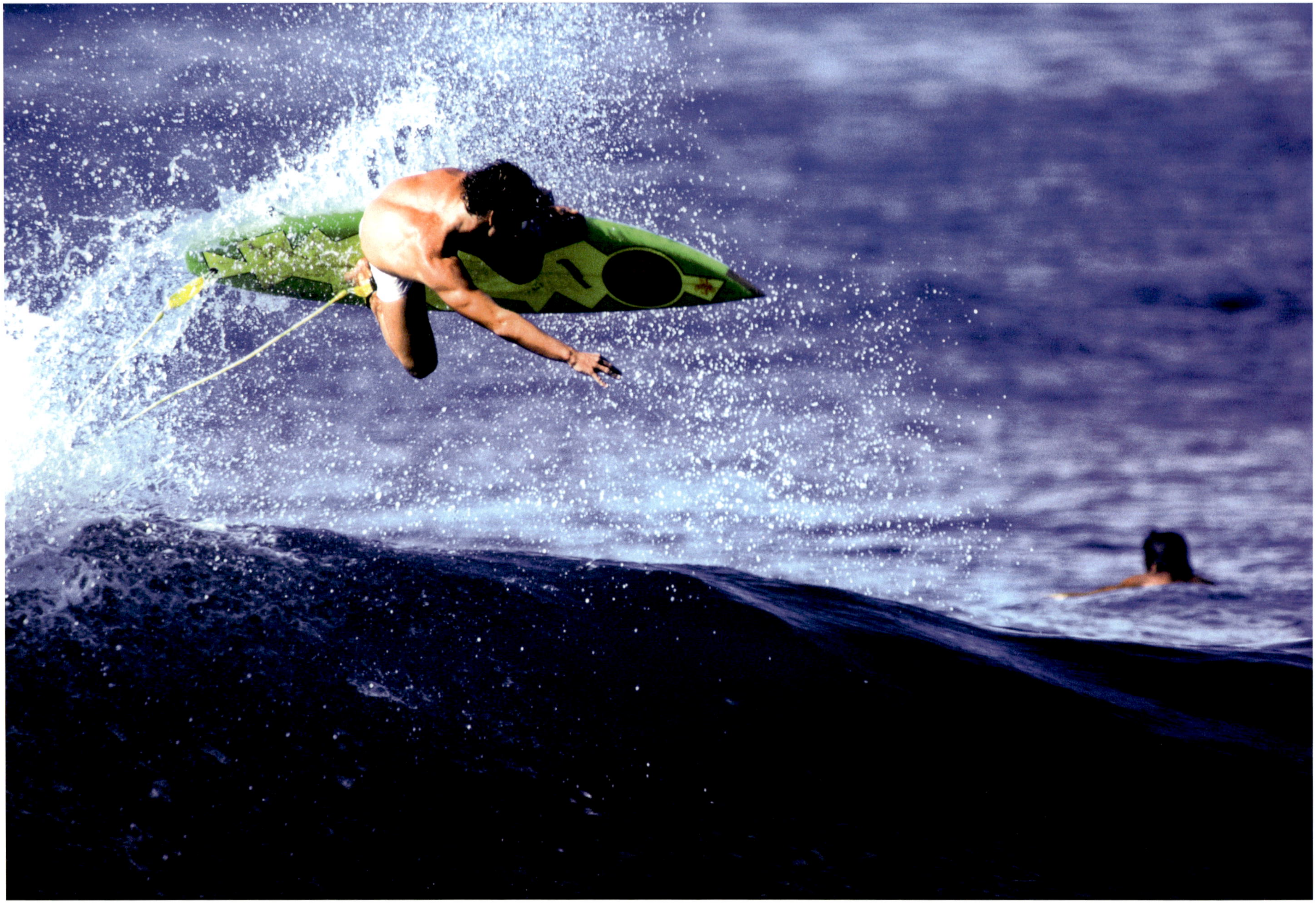

Martin Potter, first published aerial. Off the Wall, HI. 1984.

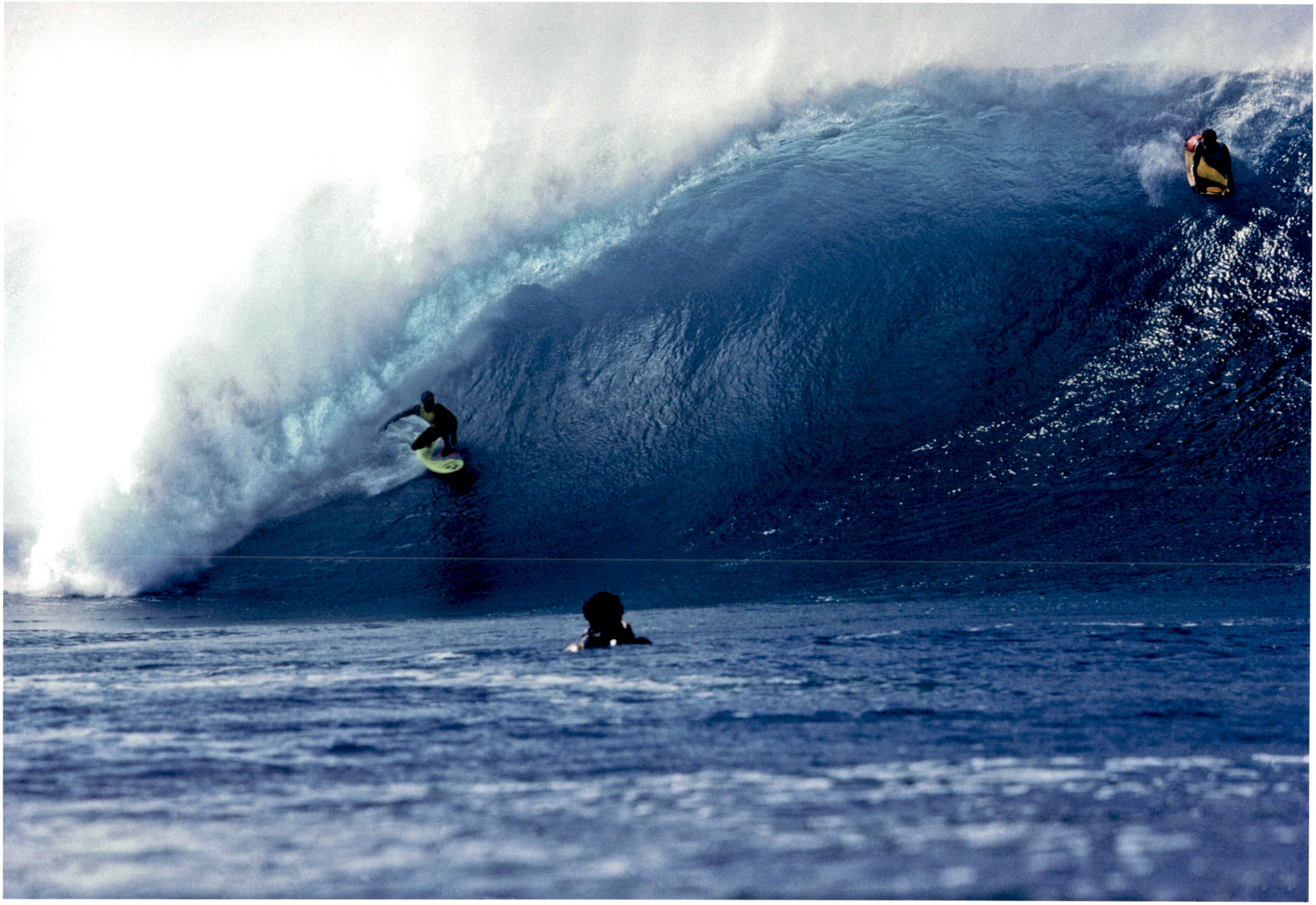

Tony Moniz, "Life in the Pit," *Surfer Magazine* poster. Pipeline, HI. 1985.

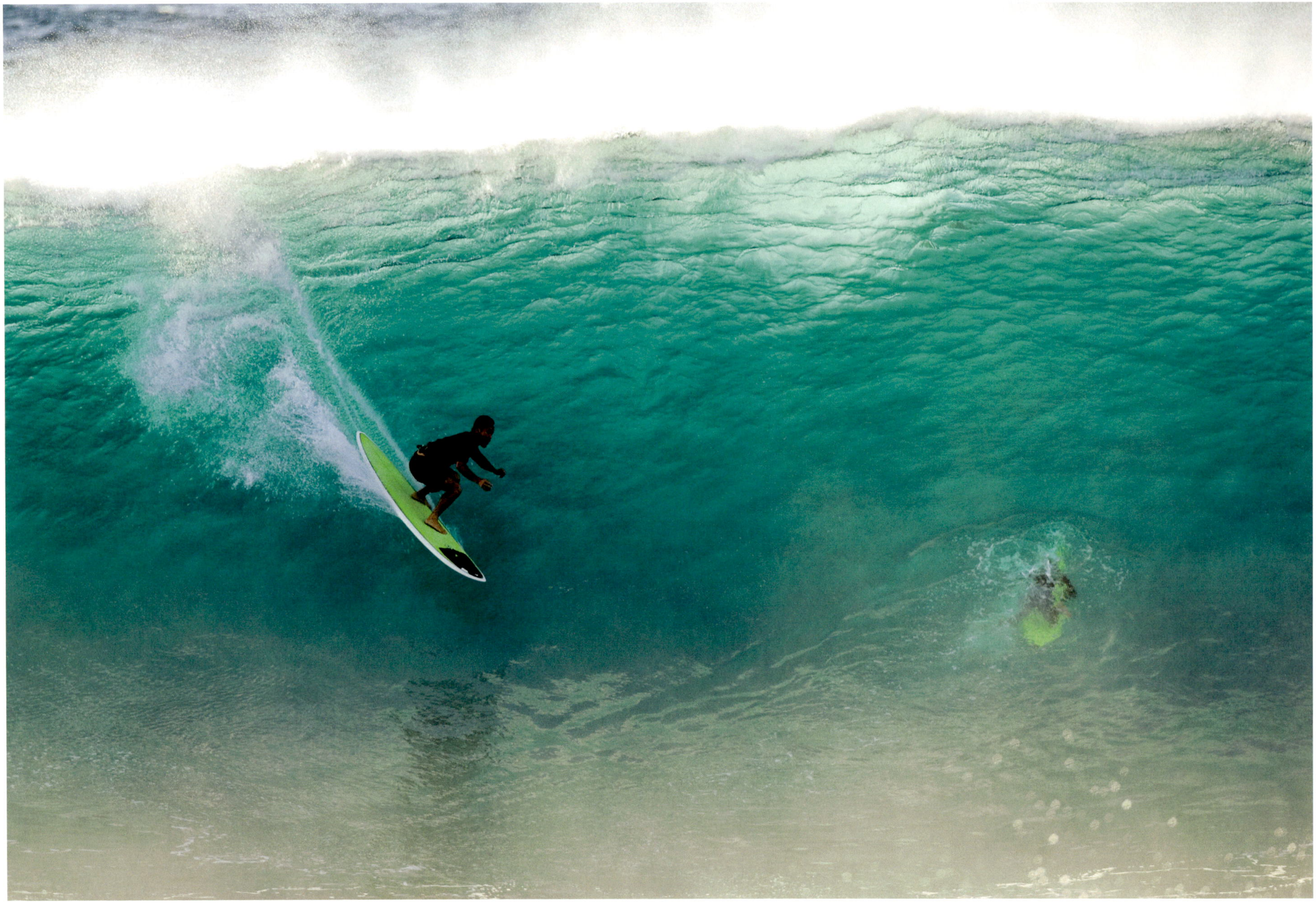

Takuji Masuda. "Respect." Pipeline, HI. 2008.

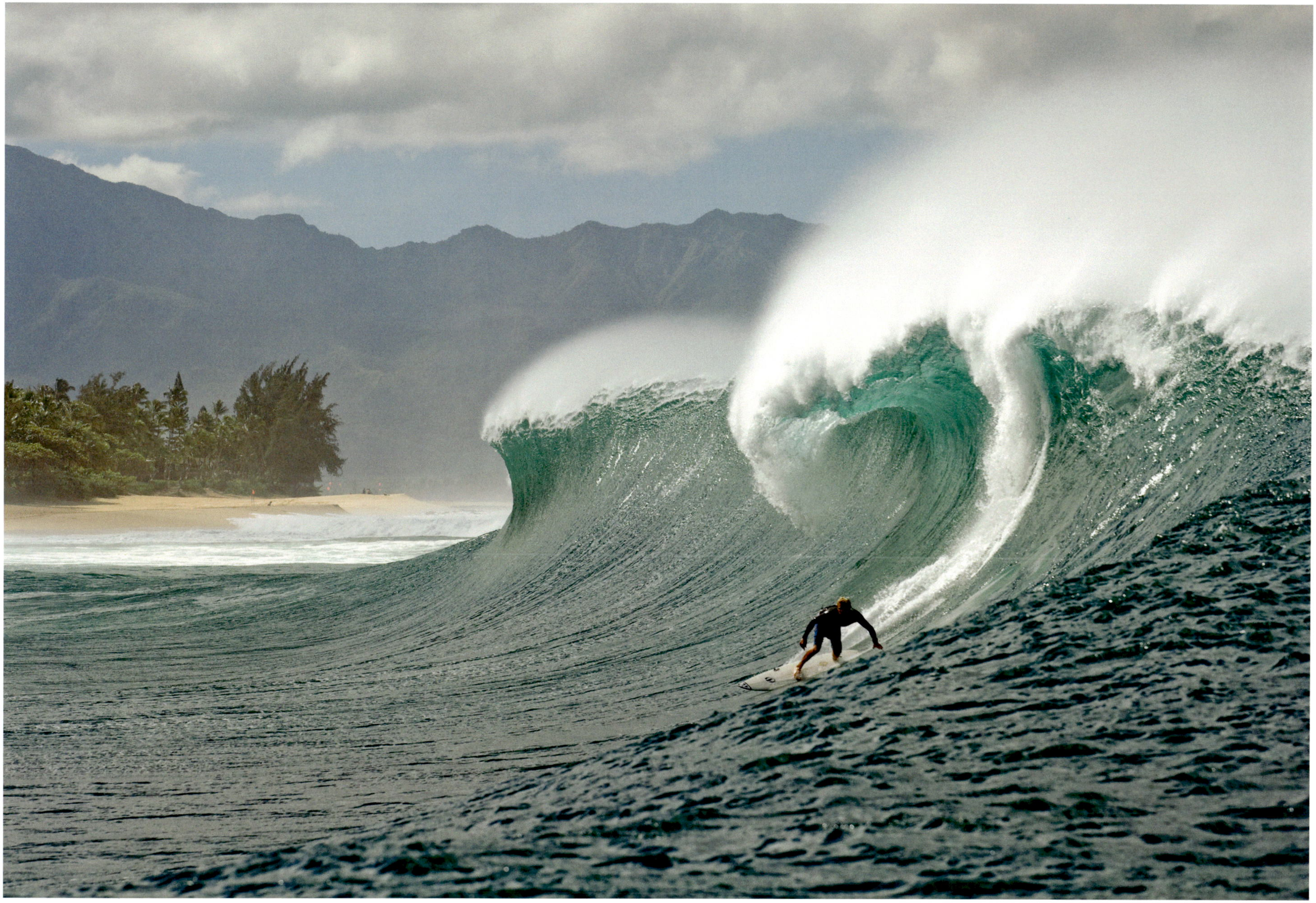

Ricky Whitlock. Tasting Hawaiian Power. Pipeline, HI. 2008.

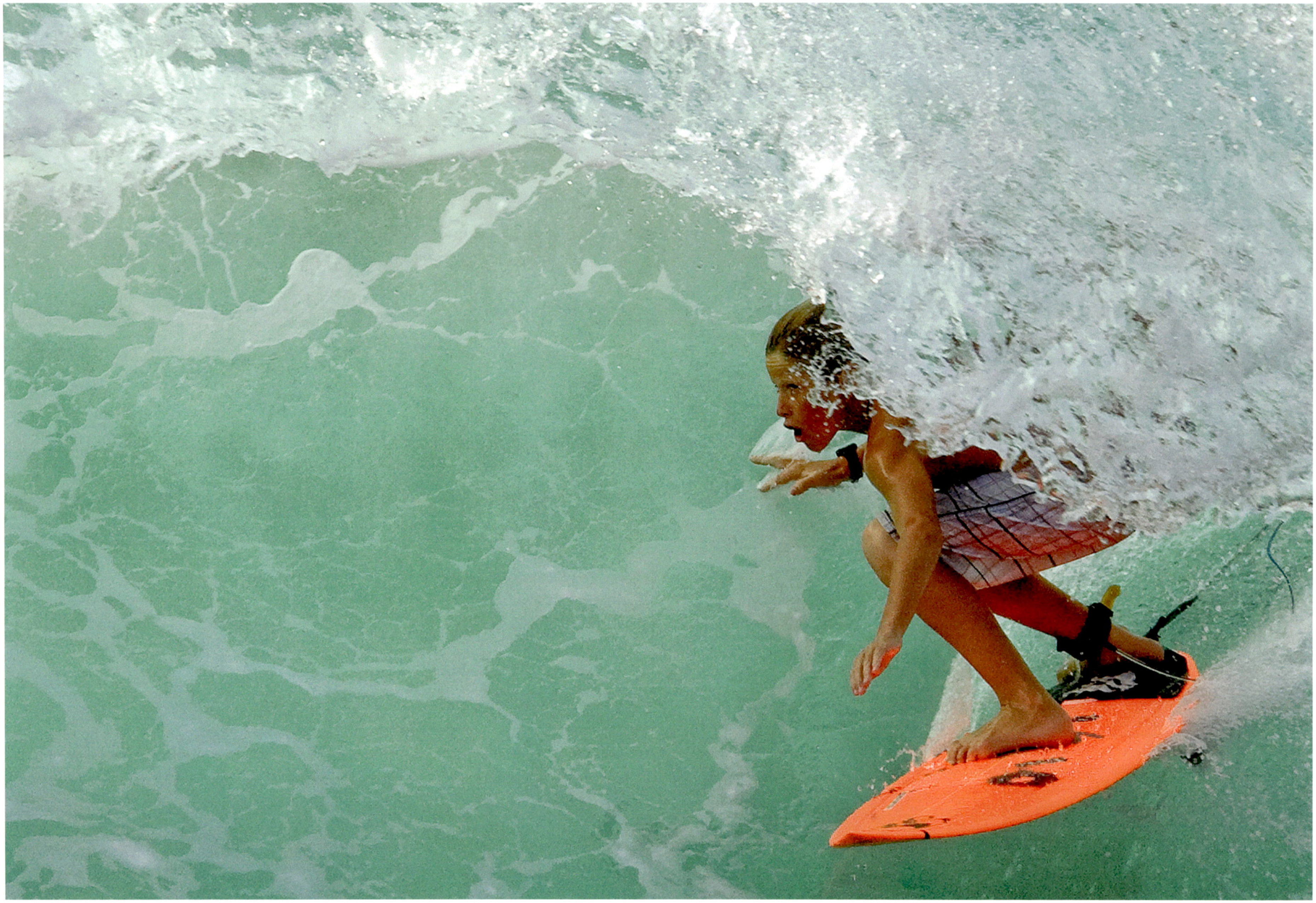

Nathan Florence, following his brother's path. Ehukai, HI. 2006.

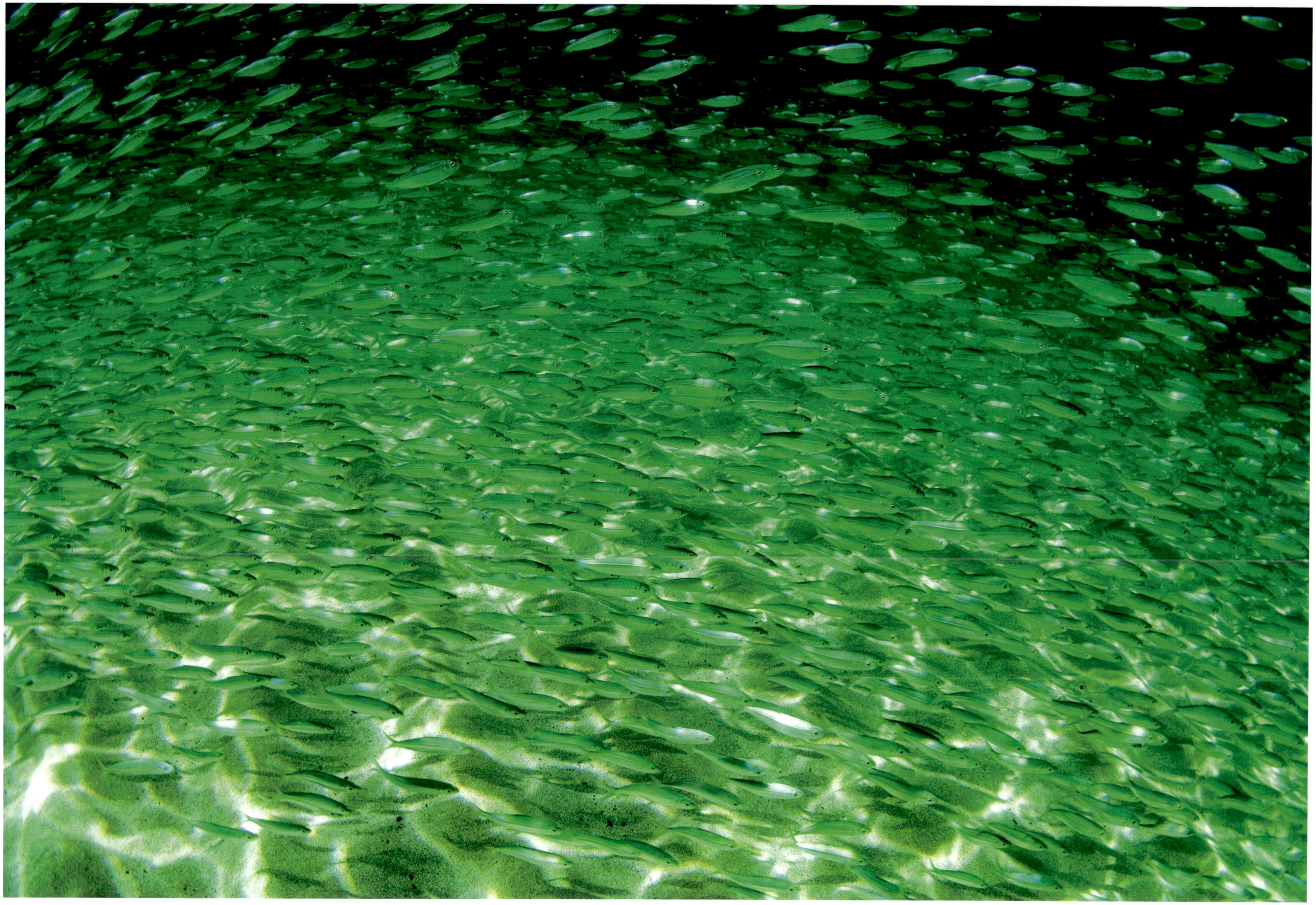

School of Waimea. Hawaii. 2006.

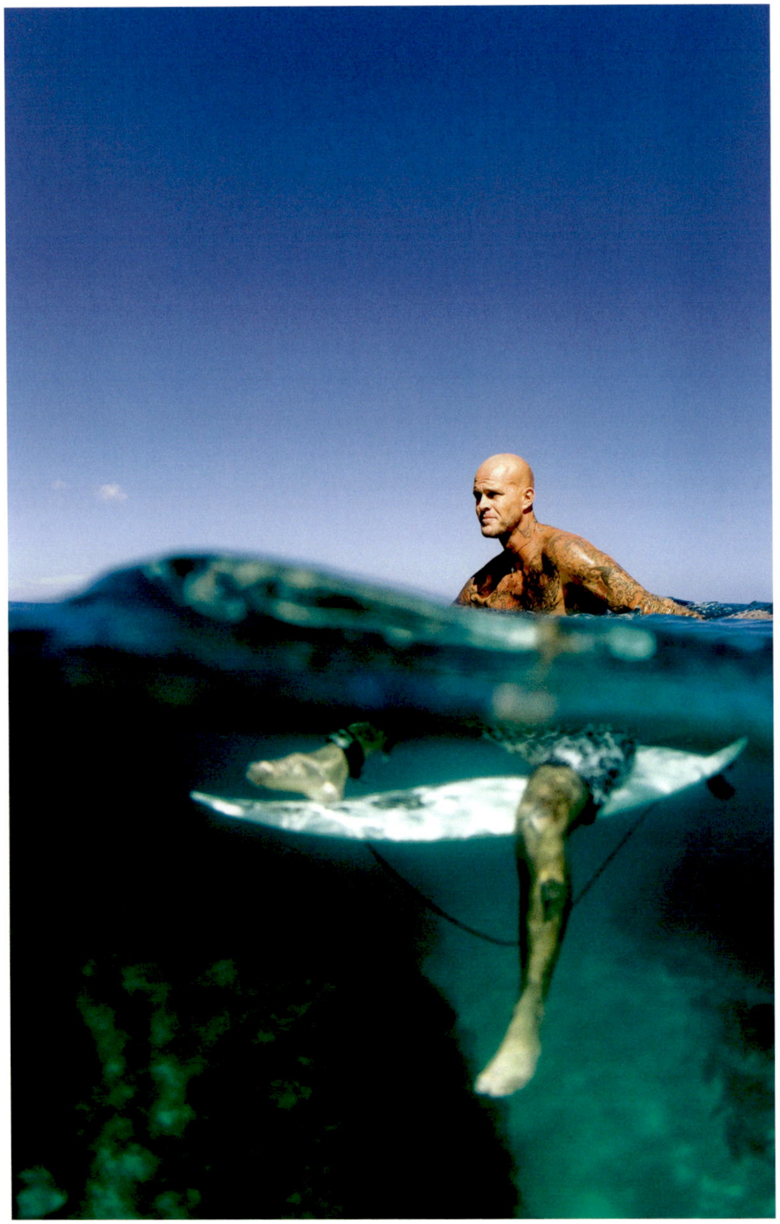

Matt Archbold. Hawaii. 2006.

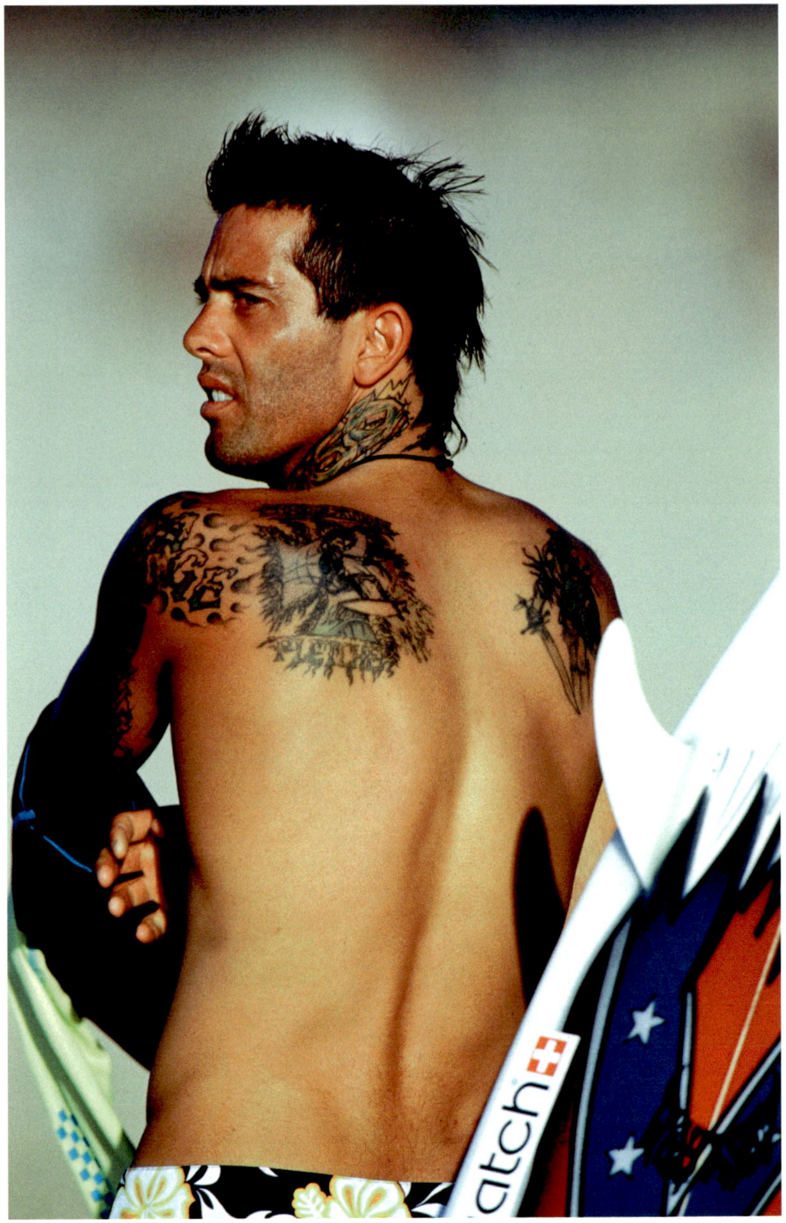

Christian Fletcher. Hawaii. 2002.

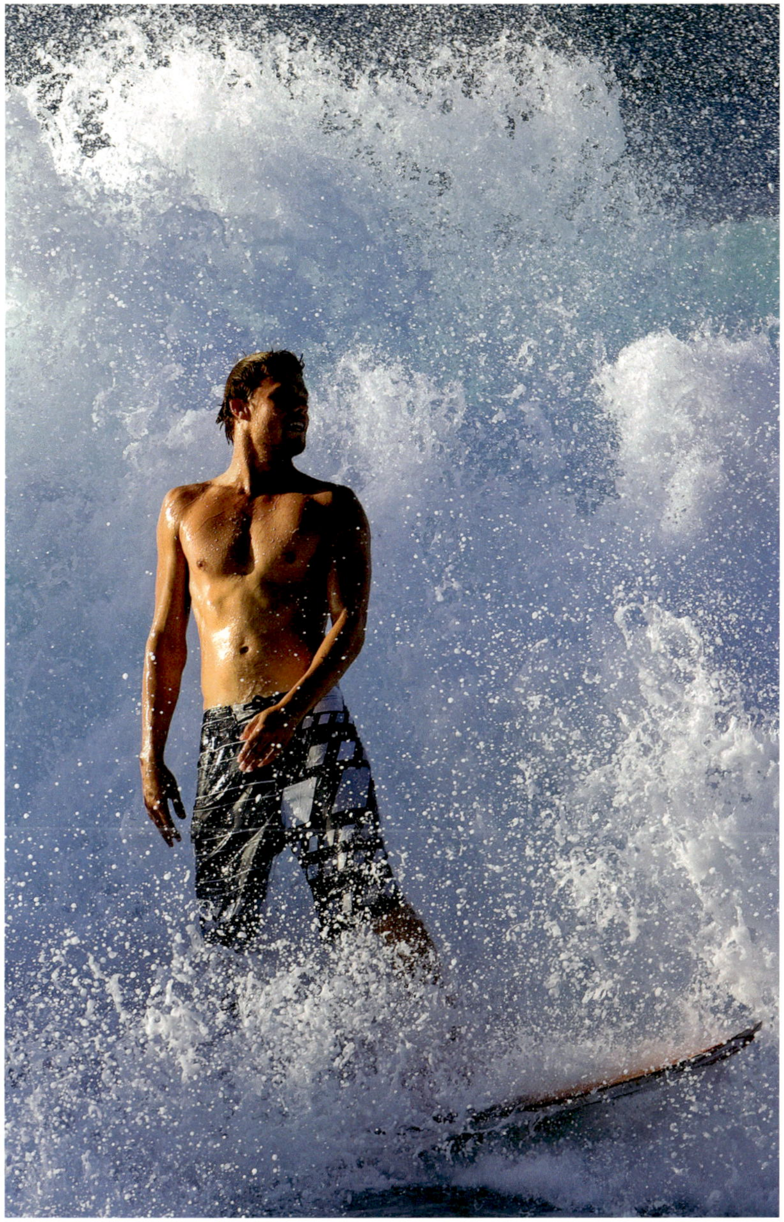

Dane Reynolds. Hawaii. 2006.

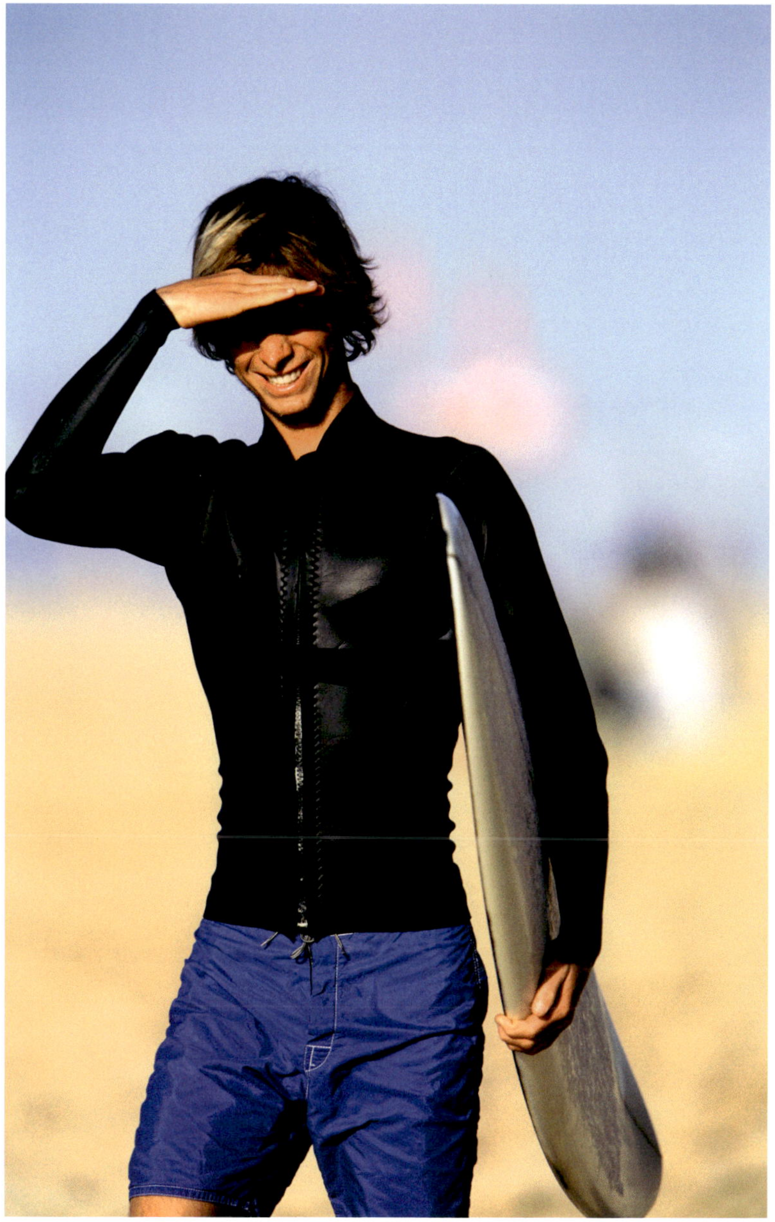

Joel Tudor. Hawaii. 1998

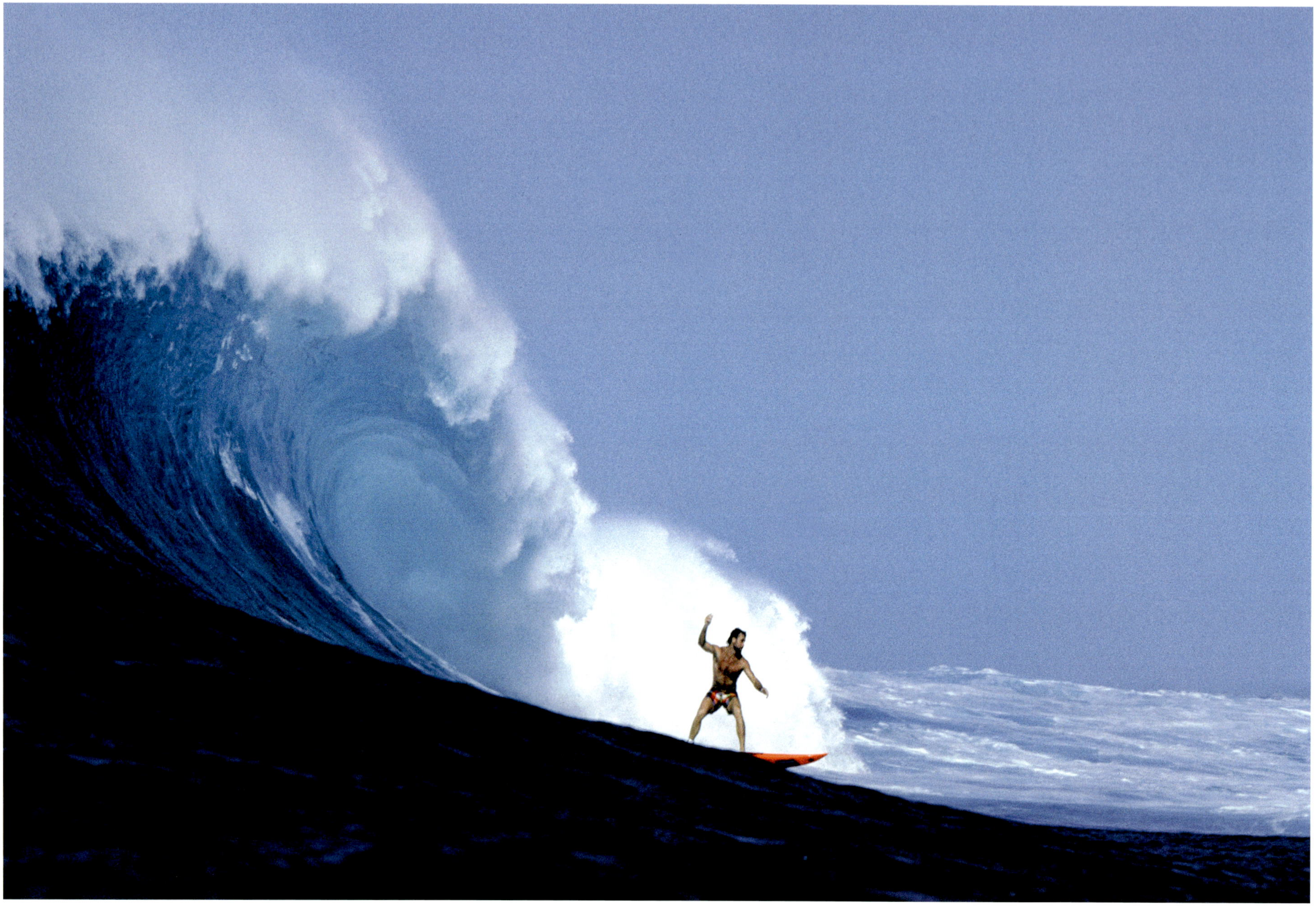

Ken Bradshaw. Mountain Man. Waimea Bay, HI. 1985.

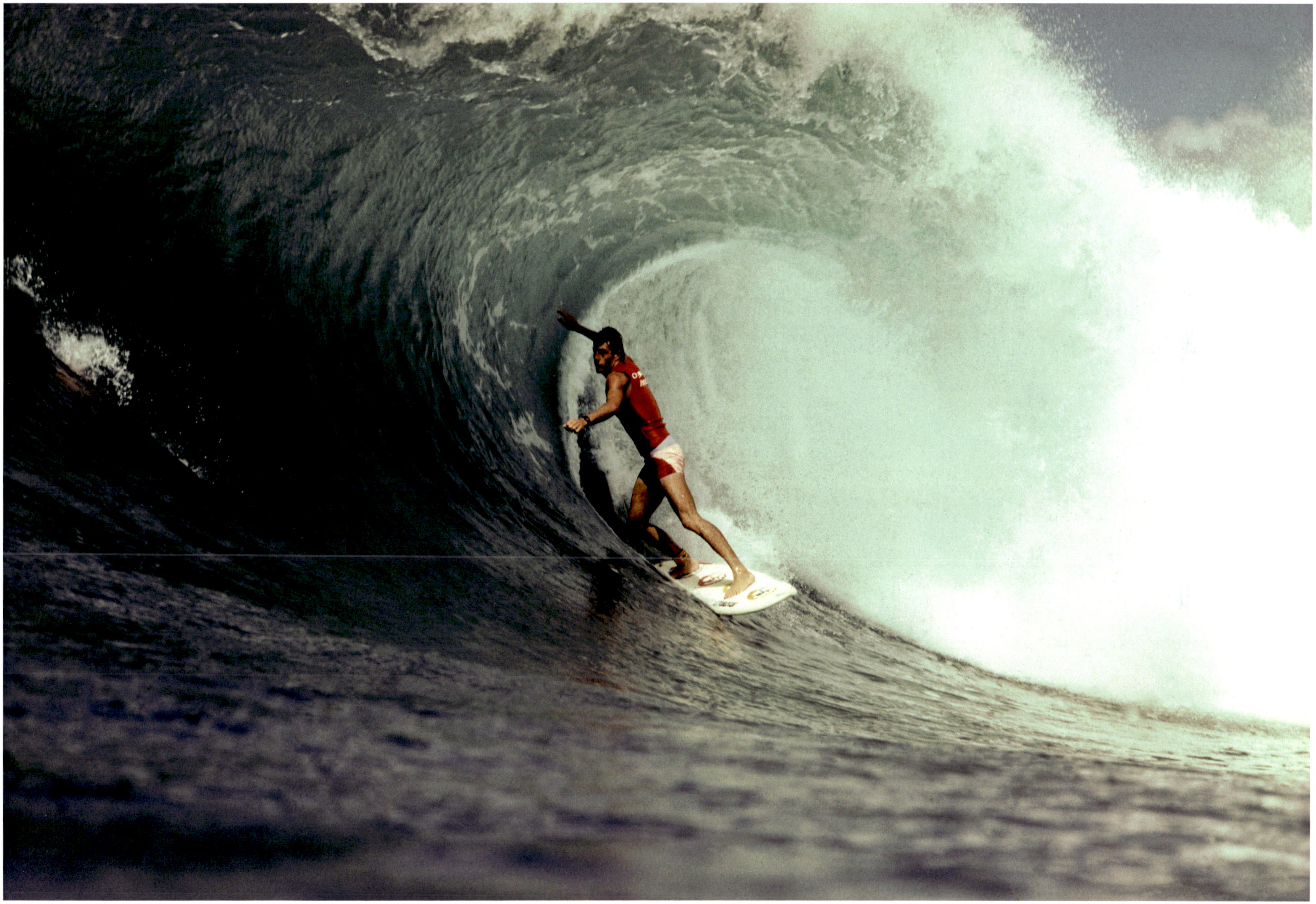

Shaun Tomson, cover shot *Surfing Magazine*. Sunset Beach, HI. 1982.

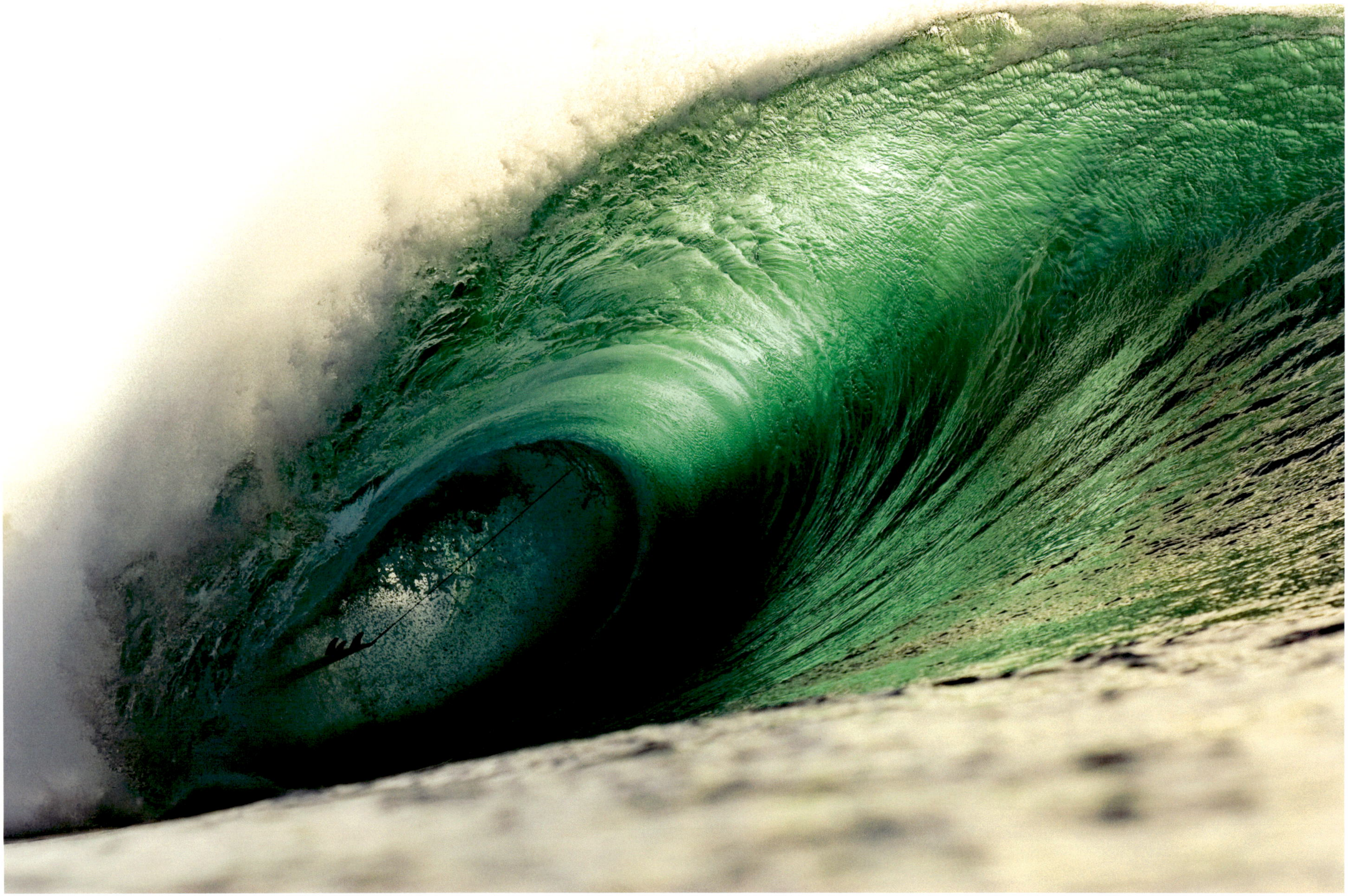

Leashes are for Dogs. Pipeline, HI. 2005.

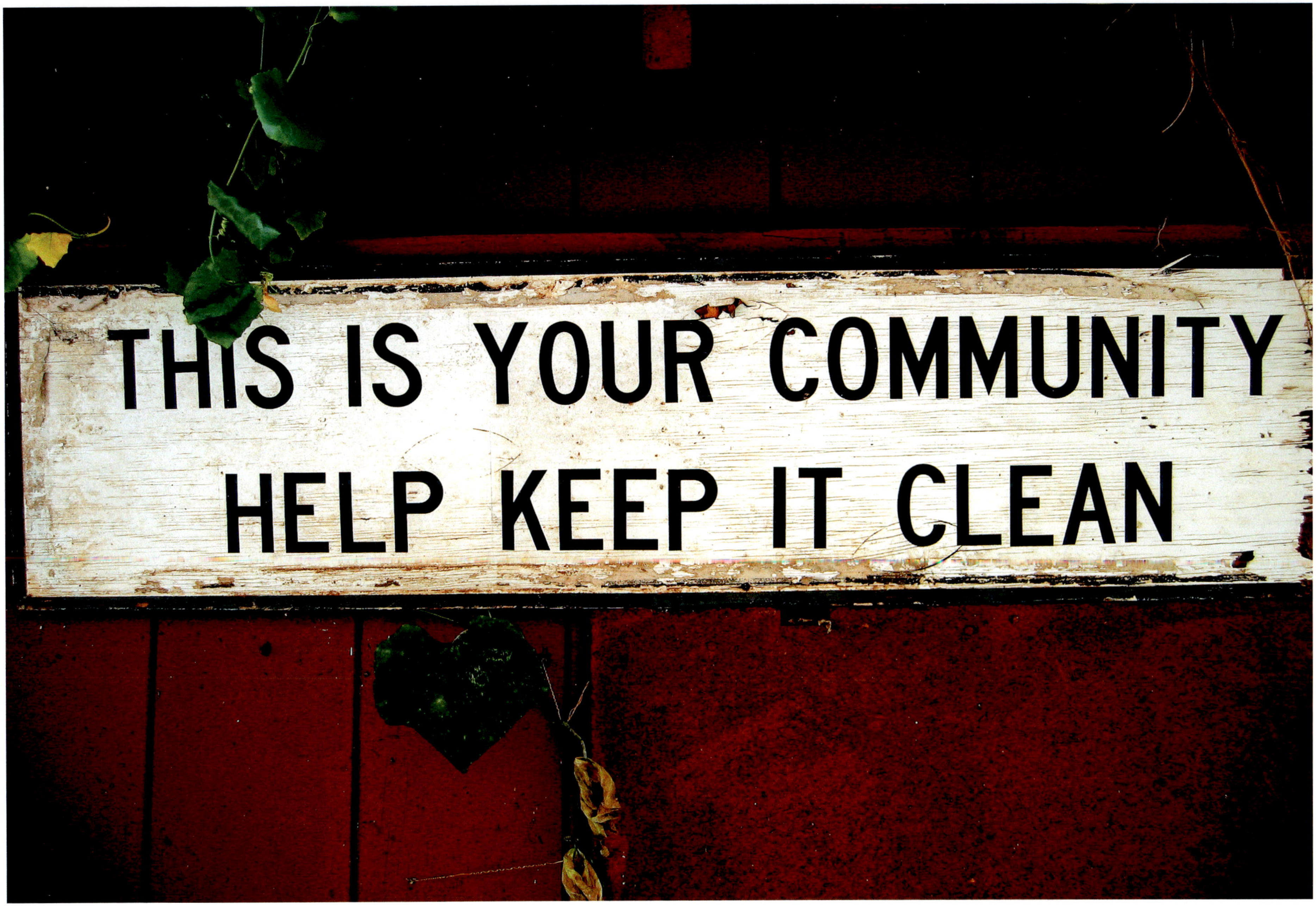

Green before green was cool. North Shore Oahu, HI. 1978.

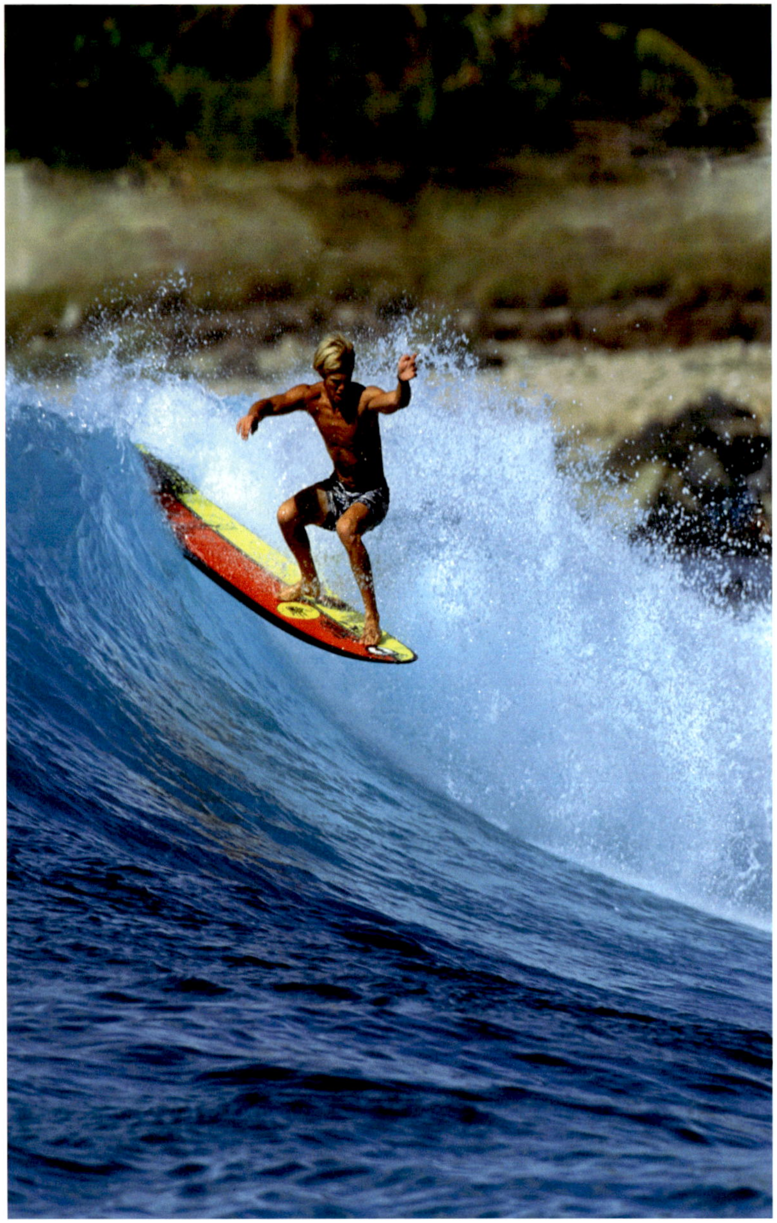

Josh Baxter cover shot *Longboard Magazine*. Makaha, HI. 1993.

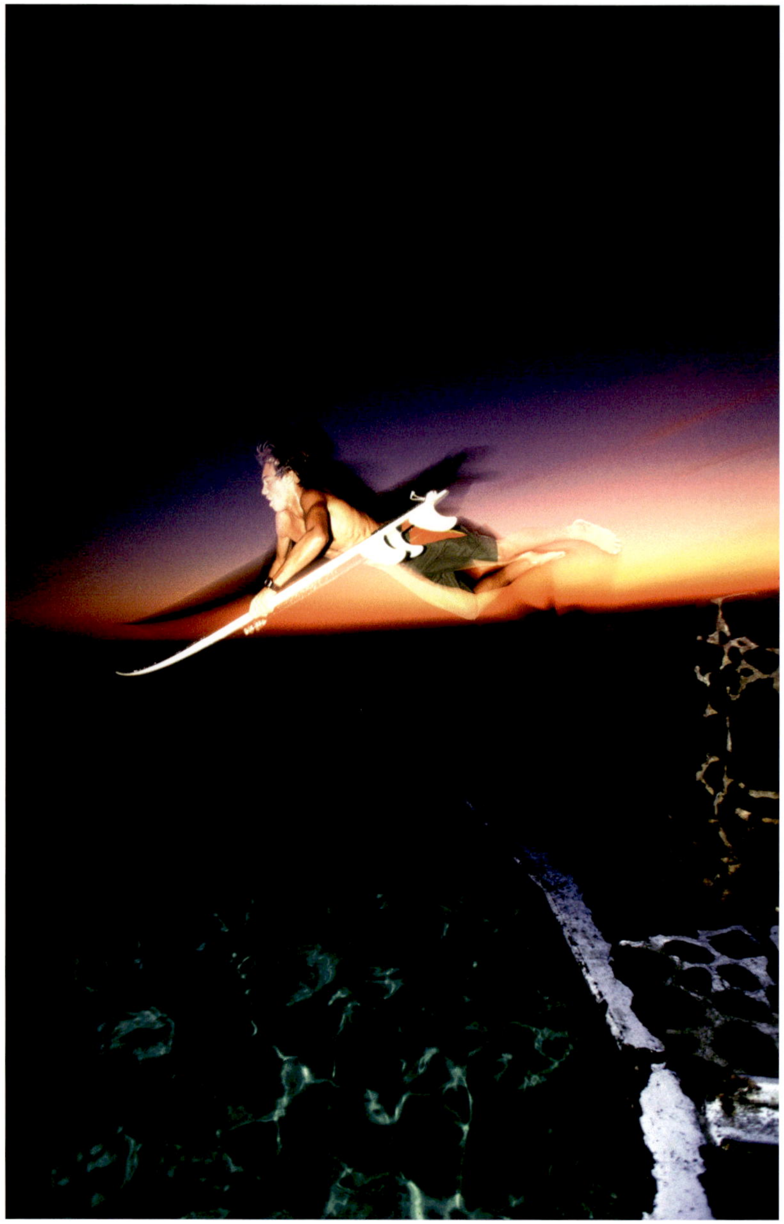

Makai McKenna. Magic Show. Big Island, HI. 1997.

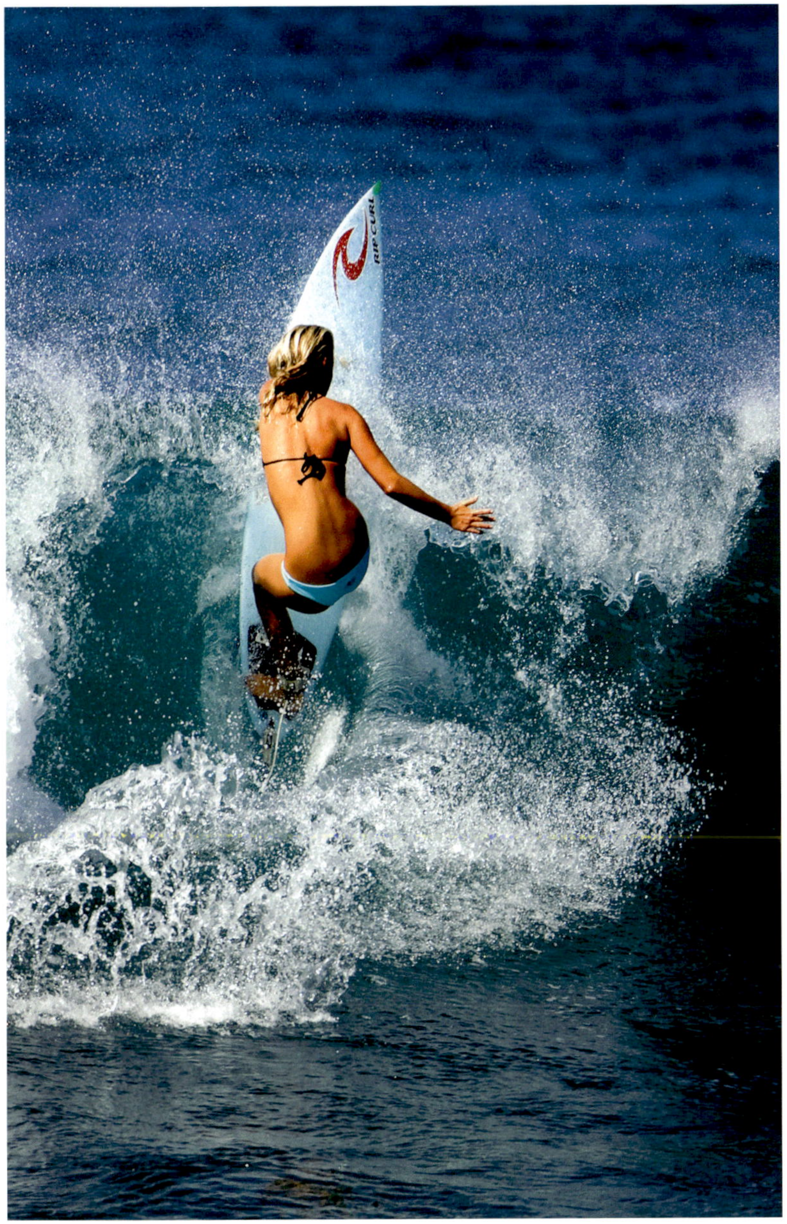

Bethany Hamilton needs no magic. Pupukea, HI. 2005.

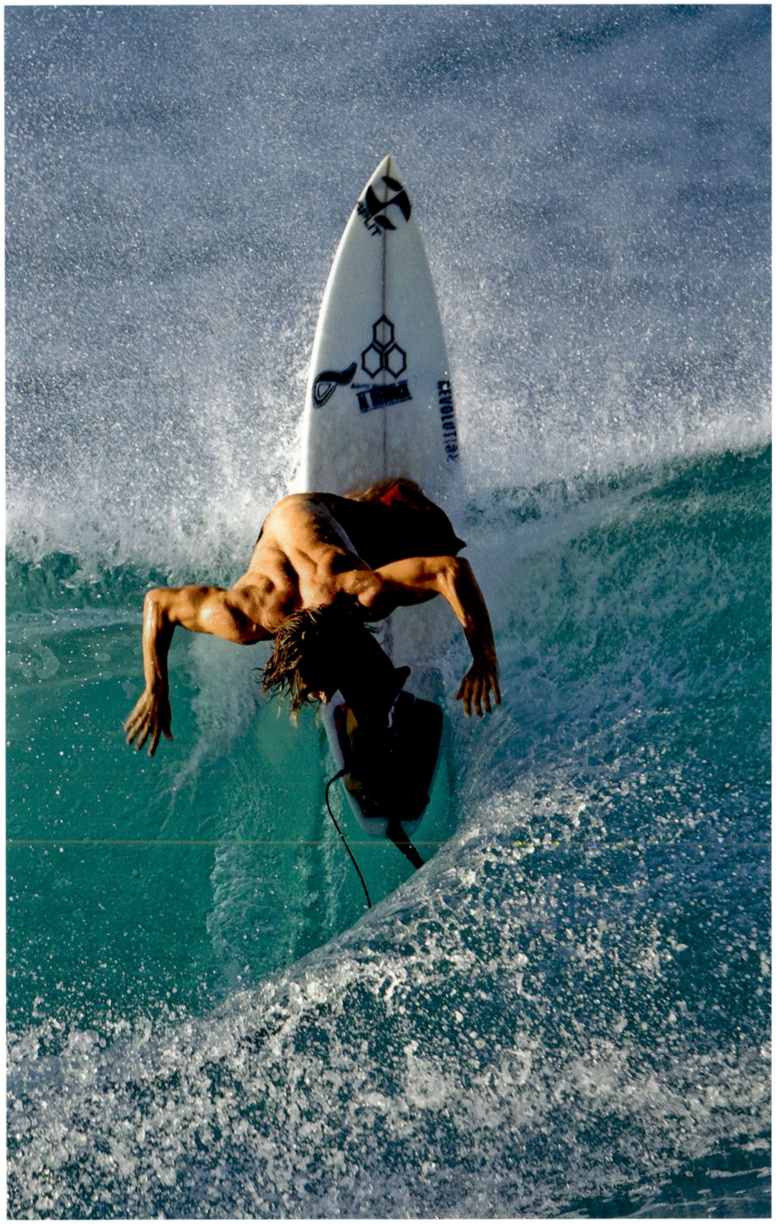

Nathaniel Curran. Backhanded Power. Pupukea, HI. 2006.

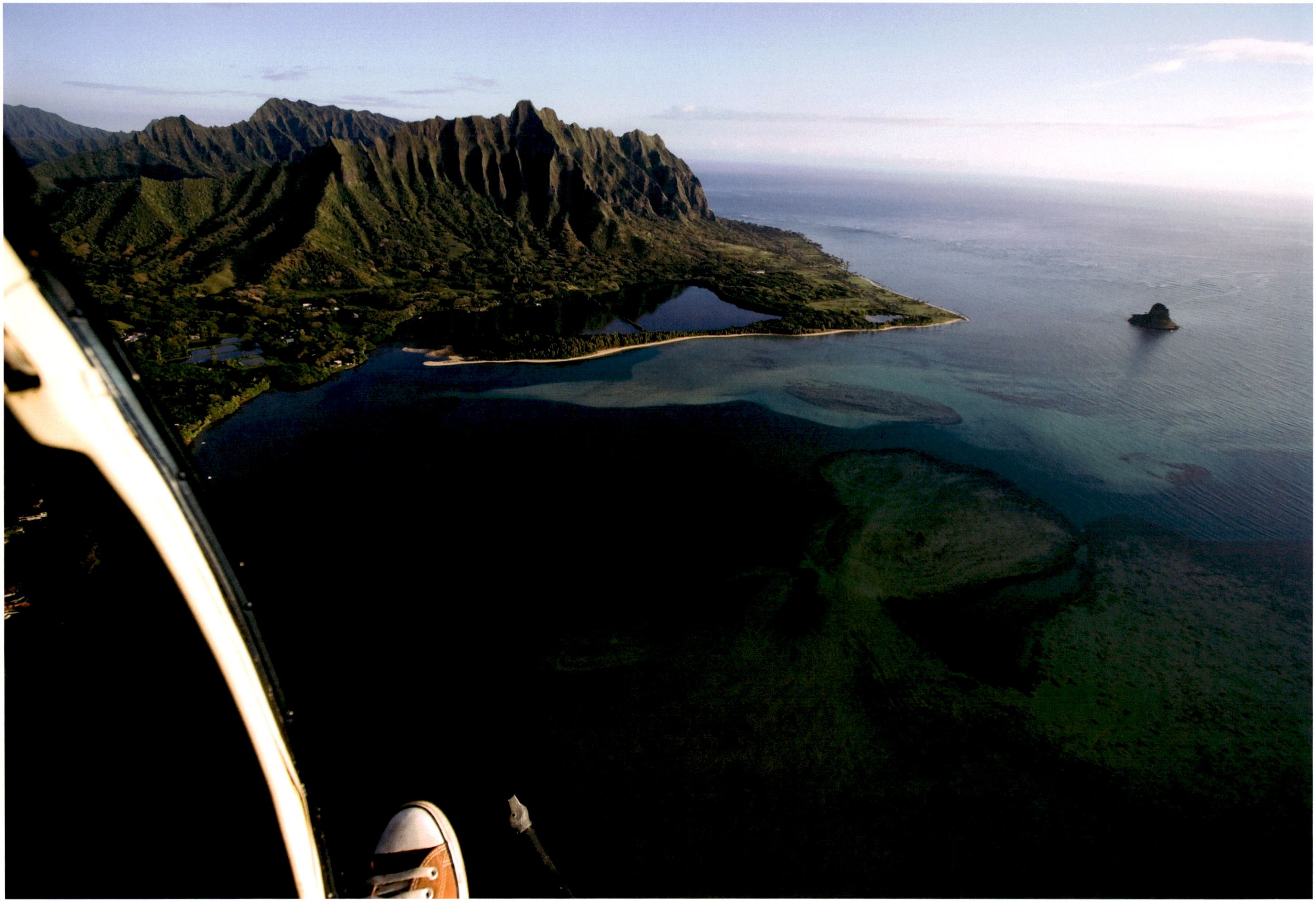

Chinaman's Hat, Russi's foot. Hawaii. 2007.

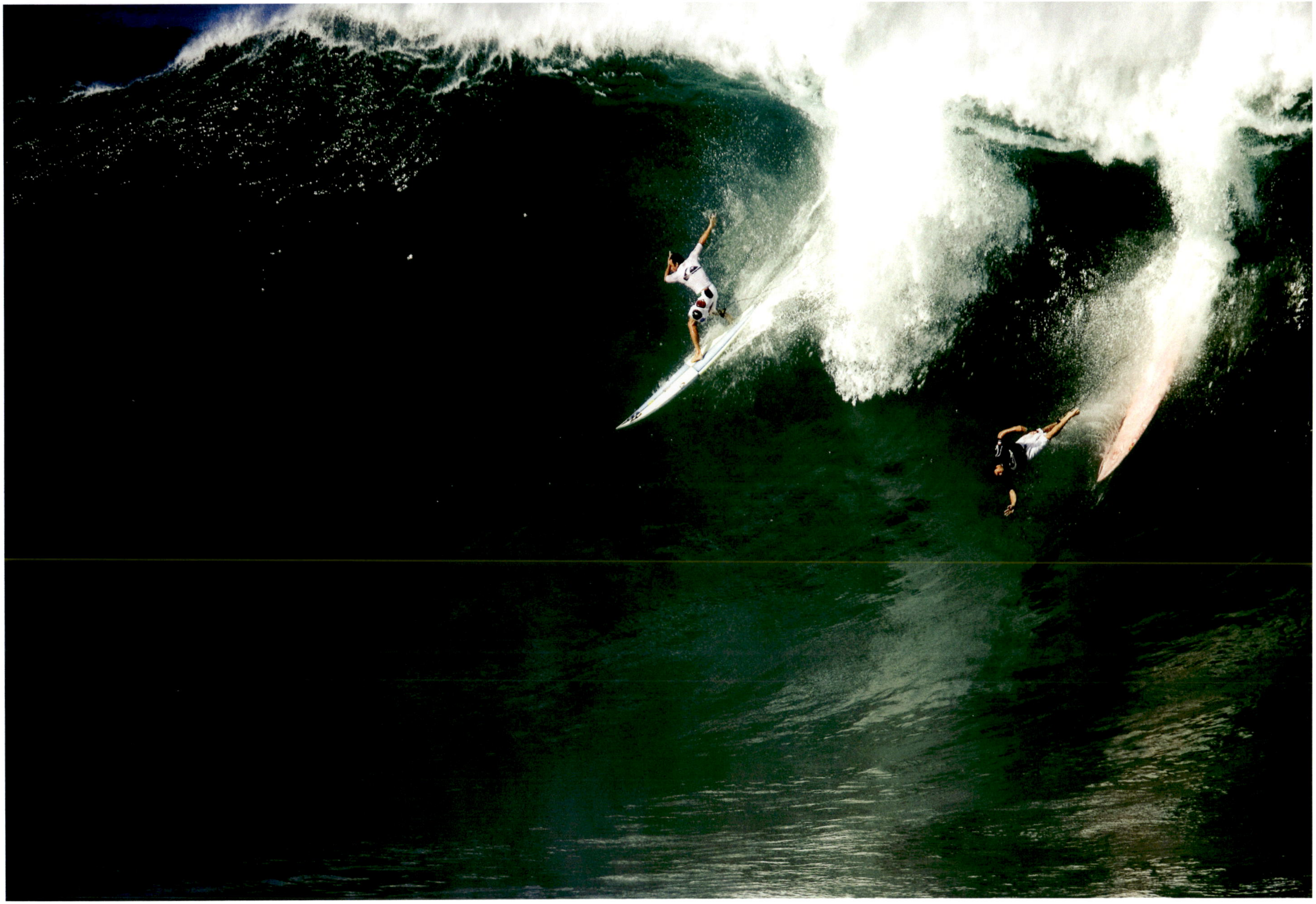

Shane Dorian and Jamie Sterling at The Eddie. Waimea Bay, HI. 2004.

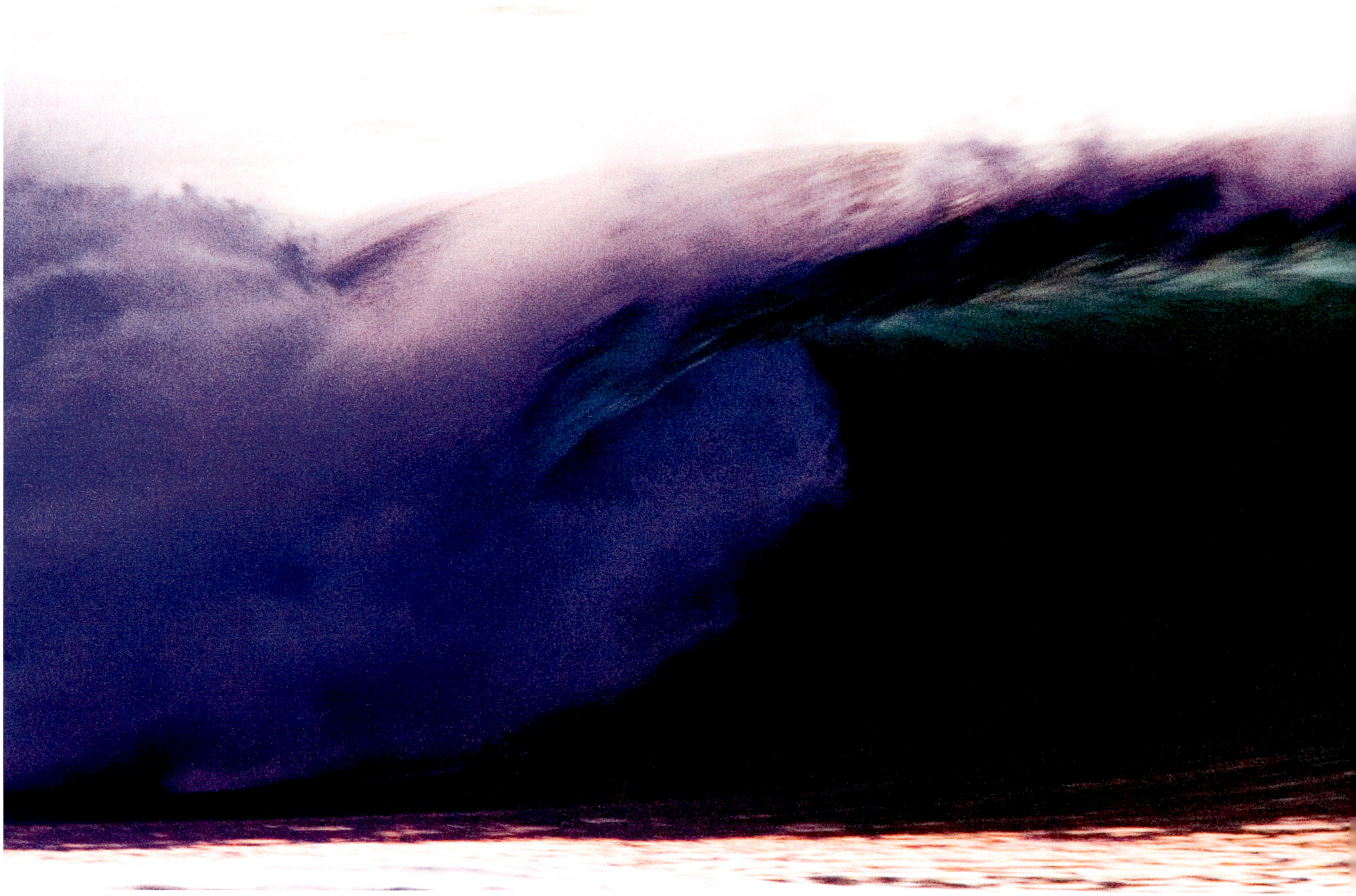

Pipe Dream. Hawaii. 2004.

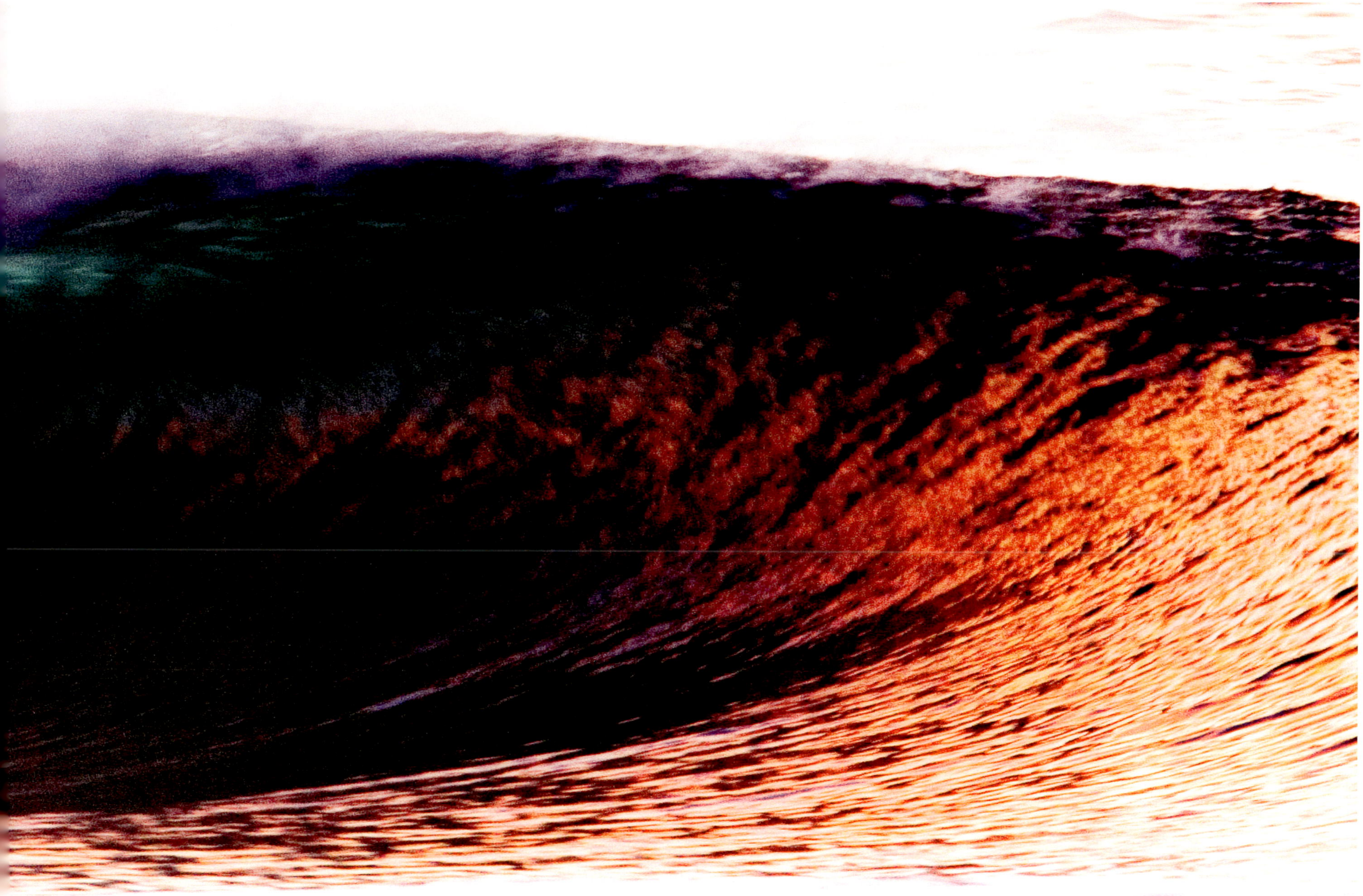

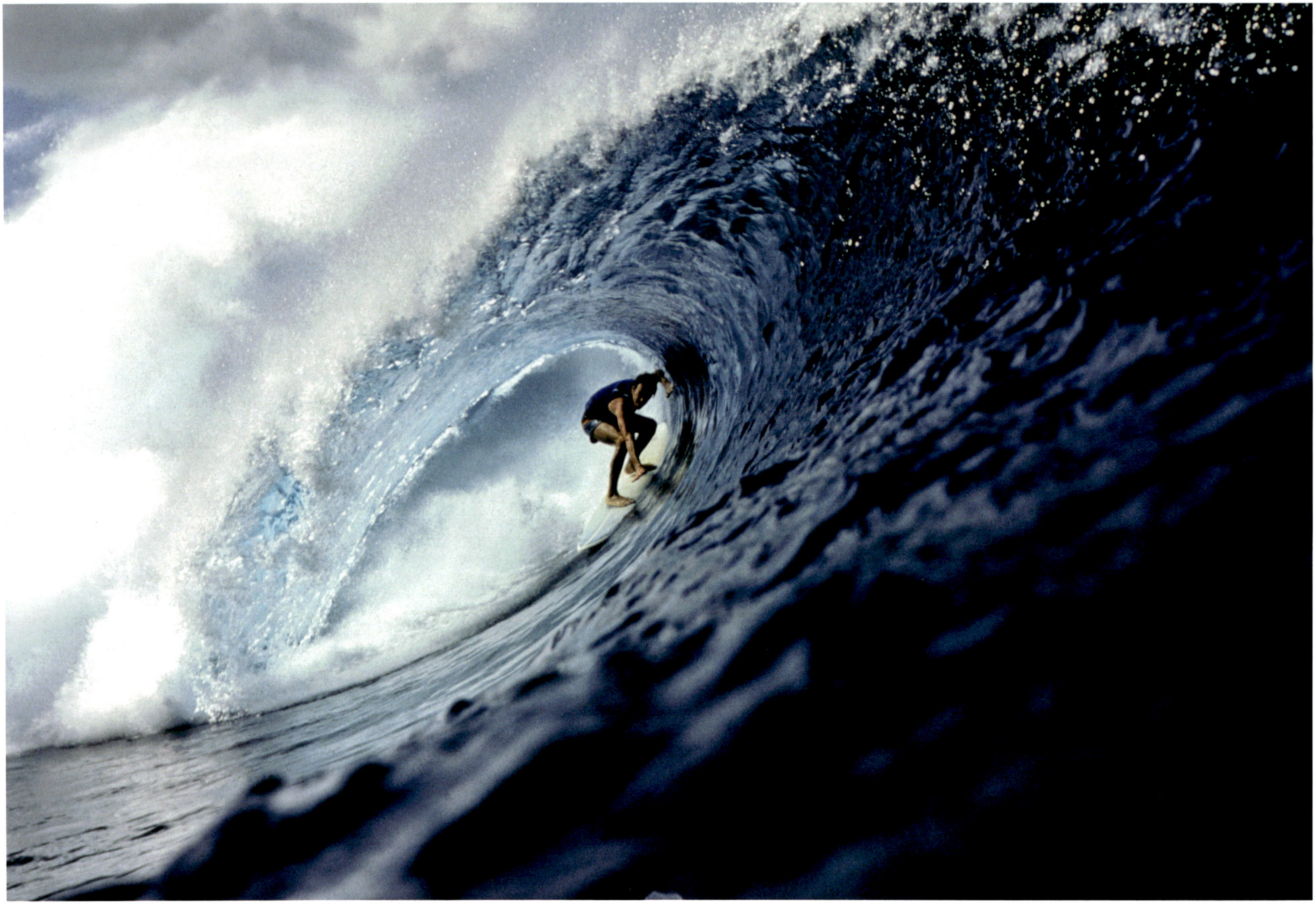

Brian Bulkley was the man at Pipeline, HI. 1979.

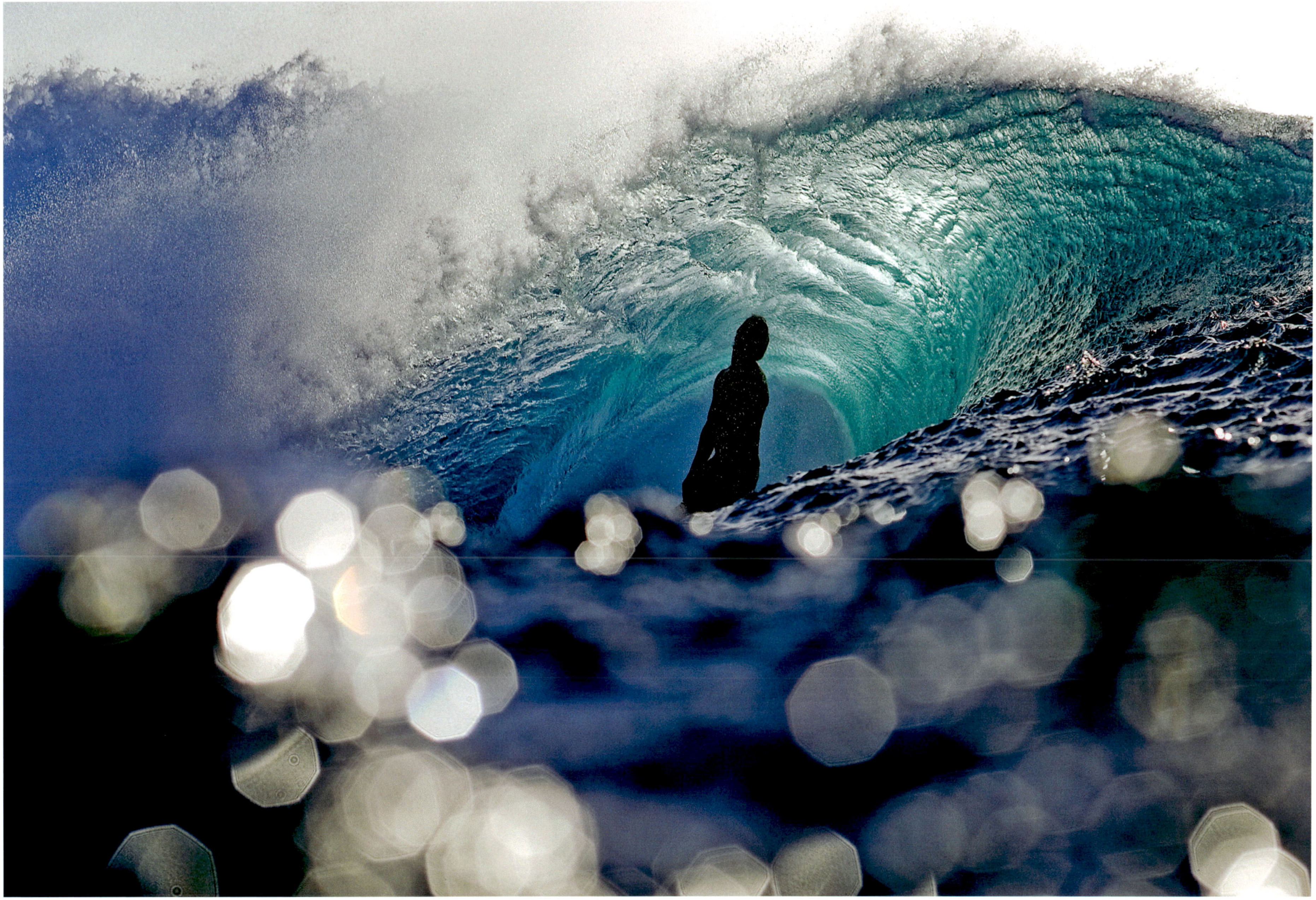

Jamie O'Brien. Mr. Casual. Pipeline, HI. 2006.

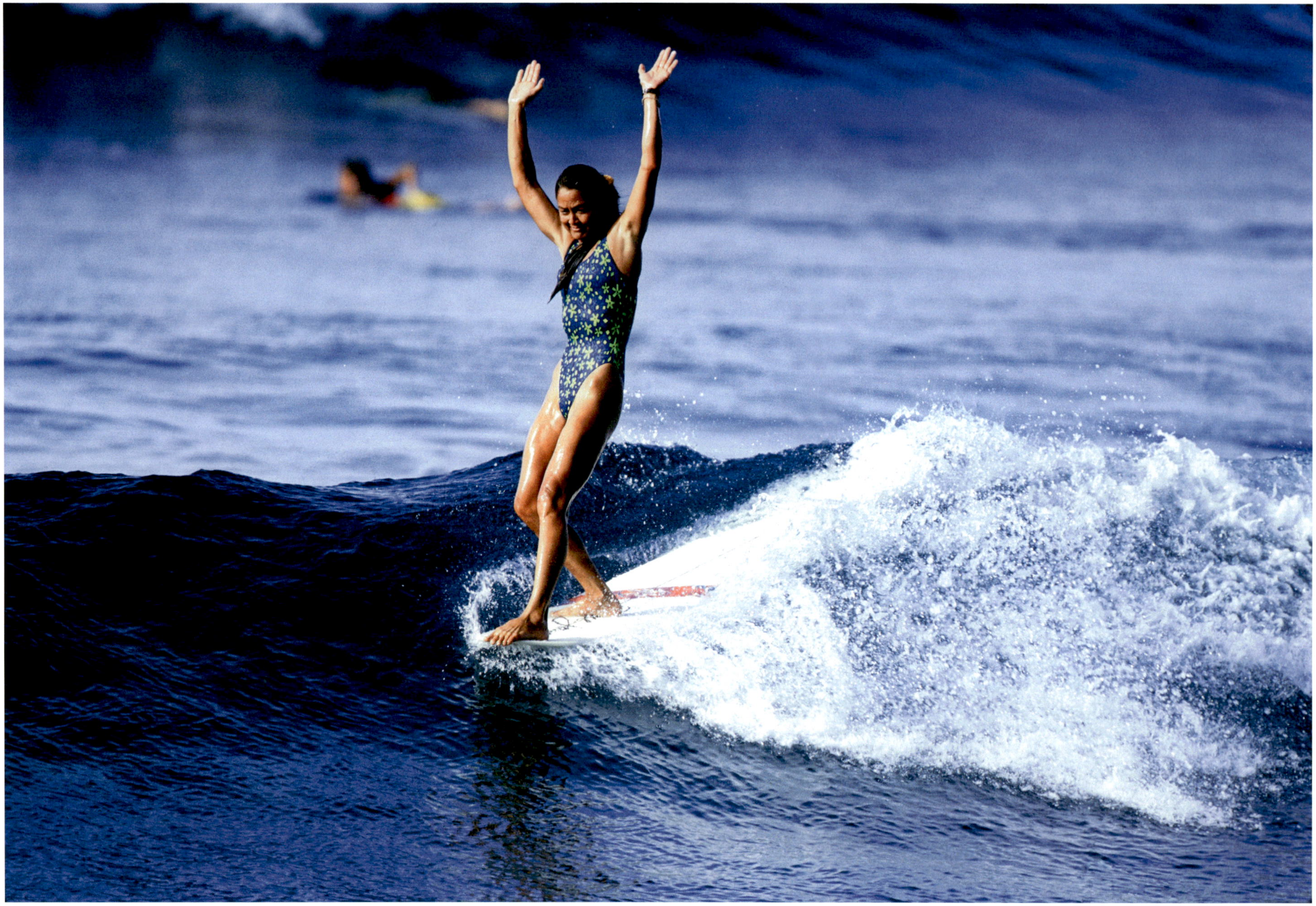

Rell Sunn. Queen of Makaha, Ambassador of Aloha. Hawaii. 1993.

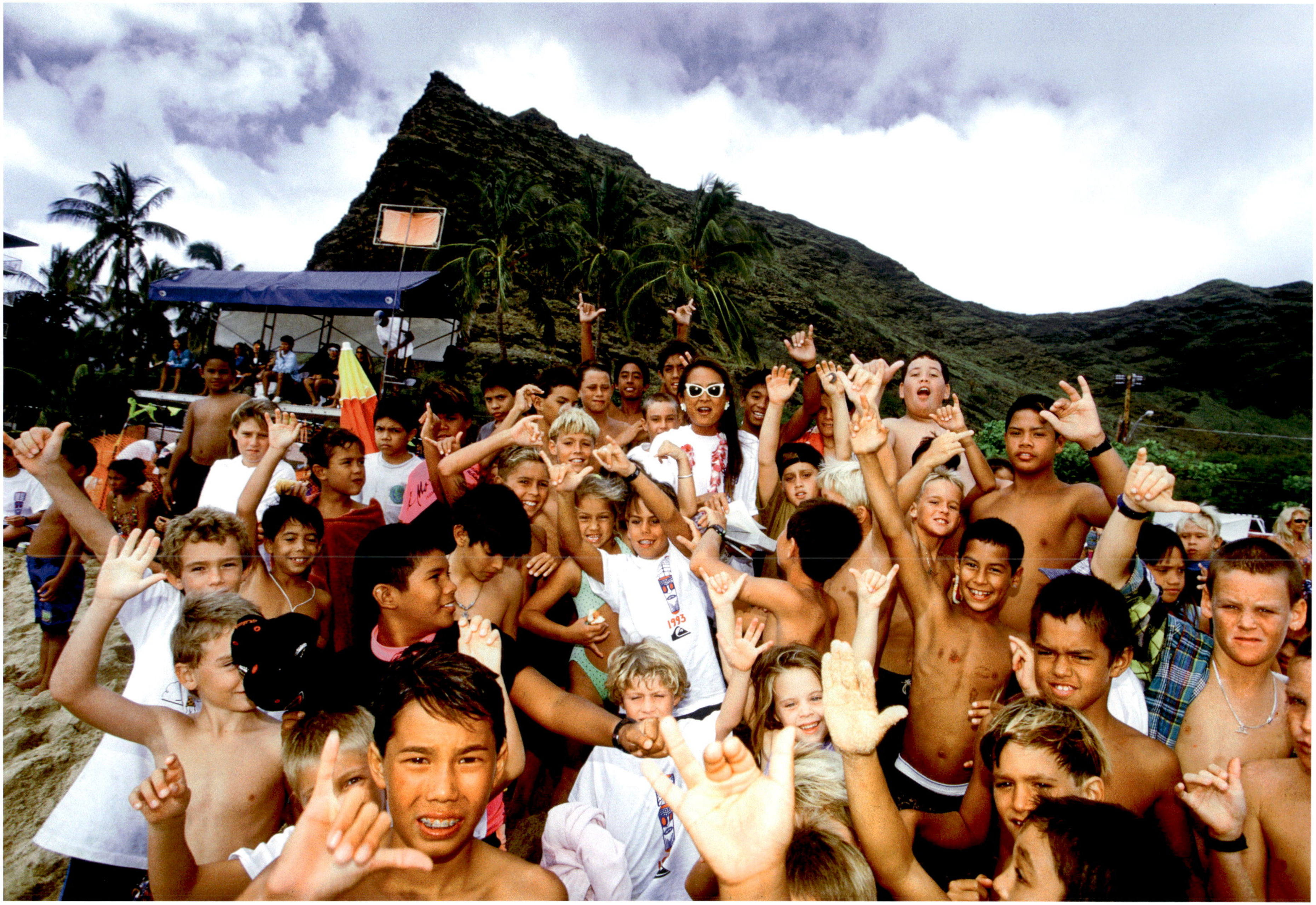

Rell Sunn Menehune Contest. Pure Love. Makaha, HI. 1993. Aloha nui.

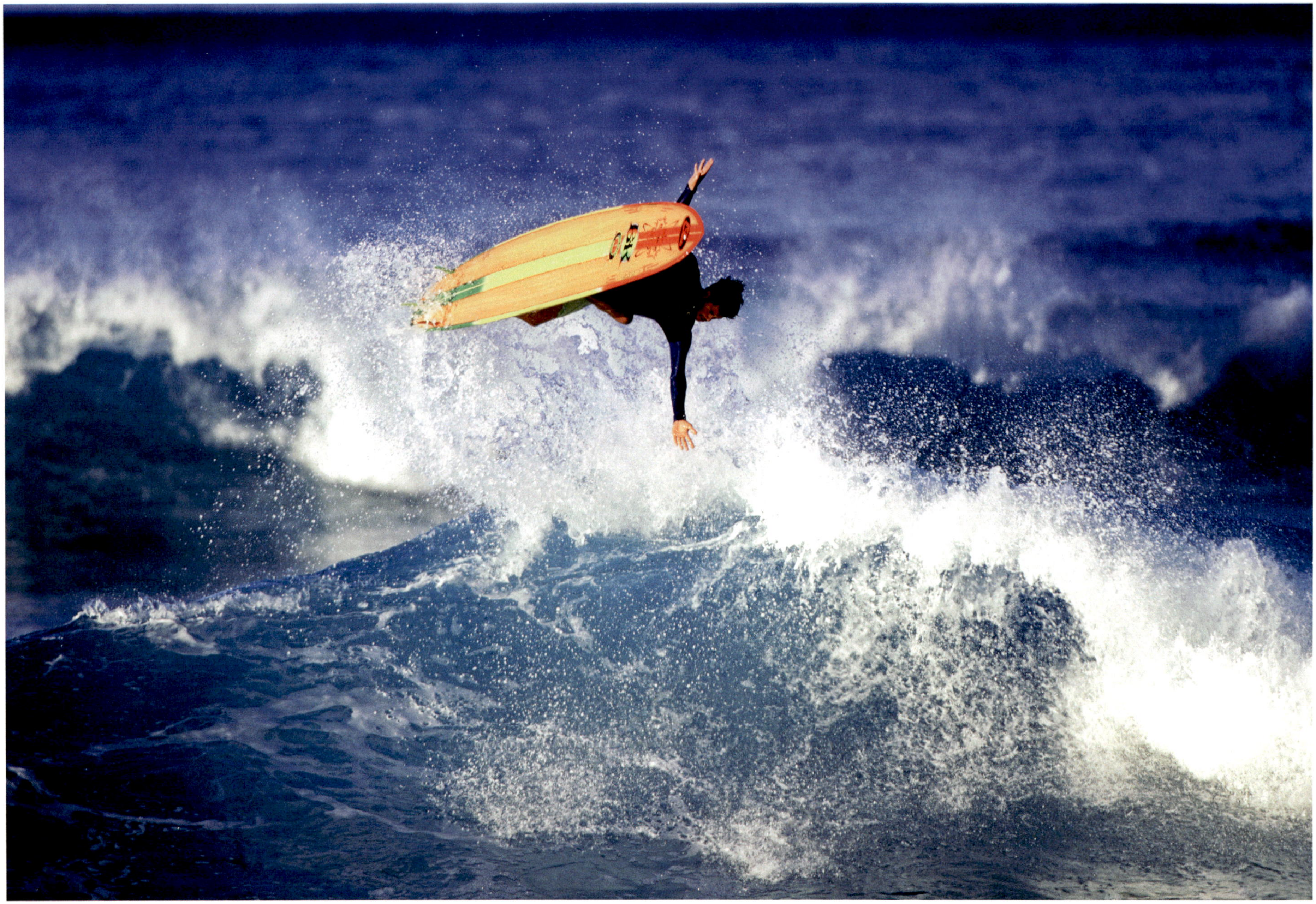

Rusty Keaulana, cover shot *Longboard Magazine*. Makaha, HI. 1996.

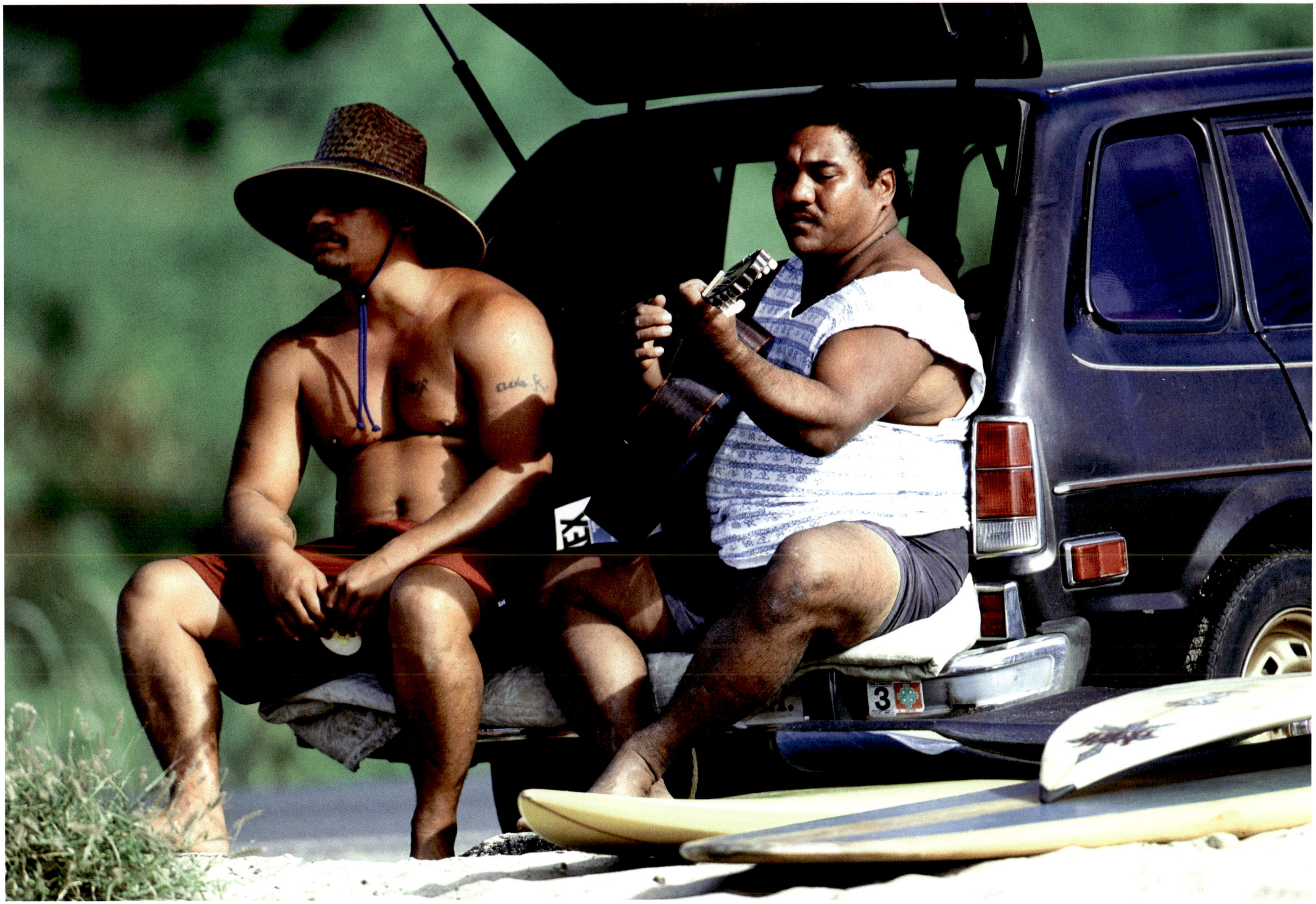

Local Boys. Makaha, HI. 1993.

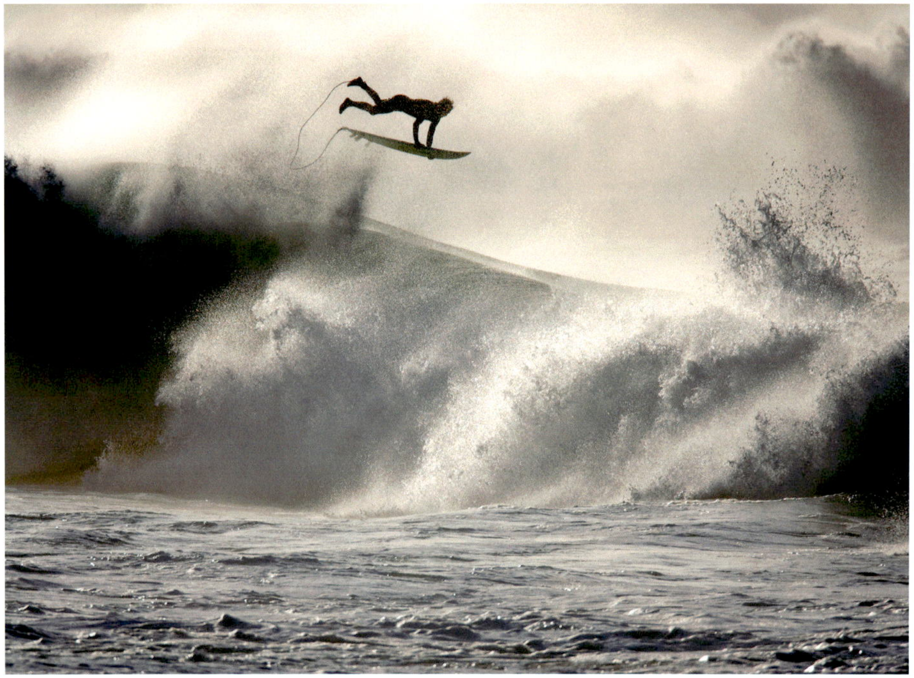

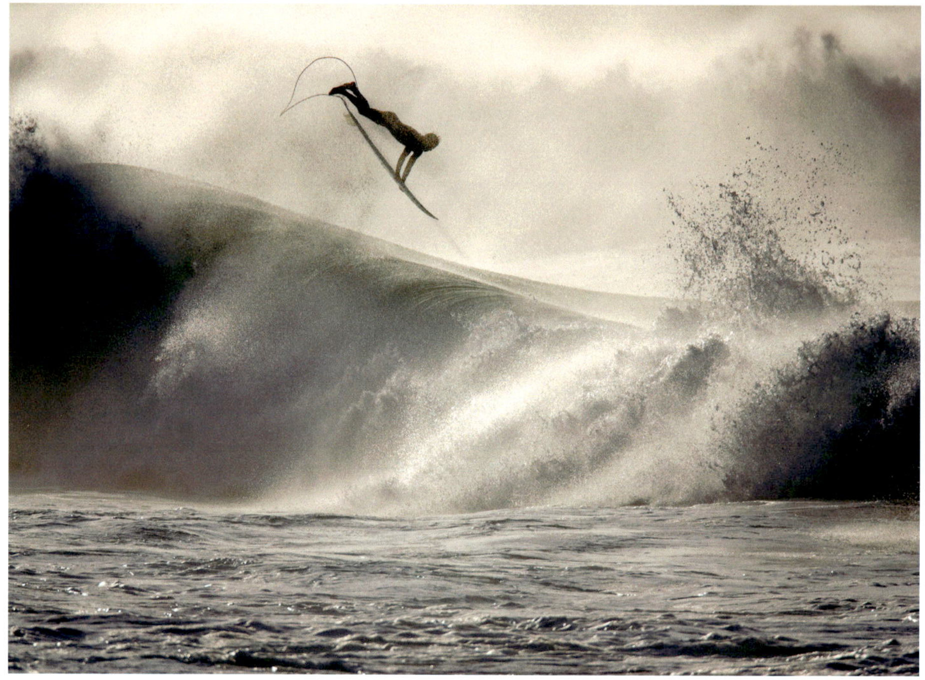

Nathan Fletcher exit stage left. Pipeline, HI. 2008.

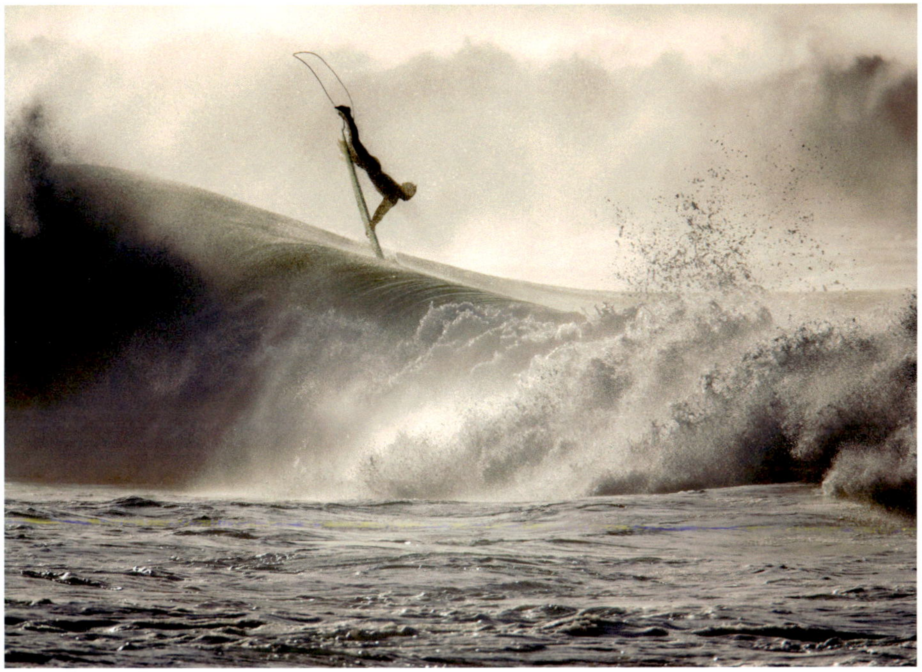

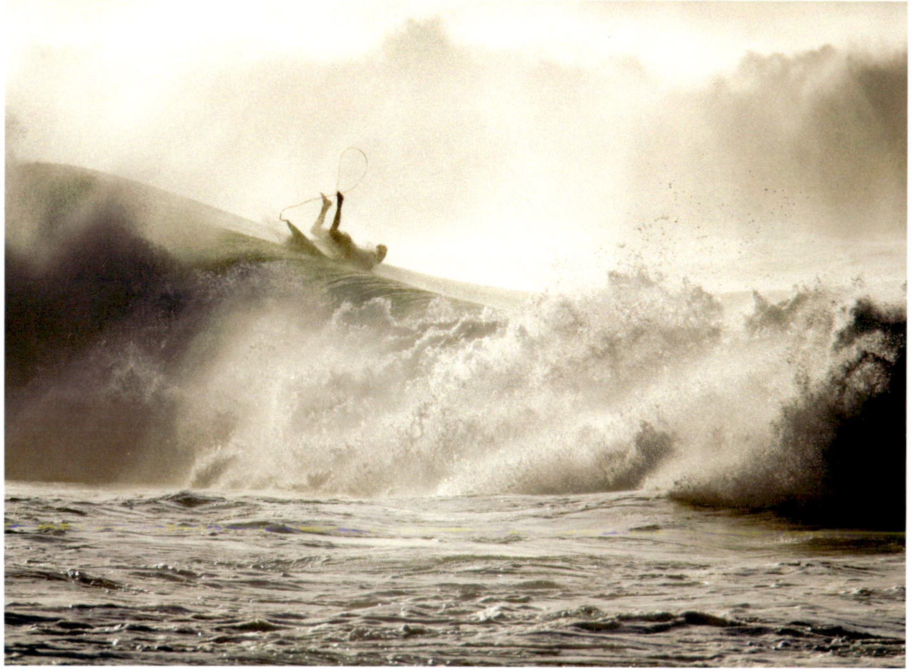

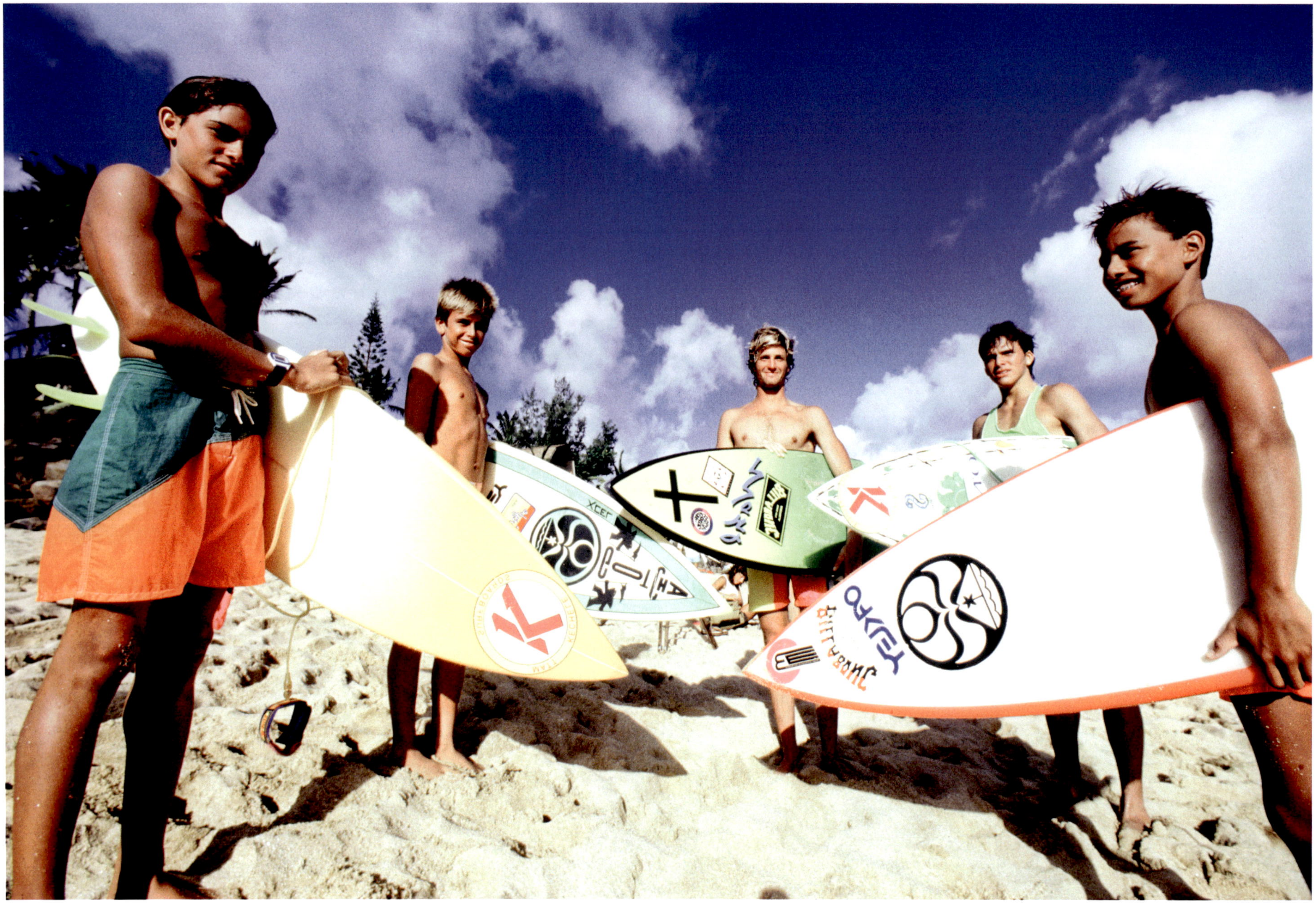

Left to right: Kelly Slater, Shane Dorian, Walter Cerney, Sean Slater, Matty Liu. Ehukai Beach Park, HI. 1987.

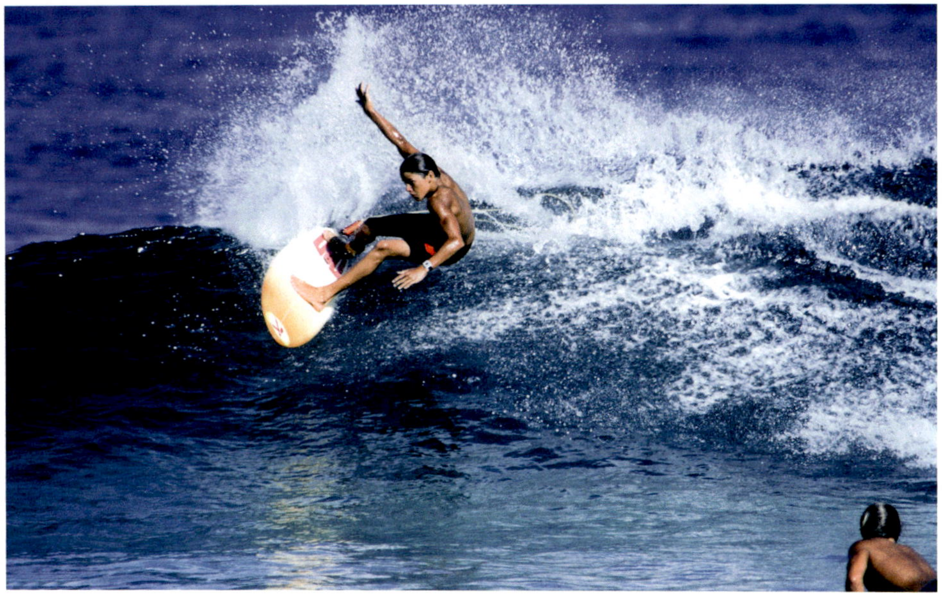

Champions

Kelly Slater changed surfing forever. Along with Rob Machado, Shane Dorian, Ross Williams, Jack Johnson, and a few others, truly advanced modern surfing. Before they came along, the surfing lifestyle and sport held the stigma of being something for slackers, stoners, and rebels. When Kelly and his friends came along, they truly made surfing a profession, turning the world's idea of surfing on its head. These guys quickly became role models for thousands and thousands of kids. This cultural impact is, in my opinion, Kelly's legacy. He also possesses that unique "freak-gene" that gives his surfing its radiance. He's the one everyone else is compared to.

The first time I saw him in the water, I was shooting a well-known surfer at Ehukai Beach Park. Out of the corner of my eye, I saw this thirteen-year-old kid just killing it. I was trying to stay focused on my task, but I couldn't stop watching this kid.

At that "pre-digital time," we didn't shoot any guys we didn't know because it was a waste of expensive film. I started turning my big lens down the beach and shooting photos of him anyway. In the years to come I was able to record much of his career, mostly here in Hawaii, but also around the world. The images have turned out to be a priceless collection of my library. I feel fortunate to have witnessed Kelly's story unfold.

It seems unlikely that a group like Kelly and his mates will turn the world upside down again. To see Kelly and Rob high-fiving each other as Rob was coming out of the barrel at the Pipe Masters was a defining moment. It spoke of their class, friendship, and camaraderie.

That group of friends gave us something classic and historic to remember.

Sadly, that respectful vibe is now being replaced by "an all about me" attitude.

We can only hope that the class of Kelly and company will someday return to surfing. In 2010, Slater won his tenth world title, Kelly is and always will be a legendary champion.

Kelly Slater. Ehukai beach park, HI. 1987.

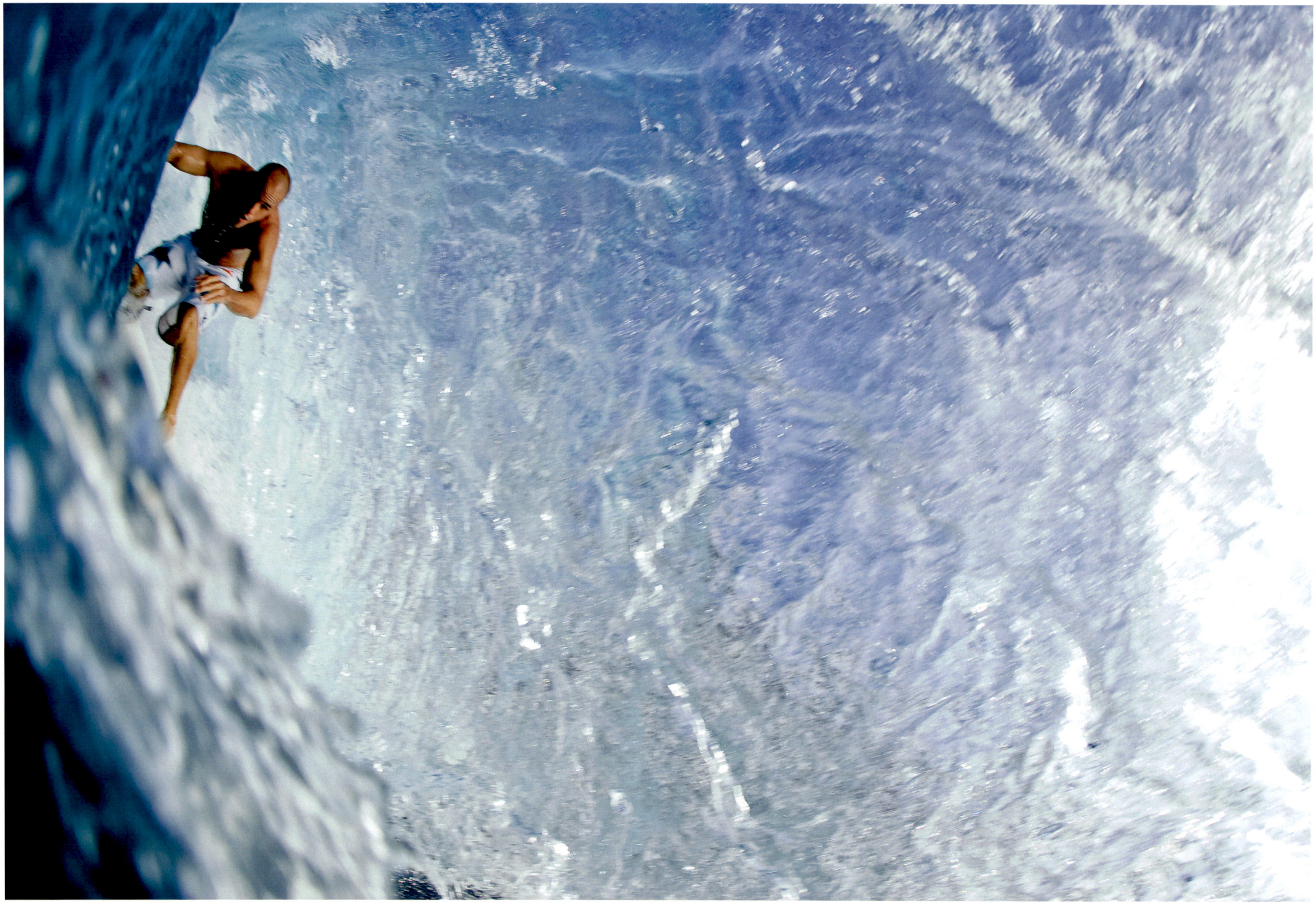

Kelly Slater. Hiding from his fans. Backdoor, HI. 2005.

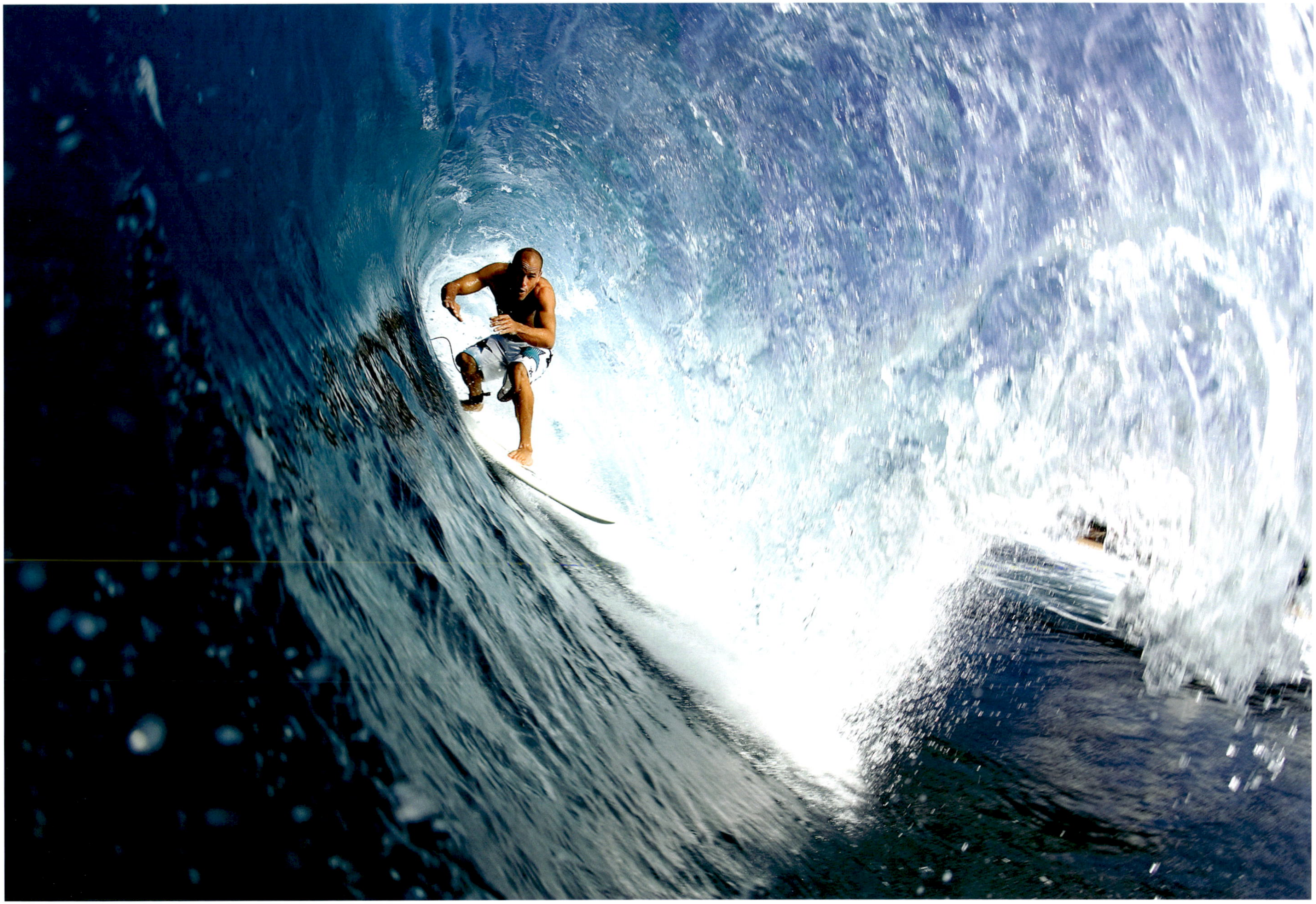

Kelly Slater. Four more would make it ten. Backdoor, HI. 2005.

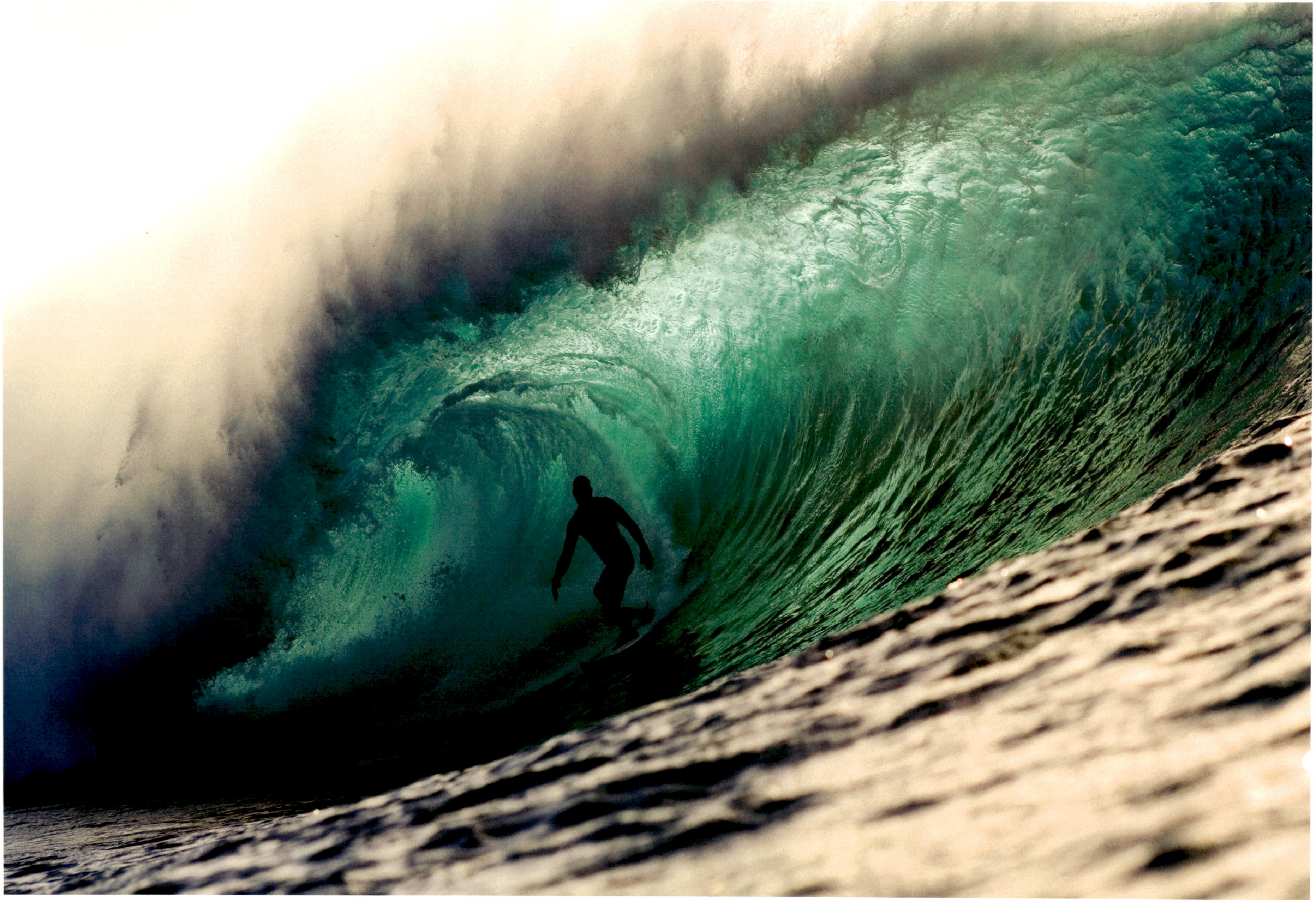

Kelly Slater. As untouchable in free surf as he is in competition. Pipeline, HI. 2006.

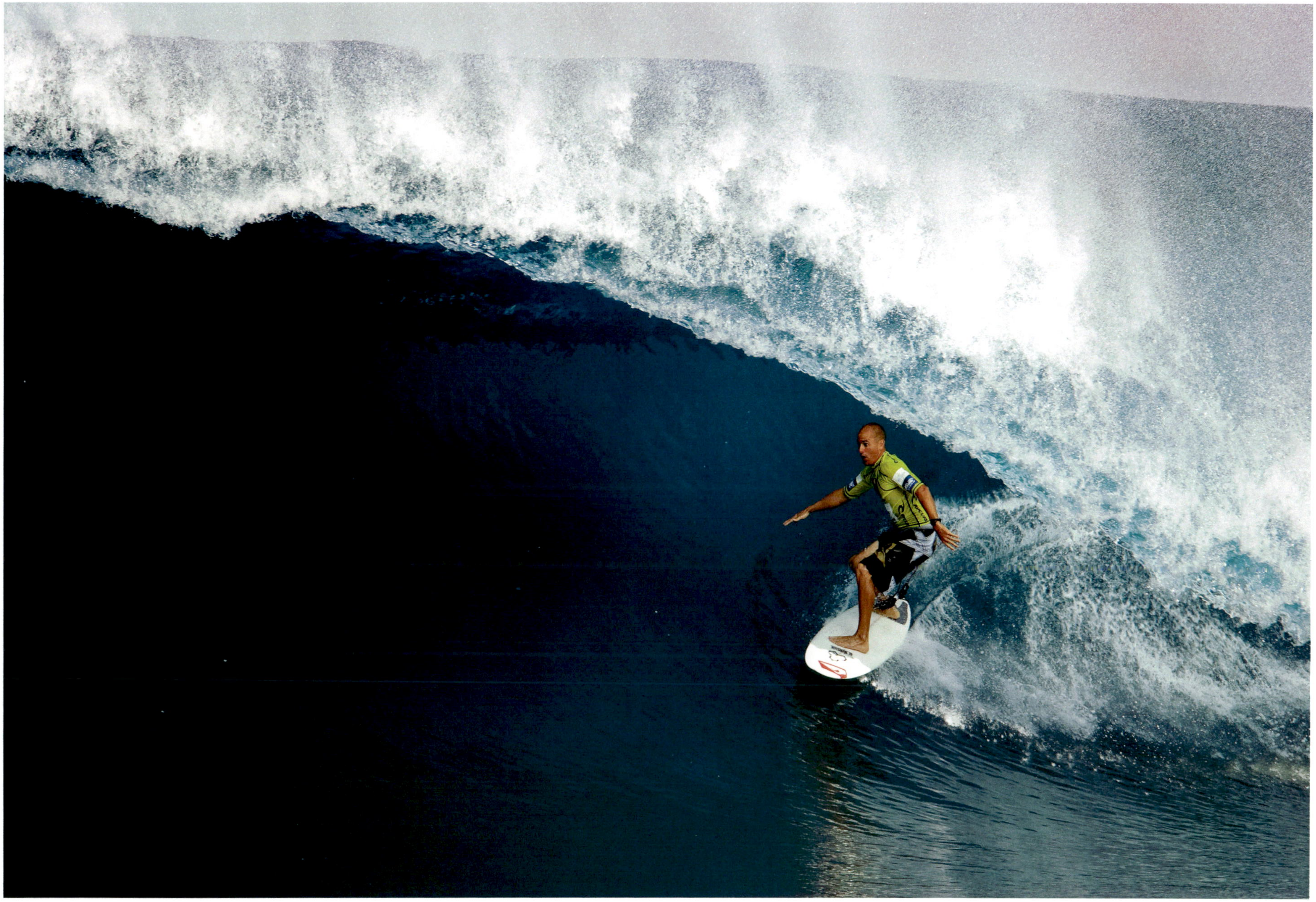

Kelly Slater. Backdoor heading for world title #7 Pipeline Masters, HI. 2005.

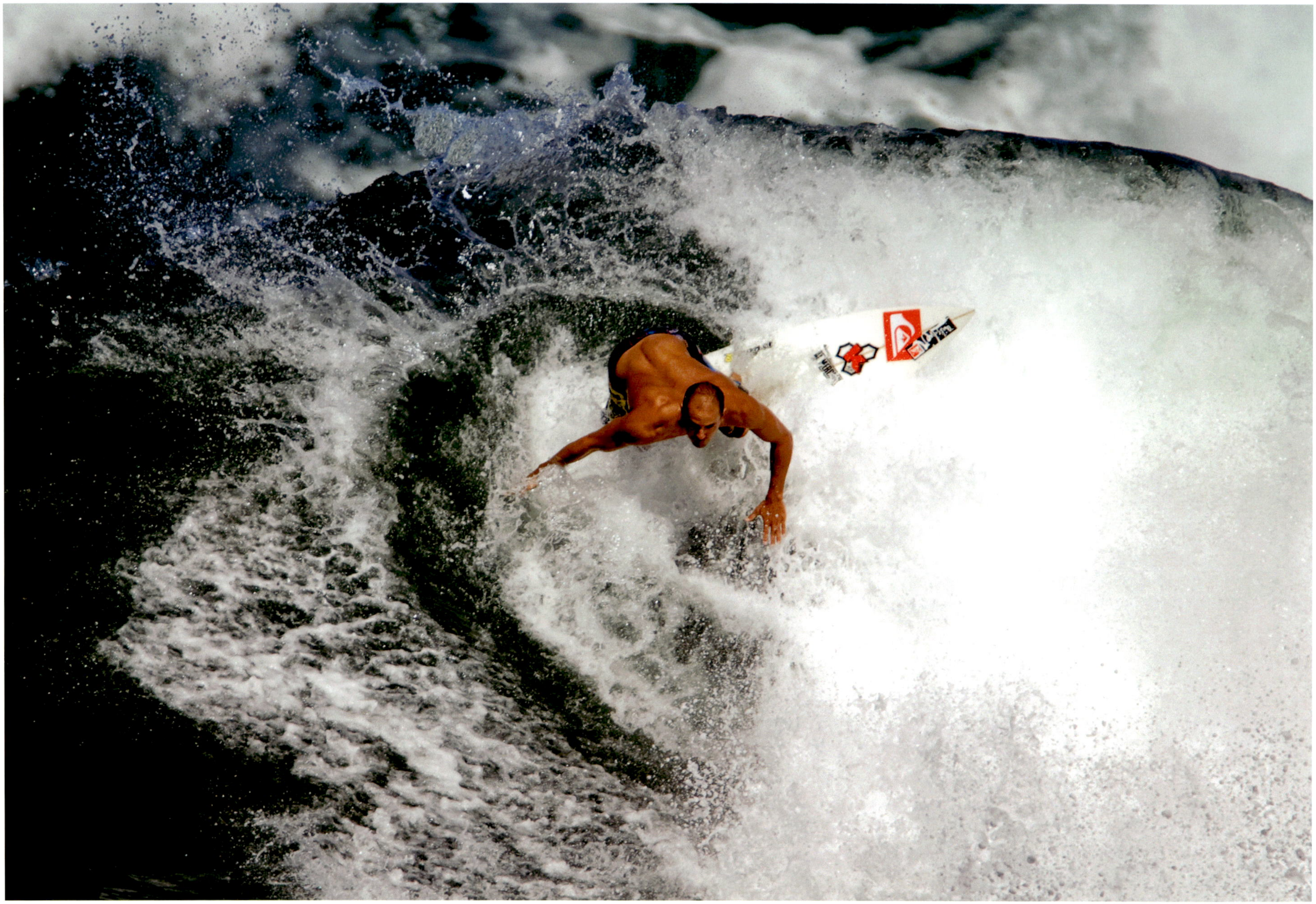

Kelly Slater, the world actually does revolve around him. Haleiwa, HI. 2004.

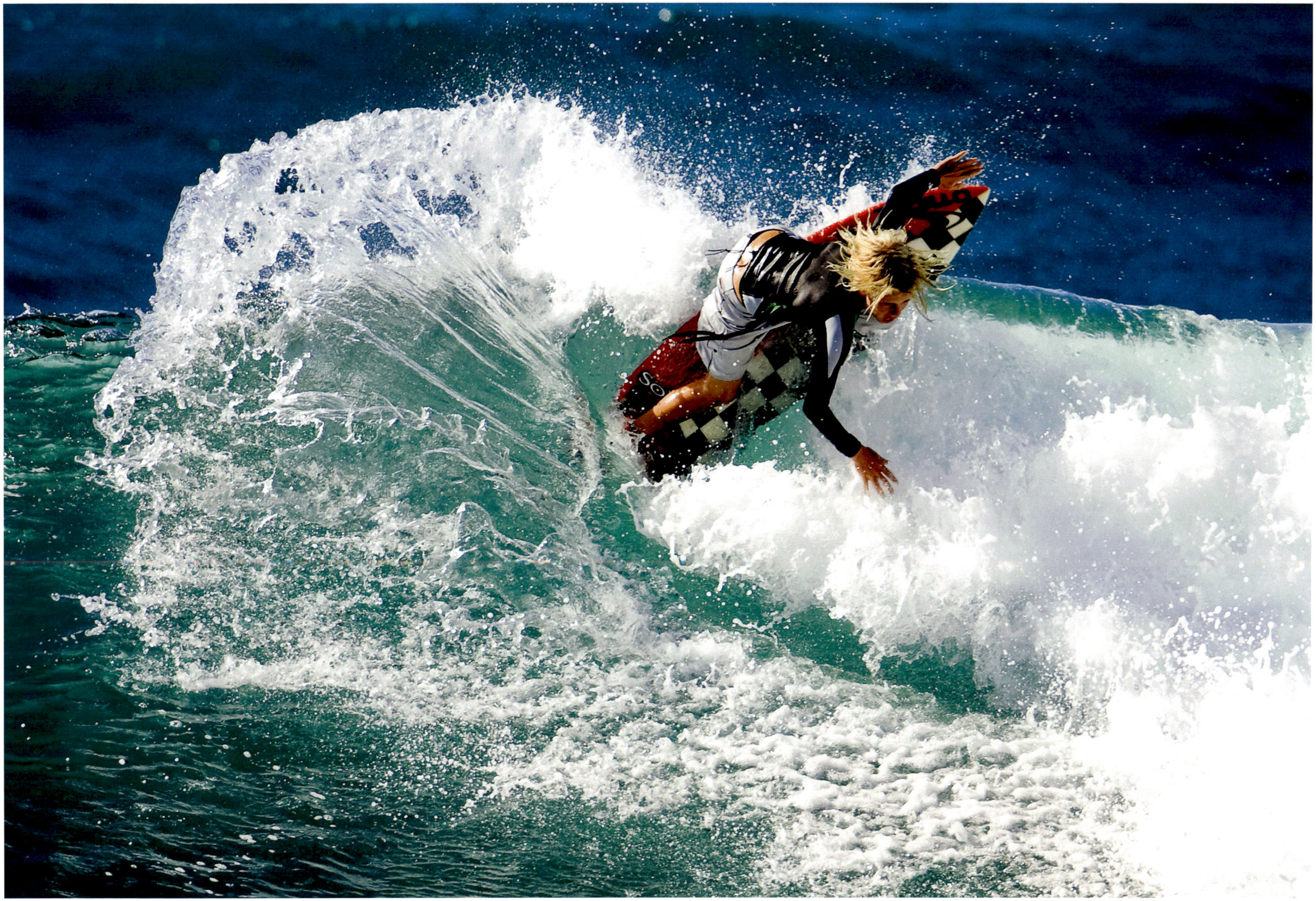

JohnJohn Florence. Twenty years younger, the same "freak" gene. Sand Bars, HI. 2006.

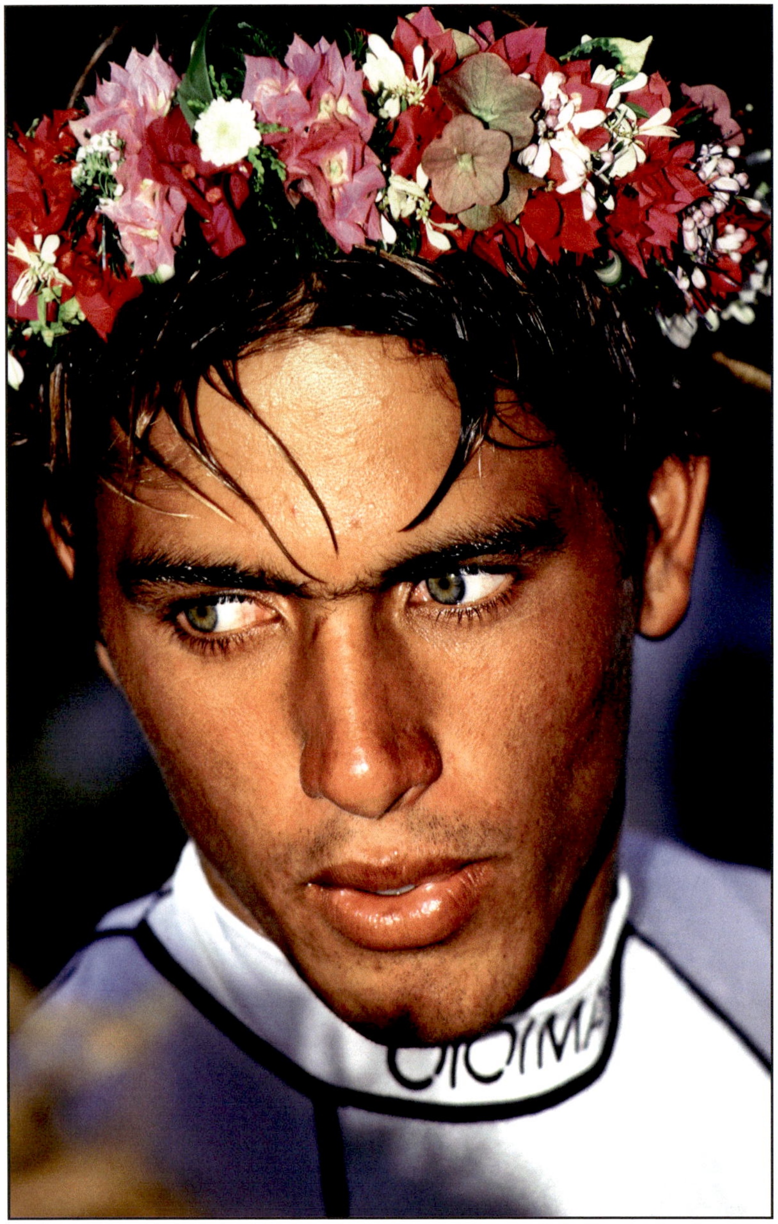

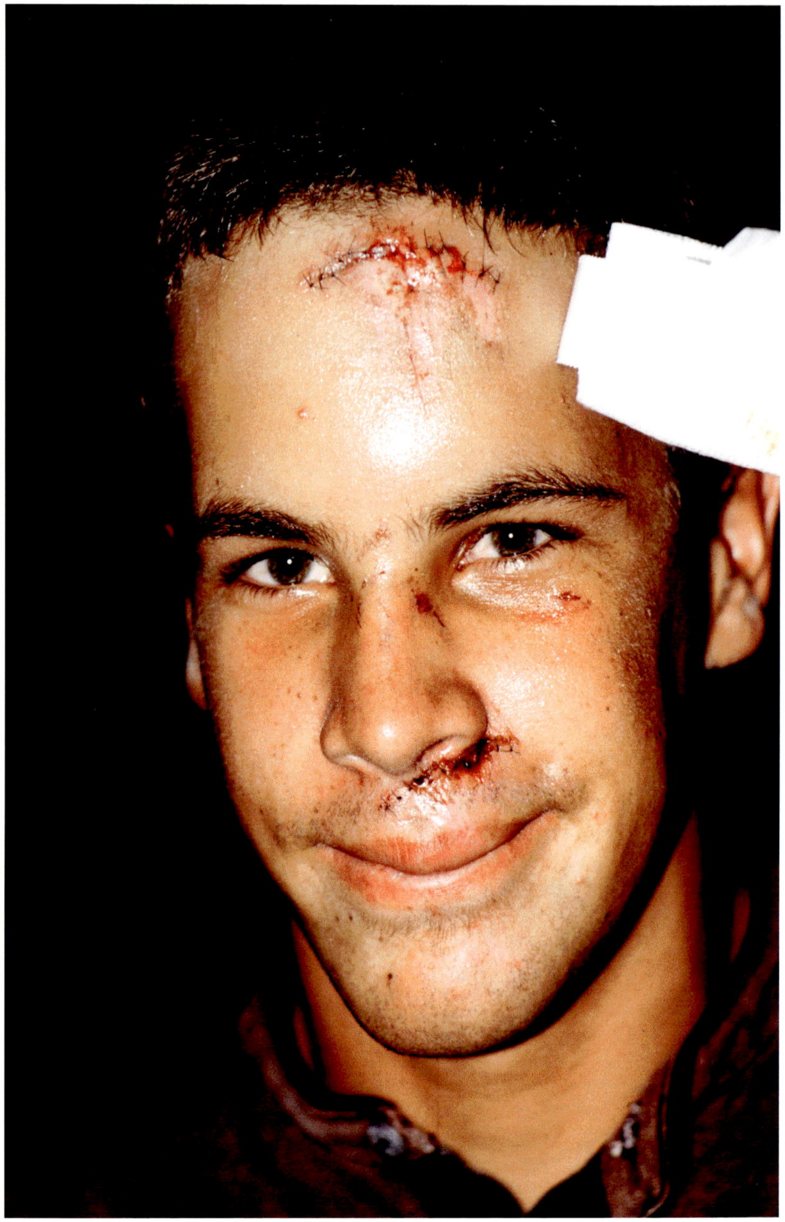

Kelly Slater. First master's win, first world title. Pipeline Masters, HI. 1992.

Jack Johnson. Pipeline reef rash. Hawaii. 1992.

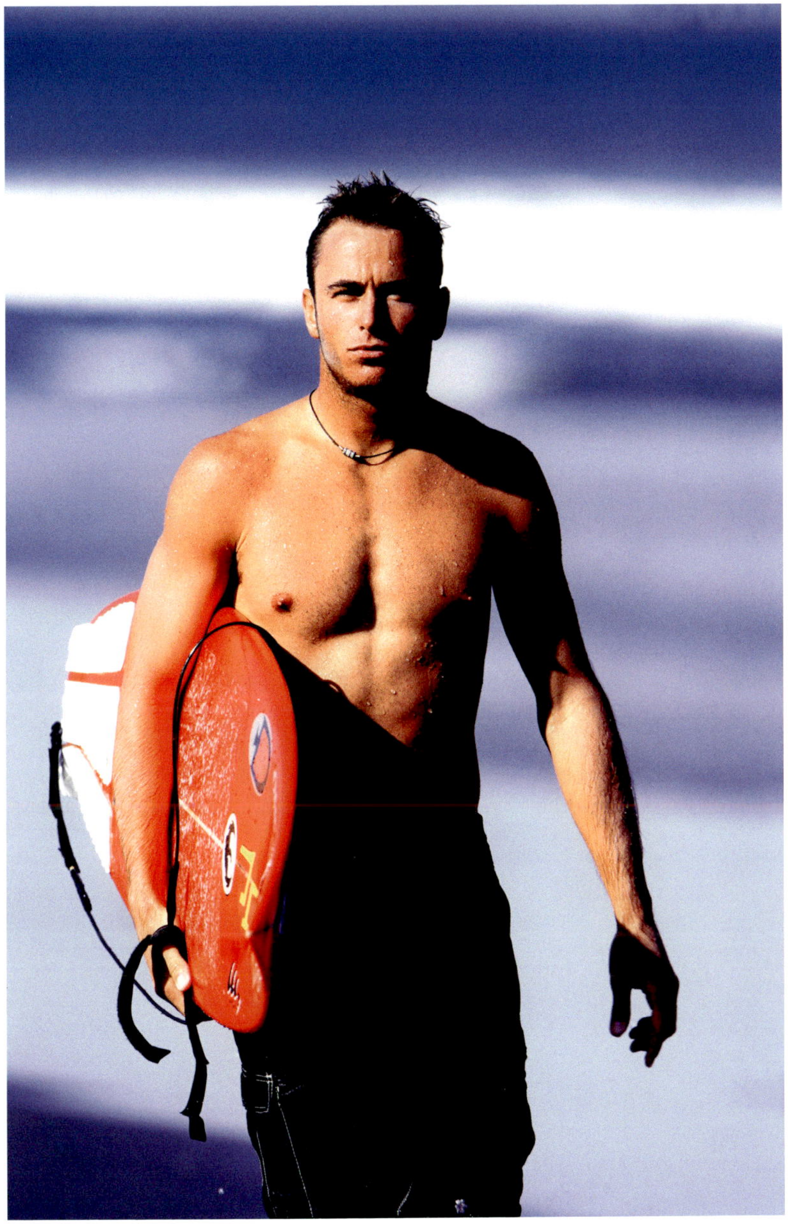

Shane Dorian. After class. Natividad Island, Mexico. 1998.

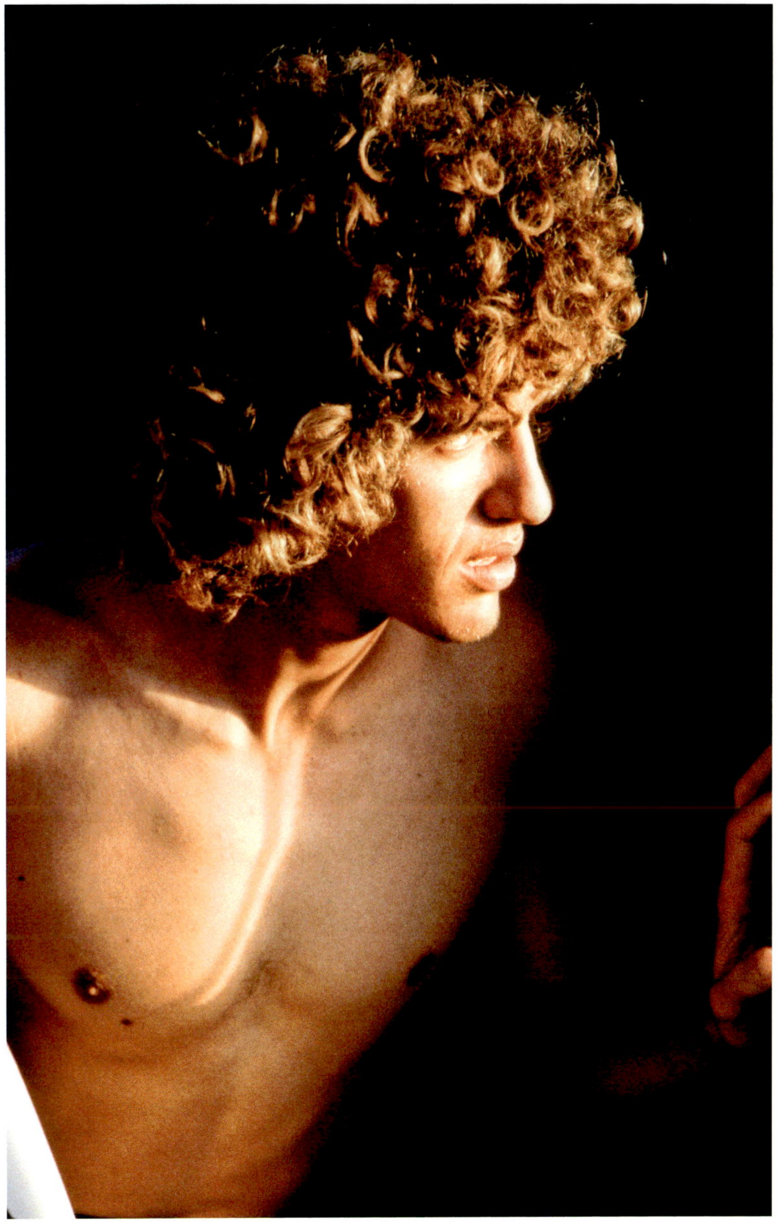

Rob Machado. Shades of Terry Fitzgerald. Hawaii. 1997.

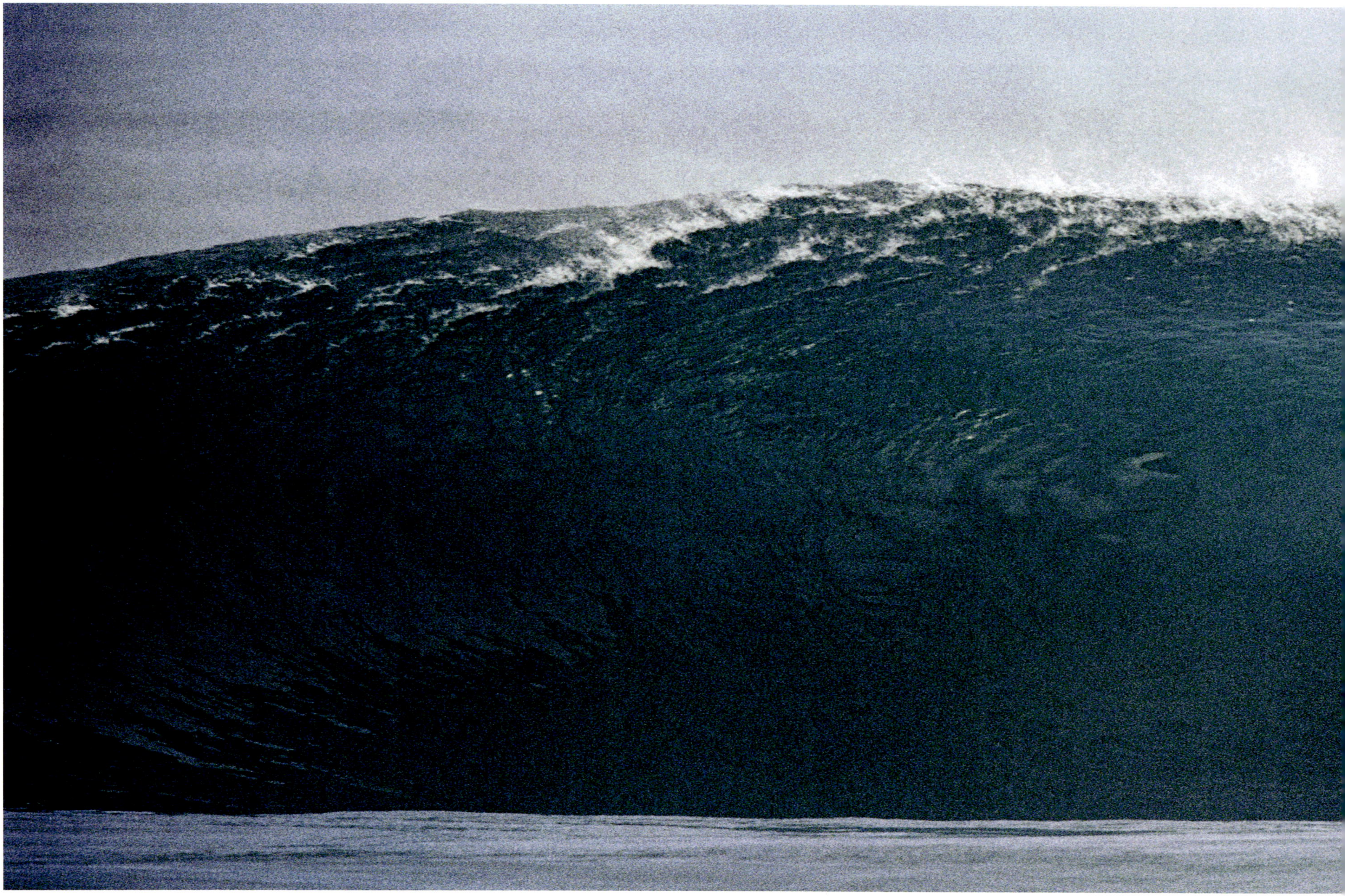

Shane "Back-Dorian." Pipeline, HI. 1999.

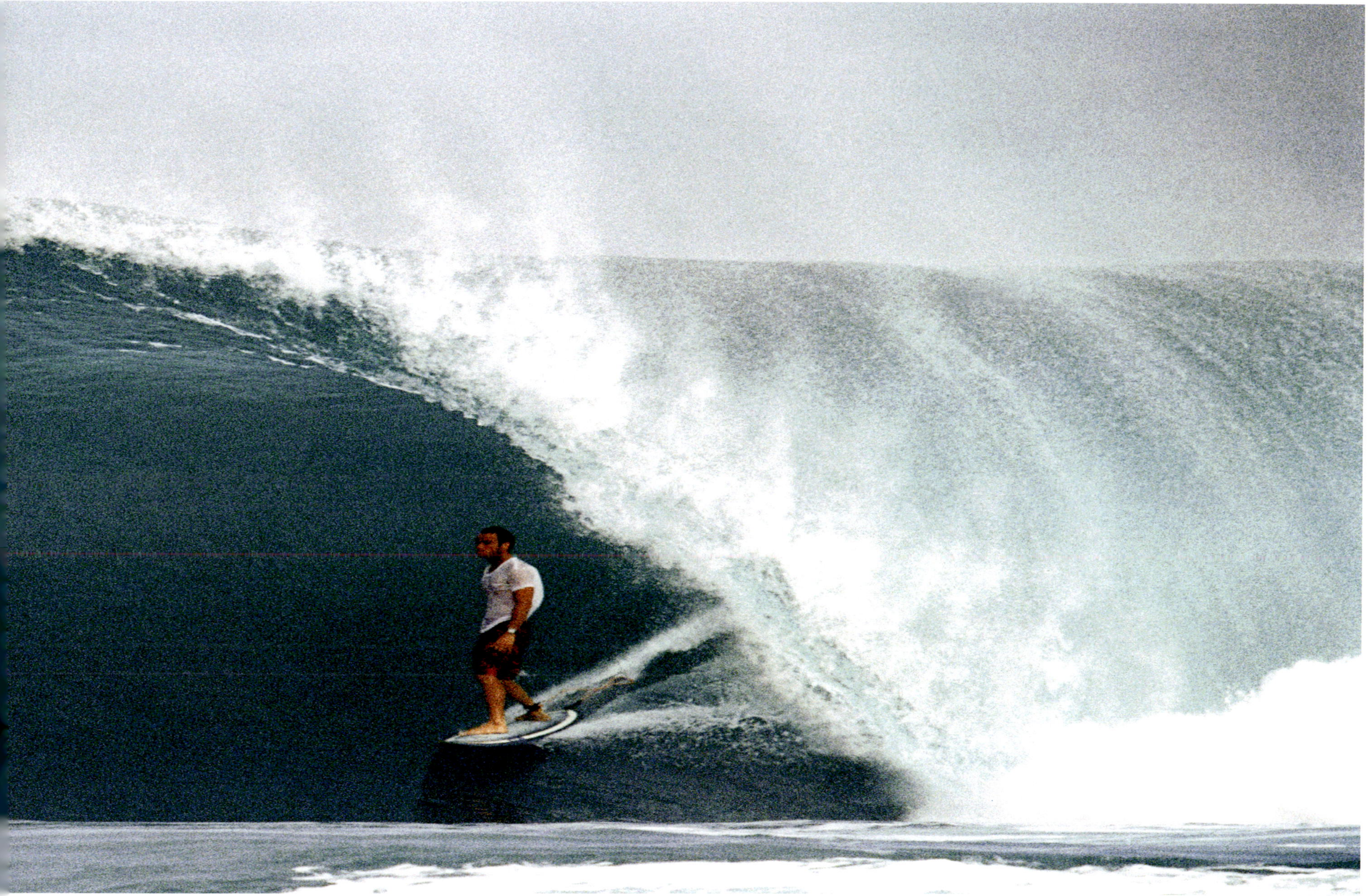

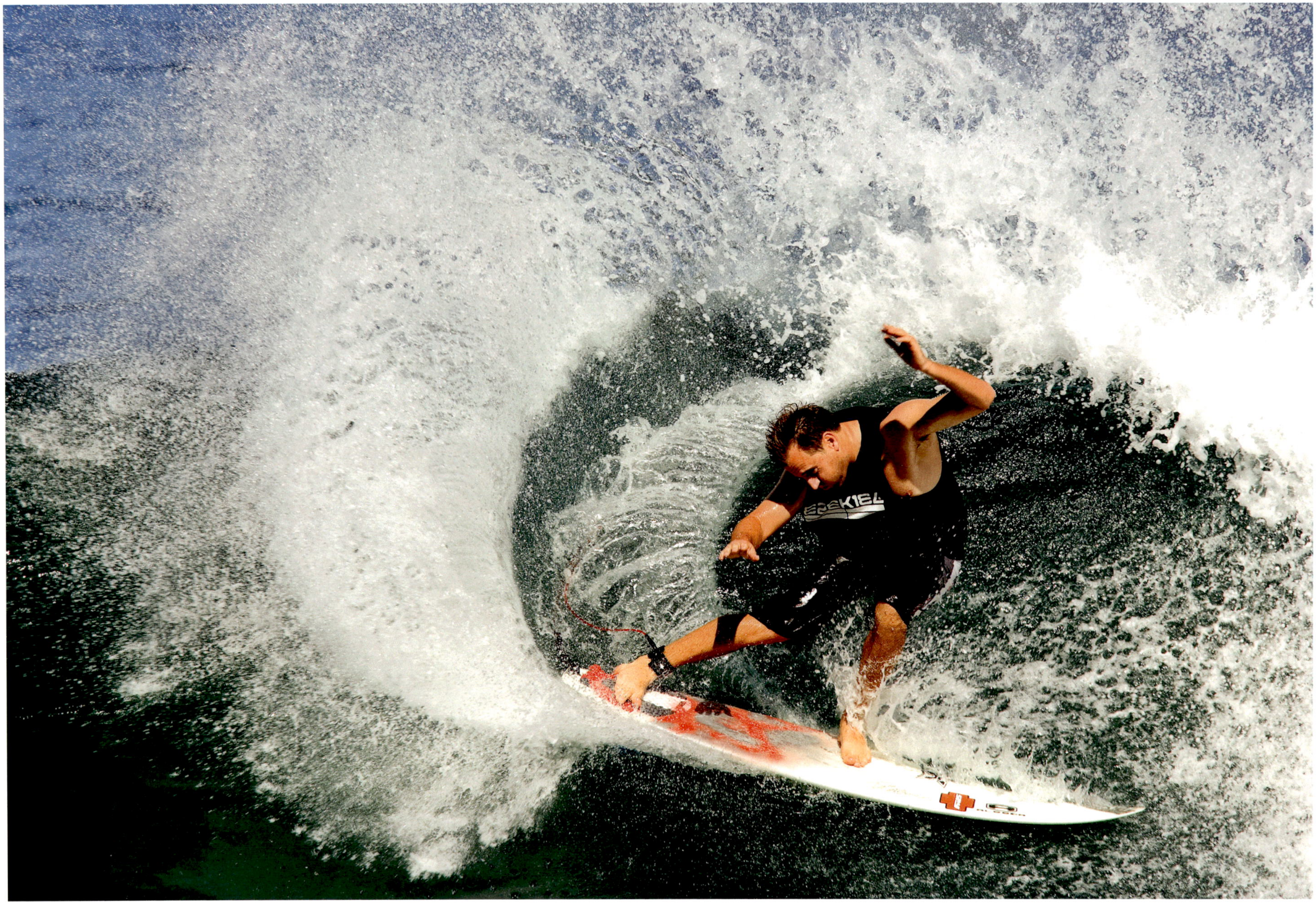

Ross Williams. Always let his surfing speak for him. Off the Wall, HI. 2004.

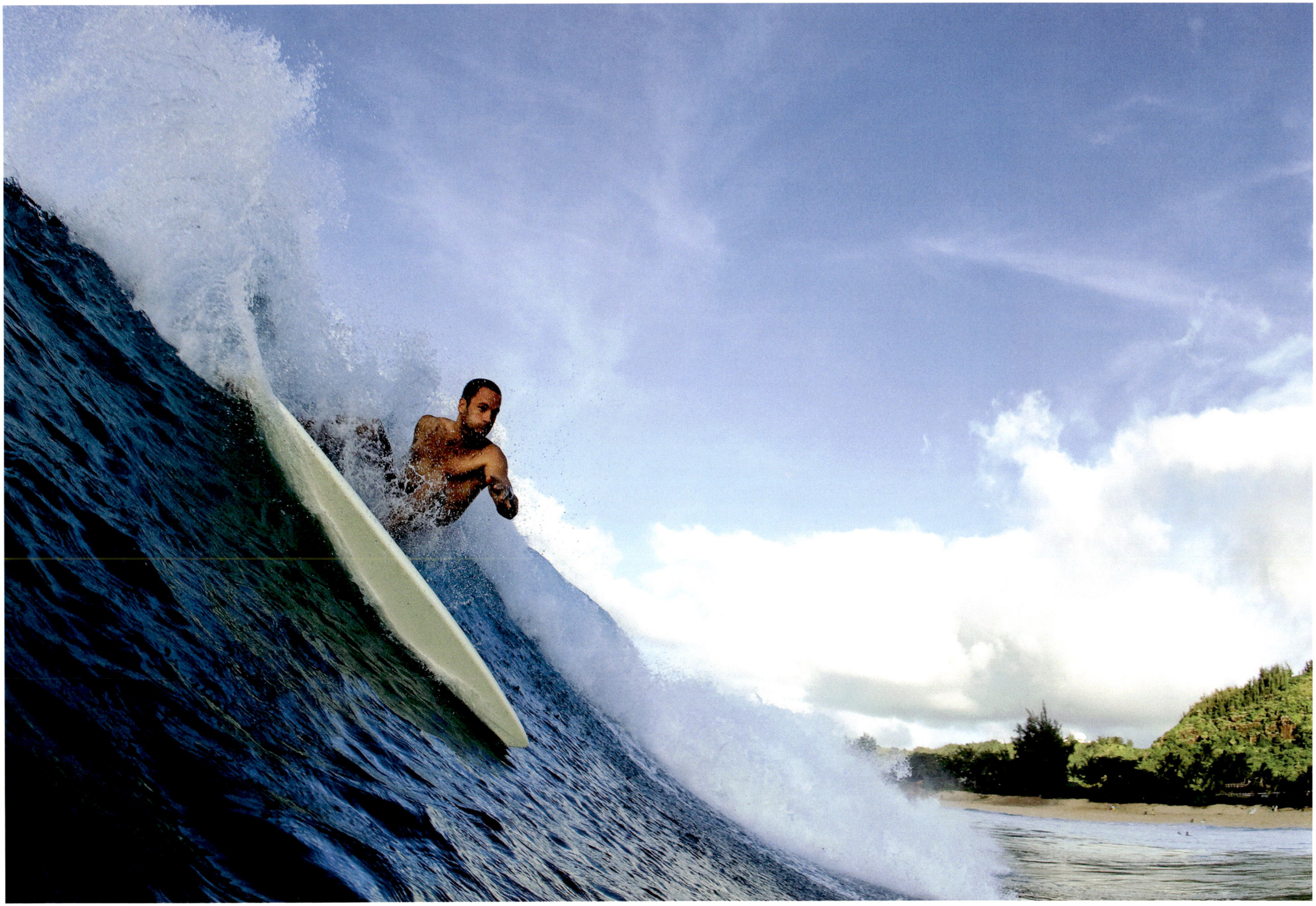

Jack Johnson. Makin' Music. Pupukea, HI. 2006.

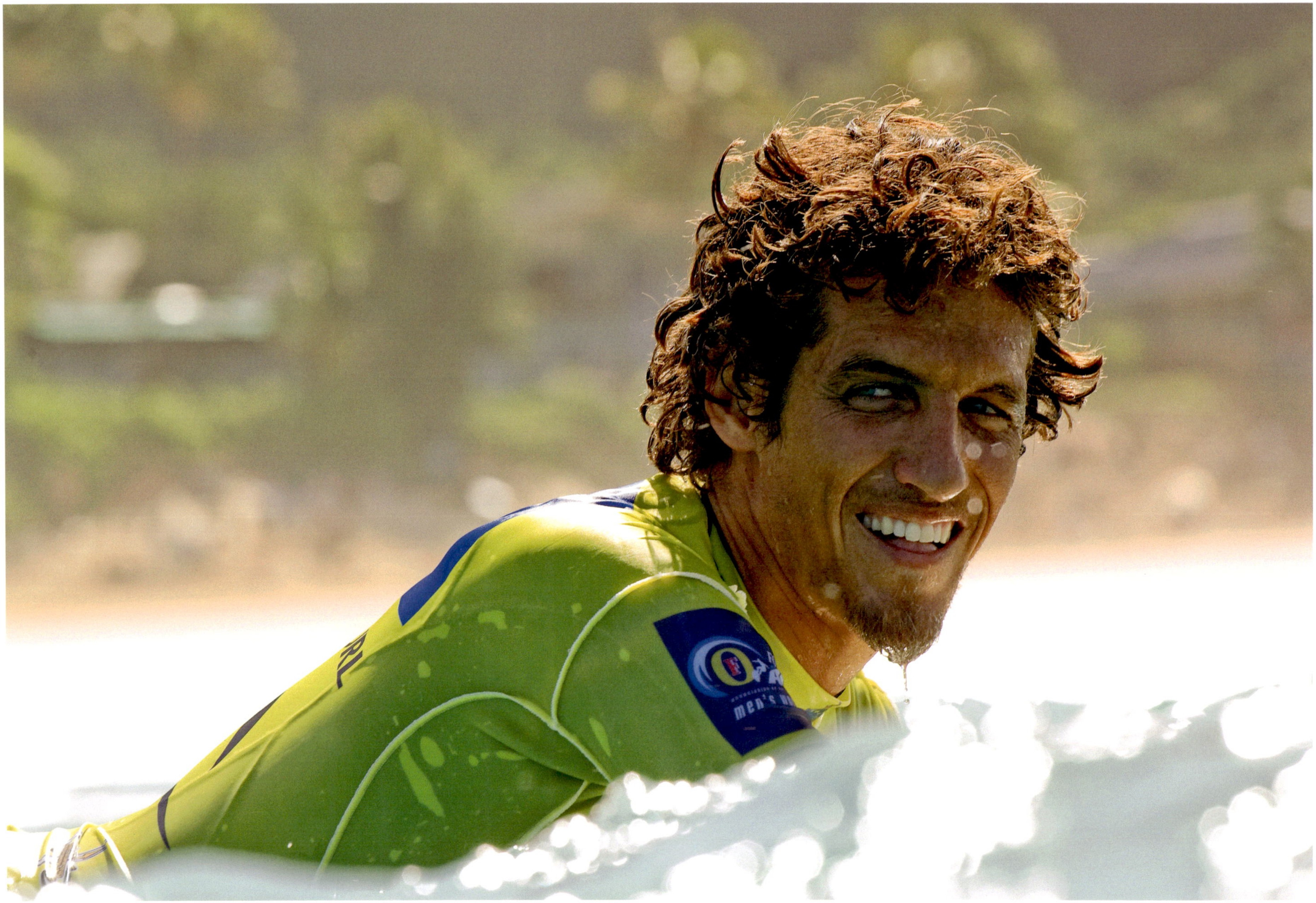

Rob Machado. Pipeline Masters, HI. 2006.

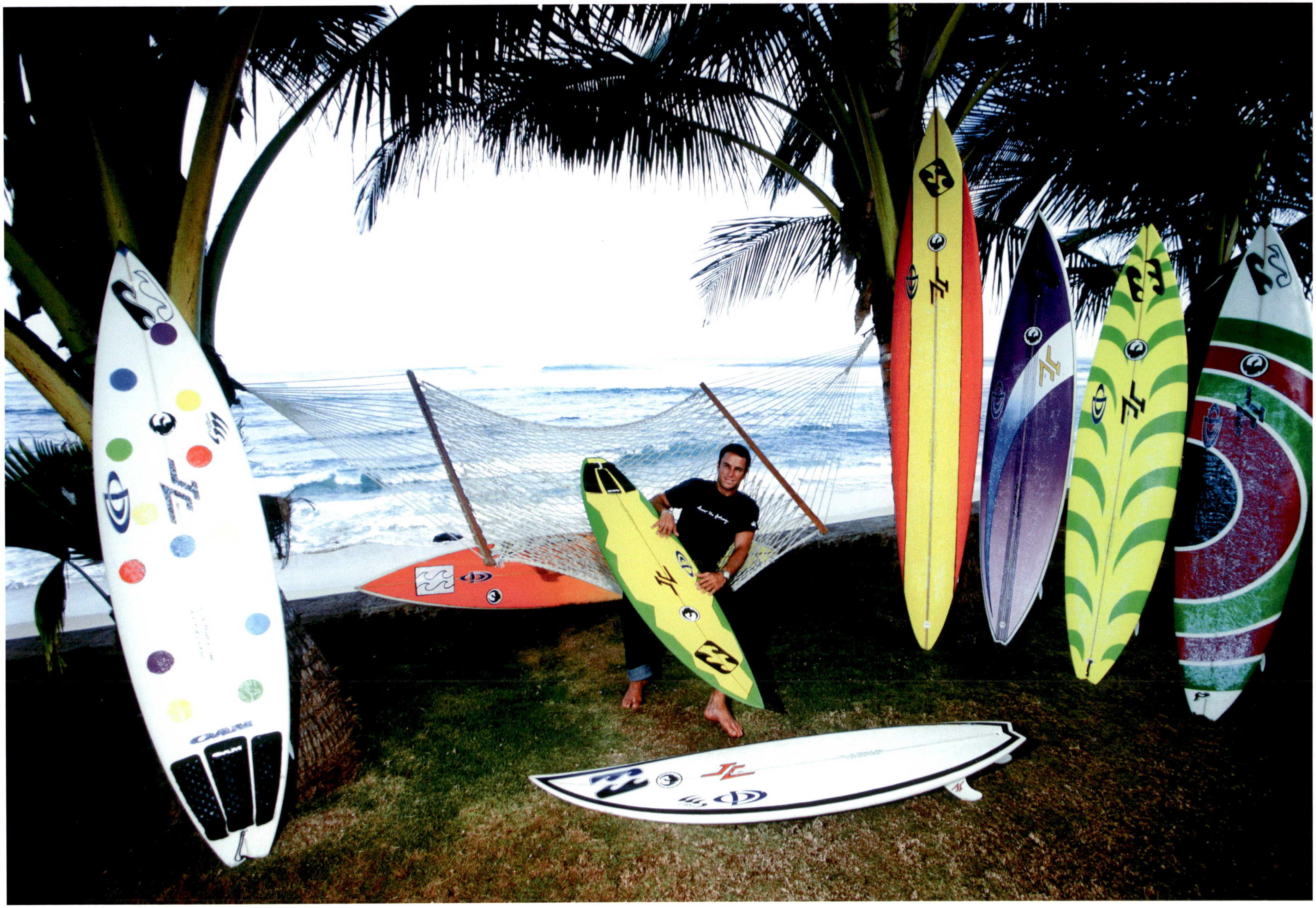

Shane Dorian. "Hero Quiver." John Carper's backyard. North Shore Oahu, HI. 2002.

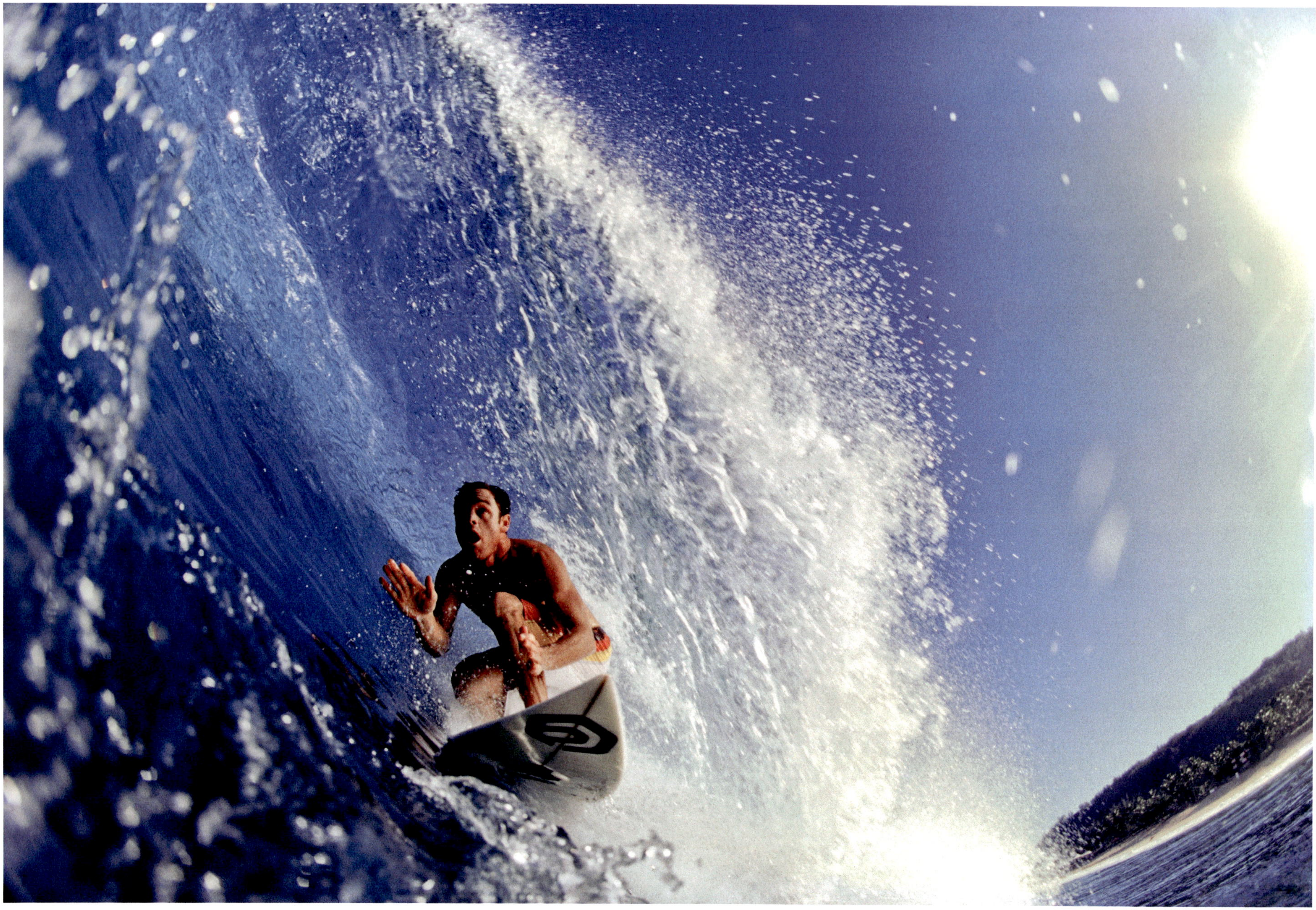

Taylor Knox taking the Highline. Backdoor, HI. 2003.

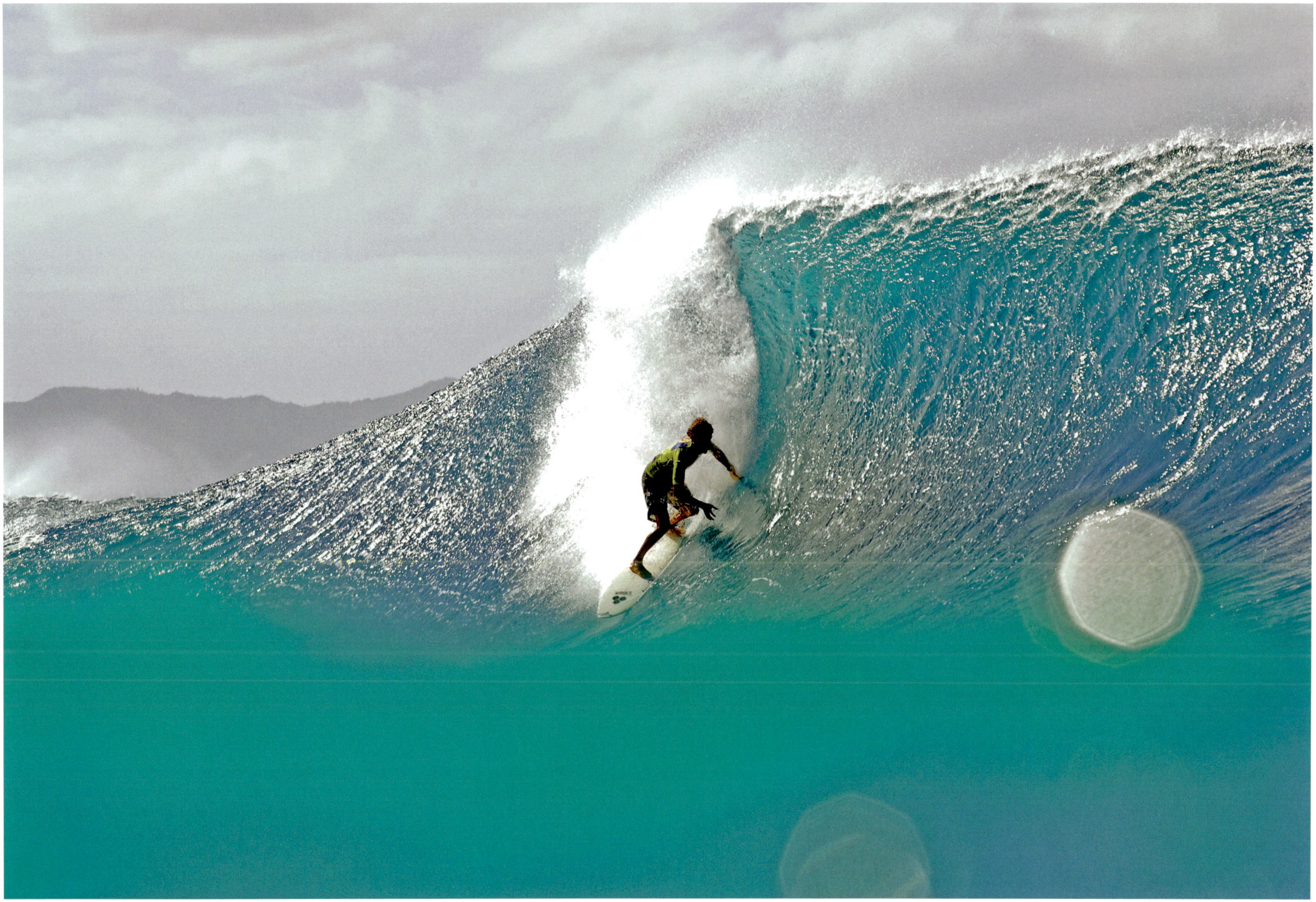

Rob Machado. Still a contender. Pipeline Masters, HI. 2006.

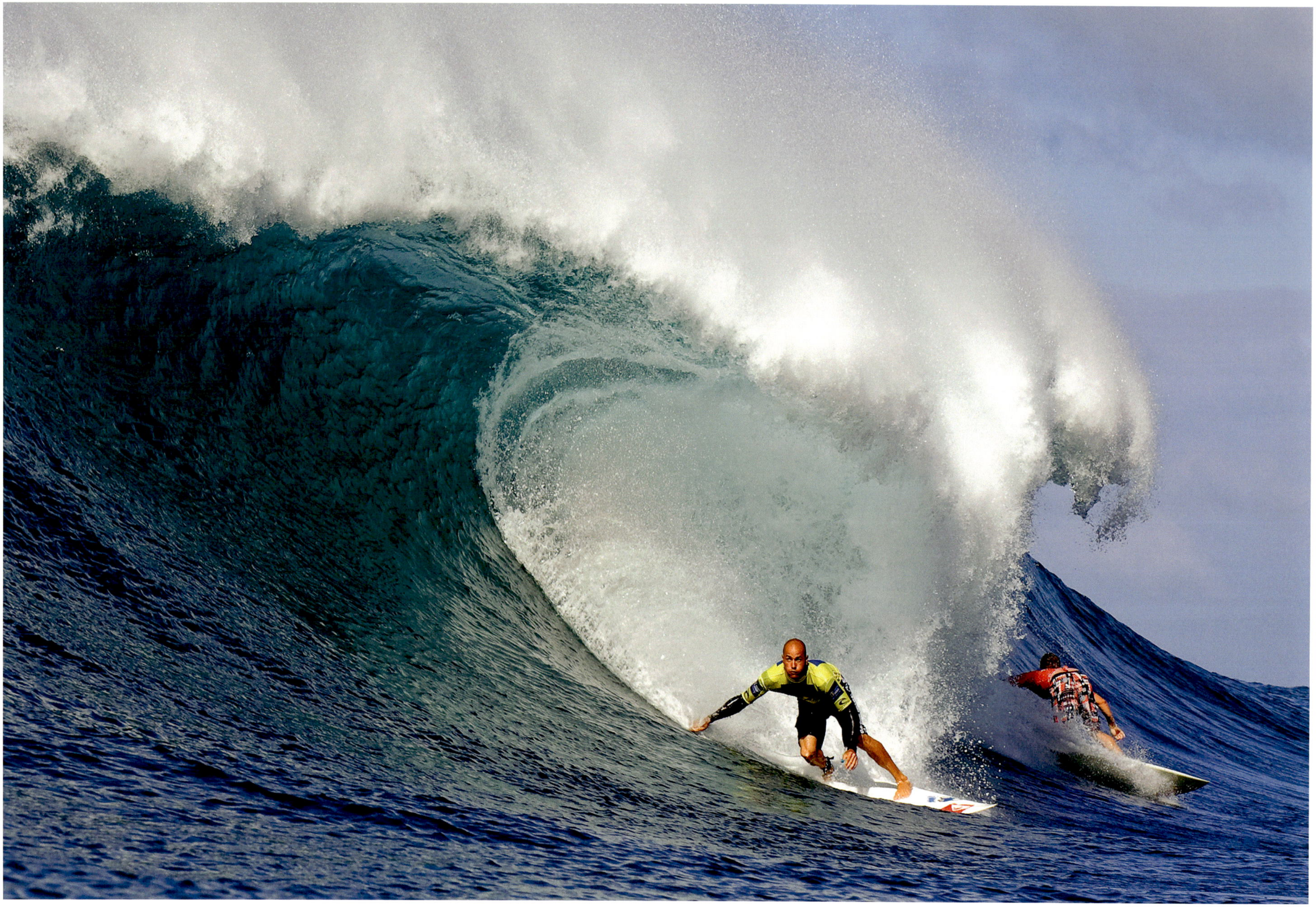

Kelly Slater and CJ Hobgood split the peak. Pipeline Masters, HI. 2006.

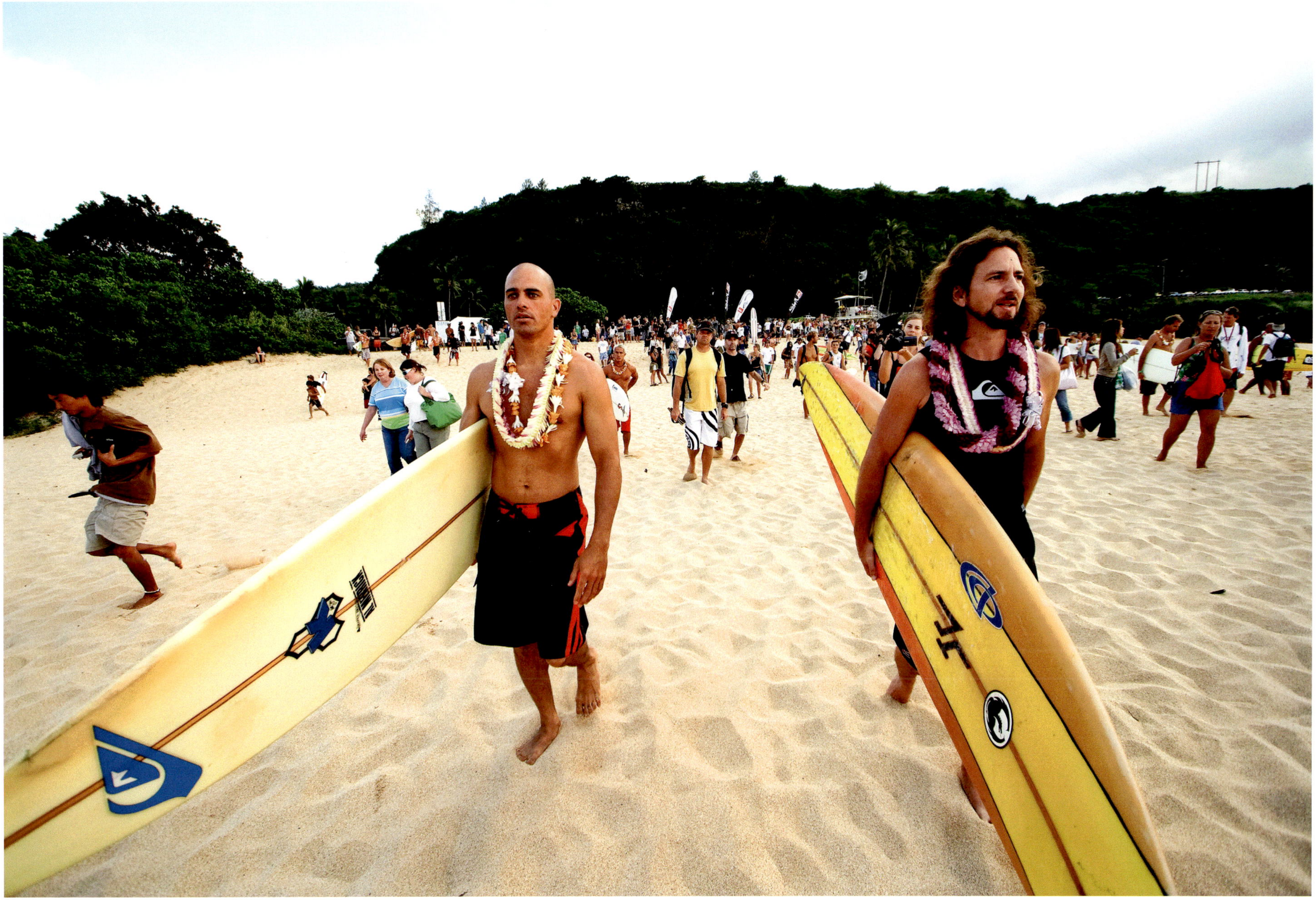

Kelly Slater and Eddie Vedder. The Eddie Aikau ceremony. Waimea, HI. 2006.

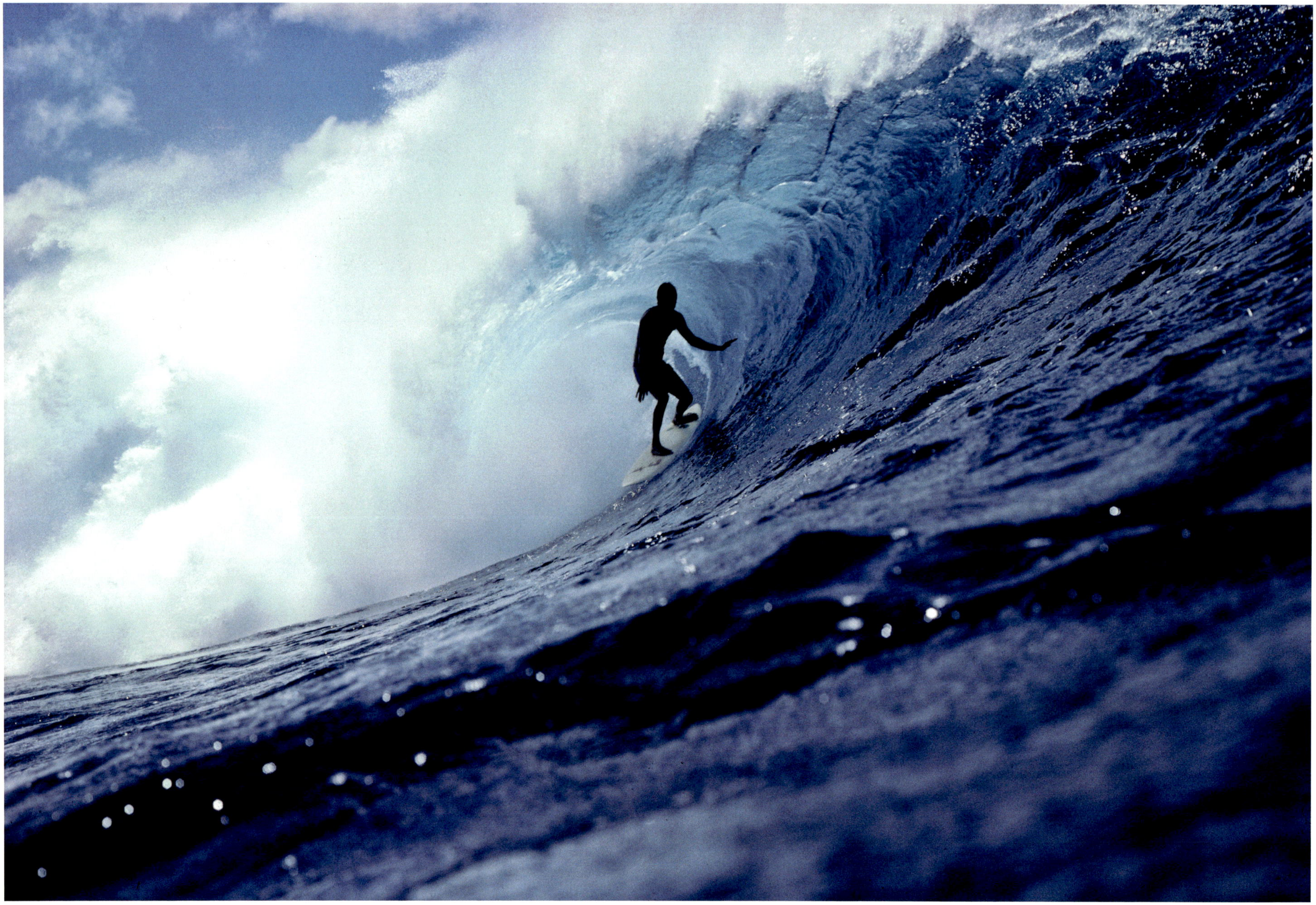

Gerry Lopez. Mr. Pipeline, HI. 1979.

The Things Legends Are Made Of

Kelly and his friends definitely had some good examples to work from, most notably Gerry Lopez, and later, Tom Curren. I am certain the New School crew got a lot of their grace and style from these two classic surfers.

I can't really say enough about Gerry Lopez and his surfing. He was very simply the "King of Pipeline" and a master of style. I feel fortunate to have lived next door to him and traveled with Gerry. He is both a soulful surfer and an amazing person.

Tom Curren was a quiet, reserved guy and never really wanted to be a role model or hero. He become one though, and was elected strictly through his surfing ability. Tom really was everybody's hero. He set the style, not just for surfing one particular break, but for surfing everywhere with power and grace. He has incredible wave knowledge and technique. He is still a legendary surfer. I'm certain Kelly would tip his hat to Curren and Lopez for everything that they have given to the sport and it's been a pleasure for me to photograph them both through their careers. These guys truly are legends.

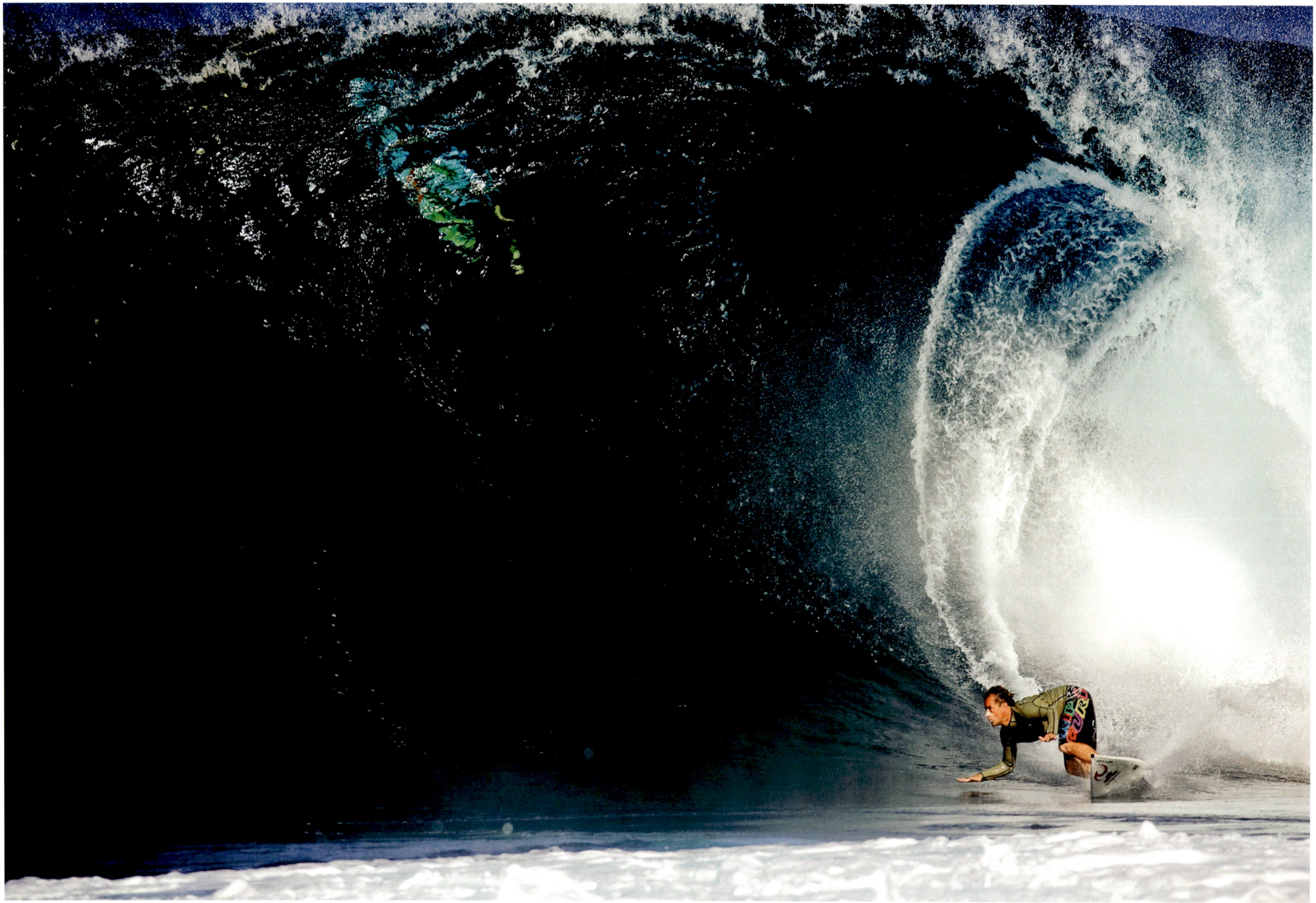

Tom Curren. Quiet and Powerful. Backdoor Pipeline, HI. 2005.

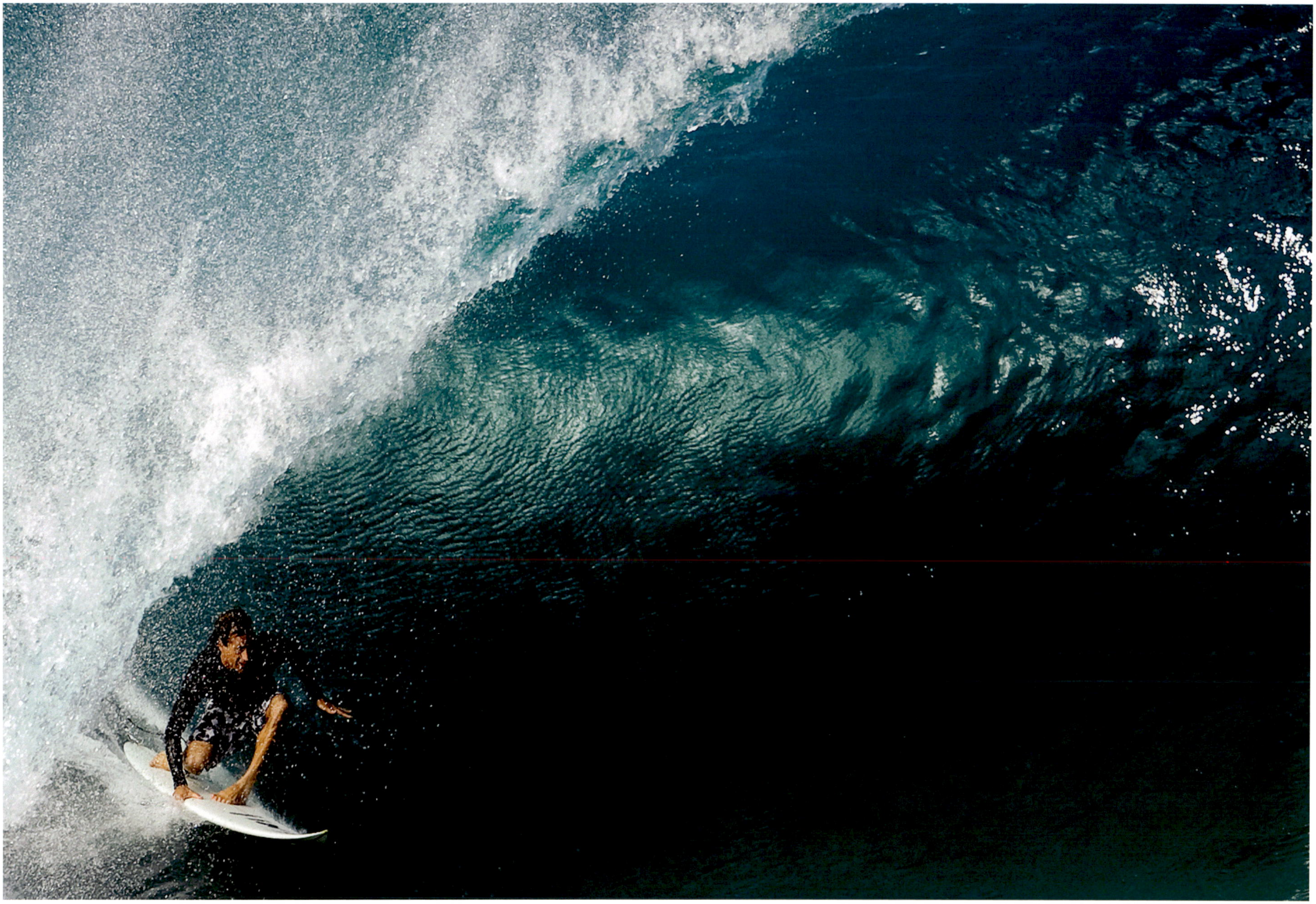

Tom Curren, even on his back hand. Pipeline, HI. 2004.

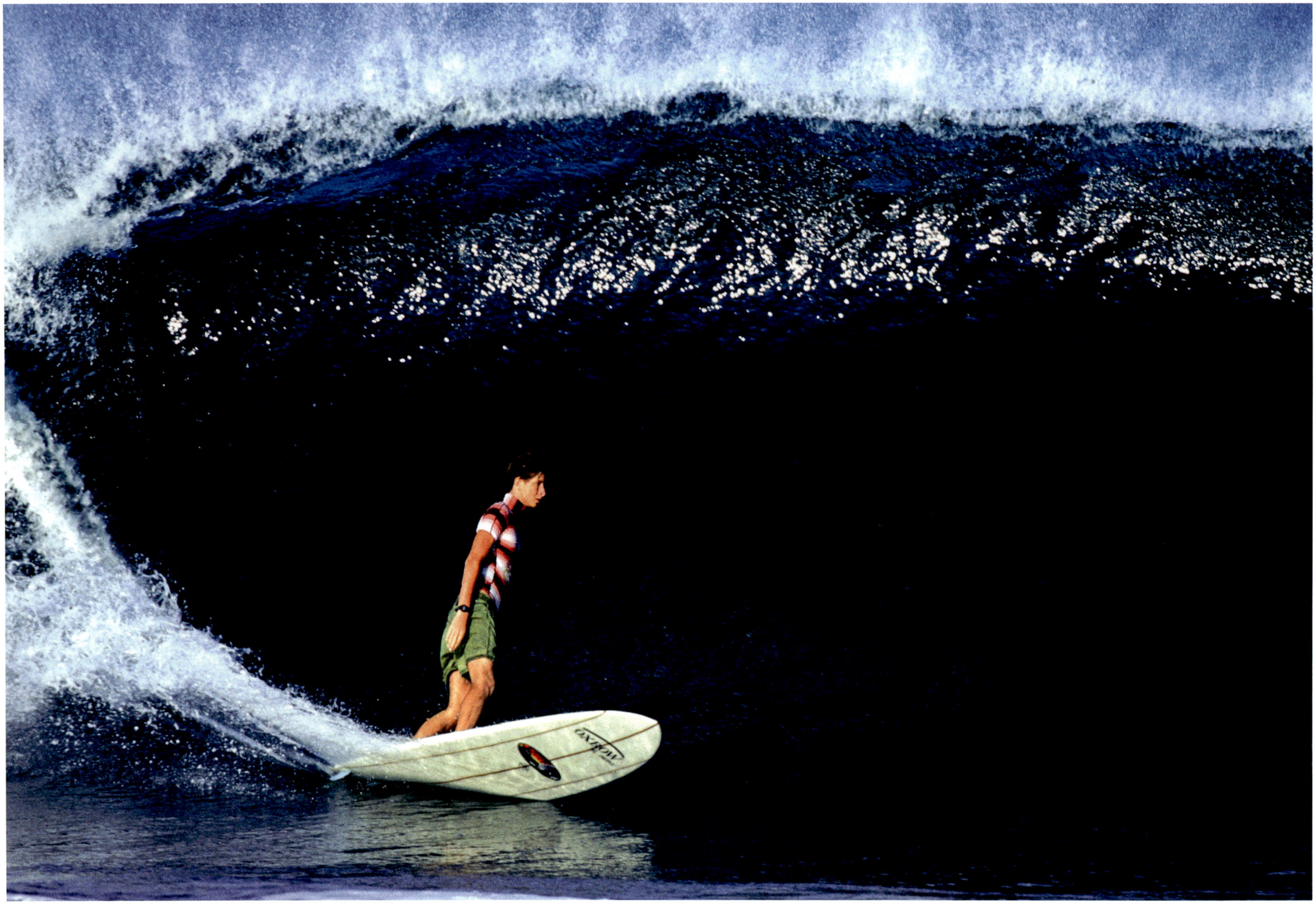

Joel Tudor, 16th Birthday. Puerto Escondido, Mexico. 1993.

Learning From the Past, Facing the Future

When I try to think of those who influence me in the world of surfing, from the great Duke Kahanamoku through all the great longboarders of the '60s, there's no one quite like Joel Tudor. As a young kid, Joel would study classic surfing style from the old films, carefully building his own version. He modeled his technique on those from the past, and watching him now you can really see the soul of all who came before him.

I met Joel when he was fifteen, taking him on his first trip for *Longboard* magazine to Puerto Escondido, a spot considered at the time as unsurfable on a longboard. I had been to Puerto several times before with friends surfing and shooting photos and I would have agreed!

Along with Joel, we took Reese Patterson, Bill Burke, and Tom Wegener on that trip. I was in awe that these guys could not only take off and catch big waves on longboards but that they could also pull into Puerto monster barrels and make them so easily. They proved us wrong.

Good surfers can handle anything and these guys certainly did. But nothing amazed me more than Tudor. He has since become the most influential surfer among the retro set, bringing back old-school longboarding and making it all his own. Using alternative surf paraphernalia, he rides all the old single-fin configurations. It's been an honor to travel all over the world with Joel and photograph him. I've shot him in just about every situation, and he is an incredible surfer and very charismatic guy.

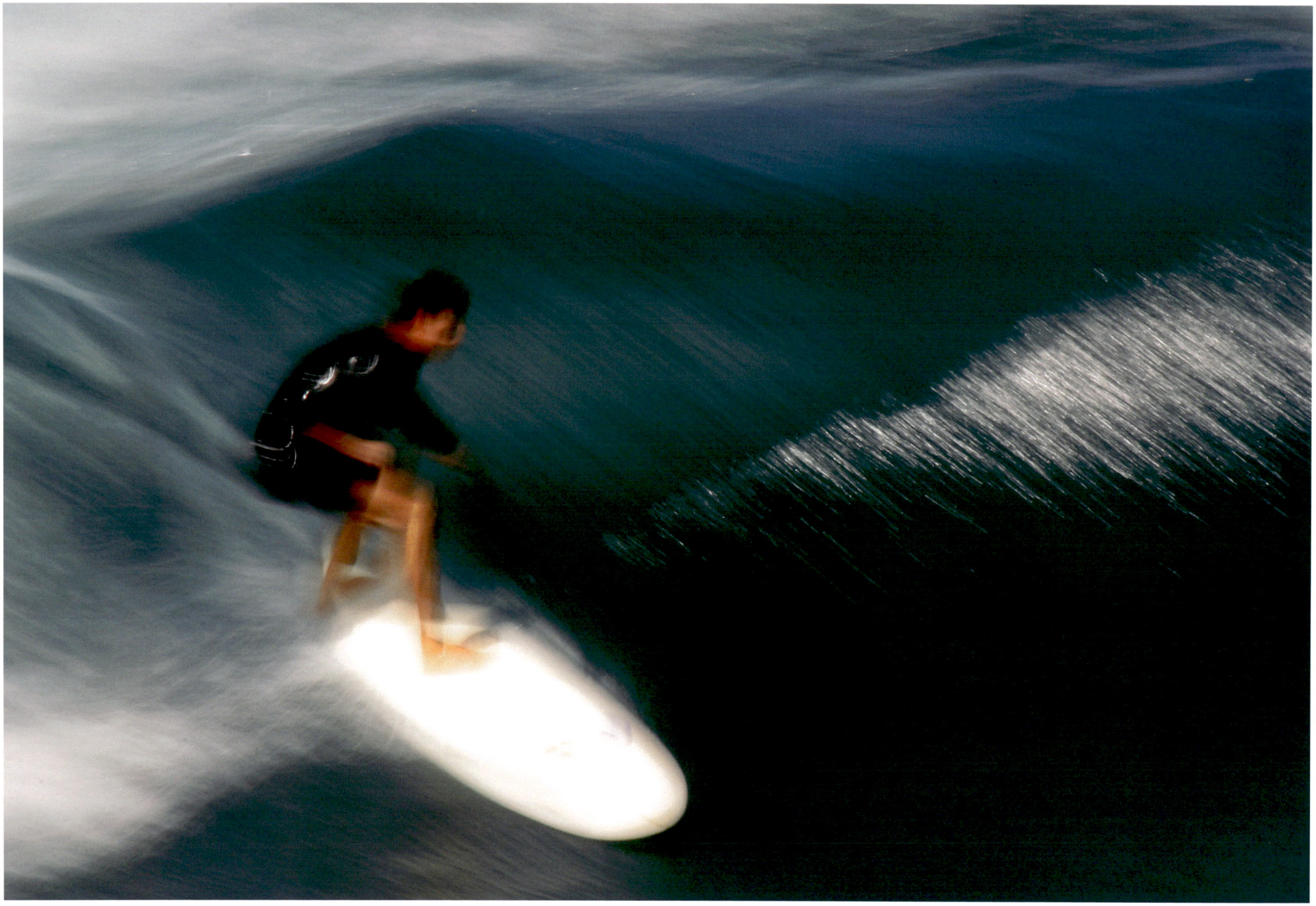

Joel Tudor painting lines. Pipeline, HI. 2003.

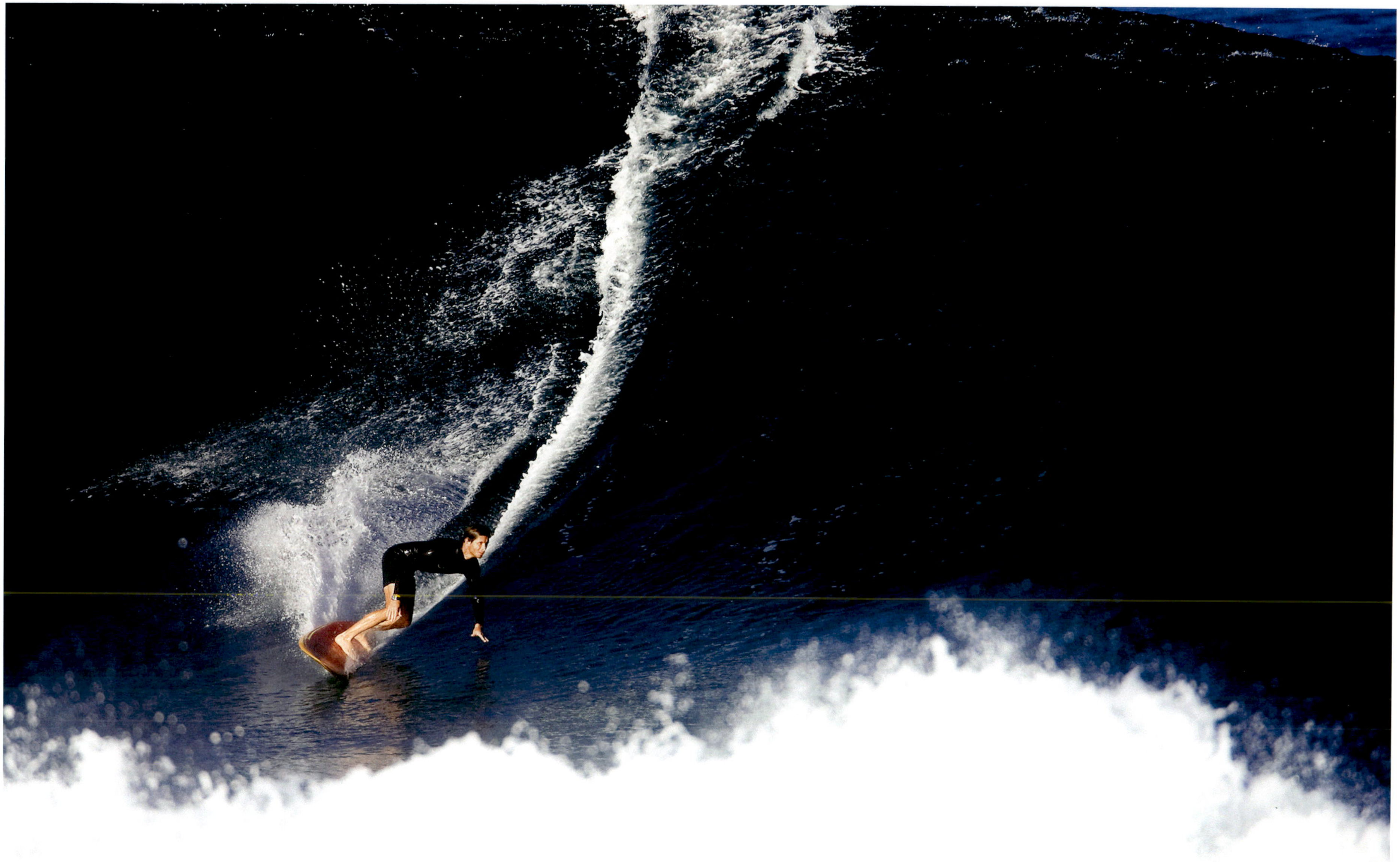

Joel Tudor drawing lines. Pipeline, HI. 2005.

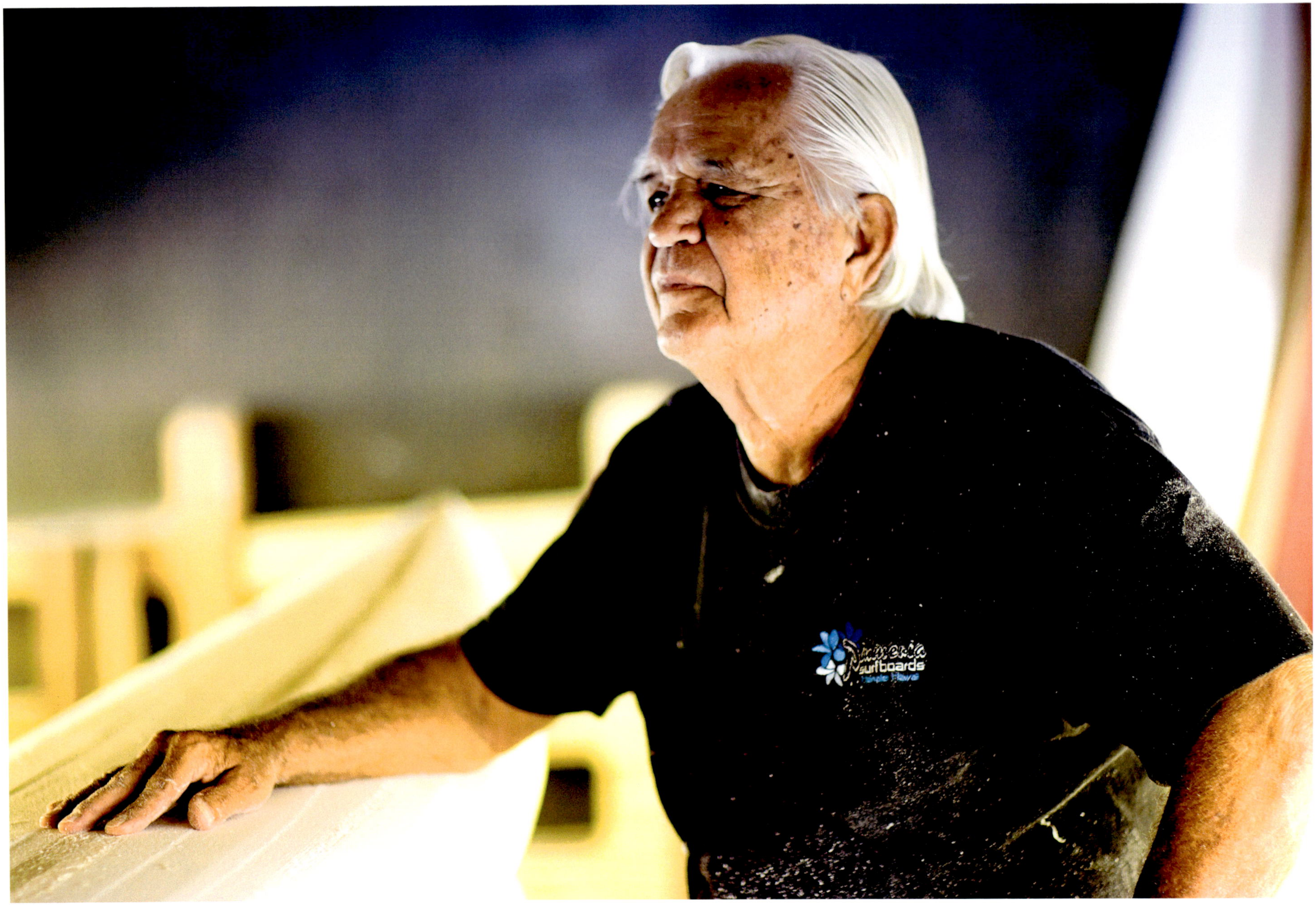

Dick Brewer. Master craftsman. North Shore Oahu, HI. 2007.

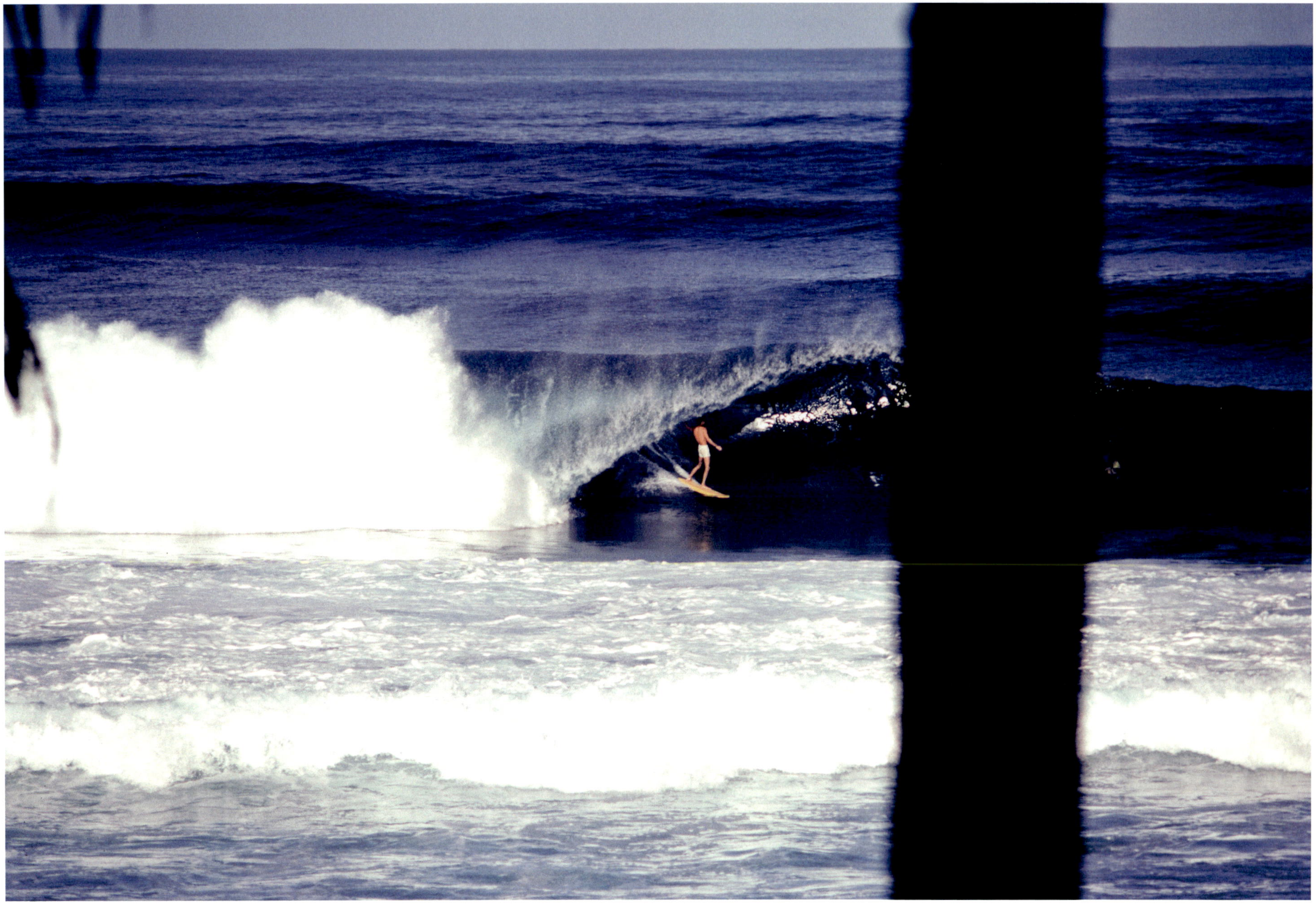

Adam "12" Salvio. From Gerry's house next door. Pipeline, HI. 1979.

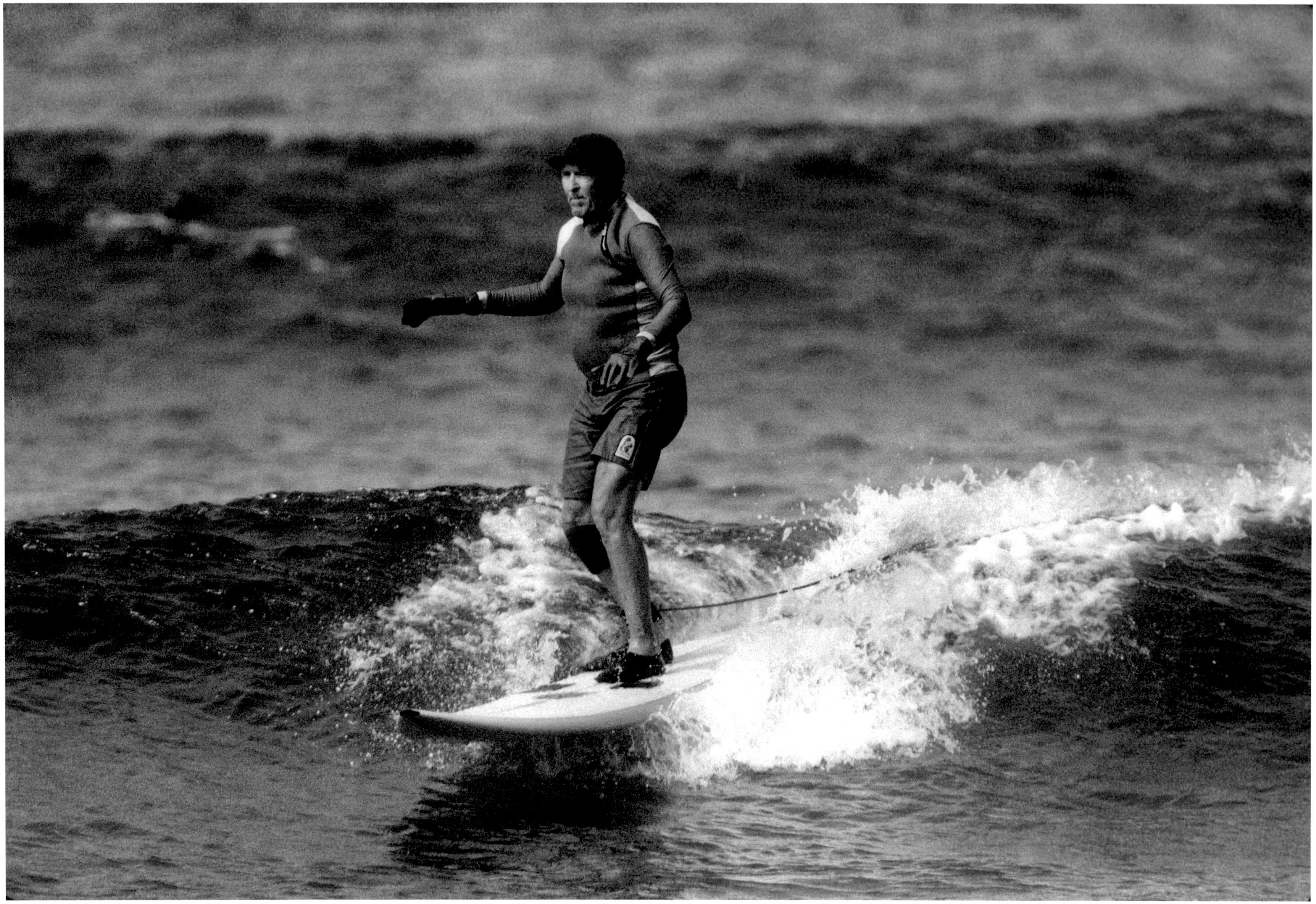

Leroy Grannis. Father of modern surf photography. Haleiwa, HI. 1993.

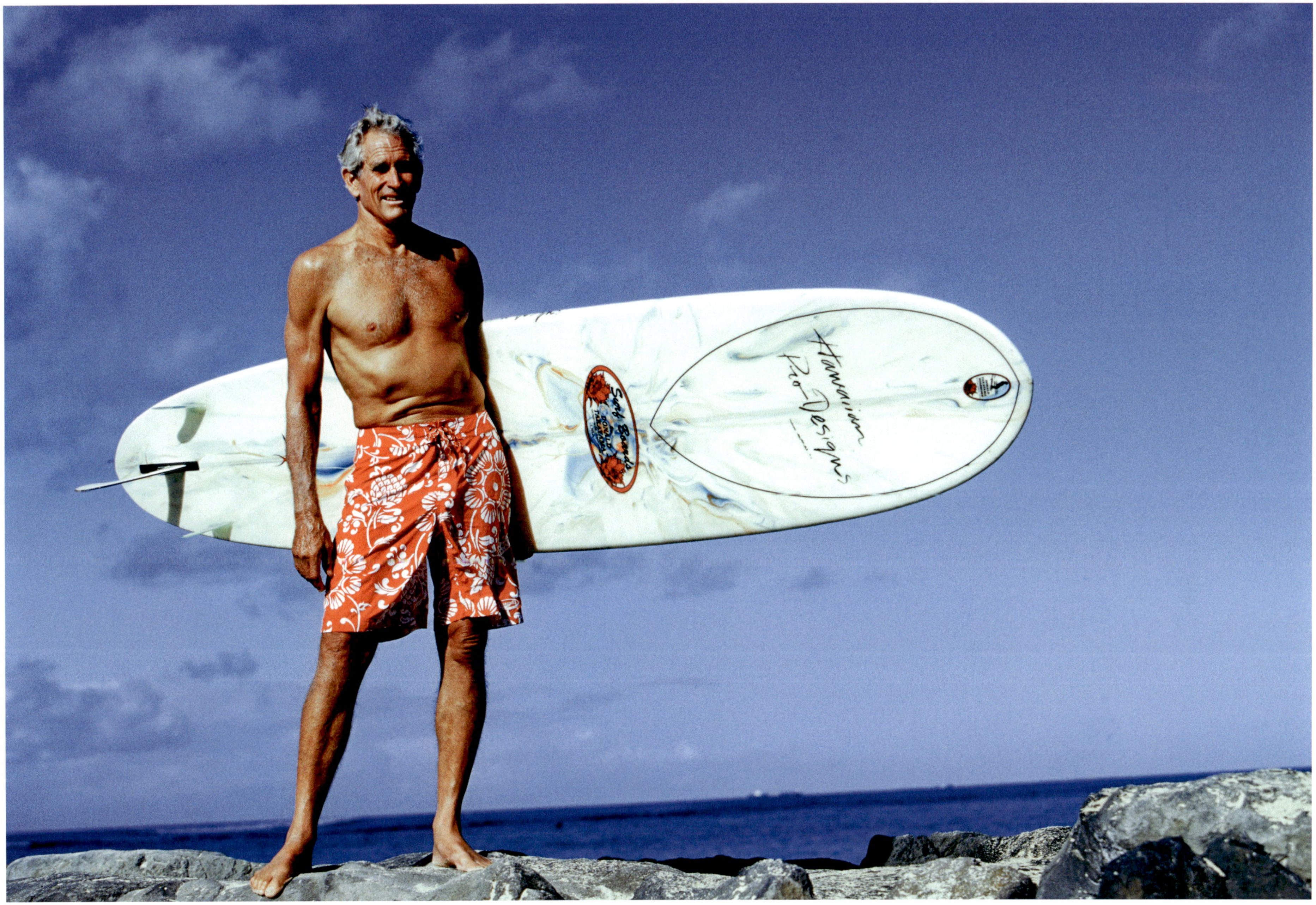

Joey Cabell. Still styling after all these years. Threes, HI. 2003.

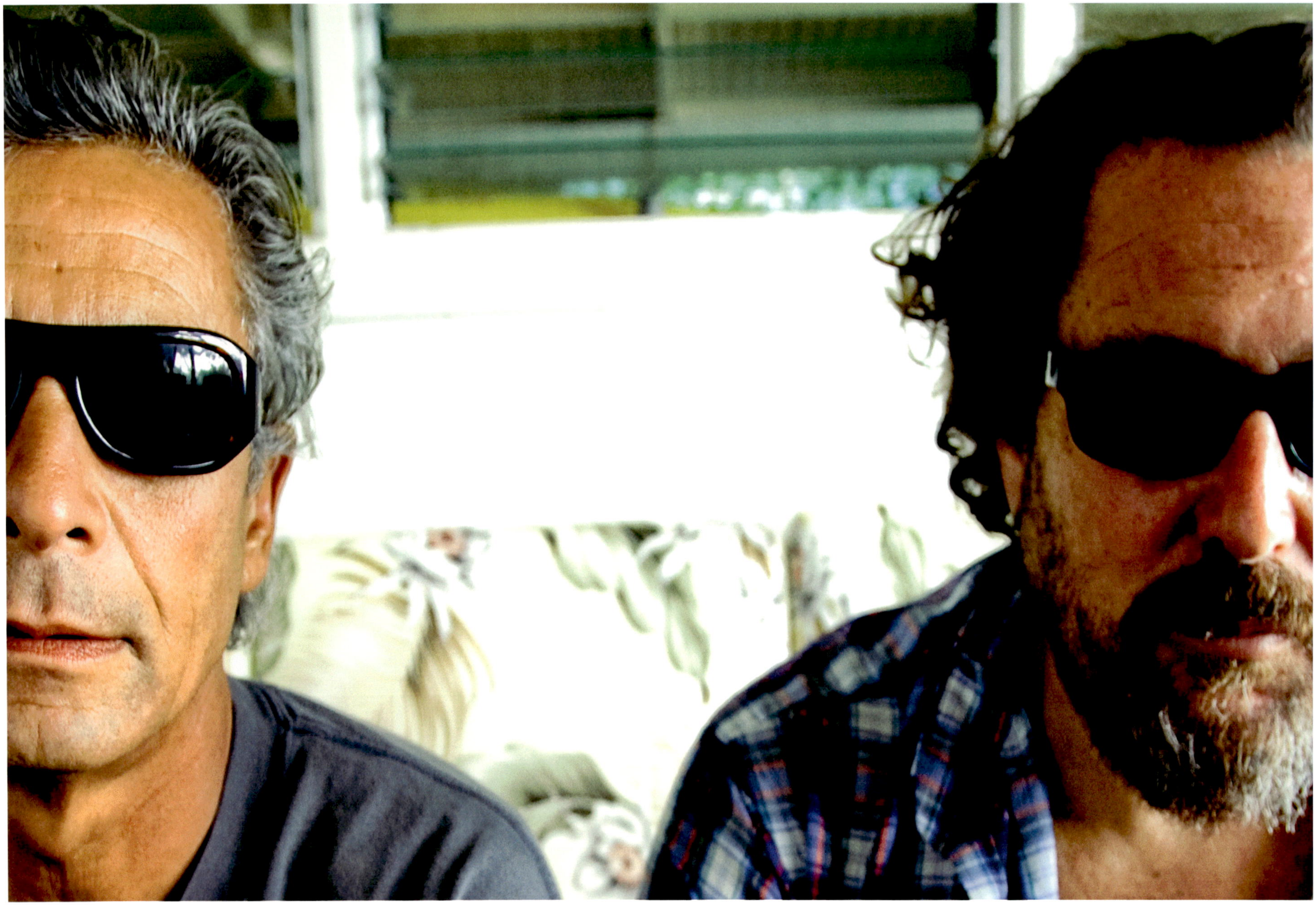

Herbie Fletcher with artist Julian Schnabel. Blues Brothers. North Shore Oahu, HI. 2004.

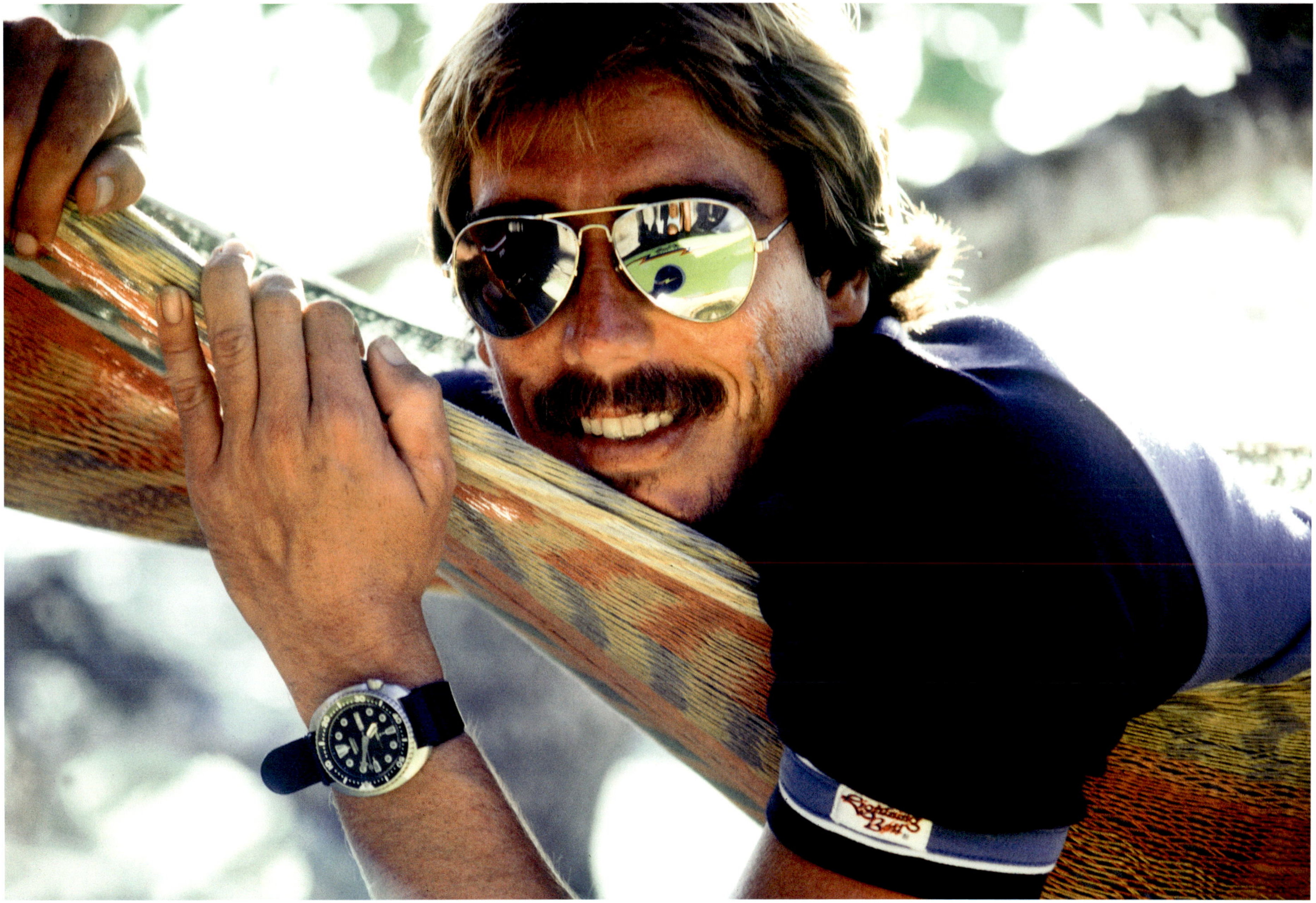

Rory Russell. My first Lightning Bolt ad. G-land, Indonesia. 1980.

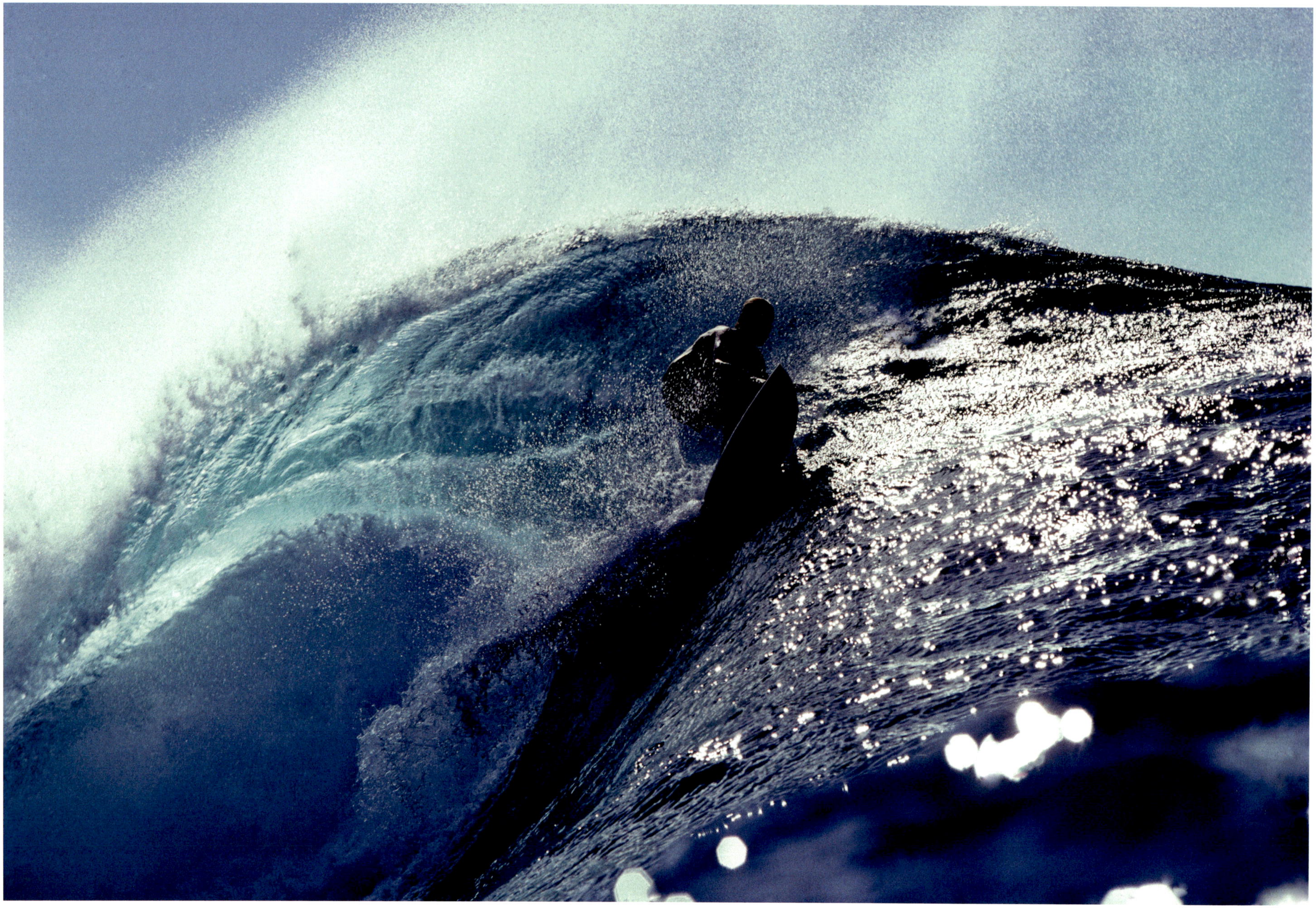

Ronnie Burns heading for heaven. Pipeline, HI. 1979.

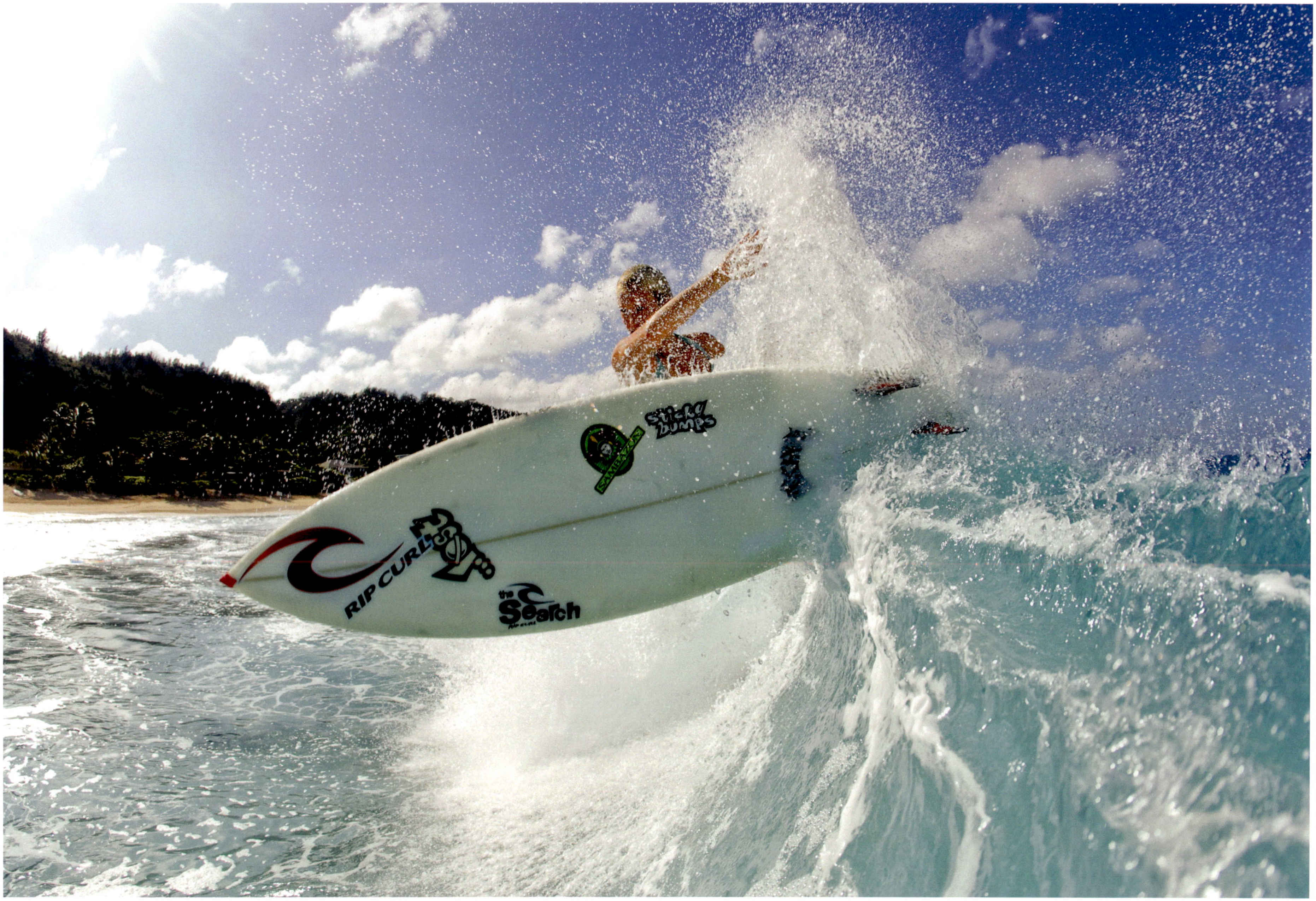

Bethany Hamilton, On a Wing and a Prayer. Pupukea, HI. 2006.

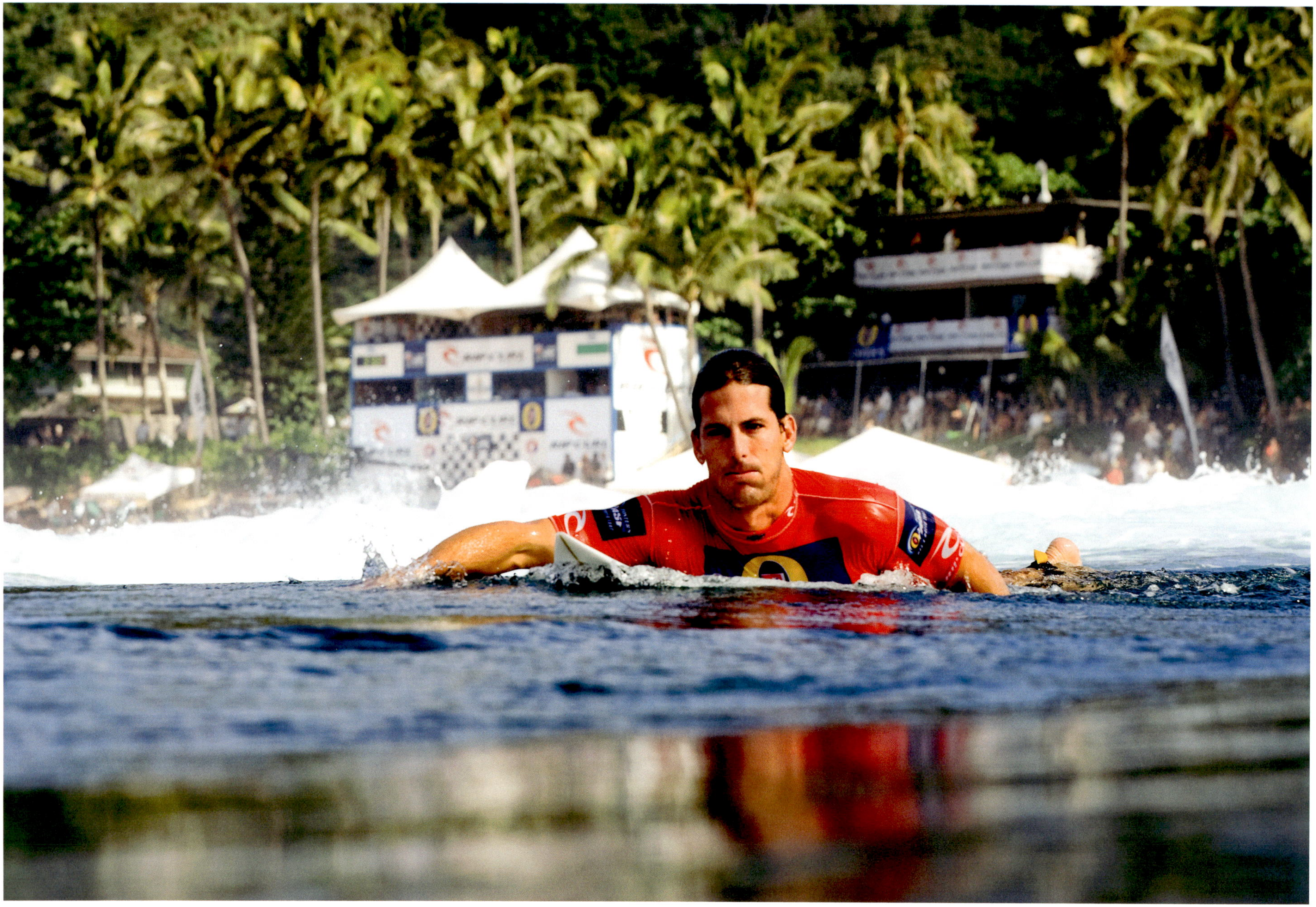

Andy Irons fully focused. Pipemasters, HI. 2006.

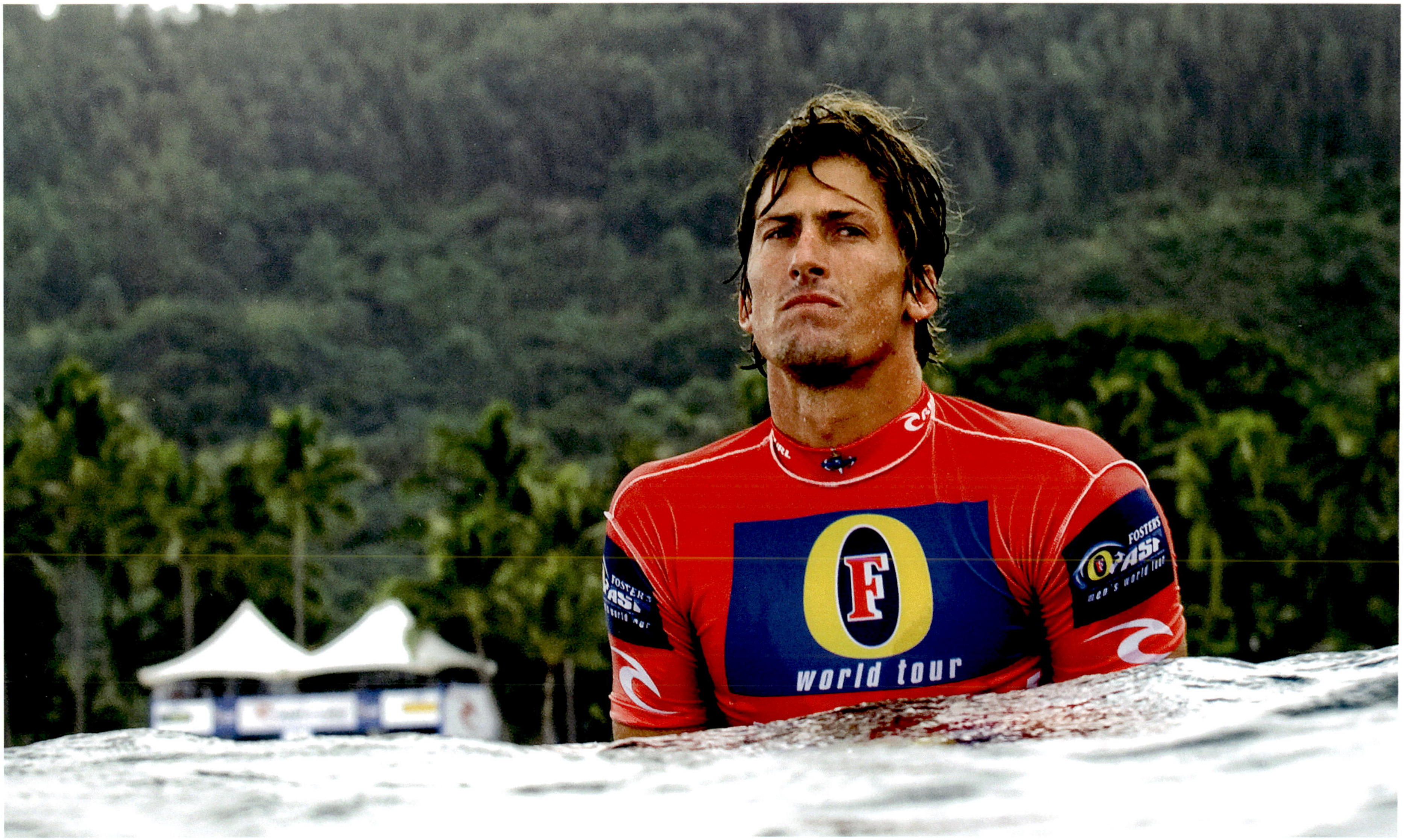

Bruce Irons. Kauai Strong. Pipemasters, HI. 2006.

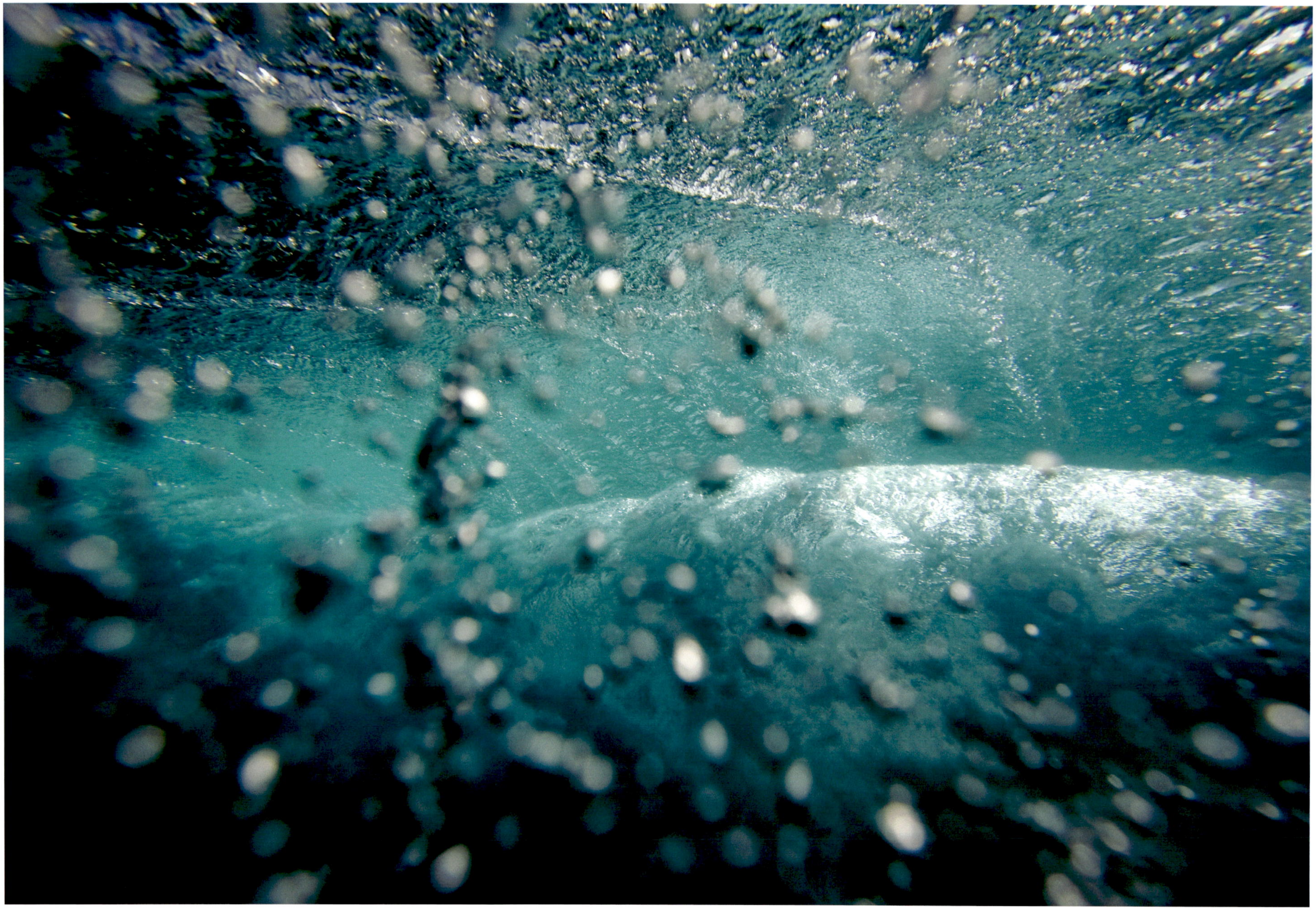

Beauty in Chaos. Hawaii 2010.

Nani Kai—Beautiful Water

Sometimes we're influenced by people—their actions, feats and defeats, their comments, conversations, and their energy—but other times inspiration can come purely from nature and creation. Photography has always been a vehicle for me to travel the world; a chance to look around and see the beauty that God has created for us to enjoy.

I am grateful that I had the freedom to roam the planet, witness all its beauty, and capture some of those elements to share with others. I really hope you enjoy viewing these images as much as I have enjoyed photographing them. I am happy to share these images with you and feel blessed in this life. Aloha nui.

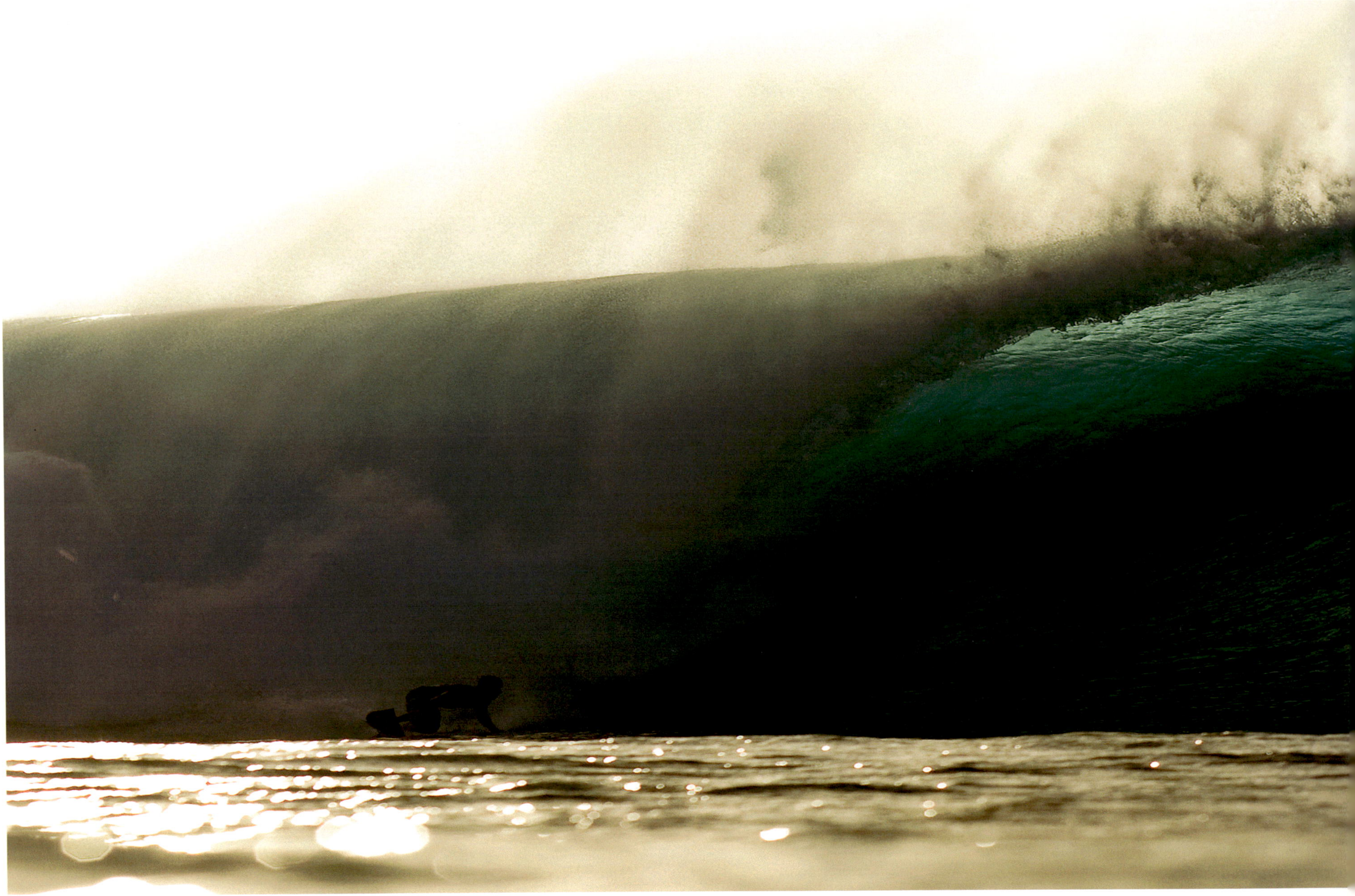

Kalani Chapman, late evening line drive. Pipeline, HI. 2006.

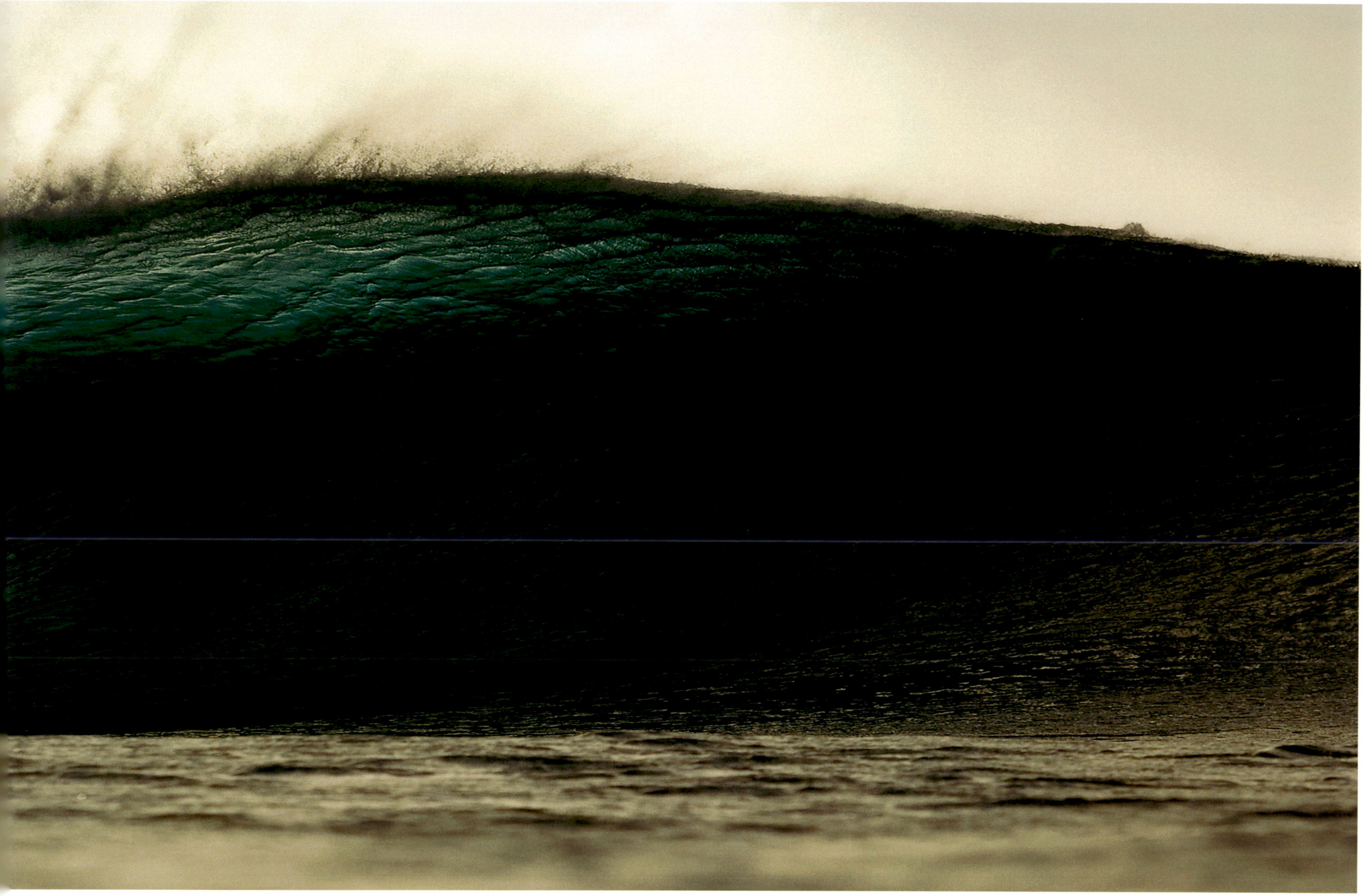

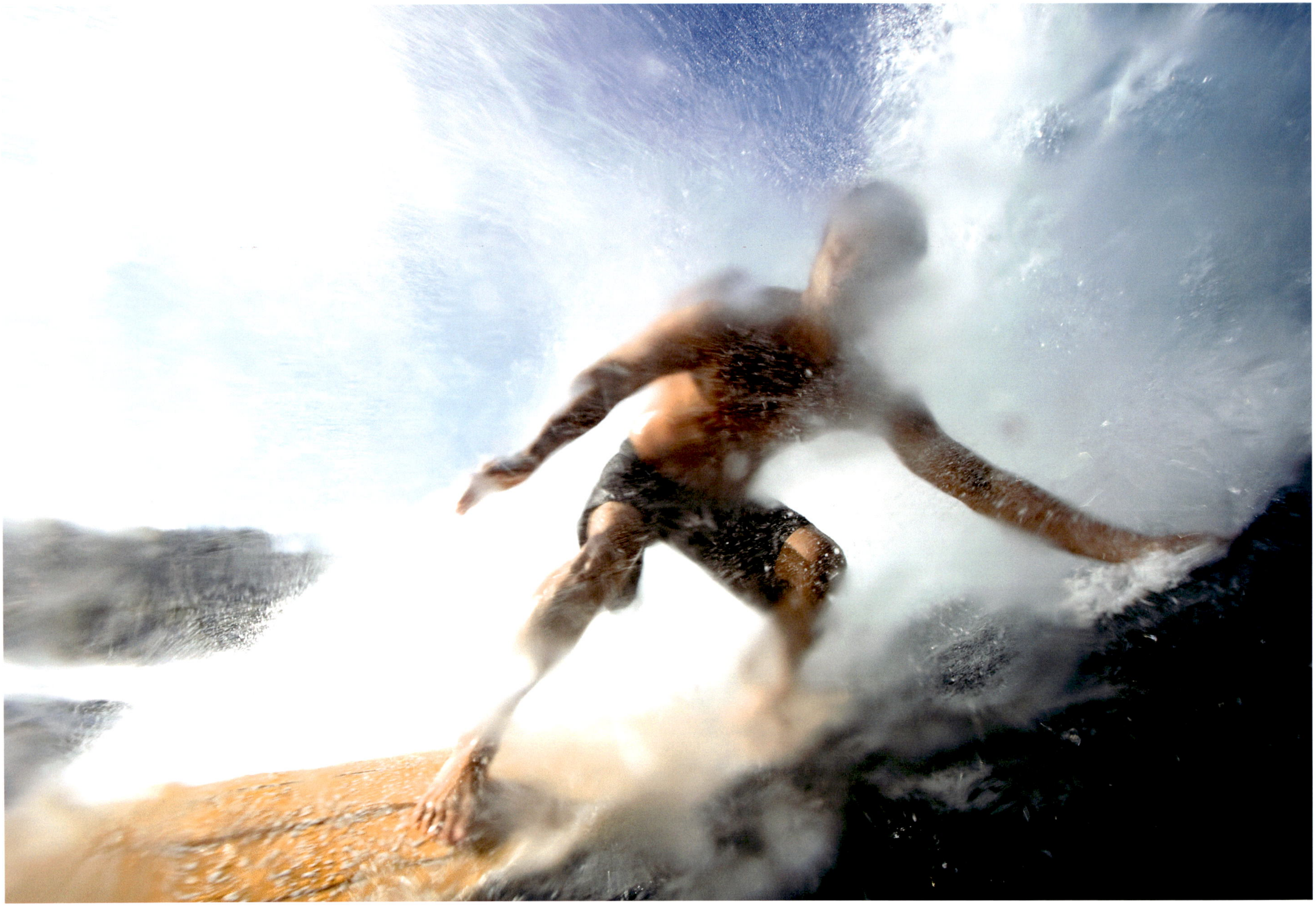

Takuji Masuda. 1963 Phil Edwards 10 ft. 3-stringer strange bedfellows at Pipeline, HI. 2008.

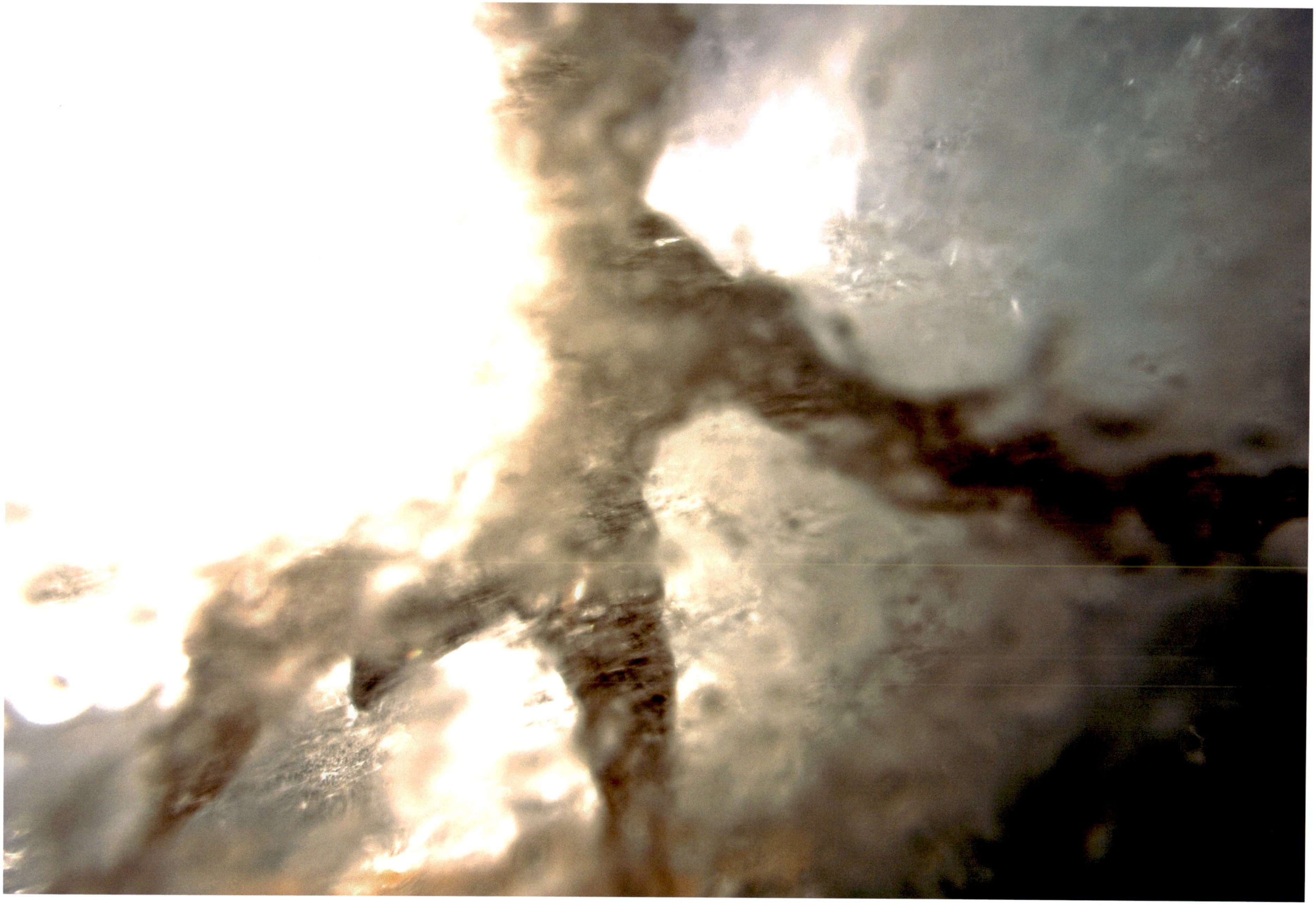

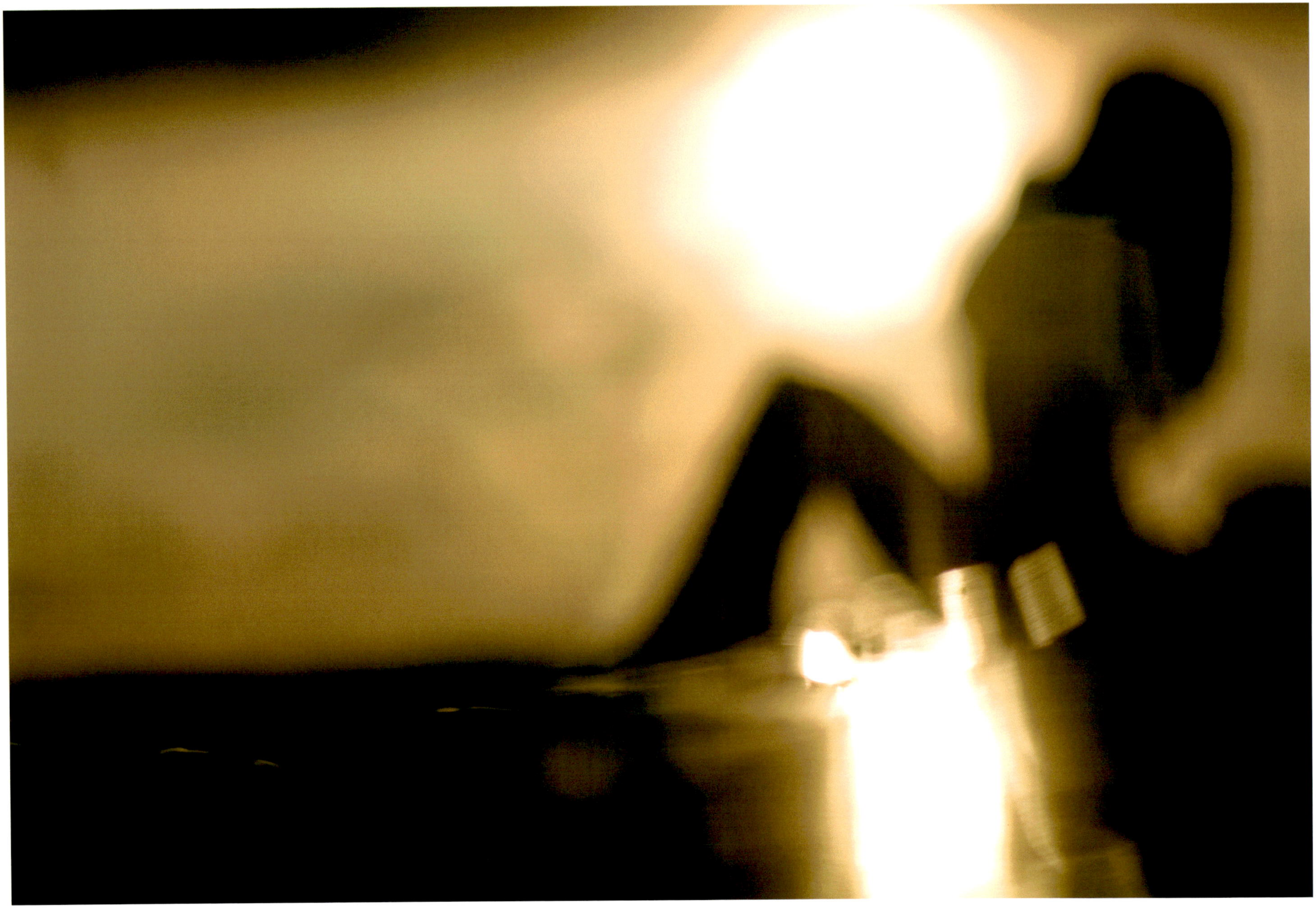

Kelia "Sister" Moniz, beauty, grace, and aloha, Hawaii. 2010.

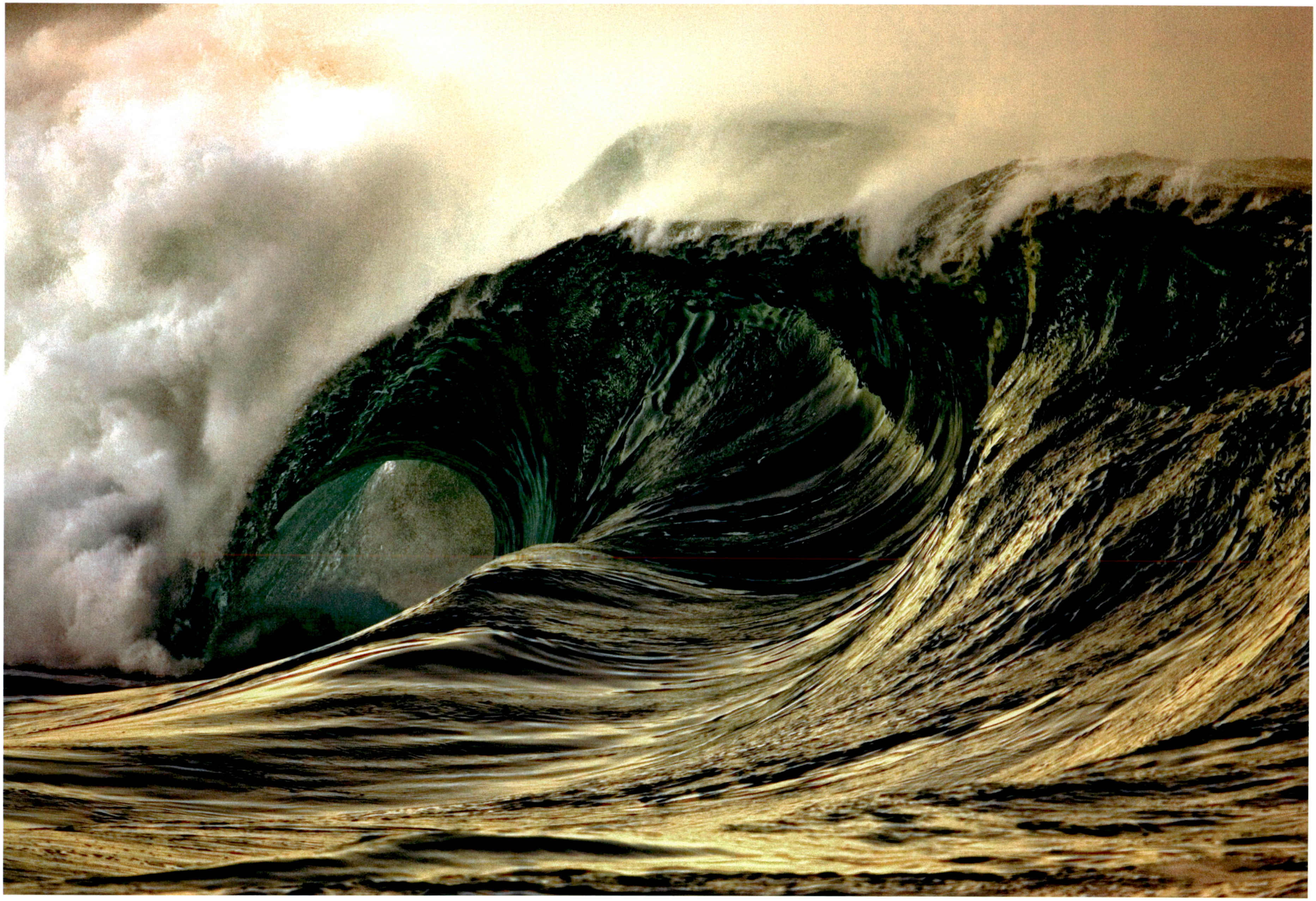

Waimea Shorebreak, beauty, No grace, No aloha, HI. 2006.

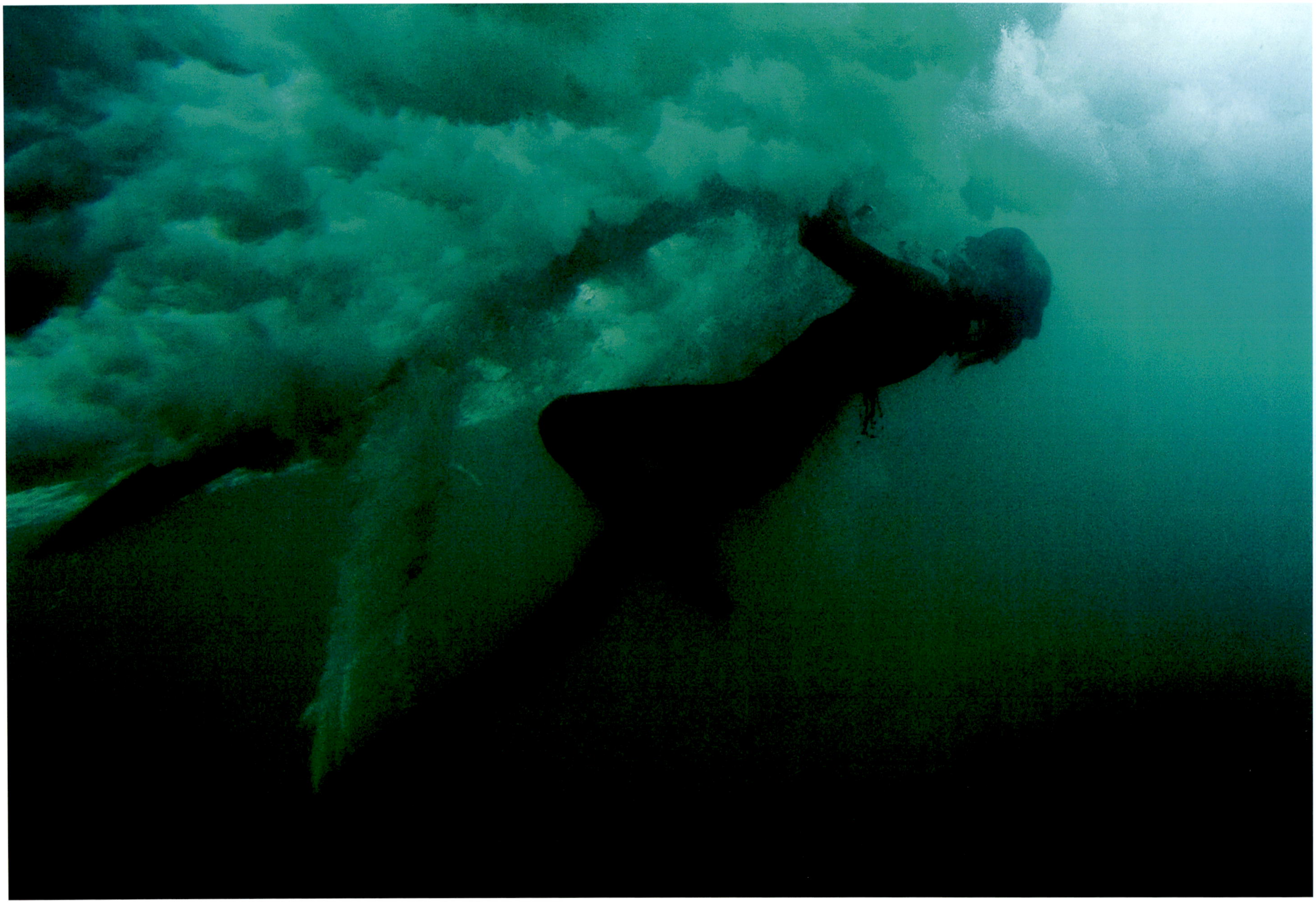

Rachel Spear, mudflap girl. Hawaii. 2008.

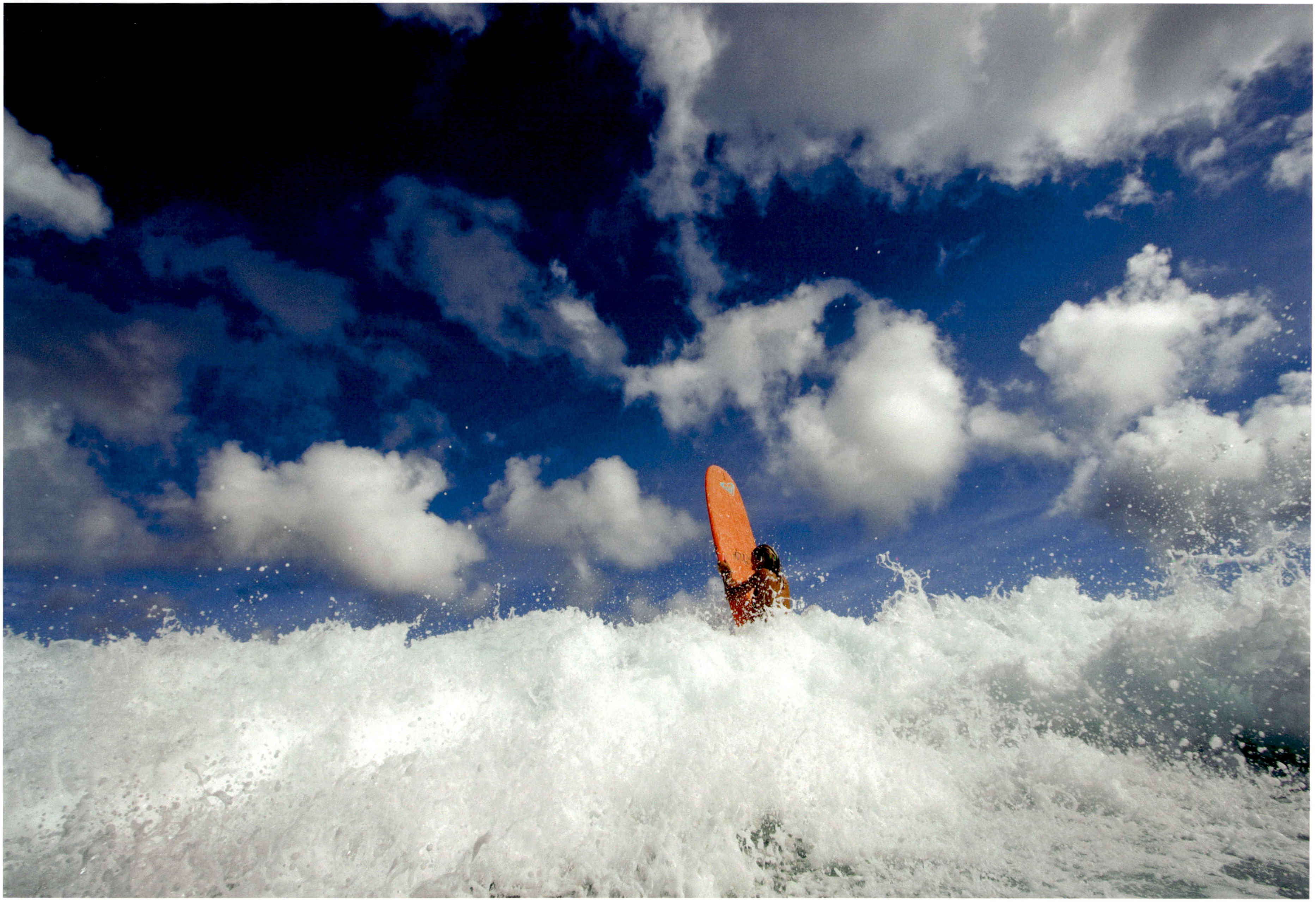

Rachel Spear. Heavenly. Pupukea, HI. 2008.

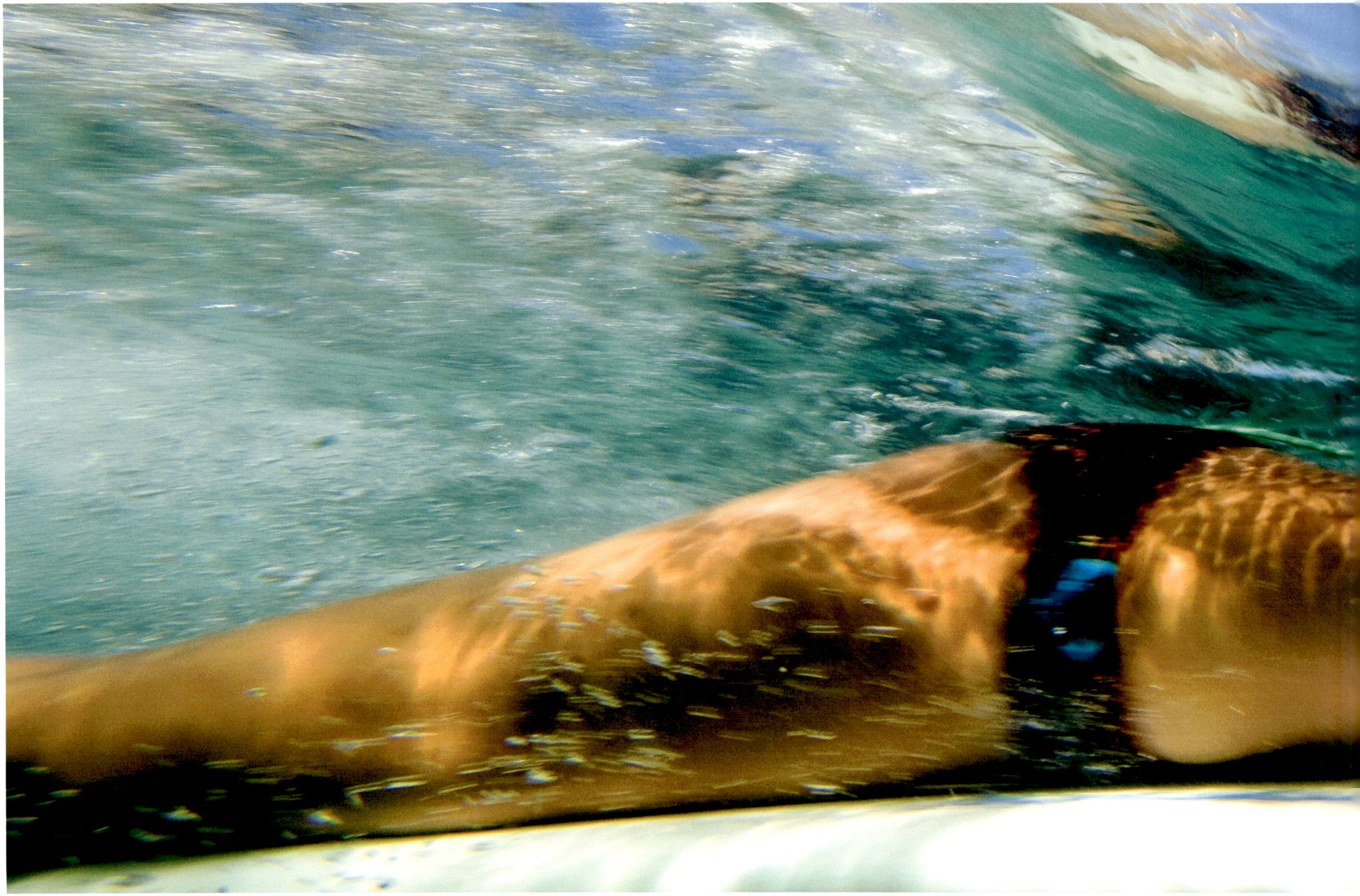

Rachel Spear. Duck and Cover. Hawaii. 2008.

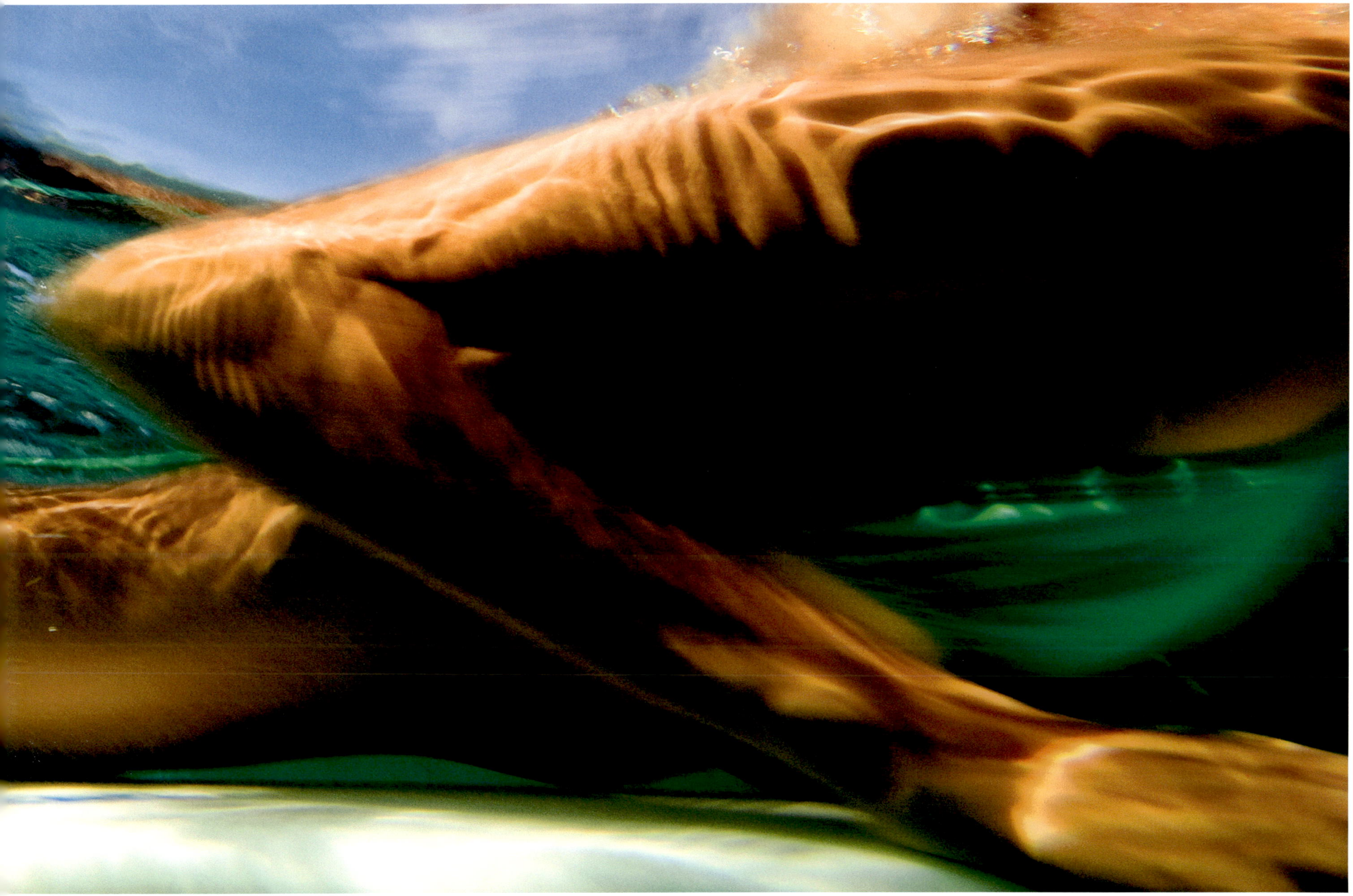

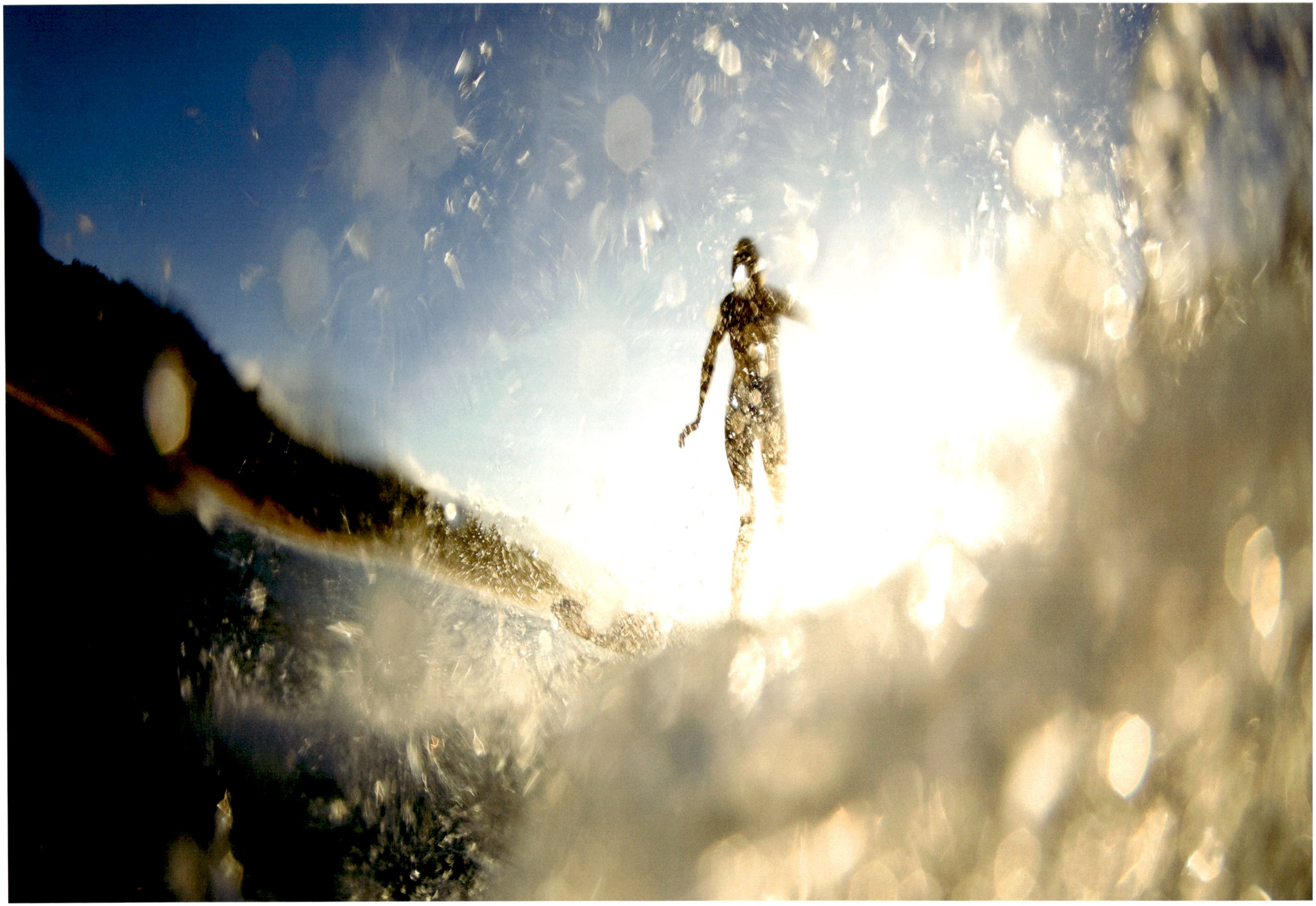

Rachel Spear. If I Was a Drop of Water. Hawaii. 2008.

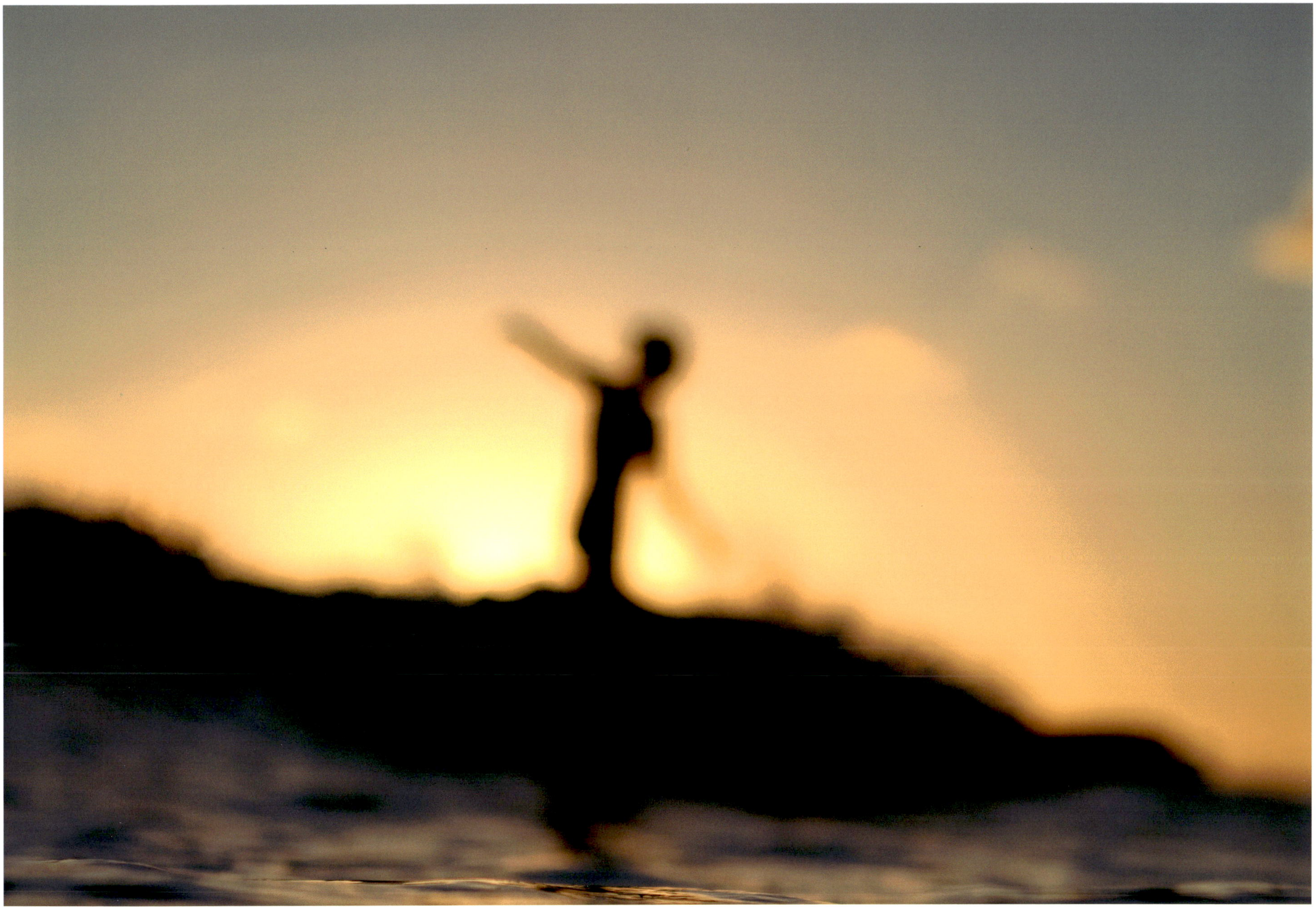

Crystal Thornburg Homcy, Soft Cross. Hawaii. 2010.

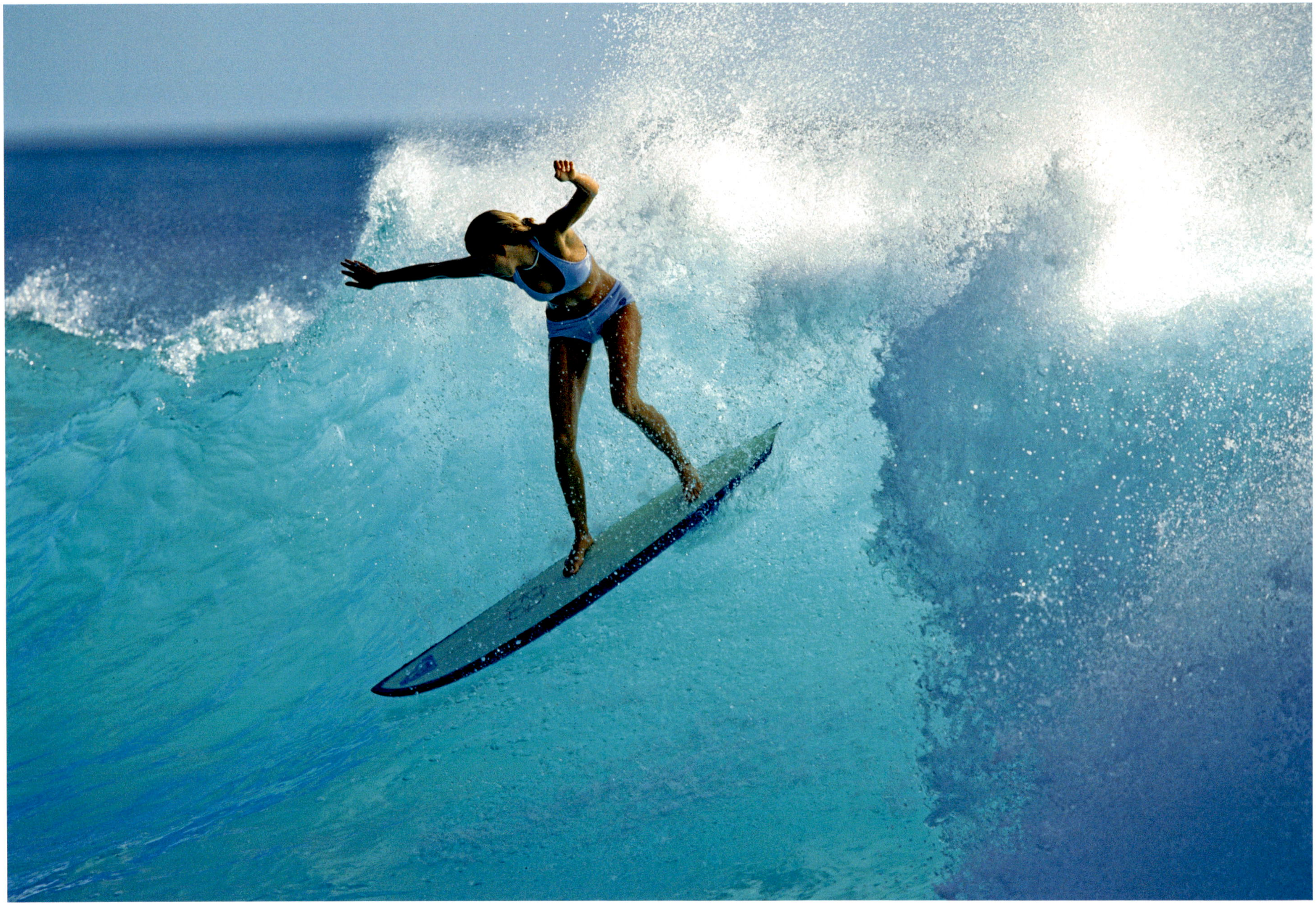

Daize Shayne Goodwin, O.G. Roxy. Makaha, HI. 2006.

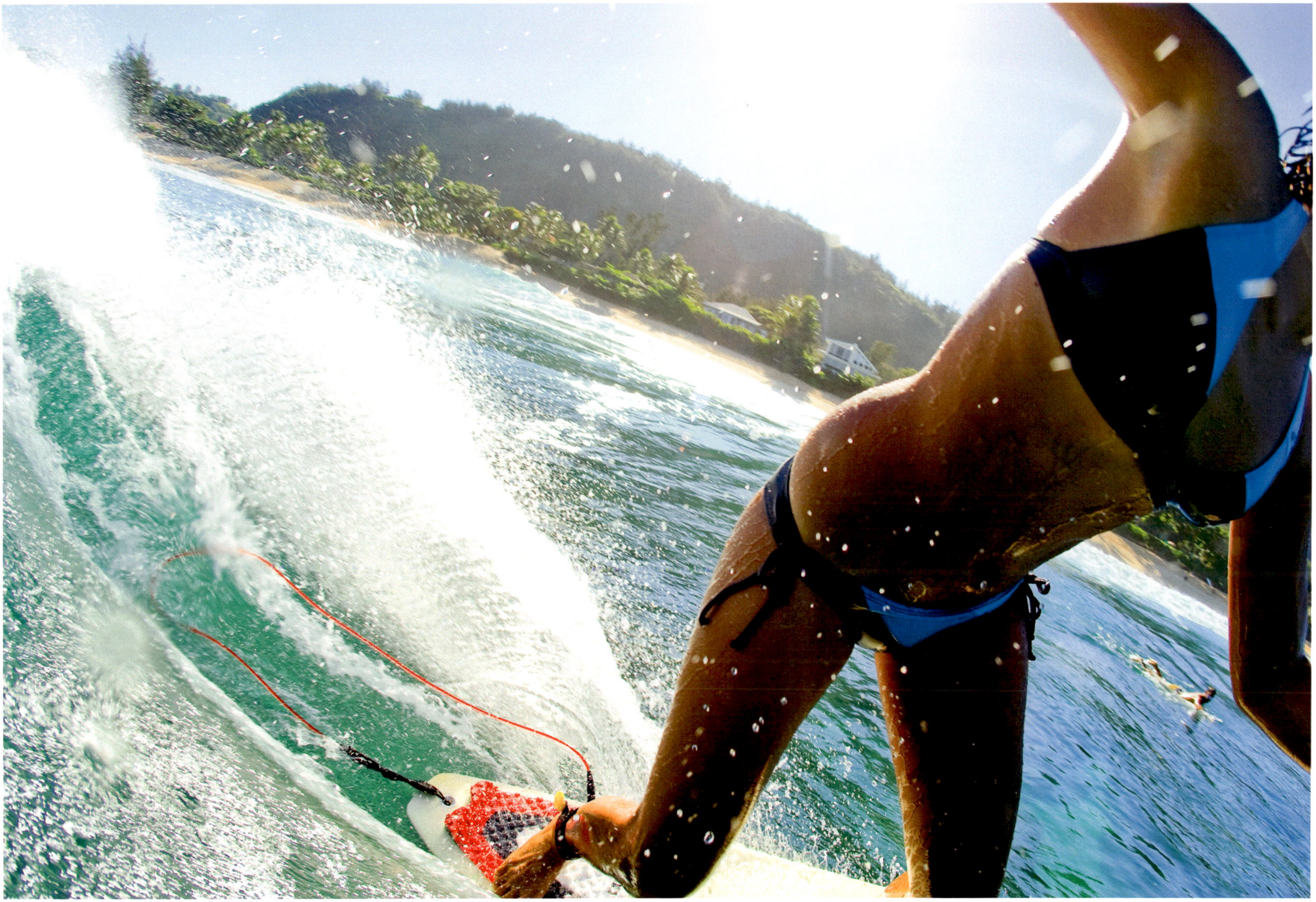

Alana Mock, Fly By. Gas Chambers, HI. 2005.

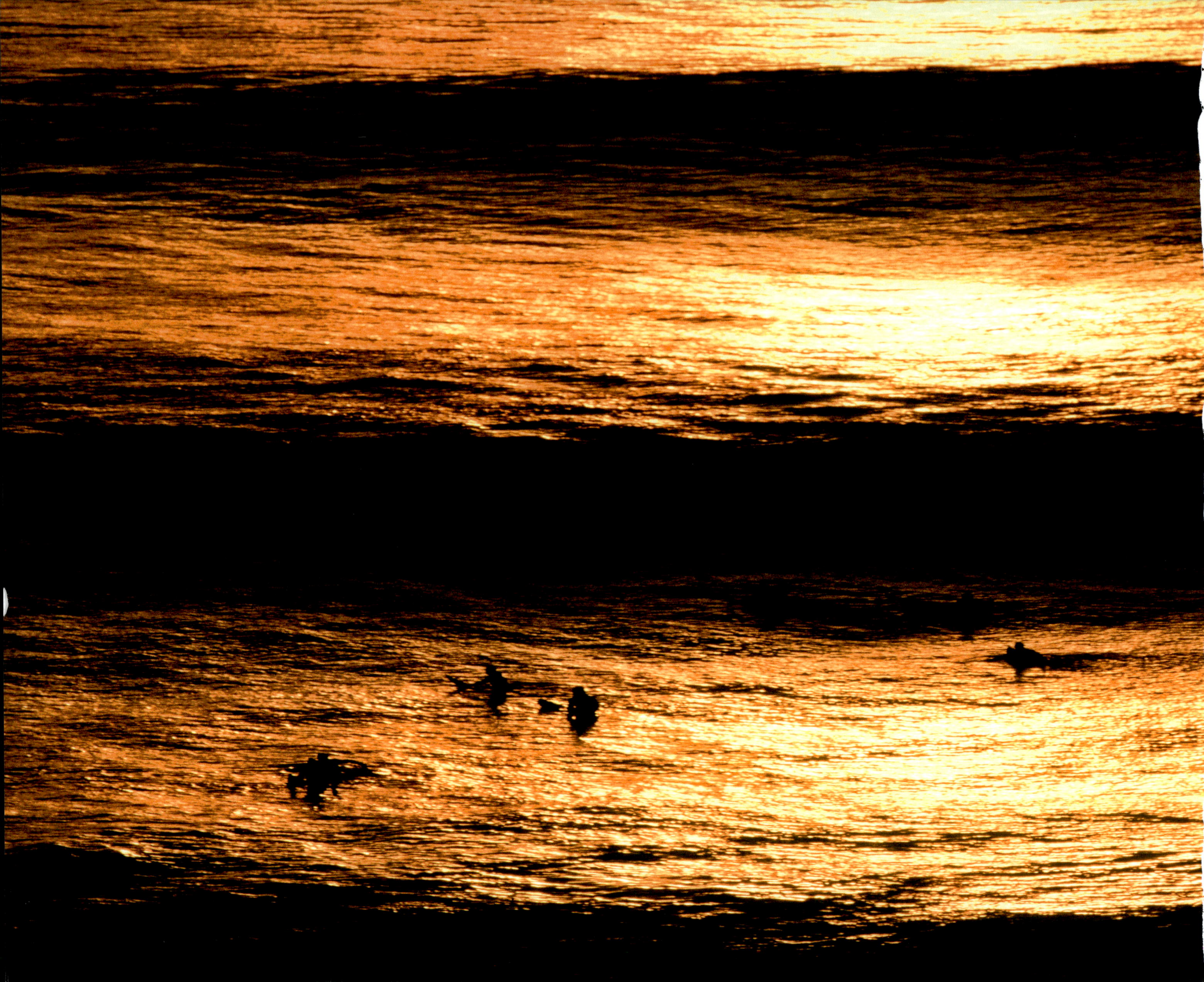